Learning Disabilities

SOURCEBOOK

SIXTH EDITION

Health Reference Series

Learning Disabilities
SOURCEBOOK

SIXTH EDITION

Basic Consumer Health Information about Dyslexia, Dyscalculia, Dysgraphia, Speech, Language, and Communication Disorders, Auditory and Visual Processing Disorders, and Other Conditions That Make Learning Difficult, Including Attention Deficit Hyperactivity Disorder, Down Syndrome and Other Chromosomal Disorders, Fetal Alcohol Spectrum Disorders, Hearing and Visual Impairment, Autism and Other Pervasive Developmental Disorders, and Traumatic Brain Injury

Along with Facts about Diagnosing Learning Disabilities, Early Intervention, the Special Education Process, Assistive Technology, and Accommodations, and Guidelines for Life-Stage Transitions, Suggestions for Coping with Daily Challenges, a Glossary of Related Terms, and a Directory of Additional Resources

OMNIGRAPHICS

615 Griswold, Ste. 520, Detroit, MI 48226

Bibliographic Note

Because this page cannot legibly accommodate all the copyright notices, the Bibliographic Note portion of the Preface constitutes an extension of the copyright notice.

* * *

OMNIGRAPHICS

Angela L. Williams, *Managing Editor*

* * *

Copyright © 2019 Omnigraphics

ISBN 978-0-7808-1703-6

E-ISBN 978-0-7808-1704-3

Library of Congress Cataloging-in-Publication Data

Names: Omnigraphics, Inc., issuing body.

Title: Learning disabilities sourcebook: basic consumer health information about dyslexia, dyscalculia, dysgraphia, speech and communication disorders, auditory and visual processing disorders, and other conditions that make learning difficult, including attention deficit hyperactivity disorder, Down syndrome and other chromosomal disorders, fetal alcohol spectrum disorders, hearing and visual impairment, autism and other pervasive developmental disorders, and traumatic brain injury; along with facts about diagnosing learning disabilities, early intervention, the special education process, legal protections, assistive technology, and accommodations, and guidelines for life-stage transitions, suggestions for coping with daily challenges, a glossary of related terms, and a directory of additional resources.

Description: Sixth Edition. | Detroit, MI: Omnigraphics, Inc., [2019] | Series: Health reference series | "Angela L. Williams, Managing Editor"--T.p. verso. | Includes bibliographical references and index.

Identifiers: LCCN 2019013874 (print) | LCCN 2019017485 (ebook) | ISBN 9780780817043 (ebook) | ISBN 9780780817036 (hardcover: alk. paper)

Subjects: LCSH: Learning disabilities--United States--Handbooks, manuals, etc. | Learning disabled children--Education--United States--Handbooks, manuals, etc. | Learning disabled--Education--United States--Handbooks, manuals, etc. | Learning disabilities--United States--Diagnosis--Handbooks, manuals, etc.

Classification: LCC LC4705 (ebook) | LCC LC4705.L434 2019 (print) | DDC 371.90973--dc23

LC record available at https://lccn.loc.gov/2019013874

Table of Contents

v

Part II: Types of Learning Disabilities

Part III: Other Disorders That Make Learning Difficult

Part IV: Learning Disabilities and the Educational Process

Part V: Living with Learning Disabilities

Part VI: Additional Help and Information

Preface

About This Book

Learning disabilities are neurological disorders that affect the brain's ability to process, store, and communicate information. They are widespread, affecting as many as 1 out of every 5 people in the United States, according to the U.S. Department of Education. In 2015–16, the number of students between the ages of 3 and 21 receiving special education services was 6.7 million, or 13 percent of all public-school students. Among students receiving special education services, 34 percent had specific learning disabilities. Learning disabilities directly impact many areas in the lives of those affected, making school difficult, making it hard to obtain and sustain employment, making daily tasks challenging, and even affecting relationships. Yet, learning disabilities are invisible obstacles. For this reason, they are often misunderstood, and their impact is often underestimated.

Learning Disabilities Sourcebook, Sixth Edition provides information about dyslexia, dyscalculia, dysgraphia, speech and communication disorders, and auditory and visual processing disorders. It also provides details about other conditions that impact learning, including attention deficit hyperactivity disorder, autism and other pervasive developmental disorders, hearing and visual impairment, and Down syndrome and other chromosomal disorders. The book offers facts about diagnosing learning disabilities, the special education process, and legal protections. Guidelines for life-stage transitions and coping with daily challenges, a glossary of related terms, and a directory of resources for additional help and information are also included.

How to Use This Book

This book is divided into parts and chapters. Parts focus on broad areas of interest. Chapters are devoted to single topics within a part.

Part I: Understanding and Identifying Learning Disabilities explains how the brain works, defines what learning disabilities are, and describes theories regarding their potential causes. It explains how learning disabilities are evaluated and provides tips on how to choose an evaluation professional.

Part II: Types of Learning Disabilities describes the most common forms of learning disabilities, including problems with reading, writing, mathematics, speech, language, and communication. It explains what these disorders are, how they are diagnosed, and how they are treated. It also discusses learning disabilities among gifted students, a fairly common—but often unrecognized—phenomenon.

Part III: Other Disorders That Make Learning Difficult discusses common disorders that have a component that affects a child's ability to learn, including attention deficit hyperactivity disorder; epilepsy; fetal alcohol spectrum disorders; pervasive developmental disorders; visual and hearing disabilities; and chromosomal disorders, such as Down syndrome.

Part IV: Learning Disabilities and the Educational Process provides information about how learning disabilities are accommodated within the schools. It describes early intervention strategies, explains how the special education process works, and details the legal supports for students with learning disabilities. Specialized teaching techniques and alternative educational options, such as tutoring and homeschooling, that are used to help learning-disabled students succeed are described, and it also offers guidelines for successfully negotiating the transitions to high school and to college.

Part V: Living with Learning Disabilities discusses how learning disabilities impact daily life. It includes tips for coping with a learning disability and for parenting a child with a learning disability. The impact of learning disabilities on self-esteem and life skills are discussed, and it offers suggestions to help those with learning disabilities deal with daily tasks, including meal preparation, money management, travel and transportation, and learning to drive. It also provides detailed guidelines for handling the employment issues faced by those with learning disabilities.

Part VI: Additional Help and Information includes a glossary of terms related to learning disabilities, a list of sources of college funding for students with disabilities, and a directory of resources for further help and support.

Bibliographic Note

This volume contains documents and excerpts from publications issued by the following U.S. government agencies: Centers for Disease Control and Prevention (CDC); Center for Parent Information and Resources (CPIR); Child Welfare Information Gateway; Education Resources Information Center (ERIC); *Eunice Kennedy Shriver* National Institute of Child Health and Human Development (NICHD); Genetic and Rare Diseases Information Center (GARD); Literacy Information and Communication System (LINCS); National Human Genome Research Institute (NHGRI); National Institute of Mental Health (NIMH); National Institute of Neurological Disorders and Stroke (NINDS); National Institute on Deafness and Other Communication Disorders (NIDCD); *NIH News in Health*; National Science Foundation (NSF); U.S. Department of Education (ED); U.S. Department of Health and Human Services (HHS); and U.S. National Library of Medicine (NLM).

It may also contain original material produced by Omnigraphics and reviewed by medical consultants.

About the Health Reference Series

The *Health Reference Series* is designed to provide basic medical information for patients, families, caregivers, and the general public. Each volume takes a particular topic and provides comprehensive coverage. This is especially important for people who may be dealing with a newly diagnosed disease or a chronic disorder in themselves or in a family member. People looking for preventive guidance, information about disease warning signs, medical statistics, and risk factors for health problems will also find answers to their questions in the *Health Reference Series*. The *Series*, however, is not intended to serve as a tool for diagnosing illness, in prescribing treatments, or as a substitute for the physician/patient relationship. All people concerned about medical symptoms or the possibility of disease are encouraged to seek professional care from an appropriate healthcare provider.

A Note about Spelling and Style

Health Reference Series editors use *Stedman's Medical Dictionary* as an authority for questions related to the spelling of medical terms and the *Chicago Manual of Style* for questions related to grammatical structures, punctuation, and other editorial concerns. Consistent adherence is not always possible, however, because the individual volumes within the *Series* include many documents from a wide variety of different producers, and the editor's primary goal is to present material from each source as accurately as is possible. This sometimes means that information in different chapters or sections may follow other guidelines and alternate spelling authorities. For example, occasionally a copyright holder may require that eponymous terms be shown in possessive forms (Crohn's disease vs. Crohn disease) or that British spelling norms be retained (leukaemia vs. leukemia).

Medical Review

Omnigraphics contracts with a team of qualified, senior medical professionals who serve as medical consultants for the *Health Reference Series*. As necessary, medical consultants review reprinted and originally written material for currency and accuracy. Citations including the phrase "Reviewed (month, year)" indicate material reviewed by this team. Medical consultation services are provided to the *Health Reference Series* editors by:

Dr. Vijayalakshmi, MBBS, DGO, MD
Dr. Senthil Selvan, MBBS, DCH, MD
Dr. K. Sivanandham, MBBS, DCH, MS (Research), PhD

Our Advisory Board

We would like to thank the following board members for providing initial guidance on the development of this series:

- Dr. Lynda Baker, Associate Professor of Library and Information Science, Wayne State University, Detroit, MI

- Nancy Bulgarelli, William Beaumont Hospital Library, Royal Oak, MI

- Karen Imarisio, Bloomfield Township Public Library, Bloomfield Township, MI

- Karen Morgan, Mardigian Library, University of Michigan-Dearborn, Dearborn, MI

- Rosemary Orlando, St. Clair Shores Public Library, St. Clair Shores, MI

Health Reference Series *Update Policy*

The inaugural book in the *Health Reference Series* was the first edition of *Cancer Sourcebook* published in 1989. Since then, the *Series* has been enthusiastically received by librarians and in the medical community. In order to maintain the standard of providing high-quality health information for the layperson the editorial staff at Omnigraphics felt it was necessary to implement a policy of updating volumes when warranted.

Medical researchers have been making tremendous strides, and it is the purpose of the *Health Reference Series* to stay current with the most recent advances. Each decision to update a volume is made on an individual basis. Some of the considerations include how much new information is available and the feedback we receive from people who use the books. If there is a topic you would like to see added to the update list, or an area of medical concern you feel has not been adequately addressed, please write to:

Managing Editor
Health Reference Series
Omnigraphics
615 Griswold, Ste. 520
Detroit, MI 48226

Part One

Understanding and Identifying Learning Disabilities

Chapter 1

The Brain and Its Function

Chapter Contents

Section 1.1

Brain Basics: How the Brain Works

This section includes text excerpted from "Brain Basics: Know Your Brain," National Institute of Neurological Disorders and Stroke (NINDS), December 12, 2018.

The brain is the most complex part of the human body. This three-pound organ is the seat of intelligence, interpreter of the senses, initiator of body movement, and controller of behavior. Lying in its bony shell and washed by protective fluid, the brain is the source of all the qualities that defines humanity. The brain is the crown jewel of the human body.

For centuries, scientists and philosophers have been fascinated by the brain, but until recently, they viewed the brain as nearly incomprehensible. Now, however, the brain is beginning to relinquish its secrets. Scientists have learned more about the brain in the last ten years than in all previous centuries because of the accelerating pace of research in neurological and behavioral science and the development of new research techniques. As a result, Congress named the 1990s the "Decade of the Brain."

This section is a basic introduction to the human brain.

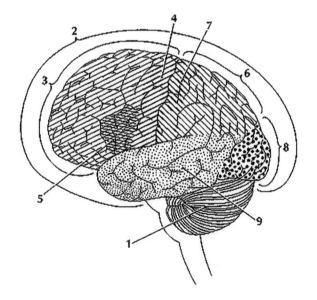

Figure 1.1. *Parts of the Human Brain*

The Architecture of the Brain

The brain is like a committee of experts. All the parts of the brain work together, but each part has its own special properties. The brain can be divided into three basic units: the forebrain, the midbrain, and the hindbrain.

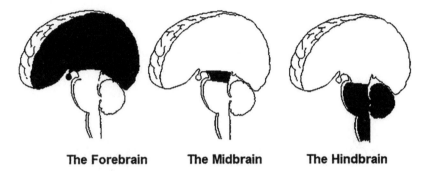

| The Forebrain | The Midbrain | The Hindbrain |

Figure 1.2. *Basic Units of the Brain*

The hindbrain includes the upper part of the spinal cord, the brain stem, and a wrinkled ball of tissue called the **"cerebellum" (1).** The hindbrain controls the body's vital functions, such as respiration and heart rate. The cerebellum coordinates movement and is involved in learned rote movements. When you play the piano or hit a tennis ball, you are activating the cerebellum. The uppermost part of the brainstem is the midbrain, which controls some reflex actions and is part of the circuit involved in the control of eye movements and other voluntary movements. The forebrain is the largest and most highly developed part of the human brain; it consists primarily of the **cerebrum (2)** and the structures hidden beneath it.

When people see pictures of the brain, it is usually the cerebrum that they notice. The cerebrum sits at the topmost part of the brain and is the source of intellectual activities. It holds your memories, allows you to plan, enables you to imagine and think. It allows you to recognize friends, read books, and play games.

The cerebrum is split into two halves (hemispheres) by a deep fissure. Despite the split, the two cerebral hemispheres communicate with each other through a thick tract of nerve fibers that lies at the base of this fissure. Although the two hemispheres seem to be mirror images of each other, they are different. For instance, the ability to form words seems to lie primarily in the left hemisphere, while the right hemisphere seems to control many abstract reasoning skills.

For some as-yet-unknown reason, nearly all of the signals from the brain to the body and vice-versa crossover on their way to and from the brain. This means that the right cerebral hemisphere primarily controls the left side of the body and the left hemisphere primarily controls the right side. When one side of the brain is damaged, the opposite side of the body is affected. For example, a stroke in the right hemisphere of the brain can leave the left arm and leg paralyzed.

The Geography of Thought

Each cerebral hemisphere can be divided into sections, or lobes, each of which specializes in different functions. To understand each lobe and its specialty, we will take a tour of the cerebral hemispheres, starting with the two **frontal lobes (3)**, which lie directly behind the forehead. When you plan a schedule, imagine the future, or use reasoned arguments, these two lobes do much of the work. One of the ways the frontal lobes seem to do these things is by acting as short-term storage sites, allowing one idea to be kept in mind while other ideas are considered. In the rearmost portion of each frontal lobe is a **motor area (4),** which helps control voluntary movement. A nearby place on the left frontal lobe called **"Broca's area" (5)** allows thoughts to be transformed into words.

When you enjoy a good meal—the taste, aroma, and texture of the food—two sections behind the frontal lobes called the **"parietal lobes" (6)** are at work. The forward parts of these lobes, just behind the motor areas, are the primary **sensory areas (7).** These areas receive information about temperature, taste, touch, and movement from the rest of the body. Reading and arithmetic are also functioning in the repertoire of each parietal lobe.

As you look at the content and images in this section, two areas at the back of the brain are at work. These lobes, called the **"occipital lobes" (8),** process images from the eyes and link that information with images stored in memory. Damage to the occipital lobes can cause blindness.

The last lobes of the cerebral hemispheres are the **temporal lobes (9),** which lie in front of the visual areas and nest under the parietal and frontal lobes. Whether you appreciate symphonies or rock music, your brain responds through the activity of these lobes. At the top of each temporal lobe is an area responsible for receiving information from the ears. The underside of each temporal lobe plays a crucial role in forming and retrieving memories, including those associated with music. Other parts of this lobe seem to integrate memories and sensations of taste, sound, sight, and touch.

The Cerebral Cortex

Coating the surface of the cerebrum and the cerebellum is a vital layer of tissue the thickness of a stack of two or three dimes. It is called the "cortex," and is from the Latin word for bark. Most of the actual information processing in the brain takes place in the cerebral cortex. When people talk about "gray matter" in the brain they are talking about this thin rind. The cortex is gray because nerves in this area lack the insulation that makes most other parts of the brain appear to be white. The folds in the brain add to its surface area and, therefore, increase the amount of gray matter and the quantity of information that can be processed.

The Inner Brain

Deep within the brain, hidden from view, lies structures that are the gatekeepers between the spinal cord and the cerebral hemispheres. These structures not only determine our emotional state, but they also modify our perceptions and responses depending on that state and allow us to initiate movements without thinking about them. As with the lobes in the cerebral hemispheres, the structures described below come in pairs: each is duplicated in the opposite half of the brain.

The **hypothalamus (10),** about the size of a pearl, directs a multitude of important functions. It wakes you up in the morning and gets the adrenaline flowing during a test or job interview. The hypothalamus is also an important emotional center, controlling the molecules that make you feel exhilarated, angry, or unhappy. Near the hypothalamus lies the **thalamus (11),** a major clearinghouse for information going to and from the spinal cord and the cerebrum.

An arching tract of nerve cells leads from the hypothalamus and the thalamus to the **hippocampus (12).** This tiny nub acts as a memory indexer—sending memories out to the appropriate part of the cerebral hemisphere for long-term storage and retrieving them when necessary. The basal ganglia (not shown) are clusters of nerve cells surrounding the thalamus. They are responsible for initiating and integrating movements. Parkinson disease (PD), which results in tremors, rigidity, and a stiff, shuffling walk, is a disease of nerve cells that lead into the basal ganglia.

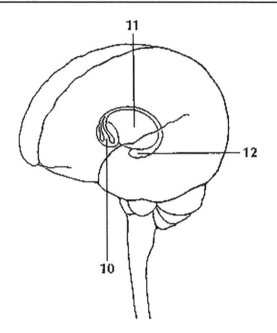

Figure 1.3. *The Inner Brain*

Making Connections

The brain and the rest of the nervous system are composed of many different types of cells, but the primary functional unit in a cell called the "neuron." All sensations, movements, thoughts, memories, and feelings are the result of signals that pass through the neurons. Neurons consist of three parts. The **cell body (13)** contains the nucleus, where most of the molecules that the neuron needs to survive and function are manufactured. **Dendrites (14)** extend out from the cell body like the branches of a tree and receive messages from other nerve cells. Signals then pass from the dendrites through the cell body and may travel away from the cell body down an **axon (15)** to another neuron, a muscle cell, or cells in some other organ. The neuron is usually surrounded by many support cells. Some types of cells wrap around the axon to form an insulating **sheath (16).** This sheath can include a fatty molecule called "myelin," which provides insulation for the axon and helps nerve signals travel faster and farther. Axons may be very short, such as those that carry signals from one cell in the cortex to another cell less than a hair's width away. Or axons may be very long, such as those that carry messages from the brain all the way down the spinal cord.

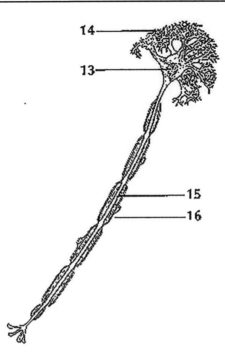

Figure 1.4. *Neuron*

Scientists have learned a great deal about neurons by studying the synapse—the place where a signal passes from the neuron to another cell. When the signal reaches the end of the axon, it stimulates the release of tiny **sacs (17).** These sacs release chemicals that are known as **"neurotransmitters" (18)** into the **synapse (19).** The neurotransmitters cross the synapse and attach to **receptors (20)** on the neighboring cell. These receptors can change the properties of the receiving cell. If the receiving cell is also a neuron, the signal can continue the transmission to the next cell.

Some Key Neurotransmitters at Work

Acetylcholine is called an **"excitatory neurotransmitter"** because it generally makes cells more excitable. It governs muscle contractions and causes glands to secrete hormones. Alzheimer disease (AD), which initially affects memory formation, is associated with a shortage of acetylcholine.

Gamma-aminobutyric acid (GABA) is called an **"inhibitory neurotransmitter"** because it tends to make cells less excitable. It helps control muscle activity and is an important part of the visual system.

Drugs that increase GABA levels in the brain are used to treat epileptic seizures and tremors in patients with Huntington disease (HD).

Serotonin is a neurotransmitter that constricts blood vessels and brings on sleep. It is also involved in temperature regulation. Dopamine is an inhibitory neurotransmitter involved in mood and the control of complex movements. The loss of dopamine activity in some portions of the brain leads to the muscular rigidity of PD. Many medications used to treat behavioral disorders work by modifying the action of dopamine in the brain.

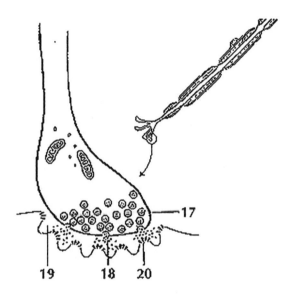

Figure 1.5. *How a Message Gets Transferred*

Neurological Disorders

When the brain is healthy, it functions quickly and automatically. But when problems occur, the results can be devastating. Some 50 million people in this country—1 in 5—suffer from damage to the nervous system.

Section 1.2

How the Brain Develops

This section includes text excerpted from "Understanding the Effects of Maltreatment on Brain Development," Child Welfare Information Gateway, U.S. Department of Health and Human Services (HHS), April 2015. Reviewed April 2019.

Our knowledge about the process of brain development helps us understand more about the roles both genetics and the environment play in our development. It appears that genetics predispose us to develop in certain ways, but our experiences, including our interactions with other people, have a significant impact on how our predispositions are expressed. In fact, research now shows that many capacities thought to be fixed at birth are actually dependent on a sequence of experiences combined with heredity. Both factors are essential for optimum development of the human brain.

Early Brain Development

The raw material of the brain is the nerve cell, called the "neuron." During fetal development, neurons are created and migrate to form the various parts of the brain. As neurons migrate, they also differentiate or specialize, to govern specific functions in the body in response to chemical signals. This process of development occurs sequentially from the "bottom up," that is, from areas of the brain controlling the most primitive functions of the body (e.g., heart rate, breathing) to the most sophisticated functions (e.g., complex thought). The first areas of the brain to fully develop are the brainstem and midbrain; they govern the bodily functions necessary for life, called the "autonomic functions." At birth, these lower portions of the nervous system are very well developed, whereas the higher regions (the limbic system and cerebral cortex) are still rather primitive. Higher functioning brain regions involved in regulating emotions, language, and abstract thought grow rapidly in the first three years of life.

The Growing Child's Brain

Brain development, or learning, is actually the process of creating, strengthening, and discarding connections among the neurons; these connections are called "synapses." Synapses organize the brain by forming pathways that connect the parts of the brain governing everything we do—from breathing and sleeping to thinking and feeling. This is the essence of postnatal brain development, because at birth, very few synapses have been formed. The synapses present at birth are primarily those that govern our bodily functions, such as heart rate, breathing, eating, and sleeping. The development of synapses occurs at an astounding rate during a child's early years in response to that child's experiences. At its peak, the cerebral cortex of a healthy toddler may create 2 million synapses per second. By the time children are 2 years of age, their brains have approximately 100 trillion synapses, many more than they will ever need. Based on the child's experiences, some synapses are strengthened and remain intact, but many are gradually discarded. This process of synapse elimination—or pruning—is a normal part of development. By the time children reach adolescence, about half of their synapses have been discarded, leaving the number they will have for most of the rest of their lives.

Another important process that takes place in the developing brain is myelination. Myelin is the white fatty tissue that forms a sheath to insulate mature brain cells, thus ensuring clear transmission of neurotransmitters across synapses. Young children process information slowly because their brain cells lack the myelin necessary for fast, clear nerve impulse transmission. As with other neuronal growth processes, myelination begins in the primary motor and sensory areas (the brain stem and cortex) and gradually progresses to the higher-order regions that control thought, memories, and feelings. Also, as with other neuronal growth processes, a child's experiences affect the rate and growth of myelination, which continues into young adulthood.

By 3 years of age, a baby's brain has reached almost 90 percent of its adult size. The growth in each region of the brain largely depends on receiving stimulation, which spurs activity in that region. This stimulation provides the foundation for learning.

Adolescent Brain Development

Studies using magnetic resonance imaging (MRI) techniques show that the brain continues to grow and develop into young adulthood (at least to the mid-twenties). White matter, or brain tissue, volume has been shown to increase in adults as old as 32 years of age. Right before puberty, adolescent brains experience a growth spurt that occurs mainly in the frontal lobe, which is the area that governs planning, impulse control, and reasoning. During the teenage years, the brain goes through a process of pruning synapses—somewhat like the infant and toddler brain—and also sees an increase in white matter and changes to neurotransmitter systems. As the teenager grows into young adulthood, the brain develops more myelin to insulate the nerve fibers and speed neural processing, and this myelination occurs last in the frontal lobe. MRI comparisons between the brains of teenagers and the brains of young adults have shown that most of the brain areas were the same—that is, the teenage brain had reached maturity in the areas that govern such abilities as speech and sensory capabilities. The major difference was the immaturity of the teenage brain in the frontal lobe and in the myelination of that area.

Normal puberty and adolescence lead to the maturation of a physical body, but the brain lags behind in development, especially in the areas that allow teenagers to reason and think logically. Most teenagers act impulsively at times, using a lower area of their brains—their "gut reaction"—because their frontal lobes are not yet mature. Impulsive behavior, poor decisions, and increased risk-taking are all part of the normal teenage experience. Another change that happens during adolescence is the growth and transformation of the limbic system, which is responsible for our emotions. Teenagers may rely on their more primitive limbic system in interpreting emotions and reacting since they lack the more mature cortex that can override the limbic response.

Plasticity—The Influence of Environment

Researchers use the term "plasticity" to describe the brain's ability to change in response to repeated stimulation. The extent of a brain's plasticity is dependent on the stage of development and the particular brain system or region affected. For instance, the lower parts of the brain, which control basic functions, such as breathing and heart rate, are less flexible, or plastic, than the higher functioning cortex, which controls thoughts and feelings. While cortex plasticity decreases as a child gets older, some degree of plasticity remains. In fact, this brain plasticity is what allows us to keep learning into adulthood and throughout our lives.

The developing brain's ongoing adaptations are the result of both genetics and experience. Our brains prepare us to expect certain experiences by forming the pathways needed to respond to those experiences. For example, our brains are "wired" to respond to the sound of speech; when babies hear people speaking, the neural systems in their brains responsible for speech and language receive the necessary stimulation to organize and function. The more babies are exposed to people speaking, the stronger their related synapses become. If the appropriate exposure does not happen, the pathways developed in anticipation may be discarded. This is sometimes referred to as the concept of "use it or lose it." It is through these processes of creating, strengthening, and discarding synapses that our brains adapt to our unique environment.

The ability to adapt to our environment is a part of normal development. Children growing up in cold climates, on rural farms, or in large sibling groups learn how to function in those environments. Regardless of the general environment, though, all children need stimulation and nurturance for healthy development. If these are lacking (e.g., if a child's caretakers are indifferent, hostile, depressed, or cognitively impaired), the child's brain development may be impaired. Because the brain adapts to its environment, it will adapt to a negative environment just as readily as it will adapt to a positive one.

Sensitive Periods

Researchers believe that there are sensitive periods for development of certain capabilities. These refer to windows of time in the developmental process when certain parts of the brain may be most susceptible to particular experiences. Animal studies have shed light on sensitive periods, showing, for example, that animals that are artificially blinded during the sensitive period for developing vision may never develop the capability to see, even if the blinding mechanism is later removed.

It is more difficult to study human sensitive periods, but it is known that, if certain synapses and neuronal pathways are not repeatedly activated, they may be discarded, and their capabilities may diminish. For example, infants have a genetic predisposition to form strong attachments to their primary caregivers, but they may not be able to achieve strong attachments, or trusting, durable bonds if they are in a severely neglectful situation with little one-on-one caregiver contact. Children from Romanian institutions who had been severely neglected had a much better attachment response if they were placed in foster care—and thus received more stable parenting—before they were 24 months old. This indicates that there is a sensitive period for attachment, but it is likely that there is a general sensitive period rather than a true cut-off point for recovery.

While sensitive periods exist for development and learning, it is also known that the plasticity of the brain often allows children to recover from missing certain experiences. Both children and adults may be able to make up for missed experiences later in life, but it is likely to be more difficult. This is especially true if a young child was deprived of certain stimulation, which resulted in the pruning of synapses (neuronal connections) relevant to that stimulation and the loss of neuronal pathways. As children progress through each developmental stage, they will learn and master each step more easily if their brains have built an efficient network of pathways to support optimal functioning.

Memories

The organizing framework for children's development is based on the creation of memories. When repeated experiences strengthen a neuronal pathway, the pathway becomes encoded, and it eventually becomes a memory. Children learn to put one foot in front of the other to walk. They learn words to express themselves. They learn that a smile usually brings a smile in return. At some point, they no longer have to think much about these processes; their brains manage these experiences with little effort because the memories that have been created allow for a smooth, efficient flow of information.

The creation of memories is part of our adaptation to our environment. Our brains attempt to understand the world around us and fashion our interactions with that world in a way that promotes our survival and, hopefully, our growth, but if the early environment is abusive or neglectful, our brains may create memories of these experiences that adversely color our view of the world throughout our life.

Babies are born with the capacity for implicit memory, which means that they can perceive their environment and recall it in certain unconscious ways. For instance, they recognize their mother's voice from an unconscious memory. These early implicit memories may have a significant impact on a child's subsequent attachment relationships.

In contrast, explicit memory, which develops around the age of two, refers to conscious memories and is tied to language development. Explicit memory allows children to talk about themselves in the past and future or in different places or circumstances through the process of conscious recollection.

Sometimes, children who have been abused or suffered other trauma may not retain or be able to access explicit memories of their experiences; however, they may retain implicit memories of the physical or emotional sensations, and these implicit memories may produce flashbacks, nightmares, or other uncontrollable reactions. This may be the case with very young children or infants who suffer abuse or neglect.

Responding to Stress

We all experience different types of stress throughout our lives. The type of stress and the timing of that stress determine whether and how there is an impact on the brain. The National Scientific Council on the Developing Child (NSCDC) outlines three classifications of stress:

- **Positive stress** is moderate, brief, and generally a normal part of life (e.g., entering a new child care setting). Learning to adjust to this type of stress is an essential component of healthy development.

- **Tolerable stress** includes events that have the potential to alter the developing brain negatively, but which occur infrequently and give the brain time to recover (e.g., the death of a loved one).

- **Toxic stress** includes strong, frequent, and prolonged activation of the body's stress response system (e.g., chronic neglect).

Healthy responses to typical life stressors (i.e., positive and tolerable stress events) are very complex and may change depending on individual and environmental characteristics, such as genetics, the presence of a sensitive and responsive caregiver, and past experiences. A healthy stress response involves a variety of hormone and neurochemical systems throughout the body, including the sympathetic-adrenomedullary (SAM) system, which produces adrenaline, and the hypothalamic-pituitary-adrenal (HPA) system, which produces cortisol. Increases in adrenaline help the body engage energy stores and alter blood flow. Increases in cortisol also help the body engage energy stores and also can enhance certain types of memory and activate immune responses. In a healthy stress response, the hormonal levels will return to normal after the stressful experience has passed.

Section 1.3

Early Brain Development and Health

This section includes text excerpted from "Early Brain
Development and Health," Centers for Disease Control
and Prevention (CDC), February 6, 2019.

The early years of a child's life are very important for later health
and development. One of the main reasons being how fast the brain
grows, starting before birth and continuing into early childhood.
Although the brain continues to develop and change into adulthood,
the first eight years can build a foundation for future learning, health,
and life success.

How well a brain develops depends on many factors in addition to
genes, such as:

• Proper nutrition starting in pregnancy

• Exposure to toxins or infections

• The child's experiences with other people and the world

Nurturing and responsive care for the child's body and mind is
the key to supporting healthy brain development. Positive or negative experiences can add up to shape a child's development and
can have lifelong effects. To nurture their child's body and mind,
parents and caregivers need support and the right resources. The
right care for children, starting before birth and continuing through
childhood, ensures that the child's brain grows well and reaches its
full potential.

The Importance of Early Childhood Experiences for Brain Development

Children are born ready to learn and have many skills to learn
over many years. They depend on parents, family members, and other
caregivers as their first teachers to develop the right skills to become
independent and lead healthy and successful lives. How the brain
grows is strongly affected by the child's experiences with other people
and the world. Nurturing care for the mind is critical for brain growth.
Children grow and learn best in a safe environment where they are
protected from neglect and from extreme or chronic stress external
with plenty of opportunities to play and explore.

Parents and other caregivers can support healthy brain growth by speaking to, playing with, and caring for their child. Children learn best when parents take turns when talking and playing, and build on their child's skills and interests. Nurturing a child by understanding their needs and responding sensitively helps to protect children's brains from stress. Speaking with children and exposing them to books, stories, and songs helps strengthen children's language and communication, which puts them on a path towards learning and succeeding in school.

Exposure to stress and trauma can have long-term negative consequences for the child's brain, whereas talking, reading, and playing can stimulate brain growth. Ensuring that parents, caregivers, and early childhood care providers have the resources and skills to provide safe, stable, nurturing, and stimulating care is an important public health goal.

When children are at risk, tracking children's development and making sure they reach developmental milestones can help ensure that any problems are detected early, and children can receive the intervention they may need.

A Healthy Start for the Brain

To learn and grow appropriately, a baby's brain has to be healthy and protected from diseases and other risks. Promoting the development of a healthy brain can start even before pregnancy. For example, a healthy diet and the right nutrients, such as sufficient folic acid, will promote a healthy pregnancy and a healthy nervous system in the growing fetus. Vaccinations can protect pregnant women from infections that can harm the brain of the fetus.

During pregnancy, the brain can be affected by many types of risks, such as by infectious diseases, such as cytomegalovirus (CMV) or Zika virus; by exposure to toxins, including from smoking or alcohol; or when pregnant mothers experience stress, trauma, or mental-health conditions, such as depression. Regular healthcare during pregnancy can help prevent complications, including premature birth, which can affect the baby's brain. Newborn screening can detect conditions that are potentially dangerous to the child's brain, such as phenylketonuria (PKU).

Healthy brain growth in infancy continues to depend on the right care and nutrition. Because children's brains are still growing, they are especially vulnerable to traumatic head injuries, infections, or toxins, such as lead. Childhood vaccines, such as the measles vaccine, can protect children from dangerous complications, such as swelling of the brain. Ensuring that parents and caregivers have access to healthy foods and places to live and play that are healthy and safe for their child can help them provide more nurturing care.

Section 1.4

Executive Function

"Executive Function," © 2016 Omnigraphics.
Reviewed April 2019.

The term "executive function" (EF) refers to a key set of mental skills that helps the brain organize information and direct behavior. Most aspects of EF are controlled by the prefrontal cortex (PFC), an area of the brain that lies directly behind the forehead. This part of the brain matures during puberty, which generally leads to an improved ability to perform higher-level tasks requiring organization and planning.

The main steps involved in EF are:

- Analyze what needs to be done

- Plan how to approach it

- Organize the steps to be accomplished

- Develop timelines for performing each step

- Adjust the approach, steps, or timelines as needed

- Complete the task within the time allowed

The brains of people with strong EF skills can execute this process very quickly. But people with weaknesses in EF tend to exhibit a pattern of chronic difficulty in organizing information and performing complex tasks. They may experience problems in getting started on a project, establishing priorities, making plans, following directions, remembering details, making decisions, using information in a logical way, paying attention, staying on task, switching focus, and managing time. Executive function disorder (EFD) also makes it more difficult for people to control impulses and regulate their behavior in response to different situations.

Causes and Symptoms

Although the cause of EFD is unknown, research suggests that genes may play an important role in its development. The different ways in which children and young people use executive skills are heavily influenced by heredity. In addition, studies have shown that EF issues often coexist with learning disabilities and attention problems, such as dyslexia and attention deficit hyperactivity disorder (ADHD). Other brain differences may affect the development of EFD as well, including neurological conditions, mood disorders, autism, fetal alcohol syndrome (FAS), and damage to the prefrontal cortex from concussions, strokes, or brain tumors.

EFD can produce a wide range of symptoms that vary by individual. Even in one individual, the symptoms may change over time. Some of the common challenges that may indicate problems with EF include:

- Deciding how to begin a task

- Figuring out how much time a task will require

- Paying attention to directions

- Concentrating on the task at hand and avoiding distractions

- Refocusing on the task after being interrupted

- Switching from one task to another, or from small details to the big picture

- Remembering multiple steps

- Incorporating outside feedback

- Changing the plan if needed

- Completing tasks in a timely manner

Weaknesses in EF skills may also manifest themselves in behavior issues, particularly in problems controlling impulses and emotions or regulating responses to different stimuli or situations. Many people with EFD have trouble with impulse control, or the ability to stop and think before speaking or acting. EFD can also affect emotional control, or the ability to manage emotions and avoid overreacting to small problems. People with EFD also tend to struggle with flexibility, or the ability to change course and come up with a new solution if one approach fails. Finally, self-monitoring can be a challenge for people with EFD. They may not be able to evaluate the effectiveness of their own strategies or use previous experience to improve future performance.

Diagnosis and Treatment

EFD is not listed as a separate condition in the American Psychiatric Association's (APA) *Diagnostic and Statistical Manual of Mental Disorders* (DSM), which provides criteria for mental-health professionals to use in making formal diagnoses. Instead, EFD usually occurs in conjunction with another health condition. Weakness in EF is one of the criteria used to diagnose ADHD, autism, and learning disabilities. In addition, people who are diagnosed with both learning disabilities and ADHD face an increased risk of severe executive dysfunction.

Although EFD is closely associated with other disorders, EF can be evaluated—and skill deficits identified—by trained mental-health professionals. The recommended process for diagnosing EFD includes the following steps:

- Keep a record of symptoms and behaviors

- Get a complete medical examination to rule out physical causes, such as hearing impairments or seizure disorders

- See a specialist for a full evaluation of EF, which may include reviewing school records, filling out questionnaires or screening forms, taking an intelligence test, and conducting observations of behavior at home, at school, or at the clinician's office

- Review the results and develop an intervention plan with strategies for dealing with the issues identified

Once EF issues have been identified, various educational strategies and behavioral approaches can help people with EFD overcome or adapt to their weaknesses. Although experts recommend early intervention during childhood, treatment can be effective at any age since the brain continues to develop. Several types of professionals may be involved in developing and administering treatment for EFD, including psychologists, speech therapists, and occupational therapists. Cognitive behavioral therapy (CBT) is a proven method that can help people with EFD develop tools to monitor their thoughts and behavior.

Children with EFD may be eligible for special education services through school systems, including academic supports and accommodations. Many schools employ response to intervention (RTI) to identify students who perform below grade level and provide them with extra help, whether within small groups or through more intensive one-on-one instruction. Classroom teachers may also use informal support strategies, such as assigning students with EFD a seat in the front row to make it easier for them to pay attention.

There are also a number of strategies parents can try at home to help children with EFD, such as:

- Making checklists to provide a visual reminder of the steps involved in completing a task, and to identify those that have already been accomplished

- Providing estimates of the time that should be budgeted for activities

- Using calendars and planners, whether on paper or on electronic devices, to keep track of schedules and aid in time management

- Explaining feedback, which may help inflexible thinkers understand the value of taking different approaches to tasks

Parents of children with EFD may also find it helpful to seek ideas, advice, and support from other parents who are dealing with the same issues. Many organizations and online communities offer such assistance. Experts also encourage parents of children with EFD to maintain a positive attitude. Since executive functioning skills continue to develop into adulthood, many children form effective strategies for dealing with EFD that enable them to reach their full potential.

References

1. Morin, Amanda. "Understanding Executive Functioning Issues," Understood.org, 2016.

2. Morin, Amanda. "Four Ways Kids Use Organization Skills to Learn," Understood.org, 2016.

Chapter 2

Early Learning, Speech, and Language Development Milestones

Chapter Contents

Section 2.1

Early Learning

This section includes text excerpted from "Early Learning: Condition Information," *Eunice Kennedy Shriver* National Institute of Child Health and Human Development (NICHD), December 1, 2016.

What Is Early Learning?

Children begin learning in the womb. From the moment they are born, interaction with the world around them helps them build crucial skills. For example:

- By 3 months of age, babies can recognize people they know.
- By 8 to 12 months of age, babies can recognize themselves in the mirror.
- From 18 months to preschool age, children can learn 9 new words each day.

Children learn all kinds of basic skills and concepts from the people and world around them.

- In the first few years of life, children start to become independent, learning how to act and how to control their emotions and behaviors.
- They learn language; math skills, such as shapes, numbers, and counting; pre-reading skills, such as how to hold a book and follow along as someone reads to them; and, with them, skills for lifelong learning.
- They also start forming relationships of trust and develop ways to handle and resolve problems.

Making sure children have good learning experiences during their early years—whether at home, in child care, or in preschool—will support their lifelong learning, health, and well-being.

Why Is Early Learning Important?

Early learning paves the way for learning at school and throughout life. What children learn in their first few years of life—and how they learn it—can have long-lasting effects on their success and health as children, teens, and adults.

Studies show that supporting children's early learning can lead to:

- Higher test scores from preschool to 21 years of age
- Better grades in reading and math
- A better chance of staying in school and going to college
- Fewer teen pregnancies
- Improved mental health
- Lower risk of heart disease in adulthood
- A longer lifespan

What Are Some Factors That Affect Early Learning?

A child's home, family, and daily life have a strong effect on his or her ability to learn. Parents and guardians can control some things in their child's life and environment, but not everything.

Some factors that can affect early learning include:

- Parents' education
- Family income
- The number of parents in the home
- Access to books and play materials
- Stability of home life
- Going to preschool
- Quality of child care
- Stress levels and exposure to stress (in the womb, as an infant, and as a child)
- Number of languages spoken at home

Why Is It Important to Study Early Learning?

Early learning can improve children's health and well-being and have long-lasting benefits. Studying which factors affect early learning and education will help researchers:

- Design better ways to help at-risk children before they start school

- Improve parent, caregiver, child care provider, and preschool teacher training

- Use research findings to design better preschool and child care programs

- Study innovative early intervention settings, such as pediatrician's offices and home-visitor programs, and ways to make these programs convenient for parents and caretakers

For example, *Eunice Kennedy Shriver* National Institute of Child Health and Human Development (NICHD) research has helped characterize a positive learning environment as one with a warm caregiver and in which the child is supported and challenged cognitively. Findings of NICHD research also link early childhood education programs to improved adult health and demonstrate that early learning programs are cost-effective.

Recent examples include findings indicating that:

- Research shows that Head Start has positive effects on children's math, literacy, and vocabulary skills across the board. The program had an even greater impact—boosting early math skills the most—among children whose parents spent little time reading to them or counting with them at home. Children whose homes provided a medium amount of such activities had the biggest gains in early literacy skills.

- Children who have trouble developing language skills may also have trouble controlling their impulses and behaviors.

- Bilingual speakers develop brain networks that help them filter out unnecessary information better than those who speak only one language. These brain networks might protect against Alzheimer disease (AD) and other age-related brain problems.

- Experience and genetic factors seem to influence whether a child will have "math anxiety"—very strong worries about math abilities that can be disabling.

How Can Parents and Caregivers Promote Early Learning?

A child's home, family, and daily life have a strong effect on her or his ability to learn.

You are your child's first teacher, and every day is filled with opportunities to help her or him learn. You can help by:

- Reading to your child, beginning when she or he is born

- Pointing out and talking with your child about the names, colors, shapes, numbers, sizes, and quantities of objects in her or his environment

- Listening and responding to your child as she or he learns to communicate

- Practicing counting together

Basic things, such as getting enough sleep and eating a healthy diet, are also important for a child's brain development and ability to learn. Creating a stable home with routines and support encourages children to learn and explore. Loud background sounds in the home (televisions, stereos, video games) can be distracting and stressful to young children and should be turned off or the volume lowered when they are present.

A good child care or preschool program also helps a child to learn and grow.

Early Learning: Other FAQs
Where Can I Find Information about Early Educational Programs for My Child?

Individual states offer different early education programs and resources. The website and contact information for the department of education in each state is accessible through a directory on The U.S. Department of Education (ED) website.

What Is "School Readiness"?

School readiness refers to having the skills, knowledge, abilities, and attitudes needed for success in school and for later learning and life.

School readiness includes:

- The child's ability to meet milestones appropriate for their stage of development, including motor skills, language development, and general knowledge; their curiosity and enthusiasm; and their ability to explore and try new things

- The environment provided by the school, including high-quality instruction, leadership, appropriate teacher training, and support of relationships with parents and the community

- Appropriate support from the child's family and community, such as daily learning opportunities and supporting the child's mental and physical health

Section 2.2

Speech and Language Development Milestones

This section includes text excerpted from "Speech and Language Developmental Milestones," National Institute on Deafness and Other Communication Disorders (NIDCD), March 6, 2017.

How Do Speech and Language Develop?

The first three years of life, when the brain is developing and maturing, is the most intensive period for acquiring speech and language skills. These skills develop best in a world that is rich with sounds, sights, and consistent exposure to the speech and language of others.

There appears to be critical periods for speech and language development in infants and young children when the brain is best able to absorb language. If these critical periods are allowed to pass without exposure to language, it will be more difficult to learn.

What Are the Milestones for Speech and Language Development?

The first signs of communication occur when an infant learns that a cry will bring food, comfort, and companionship. Newborns also begin to recognize important sounds in their environment, such as the voice of their mother or primary caretaker. As they grow, babies begin to sort out the speech sounds that compose the words of their language. By six months of age, most babies recognize the basic sounds of their native language.

Children vary in their development of speech and language skills. However, they follow a natural progression or timetable for mastering the skills of language. Sometimes a delay may be caused by hearing loss, while other times it may be due to a speech or language disorder.

What Is the Difference between a Speech Disorder and a Language Disorder?

Children who have trouble understanding what others say (receptive language) or difficulty sharing their thoughts (expressive language) may have a language disorder. Specific language impairment (SLI) is a language disorder that delays the mastery of language skills. Some children with SLI may not begin to talk until they reach three of four years of age.

Children who have trouble producing speech sounds correctly or who hesitate or stutter when talking may have a speech disorder. Apraxia of speech is a speech disorder that makes it difficult to put sounds and syllables together in the correct order to form words.

What Should You Do If Your Child's Speech or Language Appears to Be Delayed?

Talk to your child's doctor if you have any concerns. Your doctor may refer you to a speech-language pathologist, who is a health professional trained to evaluate and treat people with speech or language disorders. The speech-language pathologist will talk to you about your child's communication and general development. She or he will also use special spoken tests to evaluate your child. A hearing test is often included in the evaluation because a hearing problem can affect speech and language development.

Depending on the result of the evaluation, the speech-language pathologist may suggest activities you can do at home to stimulate your child's development. They might also recommend group or individual therapy, or they may suggest further evaluation by an audiologist (a healthcare professional trained to identify and measure hearing loss) or a developmental psychologist (a healthcare professional with special expertise in the psychological development of infants and children).

What Research Is Being Conducted on Developmental Speech and Language Problems?

The National Institute on Deafness and Other Communication Disorders (NIDCD) sponsors a broad range of research to better understand the development of speech and language disorders, improve diagnostic capabilities, and fine-tune more effective treatments. An ongoing area of study is the search for better ways to diagnose and differentiate among the various types of speech delay. A large study following approximately 4,000 children is gathering data as the children grow to establish reliable signs and symptoms for specific speech disorders, which can then be used to develop accurate diagnostic tests. Additional genetic studies are looking for matches between different genetic variations and specific speech deficits.

Researchers sponsored by the NIDCD have discovered one genetic variant in particular that is linked to SLI. The finding is the first to tie the presence of a distinct genetic mutation to any kind of inherited language impairment. Further research is exploring the role this genetic variant may also play in dyslexia, autism, and speech-sound disorders.

A long-term study looking at how deafness impacts the brain is exploring how the brain "rewires" itself to accommodate deafness. So far, the research has shown that adults who are deaf react faster and more accurately than hearing adults when they observe objects in motion. This ongoing research continues to explore the concept of "brain plasticity"—the ways in which the brain is influenced by health conditions or life experiences—and how it can be used to develop learning strategies that encourage healthy language and speech development in early childhood.

Another workshop convened by the NIDCD drew together a group of experts to explore issues related to a subgroup of children with autism spectrum disorders (ASD) who do not have functional verbal language by the age of five. Because these children are so different from one another, with no set of defining characteristics or patterns of cognitive strengths or weaknesses, development of standard assessment tests or effective treatments has been difficult. The workshop featured a series of presentations to familiarize participants with the challenges facing these children and helped them to identify a number of research gaps and opportunities that could be addressed in future research studies.

Section 2.3

Language and Linguistics: Language Acquisition

This section includes text excerpted from "Language
and Linguistics—Language Learning," National Science
Foundation (NSF), November 22, 2005. Reviewed April 2019.

Almost all human beings acquire a language (and sometimes more than one), to the level of native competency, before the age of five. How do children accomplish this remarkable feat in such a short amount of time? Which aspects of language acquisition are biologically programmed into the human brain, and which are based on experience? Do adults learn language differently from children? Researchers have long debated the answers to these questions, but there is one thing they agree on: language acquisition is a complex process.

Most researchers agree that children acquire language through interplay of biology and environmental factors. A challenge for linguists is to figure out how nature and nurture come together to influence language learning.

Emphasis on Nature

Some researchers theorize that children are born with an innate biological "device" for understanding the principles and organization common to all languages. According to this theory, the brain's "language module" gets programmed to follow the specific grammar of the language a child is exposed to early in life. Yet, the language rules and grammar children use in their speech often exceed the input to which they are exposed. What accounts for this discrepancy?

That is where the theory of universal grammar comes in. This theory posits that all languages have the same basic structural foundation. While children are not genetically "hard-wired" to speak a particular language, such as Dutch or Japanese, universal grammar lets them learn the rules and patterns of these languages—including those they were never explicitly taught. Some linguists believe that universal grammar and its interaction with the rest of the brain is the design mechanism that allows children to become fluent in any language during the first few years of life. In fact, childhood may be a critical period for the acquisition of language capabilities. Some scientists claim that if a person does not acquire any language before

31

the teenage years, they will never do so in a functional sense. Children may also have a heightened ability, compared to adults, to learn second languages—especially in natural settings. Adults, however, may have some advantages in the conscious study of a second language in a classroom setting.

No Nonsense: Babies Recognize Syllables

Babies are born into a world buzzing with new noises. How do they interpret sounds and make sense of what they hear? University of Wisconsin, Madison researcher Jenny Saffran strives to answer these types of questions by studying the learning abilities "that babies bring to the table" for language acquisition. "Studying learning gives us the chance to see the links between nature and nurture," says Saffran.

One thing the babies must learn about language is where words begin and end in a fluid stream of speech. This is not an easy task because the spaces perceived between words in sentences are obvious only if you are familiar with the language being spoken. It is difficult to recognize word boundaries in foreign speech. Yet, according to Saffran, by seven or eight months of age, babies can pluck words out of sentences.

In her studies, Saffran introduced babies to a simple nonsense language of made-up, two-syllable words spoken in a stream of monotone speech. There are no pauses between the "words," but the syllables are presented in a particular order. If the babies recognize the pattern, they can use it to identify word boundaries in subsequent experiments. To test this, Saffran plays new strings of speech where only some parts fit the previous pattern, then records how long the babies pay attention to the familiar versus novel "words." Since babies consistently pay attention to unfamiliar sounds for longer periods than to familiar ones, a difference in attention times indicates what the babies learned from their initial exposure to the nonsense language.

Saffran's research suggests babies readily identify patterns in speech and can even evaluate the statistical probability that a string of sounds represents a word. Her research reveals the sophisticated learning capabilities involved in language acquisition and demonstrates how these skills evolve as an infant matures.

Emphasis on Experience and Usage

Not all linguists believe that the innate capacities are most important in language learning. Some researchers place greater emphasis on the influence of usage and experience in language acquisition. They argue that adults play an important role in language acquisition by speaking to children—often in a slow, grammatical, and repetitious way. In turn, children discern patterns in the language and experiment with speech gradually—uttering single words at first and eventually stringing them together to construct abstract expressions. At first glance, this may seem reminiscent of how language is traditionally taught in classrooms. However, most scientists think children and adults learn language differently.

While they may not do it as quickly and easily as children seem to, adults can learn to speak new languages proficiently. However, few would be mistaken for a native speaker of the nonnative tongue. Childhood may be a critical period for mastering certain aspects of language, such as proper pronunciation. What factors account for the different language learning capabilities of adults and children? Researchers suggest accumulated experience and knowledge could change the brain over time, altering the way language information is organized and/or processed.

Chapter 3

Learning Disabilities: An Overview

Learning disabilities affect how a person learns to read, write, speak, and do math. They are caused by differences in the brain, most often in how it functions, but also sometimes in its structure. These differences affect the way the brain processes information.

Learning disabilities are often discovered once a child is in school and has learning difficulties that do not improve over time. A person can have more than one learning disability. Learning disabilities can last a person's entire life, but she or he can still be successful with the right educational supports.

A learning disability is not an indication of a person's intelligence. Learning disabilities are different from learning problems due to intellectual and developmental disabilities, or emotional, vision, hearing, or motor skills problems.

Different groups may define "learning disability" differently, often depending on the focus of the organization. You can read more on the U.S. Department of Education's (ED) website, which provides statutes, regulations, and policies on the Individuals with Disabilities Education Act (IDEA); the Learning Disabilities Association of America (LDA); and www.understood.org, which is maintained by the National Center for Learning Disabilities (NCLD).

This chapter includes text excerpted from "About Learning Disabilities," *Eunice Kennedy Shriver* National Institute of Child Health and Human Development (NICHD), September 11, 2018.

Types of Learning Disabilities

Some of the most common learning disabilities are the following:

- **Dyslexia.** People with dyslexia have problems with reading words accurately and with ease (sometimes called "fluency") and may have a hard time spelling, understanding sentences, and recognizing words they already know.

- **Dysgraphia.** People with dysgraphia have problems with their handwriting. They may have trouble forming letters, writing within a defined space, and writing down their thoughts.

- **Dyscalculia.** People with this math learning disability may have difficulty understanding arithmetic concepts and doing addition, multiplication, and measuring.

- **Apraxia of speech.** This disorder involves problems with speaking. People with this disorder have trouble saying what they want to say. It is sometimes called "verbal apraxia."

- **Central auditory processing disorder (CAPD).** People with this condition have trouble understanding and remembering language-related tasks. They have difficulty explaining things, understanding jokes, and following directions. They confuse words and are easily distracted.

- **Nonverbal learning disorders.** People with these conditions have strong verbal skills but difficulty understanding facial expressions and body language. They are clumsy and have trouble generalizing and following multi-step directions.

Because there are many different types of learning disabilities, and some people may have more than one, it is hard to estimate how many people might have learning disabilities.

What Are Some Signs of Learning Disabilities?

Many children have trouble reading, writing, or performing other learning-related tasks at some point. This does not mean they have learning disabilities. A child with a learning disability often has several related signs, and they do not go away or get better over time. The signs of learning disabilities vary from person to person.

Please note that the generally common signs included here are for informational purposes only; the information is not intended to screen for learning disabilities in general or for a specific type of learning disability.

Common signs that a person may have learning disabilities include the following:

- Problems reading and/or writing
- Problems with math
- Poor memory
- Problems paying attention
- Trouble following directions
- Clumsiness
- Trouble telling time
- Problems staying organized

A child with a learning disability also may have one or more of the following:

- Acting without really thinking about possible outcomes (impulsiveness)
- "Acting out" in school or social situations
- Difficulty staying focused; being easily distracted
- Difficulty saying a word correctly out loud or expressing thoughts
- Problems with school performance from week to week or day to day
- Speaking like a younger child; using short, simple phrases; or leaving out words in sentences
- Having a hard time listening
- Problems dealing with changes in schedule or situations
- Problems understanding words or concepts

These signs alone are not enough to determine that a person has a learning disability. Only a professional can diagnose a learning disability.

Each learning disability has its own signs. A person with a particular disability may not have all of the signs of that disability.

Children being taught in a second language may show signs of learning problems or a learning disability. The learning disability assessment must take into account whether a student is bilingual or a second language learner. In addition, for English-speaking children, the assessment should be sensitive to differences that may be due to dialect, a form of a language that is specific to a region or group.

Below are some common learning disabilities and the signs associated with them:

Dyslexia

People with dyslexia usually have trouble making the connection between letters and sounds and with spelling and recognizing words.

People with dyslexia often show other signs of the condition. These may include:

- Having a hard time understanding what others are saying

- Difficulty organizing written and spoken language

- Delay in being able to speak

- Difficulty expressing thoughts or feelings

- Difficulty learning new words (vocabulary), either while reading or hearing

- Trouble learning foreign languages

- Difficulty learning songs and rhymes

- Slow rate of reading, both silently and out loud

- Giving up on longer reading tasks

- Difficulty understanding questions and following directions

- Poor spelling

- Problems remembering numbers in sequence (for example, telephone numbers and addresses)

- Trouble telling left from right

Dysgraphia

A child who has trouble writing or has very poor handwriting and does not outgrow it may have dysgraphia. This disorder may cause a child to be tense and twist awkwardly when holding a pen or pencil.

Other signs of this condition may include:

- A strong dislike of writing and/or drawing

- Problems with grammar

- Trouble writing down ideas

- Losing energy or interest as soon as they start writing

- Trouble writing down thoughts in a logical sequence

- Saying words out loud while writing

- Leaving words unfinished or omitting them when writing sentences

Dyscalculia

Signs of this disability include problems understanding basic arithmetic concepts, such as fractions, number lines, and positive and negative numbers.

Other symptoms may include:

- Difficulty with math-related word problems

- Trouble making change in cash transactions

- Messiness in putting math problems on paper

- Trouble with logical sequences (for example, steps in math problems)

- Trouble understanding the time sequence of events

- Trouble describing math processes

What Causes Learning Disabilities

Researchers do not know all of the possible causes of learning disabilities, but they have found a range of risk factors during their work to find potential causes. Research shows that risk factors may be present from birth and tend to run in families. In fact, children who have a parent with a learning disability are more likely to develop a learning disability themselves. To better understand learning disabilities, researchers are studying how children's brains learn to read, write, and develop math skills. Researchers are working on interventions to help address the needs of those who struggle with reading the most, including those with learning disabilities, to improve learning and overall health.

Factors that affect a fetus developing in the womb, such as alcohol or drug use, can put a child at higher risk for a learning problem or disability. Other factors in an infant's environment may play a role too. These can include poor nutrition or exposure to lead in water or in paint. Young children who do not receive the support they need for their intellectual development may show signs of learning disabilities once they start school.

Sometimes, a person may develop a learning disability later in life due to injury. Possible causes in such a case include dementia or a traumatic brain injury (TBI).

How Are Learning Disabilities Diagnosed?

Learning disabilities are often identified once a child is in school. The school may use a process called "response to intervention" to help identify children with learning disabilities. Special tests are required to make a diagnosis.

Response to Intervention

Response to intervention usually involves the following:

- Monitoring all students' progress closely to identify possible learning problems

- Providing children who are having problems with help on different levels or tiers

- Moving children to tiers that provide increasing support if they do not show sufficient progress

Students who are struggling in school can also have individual evaluations. An evaluation can:

- Identify whether a child has a learning disability

- Determine a child's eligibility under federal law for special education services

- Help develop an individualized education plan (IEP) that outlines help for a child who qualifies for special education services

- Establish benchmarks to measure the child's progress

A full evaluation for a learning disability includes the following:

- A medical exam, including a neurological exam, to rule out other possible causes of the child's difficulties. These might include emotional disorders, intellectual and developmental disabilities, and brain diseases.
- Reviewing the child's developmental, social, and school performance
- A discussion of family history
- Academic and psychological testing

Usually, several specialists work as a team to do the evaluation. The team may include a psychologist, a special education expert, and a speech-language pathologist. Many schools also have reading specialists who can help diagnose a reading disability.

Role of School Psychologists

School psychologists are trained in both education and psychology. They can help diagnose students with learning disabilities and help the student and her or his parents and teachers come up with plans to improve learning.

Role of Speech-Language Pathologists

All speech-language pathologists are trained to diagnose and treat speech and language disorders. A speech-language pathologist can do a language evaluation and assess the child's ability to organize her or his thoughts and possessions. The speech-language pathologist may evaluate the child's learning skills, such as understanding directions, manipulating sounds, and reading and writing.

What Are the Treatments for Learning Disabilities?

Learning disabilities have no cure, but early intervention can lessen their effects. People with learning disabilities can develop ways to cope with their disabilities. Getting help earlier increases the chance of success in school and later in life. If learning disabilities remain untreated, a child may begin to feel frustrated, which can lead to low self-esteem and other problems.

Experts can help a child learn skills by building on the child's strengths and finding ways to compensate for the child's weaknesses. Interventions vary depending on the nature and extent of the disability.

Special Education Services

Children diagnosed with learning disabilities can receive special education services. The Individuals with Disabilities Education Act (IDEA) requires that public schools provide free special education supports to children with disabilities.

In most states, each child is entitled to these services beginning at 3 years of age and extending through high school or the age of 21, whichever comes first. The rules of IDEA for each state are available from the Early Childhood Technical Assistance Center (ECTA).

IDEA requires that children be taught in the least restrictive environment appropriate for them. This means the teaching environment should meet a child's needs and skills while minimizing restrictions on typical learning experiences.

Individualized Education Programs

Children who qualify for special education services will receive an individualized education program, or IEP. This personalized and written education plan:

- Lists goals for the child
- Specifies the services the child will receive
- Lists the specialists who will work with the child

Qualifying for Special Education

To qualify for special education services, a child must be evaluated by the school system and meet federal and state guidelines. Parents and caregivers can contact their school principal or special education coordinator to find out how to have their child evaluated. Parents can also review these resources:

- The Center for Parent Information and Resources offers information about Parent Training and Information Centers and Community Parent Resource Centers (CPRC).
- IDEA Parent Guide

Interventions for Specific Learning Disabilities

Below are just a few ways schools help children with specific learning disabilities.

Dyslexia

- **Intensive teaching techniques.** These can include specific, step-by-step, and very methodical approaches to teaching reading with the goal of improving both spoken language and written language skills. These techniques are generally more intensive in terms of how often they occur and how long they last, and they often involve small group or one-on-one instruction.

- **Classroom modifications.** Teachers can give students with dyslexia extra time to finish tasks and provide taped tests that allow the child to hear the questions instead of reading them.

- **Use of technology.** Children with dyslexia may benefit from listening to audiobooks or using word processing programs.

Dysgraphia

- **Special tools.** Teachers can offer oral exams, provide a note-taker, or allow the child to videotape reports instead of writing them. Computer software can facilitate children being able to produce written text.

- **Use of technology.** A child with dysgraphia can be taught to use word processing programs, including those incorporating speech-to-text translation, or an audio recorder instead of writing by hand.

- **Reducing the need for writing.** Teachers can provide notes, outlines, and preprinted study sheets.

Dyscalculia

- **Visual techniques.** Teachers can draw pictures of word problems and show the student how to use colored pencils to differentiate parts of the problems.

- **Memory aids.** Rhymes and music can help a child remember math concepts.

- **Computers.** A child with dyscalculia can use a computer for drills and practice.

What Conditions Are Related to Learning Disabilities?

Children with learning disabilities may be at greater risk for certain conditions compared to other kids. Recognizing and treating these conditions can help a child be more successful.

Attention Deficit Hyperactivity Disorder

Attention deficit hyperactivity disorder (ADHD) occurs more frequently in children with learning disabilities compared to children without learning disabilities. A child with a learning disability who also has ADHD may be distracted easily and find it harder to concentrate.

A *Eunice Kennedy Shriver* National Institute of Child Health and Human Development (NICHD)-supported study on reading disorders found that it is important to treat both the ADHD symptoms and reading problems. The findings show that although both disorders need separate treatments, these interventions can be done effectively at the same time.

Depression / Anxiety

A child with a learning disability may struggle with low self-esteem, frustration, worry, and other problems. Mental-health professionals can help the child understand these feelings, learn ways to cope with them, and learn how to build healthy relationships.

Three Tips for Managing a Learning Disability in Adulthood

Support from schools can improve elementary and secondary students' math, reading, and other language skills. But how can people with learning disabilities prepare for the demands of the university or working life?

Be Your Own Advocate

It is important to know and speak up for what you need. Understand your learning challenges, identify possible solutions, and ask for the resources that will allow you to reach your goals.

Ensure That Your Surroundings Facilitate Success

Work with your school or employer to create a supportive learning environment, such as access to software that will help you succeed now and in the future.

Take Advantage of Assistive Technology

Use computer tools customized to your own pace and needs that can read text aloud, help you articulate your thoughts, and provide structure to your writing.

Chapter 4

Diagnosing Learning Disabilities

Chapter Contents

Section 4.1

Identifying Learning Problems

This section includes text excerpted from "Keeping Up
in School?" *NIH News in Health*, National Institutes
of Health (NIH), September 1, 2016.

Reading, writing, and math are the building blocks of learning. Mastering these subjects early on can affect many areas of life, including school, work, and even overall health. It is normal to make mistakes and even struggle a little when learning new things. But repeated, long-lasting problems may be a sign of a learning disability.

Learning disabilities are not related to how smart a child is. They are caused by differences in the brain that are present from birth or shortly after. These differences affect how the brain handles information and can create difficulties with reading, writing, and math.

"Typically, in the first few years of elementary school, some children, in spite of adequate instruction, have a hard time and cannot master the skills of reading and writing as efficiently as their peers," says Dr. Benedetto Vitiello, a child mental-health expert at National Institutes of Health (NIH). "So, the issue is usually brought up as a learning problem."

In general, the earlier a learning disability is recognized and addressed, the greater the likelihood for success in school and later in life. "Initial screening and then ongoing monitoring of children's performance is important for being able to tell quickly when they start to struggle," explains Dr. Brett Miller, a reading and writing disabilities expert at NIH. "If you are not actively looking for it, you can miss opportunities to intervene early."

Each learning disability has its own signs. A child with a reading disability may be a poor speller or have trouble reading quickly or recognizing common words. A child with a writing disability may write very slowly, have poor handwriting, or have trouble expressing ideas in writing and organizing text. A math disability can make it hard for a child to understand basic math concepts, such as multiplication; make change in cash transactions; or do math-related word problems.

Learning difficulties can affect more than school performance. If not addressed, they can also affect health. A learning disability can make it hard to understand written health information, follow a doctor's directions, or take the proper amount of medication at the right times. Learning disabilities can also lead to a poor understanding of the benefits of healthy behaviors, such as exercise, and of health risks, such as obesity. This lack of knowledge can result in unhealthy behaviors and increased risk of disease.

Not all struggling learners have a disability. Many factors affect a person's ability to learn. Some students may learn more slowly or need more practice than their classmates. Poor vision or hearing can cause a child to miss what is being taught. Poor nutrition or exposure to toxins early in life can also contribute to learning difficulties.

If a child is struggling in school, parents or teachers can request an evaluation for a learning disability. The U.S. Individuals with Disabilities Education Improvement Act (IDEA) requires that public schools provide free special education support to children, including children with specific learning disabilities, who need such services. To qualify for these services, a child must be evaluated by the school and meet specific federal and state requirements. An evaluation may include a medical exam, a discussion of family history, and intellectual and school performance testing.

Many people with learning disabilities can develop strategies to cope with their disorder. A teacher or other learning specialist can help kids learn skills that build on their strengths to counterbalance their weaknesses. Educators may provide special teaching methods, make changes to the classroom, or use technologies that can assist a child's learning needs.

A child with a learning disability may also struggle with low self-esteem, a lack of confidence, and frustration. In the case of a math learning disability, math anxiety may play a role in worsening math abilities. A counselor can help children use coping skills and build healthy attitudes about their ability to learn.

"If appropriate interventions are provided, many of these challenges can be minimized," explains Dr. Kathy Mann Koepke, a math learning disability expert at NIH. "Parents and teachers should be aware that their own words and behavior around learning and doing math are implicitly learned by the young people around them, and may lessen or worsen math anxiety."

"We often talk about these conditions in isolation, but some people have more than one challenge," Miller says. Sometimes children with learning disabilities have another learning disorder or other condition, such as attention deficit hyperactivity disorder (ADHD).

"ADHD can be confused with a learning problem," Vitiello says. ADHD makes it difficult for a child to pay attention, stay focused, organize information, and finish tasks. This can interfere with schoolwork, home life, and friendships. But ADHD is not considered a learning disability. It requires its own treatments, which may include behavior therapy and medications.

"Parents play an important role in treatment, especially for children in elementary school," Vitiello says. Medications and behavioral interventions are often delivered at home. Teachers can usually advise parents on how to help kids at home, such as by scheduling appropriate amounts of time for learning-related activities. Parents can also help by minimizing distractions and encouraging kids to stay on task, such as when doing homework. Effective intervention requires consistency and a partnership between school and home.

Many complex factors can contribute to development of learning disabilities. Learning disorders tend to run in families. Home, family, and daily life also have a strong effect on a child's ability to learn, starting from a very early age. Parents can help their children develop skills and build knowledge during the first few years of life that will support later learning.

"Early exposure to a rich environment is important for brain development," Mann Koepke says. Engage your child in different learning activities from the start. Before they are even speaking, kids are learning. "Even if it is just listening and watching as you talk about what you are doing in your daily tasks," she says.

Point out and talk with children about the names, colors, shapes, sizes, and numbers of objects in their environment. Try to use comparison words, such as "more than" or "less than." This will help teach your child about the relationships between things, which is important for learning math concepts, says Mann Koepke. Even basic things, such as getting enough sleep and eating a healthy diet, can help children's brain development and their ability to learn.

NIH is continuing to invest in research centers that study learning challenges and their treatments, with a special focus on understudied and high-risk groups.

Although there are no "cures," early interventions offer essential learning tools and strategies to help lessen the effects of learning disabilities. With support from caregivers, educators, and health providers, people with learning disabilities can be successful at school, work, and in their personal lives.

Section 4.2

How Are Learning Disabilities Diagnosed?

"How Are Learning Disabilities Diagnosed?"
© 2016 Omnigraphics. Reviewed April 2019.

Diagnosing learning disabilities is difficult because learning disabilities show up differently in different people and a learning disability in one area may be masked by accelerated ability in another. For instance, a child who has dyscalculia may not know how to add two numbers but may write at a much higher grade level, leading teachers to think she is just being lazy about turning in her math homework.

Diagnosing Learning Disabilities in School-Aged Children and Adolescents

Learning disabilities often become evident when a child starts school. Teachers and other school professionals may identify students with suspected learning disabilities as they monitor the students' progress and their response to educational assistance. This is called the "response to intervention (RTI)" process. Parents may also bring their concerns about learning disabilities in their children to the attention of school professionals.

If a student is suspected of having learning disabilities, further testing and evaluation will be needed.

The Individuals with Disabilities Education Act (IDEA) sets out clear rules and regulations on the process for evaluating children suspected of having learning disabilities so that students with learning disabilities can take advantage of individualized educational plans (IEPs) when warranted. Under the IDEA, an evaluation must be "full and individual," meaning it needs to be comprehensive in scope but tailored to the student as a distinct individual. Tests must be given in the language and at the level that the student understands best. Tests must investigate all the skills where the student has difficulty. The results must give relevant information to make informed decisions on the next steps in the student's educational plan.

In addition, the school staff must create an evaluation plan that informs the parents of all tests, observations, and records they plan to use in the evaluation as well as providing the names of all evaluators.

The evaluation may include:

- A physical examination that looks for physical causes of learning disability, such as vision, hearing, movement, or other health issues

- A psychological evaluation to examine the student's emotional health and social skills, and determine how the student learns best

- Interviews with the student, parents, and teachers to learn more about the student's academic history, behavior in and out of school, and other information that can help the evaluators with their diagnosis

- A behavioral assessment, which is often accomplished using questionnaires filled out by teachers and parents about how the student interacts with the world in both normal and unusual situations

- Observation of the student by teachers, the school psychologist, reading specialist, speech-language pathologist, and other educational professionals

- Standardized tests are selected by educational professionals based on the student's areas of strengths and weaknesses. These tests can test general ability or specific skills

- Intelligence and achievement tests are used to measure the student's intellectual potential, what she or he knows and can do, and areas of the student's strengths and weaknesses. There are a variety of standard intelligence and achievement tests geared to a person's age. The evaluators then use the results of these tests to focus on what further testing needs to done.

- Tests for reading, writing, and math can include those that measure reading comprehension to determine the grade level at which a student should be taught; essential reading skills; oral reading (can the student read a passage aloud then answer questions on it?); pronunciation; general math skills

- Tests for language, motor, and processing skills look at issues that affect a student's learning skills. Results of this type of test may suggest problems with perception, memory, planning, motor skills, attention, and comprehension of both written and spoken communications.

- Other information already on file including report cards and state test scores

Based on the results of the evaluation, the school's IEP administrator will work with the student's teachers and family to draw up a plan of study to accommodate the student's learning disabilities and determine strategies for effective learning and living.

Diagnosing Learning Disabilities in Adults

An adult may suspect she or he has a learning disability if there are problems at work or school, such as trouble with reading, understanding charts, communicating effectively, or staying on task. There may be problems with everyday tasks, including reading the newspaper, balancing the checkbook, or making decisions. Likewise, if an adult has struggled to learn or remember for a long time, she or he may decide it is time to find out why.

Adults should seek qualified professionals to conduct the assessment. These professionals are licensed to evaluate learning disability and include psychologists and psychiatrists.

The diagnostic process for identifying learning disabilities in adults is similar to that of diagnosing a student. It includes interviews and observations, testing, an assessment of the results, and recommendations for living with the learning disability.

The assessment may include:

- An interview to gather information about the person's academic and career history, a review of any medical issues, and other information that can help the evaluator with the diagnosis

- A career-interest inventory to aid in determining what career areas are matches for the person's interests

- Standardized tests that are selected by the professional based on the information given to them. As with students, these tests can test general ability or specific skills. Standardized tests are used to look at the person's intelligence, achievement, and ability to process information. Based on those results, further tests may be administered to identify specific learning disabilities.

After the professional has gathered enough information, she or he will give the person the results of the assessment including the learning disabilities identified and make recommendations for learning and living.

Because each person is different, the diagnosing of learning disabilities must be individually tailored to that person. Age and development play a part in determining whether a person has one or more learning disabilities and which ones they are. In addition, learning disabilities may not appear until later because the person has learned to cope with the learning disabilities or it has been masked by other strengths. Regardless of when an learning disabilities is first suspected, the final diagnosis must be made by a professional or group of professionals.

References

1. "Adult Learning Disability Assessment Process," Learning Disabilities Association of America, 2016.

2. "Adults with Learning Disabilities—An Overview," Learning Disabilities Association of America, 2016.

3. "How are Learning Disabilities Diagnosed?" *Eunice Kennedy Shriver* National Institute of Child Health and Human Development (NICHD), February 28, 2014.

4. Griffin, Rayma. "Who Can Diagnose Learning and Attention Issues in Adults?" Understood.org, 2016.

5. Morin, Amanda. "Understanding the Full Evaluation Process," Understood.org, July 11, 2014.

6. Patino, Erica. "Types of Behavior Assessments," Understood. org, May 30, 2014.

7. Patino, Erica. "Types of Intelligence and Achievement Tests," Understood.org, June 5, 2014.

8. Patino, Erica. "Types of Tests for Language, Motor and Processing Skills," Understood.org, June 5, 2014.

9. Patino, Erica. "Types of Tests for Reading, Writing and Math," Understood.org, November 18, 2014.

Chapter 5

Evaluating Children for Learning Disabilities

Evaluation is an essential beginning step in the special education process for a child with a disability. Before a child can receive special education and related services for the first time, a full and individual initial evaluation of the child must be conducted to see if the child has a disability and is eligible for special education. Informed parent consent must be obtained before this evaluation may be conducted.

The evaluation process is guided by requirements in our nation's special education law, the Individuals with Disabilities Education Act (IDEA).

Purposes of Evaluation

The initial evaluation of a child is required by the Individuals with Disabilities Education Act (IDEA) before any special education and related services can be provided to that child. The purposes of conducting this evaluation are straightforward:

- To see if the child is a "child with a disability," as defined by the IDEA

This chapter includes text excerpted from "Evaluating Children for Disability," Center for Parent Information & Resources (CPIR), U.S. Department of Education (ED), September 9, 2017.

- To gather information that will help determine the child's educational needs

- To guide decision-making about appropriate educational programming for the child

The Individuals with Disabilities Education Act Definition of a "Child with a Disability"

The IDEA lists different disability categories under which a child may be found eligible for special education and related services. These categories are:

- Autism

- Deafness

- Deaf-blindness

- Developmental delay

- Emotional disturbance

- Hearing impairment

- Intellectual disability

- Multiple disabilities

- Orthopedic impairment

- Other health impairment

- Specific learning disability

- Speech or language impairment

- Traumatic brain injury (TBI)

- Visual impairment, including blindness

Having a disability, though, does not necessarily make a child eligible for special education. Consider this language from the IDEA regulations: "'Child with a disability' means a child evaluated in accordance with sections 300.304 through 300.311 as having (one of the disabilities listed above) and who, by reason thereof, needs special education and related services."

This provision includes the very important phrase "...and who, by reason thereof..." This means that, because of the disability, the child needs special education and related services. Many children have disabilities that do not have the need for extra educational assistance or individualized educational programming. If a child has a disability but is not eligible under the IDEA, she or he may be eligible for the protections afforded by other laws—such as Section 504 of the Rehabilitation Act of 1973, as amended. It is not uncommon for a child to have a 504 plan at school to address disability-related educational needs. Such a child will receive needed assistance but not under the IDEA.

Identifying Children for Evaluation

Before a child's eligibility under the IDEA can be determined, however, a full and individual evaluation of the child must be conducted. There are at least two ways in which a child may be identified to receive an evaluation under the IDEA:

- **Parents may request that their child be evaluated.** Parents are often the first to notice that their child's learning, behavior, or development may be a cause for concern. If they are worried about their child's progress in school and think she or he might need extra help from special education services, they may call, email, or write to their child's teacher, the school's principal, or the director of special education in the school district. If the school agrees that an evaluation is needed, it must evaluate the child at no cost to parents.

- **The school system may ask to evaluate the child.** Based on a teacher's recommendation, observations, or results from tests given to all children in a particular grade, a school may recommend that a child receive further screening or assessment to determine if she or he has a disability and needs special education and related services. The school system must ask parents for permission to evaluate the child, and parents must give their informed, written permission before the evaluation may be conducted.

Giving Parents Notice

It is important to know that the IDEA requires the school system to notify parents in writing that it would like to evaluate their child (or that it is refusing to evaluate the child). This is called "giving prior written notice." It is not enough for the agency to tell parents that it would like to evaluate their child or that it refuses to evaluate their child. The school must also:

- Explain why it wants to conduct the evaluation (or why it refuses)

- Describe each evaluation procedure, assessment, record, or report used as a basis for proposing the evaluation (or refusing to conduct the evaluation)

- Suggest where parents can go to obtain help in understanding the IDEA's provisions

- Inform parents of other options the school considered and why those were rejected

- Provide a description of any other factors that are relevant to the school's proposal (or refusal) to evaluate the child

The purpose behind this thorough explanation is to make sure that parents are fully informed, understand what is being proposed (or refused), understand what evaluation of their child will involve (or why the school system is refusing to conduct an evaluation of the child), and understand their right to refuse consent for evaluation, or to otherwise exercise their rights under the IDEA's procedural safeguards if the school refuses to evaluate.

All written communication from the school must be in a form the general public can understand. It must be provided in parents' native language, if they do not read English, or in the mode of communication they normally use (such as Braille or large print) unless it is clearly not feasible to do so. If parents' native language or other mode of communication is not a written language, the school must take steps to ensure:

- That the notice is translated orally (or by other means) to parents in their native language or other mode of communication

- That parents understand the content of the notice

- That there is written evidence that the above two requirements have been met

Parental Consent

Before the school may proceed with the evaluation, parents must give their informed, written consent. This consent is for the evaluation only. It does not mean that the school has the parents' permission to provide special education services to the child. That requires a separate consent.

If parents refuse consent for an initial evaluation (or simply do not respond to the school's request), the school must carefully document all its attempts to obtain parent consent. It may also continue to pursue conducting the evaluation by using the law's due process procedures or its mediation procedures, unless doing so would be inconsistent with state law relating to parental consent.

However, if the child is homeschooled or has been placed in a private school by parents (meaning, the parents are paying for the cost of the private school), the school may not override parents' lack of consent for initial evaluation of the child. As the U.S. Department of Education (ED) notes:

Once parents opt out of the public-school system, states and school districts do not have the same interest in requiring parents to agree to the evaluation of their children. In such cases, it would be overly intrusive for the school district to insist on an evaluation over a parent's objection 71 Fed. Reg. at 46635.

Timeframe for Initial Evaluation

Let us move on from the prerequisites for initial evaluation (parent notification and parent consent) to the actual process of initial evaluation and what the law requires. Let us assume that parents' informed consent has been given, and it is time to evaluate the child.

Must this evaluation be conducted within a certain period of time after parents give their consent? Yes. In its reauthorization of the IDEA in 2004, Congress added a specific time frame: the initial evaluation must be conducted **within 60 days** of receiving parental consent for the evaluation—or if the state establishes its own time frame for conducting an initial evaluation, within that time frame. (In other words: any time frame established by the state takes precedence over the 60-day timeline required by the IDEA.)

The Scope of Evaluation

A child's initial evaluation must be full and individual, focusing on that child and only that child. This is a longstanding provision of the IDEA. An evaluation of a child under the IDEA means much more than the child sitting in a room with the rest of his or her class, taking an exam for that class, that school, that district, or that state. How the child performs on such exams will contribute useful information to an IDEA-related evaluation, but large-scale tests or group-administered instruments are not enough to diagnose a disability or determine what, if any, special education or related services the child might need, let alone plan an appropriate educational program for the child.

The evaluation must use a variety of assessment tools and strategies to gather relevant functional, developmental, and academic information about the child, including information provided by the parent. When conducting an initial evaluation, it is important to examine all areas of a child's functioning to determine not only if the child is a "child with a disability," but also determine the child's educational needs. This full and individual evaluation includes evaluating the child's:

- Health
- Vision and hearing
- Social and emotional status
- General intelligence
- Academic performance
- Communicative status
- Motor abilities

As the IDEA states, the school system must ensure that: "The evaluation is sufficiently comprehensive to identify all of the child's special education and related service needs, whether or not commonly linked to the disability category in which the child has been classified."

Review Existing Data

Evaluation (and particularly reevaluation) typically begins with **a review of existing evaluation data** on the child, which may come from the child's classroom work, her or his performance on state or district assessments, information provided by the parents, and so on.

The purpose of this review is to decide if the existing data is sufficient to establish the child's eligibility and determine educational needs, or if additional information is needed. If the group determines there is sufficient information available to make the necessary determinations, the public agency must notify parents:

- Of that determination and the reason for it

- That parents have the right to request assessment to determine the child's eligibility and educational needs

Unless, the parents request an assessment, the public agency is not required to conduct one.

If it is decided that additional data is needed, the group then identifies what is needed to determine:

- Whether your son or daughter has a particular category of disability (e.g., "other health impairment," "specific learning disability")

- Your child's present levels of performance (that is, how she or he is currently doing in school) and her or his academic and developmental needs

- Whether your child needs special education and related services

- If so, whether any additions or modifications are needed in the special education and related services to enable your child to meet the goals set out in the individualized education program (IEP) to be developed and to participate, as appropriate, in the general curriculum

An example may help crystallize the comprehensive scope of evaluations: consider a first-grader with suspected hearing and vision impairments who has been referred for an initial evaluation. In order to fully gather relevant functional, developmental, and academic information and identify all of the child's special education and related service needs, evaluation of this child will obviously need to focus on hearing and vision, as well as cognitive, speech/language, motor, and social/behavioral skills to determine:

- The degree of impairment in vision and hearing and the impact of these impairments on the child

- If there are additional impairments in other areas of functioning (including those not commonly linked to hearing and/or vision) that impact the child's aptitude, performance, and achievement

- What the child's educational needs are that must be addressed

With this example, any of the following individuals might be part of this child's evaluation team: audiologist, psychologist, speech-language pathologist, social worker, occupational or physical therapist, vision specialist, regular classroom teacher, educational diagnosticians, or others.

Variety of Approaches and Sources

The evaluation must use a variety of assessment tools and strategies. This has been one of the cornerstones of the IDEA's evaluation requirements from its earliest days. Under the IDEA, it is inappropriate and unacceptable to base any eligibility decision upon the results of only one procedure. Tests alone will not give a comprehensive picture of how a child performs or what she or he knows or does not know. Only by collecting data through a variety of approaches (e.g., observations, interviews, tests, curriculum-based assessment, and so on) and from a variety of sources (parents, teachers, specialists, child) can an adequate picture be obtained of the child's strengths and weaknesses.

The IDEA also requires schools to use technically sound instruments and processes in evaluation. Technically sound instruments generally refer to assessments that have been shown through research to be valid and reliable. Technically sound processes require that assessments and other evaluation materials be:

- Administered by trained and knowledgeable personnel

- Administered in accordance with any instructions provided by the producer of the assessments

- Used for the purposes for which the assessments or measures are valid and reliable

In conjunction with using a variety of sound tools and processes, assessments must include those that are tailored to assess specific areas of educational need (for example, reading or math) and not merely those that are designed to provide a single general intelligence quotient, or IQ.

Taken together, all of this information can be used to determine whether the child has a disability under the IDEA, the specific nature of the child's special needs, whether the child needs special education and related services, and, if so, to design an appropriate program.

Consider Language, Communication Mode, and Culture

Another important component in evaluation is to ensure that assessment tools are not discriminatory on a racial or cultural basis.

Evaluation must also be conducted in the child's typical, accustomed mode of communication (unless it is clearly not feasible to do so) and in a form that will yield accurate information about what the child knows and can do academically, developmentally, and functionally. For many, English is not the native language; others use sign to communicate, or assistive or alternative augmentative communication devices. To assess such a child, using a means of communication or response not highly familiar to the child raises the probability that the evaluation results will yield minimal, if any, information about what the child knows and can do.

Specifically, consideration of language, culture, and communication mode means the following:

- If your child has limited English proficiency, materials and procedures used to assess your child must be selected and administered to ensure that they measure the extent to which your child has a disability and needs special education, rather than measuring your child's English language skills.

This provision in the law is meant to protect children of different racial, cultural, or language backgrounds from misdiagnosis. For example, children's cultural backgrounds may affect their behavior or test responses in ways that teachers or other personnel do not understand. Similarly, if a child speaks a language other than English or has limited English proficiency, she or he may not understand directions or words on tests and may be unable to answer correctly. As a result, a child may mistakenly appear to be a slow learner or to have a hearing or communication problem.

- If an assessment is not conducted under standard conditions—meaning that some condition of the test has been changed (such as the qualifications of the person giving the test or the method of giving the test)—a description of the extent to which it varied from standard conditions must be included in the evaluation report.

- If your child has impaired sensory, manual, or speaking skills, the law requires that tests are selected and administered so as best to ensure that test results accurately reflect his or her aptitude or achievement level (or whatever other factors the test claims to measure), and not merely reflect your child's impaired sensory, manual, or speaking skills (unless the test being used is intended to measure those skills).

Evaluating for Specific Learning Disabilities

The IDEA's regulations specify additional procedures required to be used for determining the existence of a specific learning disability. Sections 300.307 through 300.311 spell out what these procedures are.

It is important to note, though, that the IDEA from 2004 made dramatic changes in how children who are suspected of having a learning disability are to be evaluated.

- States must not require the use of a severe discrepancy between intellectual ability and achievement.

- States must permit the use of a process based on the child's response to scientific, research-based intervention.

- States may permit the use of other alternative research-based procedures for determining whether a child has a specific learning disability.

- The team that makes the eligibility determination must include a regular education teacher and at least one person qualified to conduct individual diagnostic examinations of children, such as a school psychologist, speech-language pathologist, or remedial reading teacher.

Determining Eligibility

Parents were not always included in the group that determined their child's eligibility and, in fact, were often excluded. Since the IDEA Amendments of 1997, parents are to be part of the group that determines their child's eligibility and are also to be provided a copy of the evaluation report, as well as documentation of the determination of the child's eligibility.

Some school systems will hold a meeting where they consider only the eligibility of the child for special education and related services. At this meeting, your child's assessment results should be explained. The specialists who assessed your child will explain what they did, why they used the tests they did, your child's results on those tests or other evaluation procedures, and what your child's scores mean when compared to other children of the same age and grade.

It is important to know that the group may not determine that a child is eligible if the determinant factor for making that judgment is the child's lack of instruction in reading or math or the child's limited

English proficiency. The child must otherwise meet the law's definition of a "child with a disability"—meaning that she or he has one of the disabilities listed in the law and, because of that disability, needs special education and related services.

If the evaluation results indicate that your child meets the definition of one or more of the disabilities listed under the IDEA and needs special education and related services, the results will form the basis for developing your child's IEP.

Disagreeing with Evaluation Results

If you, as parents of a child with a disability, disagree with the results of your child's evaluation as obtained by the public agency, you have the right to obtain what is known as an Independent Educational Evaluation, or IEE. An IEE means an evaluation conducted by a qualified examiner who is not employed by the public agency responsible for the education of your child. If you ask for an IEE, the public agency must provide you with, among other things, information about where an IEE may be obtained.

Who pays for the independent evaluation? The answer is that some IEEs are at public expense and others are paid for by the parents. For example, if you are the parent of a child with a disability and you disagree with the public agency's evaluation, you may request an IEE at public expense. "At public expense" means that the public agency either pays for the full cost of the evaluation or ensures that the evaluation is otherwise provided at no cost to you as parents. The public agency may grant your request and pay for the IEE, or it may initiate a hearing to show that its own evaluation was appropriate. The public agency may ask why you object to the public evaluation. However, the agency may not require you to explain, and it may not unreasonably delay either providing the IEE at public expense or initiating a due process hearing to defend the public evaluation.

If the public agency initiates a hearing and the final decision of the hearing officer is that the agency's evaluation was appropriate, then you still have the right to an IEE but not at public expense. As part of a due process hearing, a hearing officer may also request an IEE; if so, that IEE must be at public expense. Whenever an IEE is publicly funded, that IEE must meet the same criteria that the public agency uses when it initiates an evaluation. The public agency must tell you what these criteria are, such as location of the evaluation and the qualifications of the examiner. However, the public agency may not impose other conditions or timelines related to your obtaining an IEE at public expense.

Of course, you have the right to have your child independently evaluated at any time at your own expense. (Note: When the same tests are repeated within a short time period, the validity of the results can be seriously weakened.) The results of this evaluation must be considered by the public agency, if it meets agency criteria, in any decision made with respect to providing your child with free and appropriate public education (FAPE). The results may also be presented as evidence at a hearing regarding your child.

What Happens down the Road

After the initial evaluation, evaluations must be conducted at least every three years (generally called a "triennial evaluation") after your child has been placed in special education. Reevaluations can also occur more frequently if conditions warrant, or if you or your child's teacher request a reevaluation. Informed parental consent is also necessary for reevaluations.

As with initial evaluations, reevaluations begin with the review of existing evaluation data, including evaluations and information provided by you, the child's parents. Your consent is not required for the review of existing data on your child. As with initial evaluation, this review is to identify what additional data, if any, are needed to determine whether your child continues to be a "child with a disability" and continues to need special education and related services. If the group determines that additional data are needed, then the public agency must administer tests and other evaluation materials as needed to produce the data. Prior to collecting this additional information, the agency must obtain your informed written consent.

Or, if the group determines that no additional data are needed to determine whether your child continues to be a "child with a disability," the public agency must notify you:

- Of this determination and the reasons for it

- Of your right, as parents, to request an assessment to determine whether, for the purposes of services under the IDEA, your child continues to be a "child with a disability"

A final note with respect to reevaluations. Before determining that your child is no longer a "child with a disability" and, thus, no longer eligible for special education services under the IDEA, the public agency must evaluate your child in accordance with all of the provisions described above. This evaluation, however, is not required before terminating your child's eligibility due to graduation with a regular high school diploma or due to exceeding the age eligibility for FAPE under state law.

Chapter 6

Other Facts about Learning Disabilities

How Common Are Learning Disabilities?

Very common. As many as 1 out of every 5 people in the United States has a learning disability. Almost 1 million children (between the ages of 6 and 21) have some form of a learning disability and receive special education in school. In fact, one-third of all children who receive special education have a learning disability (Twenty-Ninth Annual Report to Congress, U.S. Department of Education (ED), 2010.

The Individuals with Disabilities Education Act Definition of "Specific Learning Disability"

Not surprisingly, the Individuals with Disabilities Education Act (IDEA) includes a definition of "specific learning disability"—as follows: Specific Learning Disability

- **General.** Specific learning disability means a disorder in one or more of the basic psychological processes involved in understanding or in using language, spoken or written, that may manifest itself in the imperfect ability to listen, think, speak, read, write, spell, or to do mathematical calculations, including

---

This chapter includes text excerpted from "Learning Disabilities (LD)," Center for Parent Information & Resources (CPIR), U.S. Department of Education (ED), June 16, 2015. Reviewed April 2019.

conditions, such as perceptual disabilities, brain injury, minimal brain dysfunction (MBD), dyslexia, and developmental aphasia.

- **Disorders not included.** Specific learning disability does not include learning problems that are primarily the result of visual, hearing, or motor disabilities, of intellectual disability, of emotional disturbance, or of environmental, cultural, or economic disadvantage.

The IDEA also lists evaluation procedures that must be used at a minimum to identify and document that a child has a specific learning disability.

Additional Evaluation Procedures for Learning Disabilities

The ways in which children are identified as having a learning disability have changed over the years. Until recently, the most common approach was to use a "severe discrepancy" formula. This referred to the gap, or discrepancy, between the child's intelligence or aptitude and her or his actual performance. However, in the 2004 reauthorization of the IDEA, how a learning disability is determined has been expanded. The IDEA now requires that states adopt criteria that:

- Must not require the use of a severe discrepancy between intellectual ability and achievement in determining whether a child has a specific learning disability
- Must permit local educational agencies (LEAs) to use a process based on the child's response to scientific, research-based intervention
- May permit the use of other alternative research-based procedures for determining whether a child has a specific learning disability

Basically, what this means is that, instead of using a severe discrepancy approach to determining the presence of a learning disability, school systems may provide the student with a research-based intervention and keep close track of the student's performance. Analyzing the student's response to that intervention (RTI) may then be considered by school districts in the process of identifying that a child has a learning disability.

There are also other aspects required when evaluating children for a learning disability. These include observing the student in her or his learning environment (including the regular education setting) to document academic performance and behavior in the areas of difficulty.

Moving on, let us suppose that the student has been diagnosed with a specific learning disability. What next?

What about School

Once a child is evaluated and found eligible for special education and related services, school staff and parents meet and develop what is known as an "Individualized Education Program," or IEP. This document is very important in the educational life of a child with learning disabilities. It describes the child's needs and the services that the public school system will provide free of charge to address those needs.

Supports or changes in the classroom (called "accommodations") help most students with a learning disability. Accessible instructional materials (AIM) are among the most helpful to students whose learning disability affects their ability to read and process printed language. Thanks to the IDEA from 2004, there are numerous places to turn now for AIMs.

Assistive technology can also help many students work around their learning disabilities. Assistive technology can range from "low-tech" equipment, such as tape recorders, to "high-tech" tools, such as reading machines (which read books aloud) and voice recognition systems (which allow the student to "write" by talking to the computer).

What If the School System Declines to Evaluate Your Child?

If the school does not think that your child's learning problems are caused by a learning disability, it may decline to evaluate your child. If this happens, there are specific actions you can take. These include:

- Contact your state's Parent Training and Information Center (PTI) for assistance. The PTI can offer you guidance and support in what to do next.

- Consider having your child evaluated by an independent evaluator. You may have to pay for this evaluation, or you can ask that the school pay for it.

- Ask for mediation, or use one of the IDEA's other dispute resolution options. Parents have the right to disagree with the school's decision not to evaluate their child and be heard.

Part Two

Types of
Learning Disabilities

Chapter 7

Auditory Processing Disorder

Children who have difficulty using the information they hear in academic and social situations may have central auditory processing disorder (CAPD), more recently termed "auditory processing disorder" (APD). These children typically can hear information but have difficulty attending to, storing, locating, retrieving, and/or clarifying that information to make it useful for academic and social purposes. This can have a negative impact on both language acquisition and academic performance.

What Is Central Auditory Processing?

When the ears detect sound, the auditory stimulus travels through the structures of the ears, or the peripheral auditory system, to the central auditory nervous system that extends from the brain stem to the temporal lobes of the cerebral cortex. The auditory stimulus travels along the neural pathways where it is "processed," allowing the listener to determine the direction from which the sound comes, identify the type of sound, separate the sound from background noise, and interpret the sound. The listener builds upon what is heard by

This chapter includes text excerpted from "Auditory Processing Disorders: An Overview," Education Resources Information Center (ERIC), U.S. Department of Education (ED), December 2012. Reviewed April 2019.

storing, retrieving, or clarifying the auditory information to make it functionally useful.

What Is a Disorder of Auditory Processing?

APD is an impaired ability to attend to, discriminate, remember, recognize, or comprehend information presented auditorily in individuals who typically exhibit normal intelligence and normal hearing. This definition has been expanded to include the effects that peripheral hearing loss may contribute to auditory processing deficits. Auditory processing difficulties become more pronounced in challenging listening situations, such as noisy backgrounds or poor acoustic environments, at great distances from the speaker, speakers with fast speaking rates, or speakers with foreign accents.

What Are the Behaviors of Children with Auditory Processing Disorder?

Children who have auditory processing disorders may behave as if they have a hearing loss. While not all children present all behaviors, The following are examples of behaviors that may be displayed by children who have APD:

- Inconsistent response to speech
- Frequent requests for repetition ("What?" "Huh?")
- Difficulty listening or paying attention in noisy environments
- Often misunderstanding what is said
- Difficulty following long directions
- Poor memory of information presented verbally
- Difficulty discerning direction from which sound is coming
- History of middle ear infection

What Are Academic Characteristics of Children Who Have Auditory Processing Disorder?

In addition to the preceding behaviors, children may also present a variety of academic characteristics that may lead teachers and parents to suspect APD. The following are some of the characteristics. Again, all children will not present all characteristics.

- Poor expressive and receptive language abilities

- Poor reading, writing, and spelling

- Poor phonics and speech sound discrimination

- Difficulty taking notes

- Difficulty learning foreign languages

- Weak short-term memory

- Behavioral, psychological, and/or social problems resulting from poor language and academic skills

How Is Auditory Processing Disorder Diagnosed?

Given the complexity of auditory processing disorders, it is important to involve a multidisciplinary team, which includes psychologists, physicians, teachers, parents, audiologists, and speech-language pathologists. Audiologists diagnose the presence of APD (hearing and processing problems), and speech-language pathologists evaluate a child's perception of speech and receptive-expressive language use. Other team members conduct additional assessments to determine a child's educational strengths and weaknesses. Checklists that ask teachers and parents to observe the child's auditory behaviors may be used to determine a need for the APD evaluation. The parent's description of the child's auditory behavior at home is an especially important contribution to the diagnosis of APD.

What Does the Audiologist Do?

The audiologist assesses the peripheral and central auditory systems using a battery of tests, which may include both electrophysiological and behavioral tests. Peripheral hearing tests determine if the child has hearing loss and, if so, the degree to which the loss is a factor in the child's learning problems. Assessment of the central auditory system evaluates the child's ability to respond under different conditions of auditory signal distortion and competition. It is based on the assumption that a child with an intact auditory system can tolerate mild distortions of speech and still understand it, while a child with APD will encounter difficulty when the auditory system is stressed by signal distortion and competing messages. The test results allow the audiologist to identify strengths and weaknesses in the child's auditory system that can be used to develop educational and remedial intervention strategies.

How Should Test Results Be Interpreted?

As with any kind of evaluation, test results should be interpreted with caution. The effects of neurological maturation may influence test results for children under the age of 12. A true diagnosis of APD cannot be determined until that time. However, there are much younger children whose auditory behaviors, language, and academic characteristics indicate that APD is a strong possibility, and, even without a formal diagnosis, these children would benefit from intervention. Remediation should address their strengths and areas of need based on available speech-language and psychoeducational testing.

What Can Be Done to Help Children with Auditory Processing Disorder in the Classroom?

Traditional educational and therapeutic approaches can be employed to remediate areas of need in language, reading, and writing. Many techniques that have shown to be effective with children with APD would be beneficial to all children, with and without APD, if the strategies employed are specific to the child's areas of need. Some of these are described below:

Modify the environment by reducing background noise and enhancing the speech signal to improve access to auditory information.

- Eliminate or reduce sources of noise in the classroom (air vent, street traffic, playground, hallway, furniture noises, etc.).

- Use assistive listening devices (ALDs), such as a sound field amplification system or an FM auditory trainer.

- Allow preferential or roving seating to ensure that the child is seated as close to the speaker possible.

- Allow the child to use a tape recorder and/or a peer note taker.

- Ensure that the speaker gets the child's attention before speaking, and considers using a slower speaking rate, repeating directions, allowing time for the child to respond to questions, pausing to allow the child to catch up, and presenting information in a visual format through overheads, illustrations, and print.

Teach the child to use compensatory strategies, "meta" strategies, or executive functions to teach how to listen actively. The child should:

- Learn to identify and resolve difficult listening situations.

- Develop skills to understand the demands of listening, such as attending, memory, identifying important parts of the message, self-monitoring, clarifying, and problem-solving.

- Develop memory techniques, such as verbal rehearsal (reauditorization), mnemonics (chunking, cueing, and chaining).

- Encourage the use of external organizational aids, such as a checklist, notebook, calendar, etc.

- Develop vocabulary, syntax, and pragmatic skills to facilitate language comprehension.

Provide auditory training to remediate specific auditory deficits.

- Children who have poor reading, writing, and spelling skills may benefit from phonological awareness activities.

- Auditory closure activities may assist children in filling in or predicting the information they are listening to in the classroom and conversations.

- Instruction in interpreting intonation, speaking rate, or vocal intensity, and in the relationship between syllable and word may assist children in determining important parts of the message.

- When the child has demonstrated success on the above tasks in a quiet environment, give the child practice engaging in the same tasks in an environment that includes background noise.

- Explore the use of commercially available computer programs designed to develop the child's attention to the phonological aspects of speech. These should be recommended by a professional who can determine their applicability to the child's needs.

Chapter 8

Developmental Dyscalculia

Developmental dyscalculia is generally defined as a disorder in mathematical abilities, presumed to be due to a specific impairment in brain function. Developmental dyscalculia is supposed to be a unique deficit that is not caused by a reading disorder (dyslexia), attentional disorder, or general intelligence (IQ) problems. The present study aims to examine attention in developmental dyscalculia by employing a recently designed test of three attentional networks and their interactions.

Characteristics of Developmental Dyscalculia

Children with developmental dyscalculia fail in a wide range of numerical tasks. For example, they present difficulties in the retrieval of arithmetical facts, in using arithmetical procedures, and in solving arithmetical operations in general. Recently, studies on developmental dyscalculia concentrated on basic numerical processing and found that those with developmental dyscalculia exhibited an atypical effect, size congruency magnitude comparisons, and subitizing.

Neuro-functional studies indicate that mathematical difficulties involve abnormalities in the structure or the activity of the parietal lobes, mostly the intraparietal sulcus. A focused infarct to the left

This chapter includes text excerpted from "Attentional Networks in Developmental Dyscalculia," U.S. National Library of Medicine (NLM), January 7, 2010. Reviewed April 2019.

intraparietal sulcus could produce primary acalculia. Some researchers found a reduction in gray matter in the left intraparietal sulcus in children born preterm who suffered from calculation deficits. A structural and functional abnormality in the right intraparietal sulcus was found in women with Turner syndrome who had dyscalculia. Recent work by researchers examined the activity in the brains of those with developmental dyscalculia and discovered reduced activity in the right intraparietal sulcus during non-symbolic magnitude processing. Finally, researchers showed that transcranial magnetic stimulation (TMS) to the right intraparietal sulcus in normal control participants induced a dyscalculia-like pattern. Accordingly, one line of thinking is that developmental dyscalculia is a domain-specific (pure) disorder that involves only deficits in basic numerical processing and is related to one biological marker (i.e., a deficit in the intraparietal sulcus).

Alternatively, some refer to deficits in arithmetic as a "domain-general phenomenon." One of the main deficits in developmental dyscalculia is difficulty in the retrieval of arithmetical facts. It has been suggested that this difficulty is more related to deficits in attention, working memory, or long-term memory than to deficits in conceptual knowledge of arithmetic. In addition, there are indications that mathematical abilities are directly related to general abilities, such as executive functions and verbal or visuospatial working memory. Finally, there are indications that the developmental course of the numerical distance effect is domain-general rather than domain-specific. Moreover, it has been suggested that mathematical learning difficulties are characterized by heterogeneity in symptoms and, possibly, in deficient mechanisms.

Some researchers suggested that developmental disorders characterized by a domain-specific end state can stem from a domain-general starting point. In addition, it has been suggested that neuropsychological dissociation studies of brain injuries and stroke patients that have dramatically influenced cognitive research may not apply to developmental disorders, such as developmental dyscalculia. First, the basis of developmental disorders is believed to be genetic, and one could not expect a one-to-one correlation between genes and specific cognitive functions (such as a deficit in the processing of quantities in developmental dyscalculia). Second, there are compensation mechanisms that operate throughout development and change the observed deficits during adolescence. Third, some of the tests employed in the screening process of research participants (e.g., screening for attentional deficits in developmental dyscalculia) are not sensitive enough to reveal deficits in the "preserved" domain. Hence, it is possible that an abnormal expression of genes affects multiple aspects of development, with the strongest effect being on one specific aspect. In the case of developmental dyscalculia, this could be core numerical processing.

The present study investigates attention, in a group of those with "pure" developmental dyscalculia. Namely, the participants have no indication of deficits in commonly used tests of attention and reading and have a normal level of intelligence. The study focuses on attention because the intraparietal sulcus, involved in number processing and possibly abnormal in those with developmental dyscalculia, has a critical role in orienting of attention. Moreover, several researchers have suggested that some of the difficulties in developmental dyscalculia may be related to attention.

Attention and Developmental Dyscalculia

Researchers also found that children diagnosed as having developmental dyscalculia had a higher mean score on an attentional problem subscale than matched controls. A similar pattern of results was found in the study of developmental dyscalculia group, and the study presented more commission and omission errors compared to the controls in the computerized continuous performance test (CPT). In addition, many deficits that characterize developmental dyscalculia can be connected to deficits in recruiting attention.

Researchers examined developmental dyscalculia participants using the numerical Stroop task, in which differently valued numbers are displayed in various sizes, and discovered a lack of facilitation. They concluded that the ability to connect Arabic numerals to internal magnitudes is damaged in those with developmental dyscalculia. However, deficits in the executive functions network in the developmental dyscalculia population can also influence performance in the numerical Stroop task. In Stroop and Stroop-like tasks, a multi-dimensional object is presented and participants have to attend to one dimension while ignoring other dimensions. Performance in these tasks is considered to be based, among other things, on selective attention abilities, and on executive functions, examined frequently in conflict situations. Moreover, the anterior cingulate cortex is considered to be involved in conflict monitoring. The activity in the anterior cingulate cortex was discovered during the numerical Stroop task. In addition, it was recently found that normal participants presented a developmental dyscalculia-like pattern in the numerical Stroop task under a condition of attentional load, namely, they showed a lack of facilitation.

Those with developmental dyscalculia have a smaller subitizing range. Subitizing is a fast and accurate evaluation of a small set of objects. However, it was recently suggested that subitizing may be modulated by attention. A recent study examined the role of attention in the subitizing process and discovered that when attention is limited, the subitizing range decreases to 2 dots. In addition, attentional training increases the subitizing range.

Several studies directly proposed that those with developmental dyscalculia suffer from deficits in executive functions or in working memory. In contrast, some researchers found no evidence for deficient executive functioning in mathematically disabled (MD) children. They used the Stroop and the flanker tasks to examine the inhibition ability in MD children and matched controls. The ability to inhibit irrelevant information is considered to be part of the executive function network. Their results indicated that MD children showed normal performance on these tasks. No group differences were found in their study.

Some of the studies that were described above did not differentiate between pure developmental dyscalculia and the co-morbidity between developmental dyscalculia and attention deficit hyperactivity disorder (ADHD), thus it is not clear whether the attentional difficulties in those with developmental dyscalculia are part and parcel of their dyscalculia or of the co-morbid deficit (i.e., ADHD). To this end, it is important to exclude participants with co-morbidity between ADHD and developmental dyscalculia.

Chapter 9

Dysgraphia

Dysgraphia is a neurological disorder characterized by writing disabilities. Specifically, the disorder causes a person's writing to be distorted or incorrect. In children, the disorder generally emerges when they are first introduced to writing. They make inappropriately sized and spaced letters, or write wrong or misspelled words, despite thorough instruction. Children with the disorder may have other learning disabilities; however, they usually have no social or other academic problems. Cases of dysgraphia in adults generally occur after some trauma. In addition to poor handwriting, dysgraphia is characterized by wrong or odd spelling, and production of words that are not correct (i.e., using "boy" for "child"). The cause of the disorder is unknown, but in adults, it is usually associated with damage to the parietal lobe of the brain.

Treatment

Treatment for dysgraphia varies and may include treatment for motor disorders to help control writing movements. Other treatments

This chapter contains text excerpted from the following sources: Text in this chapter begins with excerpts from "Dysgraphia Information Page," National Institute of Neurological Disorders and Stroke (NINDS), March 27, 2019; Text under the heading "Handwriting and Dysgraphia" is excerpted from "Inter-Relationships between Objective Handwriting Features and Executive Control among Children with Developmental Dysgraphia," U.S. National Library of Medicine (NLM), April 24, 2018.

may address impaired memory or other neurological problems. Some physicians recommend that individuals with dysgraphia use computers to avoid the problems of handwriting.

Prognosis

Some individuals with dysgraphia improve their writing ability, but for others, the disorder persists.

Handwriting and Dysgraphia

Handwriting still serves as the most immediate form of graphic communication, despite the expanding use of technology. Skilled handwriting is essential for school-aged children. This skill allows them to write within a reasonable amount of time and to create a readable product through which thoughts and ideas can be communicated.

Children typically acquire skillful handwriting performance during the first three years of school. With this skill, they are able to automatically write a legible product while keeping in line with the expected time demands of the class schedule, (although, previous research has established that a large number of children do not yet write automatically by this age). These children are either diagnosed with dysgraphia or need to cope with ongoing difficulties with handwriting. In the *Diagnostic and Statistical Manual of Mental Disorders, Fifth Edition* (DSM-5) dysgraphia is coded as a "Specific Learning Disorder with impairment in the written expression." However, no specific diagnostic criteria are provided. Some researchers describe dysgraphia as a disturbance or difficulty in the production of written language related to the mechanics of writing. The inadequate handwriting performance is seen among children who have at least an average intelligence level and who have not been diagnosed with any apparent neurological or perceptual-motor difficulties.

Despite evidence of dysgraphia among 10 to 34 percent of all school-aged children, research on developmental dysgraphia is sparse. Fine motor activities and predominantly writing tasks compose 30 to 60 percent of an average school day. Therefore, handwriting deficits as such, or dysgraphia, can harm children's confidence and self-image, and consequently affect their academic achievements.

Handwriting is a complex activity that entails an intricate blend of cognitive, kinesthetic, and perceptual-motor components. In order to produce a handwritten product, the child needs to simultaneously activate sensory-motor and cognitive skills, devise an idea, plan the structure of the sentence syntax and spelling, attain motor-orthographic integration to create the text and achieve the desired result.

Chapter 10

Dyslexia

Chapter Contents

Section 10.1

Dyslexia Basics

This section contains text excerpted from the following sources:
Text in this section begins with excerpts from "Dyslexia Information
Page," National Institute of Neurological Disorders and Stroke
(NINDS), November 2, 2018; Text beginning with the heading
"Dyslexia Symptoms" is excerpted from "What Is Dyslexia?"
MedlinePlus, National Institutes of Health (NIH), July 6, 2016.

Dyslexia is a brain-based type of learning disability that specifically impairs a person's ability to read. These individuals typically read at levels significantly lower than expected, despite having normal intelligence. Although the disorder varies from person to person, common characteristics among people with dyslexia are difficulty with phonological processing (the manipulation of sounds), spelling, and/or rapid visual-verbal responding. In individuals with adult onset of dyslexia, it usually occurs as a result of brain injury or in the context of dementia; this contrasts with individuals with dyslexia who simply were never identified as children or adolescents. Dyslexia can be inherited in some families, and recent studies have identified a number of genes that may predispose an individual to developing dyslexia.

Dyslexia Symptoms

People with dyslexia often show:

- Difficulty and slowness in reading words
- Difficulty understanding text that is read (poor comprehension)
- Problems with spelling
- Delayed speech (learning to talk later than most other children)
- Difficulty with rhyming

Treating Dyslexia

The main focus of treatment should be on a person's specific learning problems, typically by modifying the teaching environment and methods.

- **Special teaching techniques.** The use of explicit, systematic instruction to teach and directly support children's efforts to learn to read and recognize words. This occurs over time.

- **Classroom modifications.** For example, teachers can give students with dyslexia extra time to finish tasks and provide taped tests that allow the child to hear the questions instead of reading them.

- **Use of technology.** Children with dyslexia may benefit from listening to books on tape or using word-processing programs with spell-check features.

Prognosis for Dyslexia

For those with dyslexia, the prognosis is mixed. The disability affects such a wide range of people and produces such different symptoms and varying severity that predictions are hard to make. Prognosis is generally good, however, for individuals whose dyslexia is identified early, who have supportive family and friends and a strong self-image, and who are involved in proper remediation.

Information for the Parents
Is There a Key to Helping People with Dyslexia?

Early, systematic, and explicit reading instruction—teaching the link between the written word and its specific sounds—is critical for dyslexia. The written word maps directly onto spoken language. So, the challenge is to link the sounds of English, for example, to the specific letters of the alphabet.

How Can Parents Help Their Children?

Since learning begins at home, the best thing parents can do is to talk with their children and read to them every day. Let them soak in what they are hearing and learn how to converse. This is a great opportunity to bond with your children and helps them build their oral vocabulary and learn the structure of language, which are part of the foundation for reading.

What Is the Goal?

The goal is to build a foundation for reading, which takes lots of time and practice.

When Should Special Instruction Begin?

For children who are struggling to read, special instruction should begin as early as possible. Some children need more time to learn, while others do better in smaller groups. So, parents should build relationships with their children's teachers and school administrators to advocate for the best possible support.

Early intervention reduces long-term problems. Children who are not improving by the fourth or fifth grade may need continued instructional support on foundational skills of reading in later grades.

Section 10.2

Brain Activity Pattern Signals Ability to Compensate for Dyslexia

This section includes text excerpted from "Brain Activity Pattern Signals Ability to Compensate for Dyslexia," *Eunice Kennedy Shriver* National Institute of Child Health and Human Development (NICHD), December 20, 2010. Reviewed April 2019.

Brain scans of dyslexic adolescents who were later able to compensate for their dyslexia showed a distinct pattern of brain activity when compared to scans of adolescents who were unable to compensate, reported researchers funded in part by the National Institutes of Health (NIH).

The finding raises the possibility that, one day, imaging or other measures of brain activity could be used to predict which individuals with dyslexia would most readily benefit from various specific interventions.

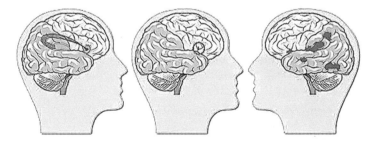

Figure 10.1. *Brain Scans of Dyslexic Adolescents*

In Figure 10.1, (left) brains of adolescents who compensated for dyslexia had strong connections on the right side of the brain, between a brain area that processes images and an area that stores images in long term memory. When involved in rhyming tasks, the brains of youth who compensated for dyslexia showed increased activity in a brain area known as the "inferior frontal gyrus" (center). In contrast, (right) brains of typically developing readers show increased activity on the left side of the brain when involved in rhyming.

"This finding provides insight into how certain individuals with dyslexia may compensate for reading difficulties," said Alan E. Guttmacher, M.D., Director of the NIH's *Eunice Kennedy Shriver* National Institute of Child Health and Human Development (NICHD), which provided funding for the study. "Understanding the brain activity associated with compensation may lead to ways to help individuals with this capacity draw upon their strengths. Similarly, learning why other individuals have difficulty compensating may lead to new treatments to help them overcome reading disability."

The study findings were published online in *Proceedings of the National Academy of Sciences*. The study's first author was Fumiko Hoeft, M.D., Ph.D., of the Stanford University School of Medicine.

The researchers used two types of brain imaging technology to conduct their study. The first, functional magnetic resonance imaging (fMRI), depicts oxygen use by brain areas involved in a particular task or activity. The second, diffusion tensor magnetic resonance imaging (DTI), maps the brain's wiring, revealing connections between brain areas.

The adolescents were shown pairs of printed words and asked to identify pairs that rhymed. The adolescents who would later compensate for their dyslexia showed a pattern of increased activity in the inferior frontal gyrus, an area on the right side of the head, slightly below and behind the temple. This brain area governs the ability to halt an ongoing activity, such as stopping at a traffic light. Similarly, DTI scans of the brain also revealed stronger connections in the superior longitudinal fasciculus (also on the right side), a network of neural fibers linking the front and rear of brain. The fibers are involved in the processing of visual aspects of text. The researchers do not know how the inferior frontal gyrus and superior longitudinal fasciculus are involved in compensating for dyslexia.

The 45 adolescents who took part in the study ranged from 11 to 14 years of age. Each child underwent a battery of tests to determine reading abilities. Among the series of tests were measures of phonemic awareness (the ability to distinguish between the sounds that make up spoken words); how well they could comprehend what they read; how fluently and accurately they could read; how fast they could read; spelling ability; the ability to rapidly name objects, letters, numbers, and colors; and the size of their vocabularies.

The researchers classified 25 adolescents as having dyslexia based on their scores in these tests.

The researchers used the term "dyslexia" to describe the reading difficulties experienced by the adolescents in the study. These individuals have a learning disability that makes learning to read much more challenging and often requires more intensive interventions to help them succeed.

Dr. Hoeft said that, in the study, the adolescents who were classified as having dyslexia had difficulty learning to read, despite adequate teaching and exposure to written language.

The researchers adapted computer algorithms used in artificial intelligence research to refine the data collected by the scanner, to gauge subtle brain functioning and structure with a high degree of accuracy.

FMRI scans of the remaining adolescents without dyslexia who are reading normally showed strong brain activation patterns on the left side of the brain when the adolescents were involved in the rhyming task. In contrast, brain scans of the dyslexic adolescents revealed weak activation on the left side of the brain. However, 13 of the dyslexic adolescents who later were able to compensate for their disability showed strong activation in the right inferior frontal gyrus. Similarly, DTI scans for the compensating group showed a strong network of connections in the superior longitudinal fasciculus on the right side of the brain.

When the researchers administered the reading test battery to the adolescents 2½ years later, they found that the 13 adolescents who showed the strong activation pattern in the inferior frontal gyrus were much more likely to have compensated for their reading difficulty than were the remaining 12 dyslexic adolescents.

Dr. Hoeft, explained, that the largest improvement was seen in reading comprehension, which she said is the ultimate goal of reading. The adolescents showed less improvement in other reading-related skills, such as phonemic awareness. Good readers tend to develop phonemic awareness skills before developing fluency and comprehension skills. Dr. Hoeft said that the findings suggest that the brains of the dyslexic adolescents relied on the right side of the brain to compensate for their reading difficulties, rather than on developing regions in the left side of their brains (involved with phonemic awareness), as typical readers do.

In fact, through their analysis of brain activation patterns and brain structure, the researchers could predict with more than 90 percent accuracy which adolescents would compensate for their dyslexia.

"Our findings add to a body of studies looking at a wide range of conditions that suggest brain imaging may help determine when a treatment is likely to be effective or which patients are most susceptible to risks," said Dr. Hoeft.

In contrast, the testing battery the researchers used did not indicate which of the dyslexic adolescents would improve their reading ability.

Chapter 11

Gifted but Learning Disabled

Identification of Gifted/Learning Disabled

The identification of gifted/learning disabled (GLD) students is not a straightforward process. A student with two exceptionalities is often described as "twice-exceptional," and these students have been noted throughout our history. Many of these GLD people have made significant contributions to our society. For instance, in her article "A Diamond in the Rough," Lisa Fine Goldstein, a writer for *Education Week*, reminds us that, despite Einstein's brilliance in visual and spatial reasoning and problem-solving, he had behavioral problems as a schoolboy, was a rotten speller, and had trouble expressing himself. His report cards were dismal.

It is these traits that are often linked to the twice-exceptional or GLD person. The gifted/learning disabled have been identified as a unique group of individuals with unique educational needs for three decades; however, identification and programming strategies have remained elusive for this particular group of students. To succeed, these students require remediation in their areas of need or disability, and at the same time, they also require opportunities to enhance their strengths in their areas of giftedness.

Gifted/learning disabled students are also students at risk. School comes easily for these students, yet they are often unprepared for

This chapter includes text excerpted from "The Challenge of Identifying Gifted/ Learning Disabled Students," Education Resources Information Center (ERIC), U.S. Department of Education (ED), March 2013. Reviewed April 2019.

the challenges their disabilities create when they are presented with higher-level tasks as they progress in school. This ability/disability can produce, among many possible emotions and behaviors, frustration, anger, depression, carelessness, off-task behavior, and classroom disruption. These students may also suffer from low self-esteem and they can feel as if they are a disappointment to their teachers and parents, and they tend to focus on what they cannot do, rather on what they can do.

Definitions
Learning Disabled

The term "learning disabled" refers to a number of disorders that may affect the acquisition, organization, retention, understanding, or use of verbal or nonverbal information. These disorders affect learning in individuals who otherwise demonstrate at least average abilities essential for thinking and/or reasoning. As such, learning disabilities are distinct from global intellectual deficiency. Learning disabilities result from impairments in one or more processes related to perceiving, thinking, remembering, or learning. These disorders are not due primarily to hearing and/or vision problems, socioeconomic factors, cultural or linguistic differences, lack of motivation, or ineffective teaching.

In addition, a learning disorder evident in both academic and social situations involves one or more of the processes necessary for the proper use of spoken language or the symbols of communication and is characterized by a condition that:

1. Is not primarily the result of:

    - Impairment of vision

    - Impairment of hearing

    - Physical disability

    - Developmental disability

    - Primary emotional disturbance

    - Cultural difference

2. Results in a significant discrepancy between academic achievement and assessed intellectual ability, with deficits in one or more of the following:

    - Receptive language (listening, reading)

- Language processing (thinking, conceptualizing, integrating)
- Expressive language (talking, spelling, writing)
- Mathematical computations

3. May be associated with one or more conditions diagnosed as:
   - A perceptual handicap
   - A brain injury
   - Minimal brain dysfunction
   - Dyslexia
   - Developmental aphasia

Gifted

"Giftedness" is an exceptional potential and/or performance across a wide range of abilities in one or more of the following areas:

- General intellectual
- Specific academic
- Creative thinking
- Social
- Musical
- Artistic
- Kinesthetic

Exactly how to measure this potential is not indicated; however, the need to focus on the exceptional potential and/or performance in general intellectual and specific academic abilities is clear.

A gifted student has an unusually advanced degree of general intellectual ability that requires differentiated learning experiences of a depth and breadth beyond those normally provided in the regular school program in order to satisfy the level of educational potential indicated.

Gifted / Learning Disabled

Combining the definitions for gifted and learning disabled results in the following definition for gifted/disabled that will be used for the remainder of this chapter. A gifted/learning disabled (GLD) student is a student of superior intellectual ability who demonstrates a significant discrepancy between their level of performance in a particular academic area and their expected level of performance based on their intellectual ability. In addition to superior intellectual ability and a performance/potential discrepancy, a processing deficit is also evident.

Although GLD students have been identified as a unique group since the 1970s, they remain under-identified in the population of disabled students. Because criteria used to establish giftedness varies between school jurisdictions, it is difficult to make identification comparisons. It is also difficult to establish common identification criteria.

In sum, the characteristics of the gifted/learning disabled can impinge negatively on the identification process.

Types of Gifted / Learning Disabled

Because of their academic potential, the gifted/learning disabled student's achievement may not be as low as other students with learning disabilities. For this reason, they may be referred for special education less often than their non-gifted counterparts. Researchers speculate that these students may fail to receive the specialized services they require because they fail to meet the criteria for either gifted or learning disabled programs. Gifted students are often able to compensate for their disabilities and are not achieving below grade level. They may not receive referrals unless there are behavioral issues. On the other hand, students who have learning disabilities may not be identified as gifted because they do not consistently display high achievement. Looking at the reasons behind the lack of referrals, researchers have identified three different types of GLD students:

- Gifted with mild learning disabilities

- Gifted with severe learning disabilities

- Masked abilities and disabilities

Type I—Mild Learning Disability

The first type of GLD students are those who are gifted with mild learning disabilities. These students tend to do well throughout elementary school and often participate in gifted programs at that level. They do not run into difficulty until they must do higher level work in the area of their disability and may go through periods of underachievement.

Because they have previously done well, they are often not identified as learning disabled but may be looked upon as lazy, lacking motivation, or as having poor self-esteem.

Type II—Severe Learning Disability

The second type of GLD student has severe learning disabilities but is also gifted. These students are often identified as learning disabled but rarely identified as gifted. They are noted for what they cannot do, rather than what they can do, and attention becomes focused on their problems. Unless they are correctly identified and provided with appropriate programming, it is difficult for these students to reach their full potential.

Type III—Masked Abilities and Disabilities

The final type of student is generally not identified as gifted or learning disabled. Their gifts mask their disabilities, and their disabilities mask their gifts. As a result of this masking, they appear average and are not often referred for evaluation. Without a formal assessment, the discrepancy between their ability and their achievement is not noticed. These students may perform at grade level but do not reach their full potential. This third group presents an interesting challenge, as their disability may lower their IQ (intelligence quotient) score so significantly that even with testing they may not be identified as gifted.

Compensation

Further complicating the identification of gifted/learning disabled students is the idea of compensation. Gifted students are excellent problem solvers. The more abstract reasoning they have, the better able they are to use reasoning in place of modality strength to solve problems. Compensation can be unconscious or conscious. One part of the brain may take over when another part is damaged. In some cases, students may be taught specific compensation techniques. While compensation can help the student adapt, it can also make an accurate diagnosis of a learning disability more difficult.

Recommended Methods of Identification
A Multi-Faceted Approach

Determining the best method to identify gifted/learning disabled students is not an easy task due to their dual issues. The

Twice-Exceptional Child Projects (a research project funded by the U.S. government), found that gifted/learning disabled student's scores on the Wechsler Intelligence Scale for Children-Revised (WISC-R)—an intelligence test for children between the ages of 6 and 16—resembled their gifted peers, while their reading and written language ability more closely resembled that of learning disabled students. Researchers suggest that since gifted/learning disabled students represent a variety of giftedness in combination with various forms of learning disabilities, one pattern or set of scores that identifies all gifted/learning disabled students is not very likely. There is, however, a set of characteristics that seems to apply to all gifted/learning disabled students and should be the focus when identifying these students:

- Evidence of an outstanding talent or ability

- Evidence of a discrepancy between expected and actual achievement

- Evidence of a processing deficit

Chapter 12

Nonverbal Learning Disability

Nonverbal learning disability (NLD) is a brain-based learning disability where individuals have difficulty with abstract thinking, spatial relationships, and identifying and interpreting concepts and patterns. Nonverbal learning disability occurs in 0.1 to 1 percent of the general population. It is also called "nonverbal learning disorder" (NVLD) or a "right-hemisphere learning disorder."

People use the spoken word in various ways. Sometimes, they say exactly what they mean. Sometimes, they expect the listener to pick up another meaning from their facial expression or tone of voice. Sometimes, they expect the listener to fill in information from past experience or some other source of information. For example, when said directly, "I love rainy days" is the truth. But, if the same phrase is said with a frown or eye roll and a growly tone, the speaker is being sarcastic and is really telling the listener that she or he hates rainy days. Finally, if the speaker says, "You know how I feel about rainy days," the listener is expected to fill in some previously learned information. A person with a nonverbal learning disability cannot interpret the facial expressions and tone of voice of the sarcasm and thus takes the untrue statement as true. Nor can the listener draw on a pattern of previously learned information, and thus truly does not know how the speaker feels.

"Nonverbal Learning Disability," © 2016 Omnigraphics. Reviewed April 2019.

Signs of Nonverbal Learning Disability

Children with NLD tend to be very smart. They talk freely, develop large vocabularies in comparison to other children their age, memorize facts, and read early. Intelligence tests show high verbal IQ but low performance IQ due to visual-spatial difficulties.

There are five main areas of weakness in people with NLD. People with NLD may not exhibit weakness in all five areas, nor may they exhibit them all at once. The weaknesses tend to become more obvious as children progress in school and are required to rely more on identifying patterns and less on memorized facts.

The five main areas of weakness have been identified as:

- **Visual/spatial awareness.** Children with NLD may have problems estimating distance, size, and/or shape of objects. They may be clumsy, spill drinks, bump into people or objects, or not be able to catch a ball. They may also have a poor sense of direction, such as being able to distinguish left from right.

- **Motor skills.** Children with NLD may have trouble mastering basic motor skills both large (such as dressing themselves, running, or riding a bike) or small (such as writing or using scissors).

- **Abstract thinking.** Children with NLD may have difficulty seeing or understanding the big picture. They can read a story and relate the details, but cannot answer questions about how the details fit together.

- **Conceptual skills.** Children with NLD may have trouble grasping the larger concept of a situation. For example, determining how pieces of a puzzle fit together to make a whole or identifying the steps needed to solve a problem. This contributes to problems especially with math.

- **Social skills.** Children with NLD may have trouble making friends or socializing in a group. They may interrupt or behave inappropriately in social situations. They use previously learned skills to cope with new social situations, whether appropriate or not.

In addition, because NLD occurs in the right side of the brain, children with NLD may have a distorted sense of touch or feel and poor coordination on the left side of the body.

These areas of weakness are often masked in preschool and the early elementary grades when students are learning basic (rote) skills, such as reading and arithmetic. By the fourth or fifth grade, when students are required to process what they read or remember patterns from previous examples, the weaknesses start to become evident. At the same time, these very smart children may start exhibiting behavioral problems brought on by frustration in not "getting it" or feelings of being a social reject.

Diagnosis of Nonverbal Learning Disorder

The diagnosis of NLD is controversial. NLD is not listed in the American Psychiatric Association's *Diagnostic and Statistical Manual of Mental Disorders, 5th ed.* (DSM-5), the manual used by doctors and therapists to diagnose learning disabilities. Nor is NLD recognized as a disability covered by the Individuals with Disabilities Education Act (IDEA). Nonetheless, if a child is exhibiting signs of NLD, there are steps parents should take to identify the problem.

- **A medical exam.** A thorough physical examination and a discussion of the child's learning problems will help the doctor rule out any physical causes for the learning problems.

- **A mental-health professional.** Most likely, the family doctor will refer the child to a neurologist or other specialist. The specialist will talk to the parents and child about what is happening and may administer a variety of tests in the areas of speech and language, motor skills, and visual-spatial relationships. The results coupled with information from the parents and child will help the specialist analyze the strengths and weaknesses associated with NLD and make a diagnosis.

As with many learning disorders, the symptoms of NLD vary from child to child; thus, a comprehensive assessment is needed to determine the individual child's needs. With the input and support of learning professionals and therapists, as well as the family, steps can be taken to help the student with NLD.

Help for Those with Nonverbal Learning Disorder

It is important to work with the child's school specialists to develop accommodations for the child's NLD. Formal accommodations may be developed through an Individualized Education Program (IEP) or 504 Plan. If the child does not qualify for either plan, informal accommodations may be made in the classroom. Classroom accommodations may include modifying homework assignments and tests for time and content, presenting lectures with PowerPoint (PPT) slides so the student can see as well as hear the material being covered, and/or working with a reading specialist to read a passage aloud then extract key terms and ideas.

Parents can help their child in various ways that will make things easier for both the student and the family. They can:

- Establish structure and routine.

- Give clear instructions.

- Keep a chart of the day's activities, both social and academic.

- Make transitions easier by giving logical, step-by-step explanations of what is going to happen. (We are going to IHOP for dinner. We need to leave in an hour.)

- Break down tasks into small steps in a logical sequence.

- Play games with the child to have her or him identify emotions from facial expressions or voice tone.

- Avoid sarcasm, or if it happens, use the experience to help the child identify the signs of sarcasm.

- Set up one-on-one play dates with another child who shares an interest with yours. Playdates should be structured, monitored, and time-bound.

- Avoid situations that may overwhelm the child with too much sensory input—noise, smell, and activity.

There are other sources of help for parents and students. Social skills groups help the student in social situations. Parent behavioral training helps parents learn how to collaborate with teachers. Occupational and physical therapy may help the child improve movement and writing skills, as well as build tolerance for outside experiences. Cognitive therapy can help the child deal with anxiety, depression, and other mental-health issues.

Although NLD presents many challenges for both the student and the family, there is help available, and with patience and effort, there will be improvement.

References

1. Epstein, Varda. "Nonverbal Learning Disorder: Is This What Your Child Has?" Kars4Kids, July 1, 2015.

2. Miller, Caroline. "What Is Nonverbal Learning Disorder?" Child Mind Institute, 2016.

3. Patino, Erica. "Understanding Nonverbal Learning Disabilities," Understood.org, May 21, 2014.

4. "Quick Facts on Nonverbal Learning Disorder," Child Mind Institute, 2016.

5. Thompson, Sue. "Nonverbal Learning Disorders," LDonline, 1996.

Chapter 13

Speech, Language, and Communication Disorders

Chapter Contents

Section 13.1

Voice, Speech, and Language

This section includes text excerpted from "What Is Voice?, What Is Speech?, What Is Language?" National Institute on Deafness and Other Communication Disorders (NIDCD), March 6, 2017.

The functions, skills, and abilities of voice, speech, and language are related. Some dictionaries and textbooks use the terms almost interchangeably. But for scientists and medical professionals, it is important to distinguish among them.

What Is Voice?

Voice (or vocalization) is the sound produced by humans and other vertebrates using the lungs and the vocal folds in the larynx, or voice box. Voice is not always produced as speech, for instance, infants babble and coo; animals bark, moo, whinny, growl, and meow; and adult humans laugh, sing, and cry. Voice is generated by airflow from the lungs as the vocal folds are brought close together. When air is pushed past the vocal folds with sufficient pressure, the vocal folds vibrate. If the vocal folds in the larynx did not vibrate normally, speech could only be produced as a whisper. Your voice is as unique as your fingerprint. It helps define your personality, mood, and health.

Approximately 17.9 million adults in the United States have trouble using their voices. Disorders of the voice involve problems with pitch, loudness, and quality. Pitch is the highness or lowness of a sound based on the frequency of the sound waves. Loudness is the perceived volume (or amplitude) of the sound, while quality refers to the character or distinctive attributes of a sound. Many people who have normal speaking skills have great difficulty communicating when their vocal apparatus fails. This can occur if the nerves controlling the larynx are impaired because of an accident, a surgical procedure, a viral infection, or cancer.

What Is Speech?

Humans express thoughts, feelings, and ideas orally to one another through a series of complex movements that alter and mold the basic tone created by voice into specific, decodable sounds. Speech is produced by precisely coordinated muscle actions in the head, neck, chest, and abdomen. Speech development is a gradual process that requires years of practice. During this process, a child learns how to regulate these muscles to produce understandable speech.

However, by the first grade, roughly 5 percent of children have noticeable speech disorders; the majority of these speech disorders have no known cause. One category of speech disorder is fluency disorder, or stuttering, which is characterized by a disruption in the flow of speech. It includes repetitions of speech sounds, hesitations before and during speaking, and the prolonged emphasis of speech sounds. More than 15 million individuals in the world stutter, most of whom began stuttering at a very early age. The majority of speech-sound disorders in the preschool years occur in children who are developing normally in all other areas. Speech disorders also may occur in children who have developmental disabilities.

What Is Language?

Language is the expression of human communication through which knowledge, belief, and behavior can be experienced, explained, and shared. This sharing is based on systematic, conventionally used signs, sounds, gestures, or marks that convey understood meanings within a group or community. Recent research identifies "windows of opportunity" for acquiring language—written, spoken, or signed—that exist within the first few years of life.

Between six and eight million individuals in the United States have some form of language impairment. Disorders of language affect children and adults differently. For children who do not use language normally from birth, or who acquire an impairment during childhood, language may not be fully developed or acquired. Many children who are deaf in the United States use a natural sign language known as "American Sign Language" (ASL). ASL shares an underlying organization with spoken language and has its own syntax and grammar. Many adults acquire disorders of language because of stroke, head injury, dementia, or brain tumors. Language disorders also are found in adults who have failed to develop normal language skills because of mental retardation, autism, hearing impairment, or other congenital or acquired disorders of brain development.

Section 13.2

Watch for Signs of Speech or Language Delay

This section includes text excerpted from "Watch for Signs of Speech or Language Delay," Office of Disease Prevention and Health Promotion (ODPHP), U.S. Department of Health and Human Services (HHS), July 18, 2018.

The Basics

The first three years of your child's life are the most important for learning to talk. Watch for signs that your child is learning to talk on schedule.

How Do Children Learn to Talk?

Children start learning how to talk before they start using words. They learn by watching, listening, and responding to people around them.

In the first few months, your baby listens to your voice and tries to make the same sounds you do. When you respond to your baby's sounds, you are helping your child learn how to communicate.

Smiles, babbles, and cooing sounds are your baby's way of "talking" to you. Over time, your child will learn many more sounds and words.

How Do I Know My Child Is Learning to Talk on Schedule?

You can watch for signs (called "developmental milestones") to see if your child is learning to talk on schedule. Here are some milestones to look for:

- By 2 months of age, your baby starts to coo and make gurgling sounds.

- By 4 months of age, your baby starts to babble.

- By 6 months of age, your baby responds to sounds by making sounds.

- By 1 year of age, your child says a few simple words—such as "mama," "dada," and "uh-oh!"

- By 18 months of age, your child says several single words.

- By 2 years of age, your child puts words together, such as "more milk."

- By 3 years of age, your child says two to three sentences at a time.

What If My Child Is Not Talking on Schedule?

If you think your child may have a speech or language problem, talk to a doctor. The doctor may send your child to a specialist for tests.

The best way to help your child with language delays is to find and treat problems early. With early treatment, there is a good chance your child's speech and language will improve.

Take Action

You can help your child learn to talk. Try these tips.

Talk to Your Baby

- Start talking and singing to your baby as soon as she or he is born. This will help your baby learn to make sounds.

- Look at your baby when she or he babbles and laughs.

- Smile and talk to your baby when she or he "talks" to you with gurgles, coos, babbles, and laughs. This helps your baby learn how to communicate.

- Repeat the sounds your baby makes, such as "ba-ba" or "goo-goo."

- Smile at your baby, and copy the facial expressions she or he makes.

Talk to Your Child

- Use words, as well as hand signals or signs. Using both together can help your child understand what you mean.

- Respond to your child's words and sounds. For example, your child might point to a banana and say "na, na." You can respond by asking, "Do you want to eat the banana?"

- Talk to your child throughout the day. Whether you are outside or at home, name things and describe what you are doing.

- Always respond to your child's questions.

Read to Your Child

Listening to you read aloud can help your baby learn sounds. Being read to can also help children understand language and learn new words. You can start reading to your child as soon as she or he is born.

Choose books with:

- Big pictures in bright colors

- Simple stories

- Numbers and counting, the alphabet, shapes, or sizes

- Rhymes

To get your child more involved, talk or sing about the pictures as you read.

- Point to the pictures, and name what you see.

- Ask your child to point to things on the page.

- As your child gets older, ask questions about the story.

Watch for Developmental Milestones

Babies and young children develop at their own pace. Checklists of developmental milestones can give you a general idea of what your child will be learning at each stage and what to expect next.

It is also important to take your child to the doctor for regular checkups so the doctor can make sure your child is healthy and developing normally.

If You Have Concerns, Talk with Your Child's Doctor

If you are concerned about your child's speech and language, talk with your child's doctor. Ask for a hearing test and a speech and language evaluation for your child.

Your doctor may also suggest you contact the early intervention program in your community. Early intervention programs provide services to help children under three years of age who have a disability or developmental delay.

Section 13.3

Language and Speech Disorders in Children

This section includes text excerpted from "Language and
Speech Disorders in Children," Centers for Disease Control
and Prevention (CDC), February 6, 2019.

Helping Children Learn Language

Parents and caregivers are the most important teachers during
a child's early years. Children learn language by listening to others
speak and by practicing. Even young babies do tend to notice when
others repeat and respond to their noises and sounds. Children's language and brain skills get stronger if they hear many different words.
Parents can help their child learn in many different ways, such as:

- Responding to the first sounds, gurgles, and gestures a baby
  makes
- Repeating what the child says and adding to it
- Talking about the things that a child sees
- Asking questions and listening to the answers
- Looking at or reading books
- Telling stories
- Singing songs and sharing rhymes

This can happen both during playtime and during daily routines.
Parents can also observe the following:

- How their child hears and talks and compare it with typical
  milestones for communication skills
- How their child reacts to sounds and have their hearing tested if
  they have concerns

What to Do If There Are Concerns

Some children struggle with understanding and speaking, and they
need help. They may not master the language milestones at the same
time as other children, and it may be a sign of a language or speech
delay or disorder.

Language development has different parts, and children might have problems with one or more of the following:

- Understanding what others say (receptive language). This could be due to:

  - Not hearing the words (hearing loss)

  - Not understanding the meaning of the words

- Communicating thoughts using language (expressive language). This could be due to:

  - Not knowing the words to use

  - Not knowing how to put words together

  - Knowing the words to use but not being able to express them

Language and speech disorders can exist together or by themselves. Examples of problems with language and speech development include the following:

- Speech disorders

  - Difficulty with forming specific words or sounds correctly

  - Difficulty with making words or sentences flow smoothly, such as stuttering or stammering

- Language delay—the ability to understand and speak develops more slowly than is typical

- Language disorders

  - Aphasia (difficulty understanding or speaking parts of language due to a brain injury or how the brain works)

  - Auditory processing disorder (difficulty understanding the meaning of the sounds that the ear sends to the brain)

Language or speech disorders can occur with other learning disorders that affect reading and writing. Children with language disorders may feel frustrated that they cannot understand others or make themselves understood, and they may act out, act helpless, or withdraw. Language or speech disorders can also be present with emotional or behavioral disorders, such as attention deficit hyperactivity disorder (ADHD) or anxiety. Children with developmental disabilities, including autism spectrum disorder (ASD), may also have difficulties with speech and language. The combination of challenges can make it particularly hard for a child to succeed in school. Properly diagnosing a child's disorder is crucial so that each child can get the right kind of help.

Detecting Problems with Language or Speech

If a child has a problem with language or speech development, talk to a healthcare provider about an evaluation. An important first step is to find out if the child has any hearing loss. Hearing loss may be difficult to notice, particularly if a child has hearing loss only in one ear or has partial hearing loss, which means they can hear some sounds but not others.

A language-development specialist, such as a speech-language pathologist, will conduct a careful assessment to determine what type of problem with language or speech the child may have.

Overall, learning more than one language does not cause language disorders, but children may not follow exactly the same developmental milestones as those who learn only one language. Developing the ability to understand and speak in two languages depends on how much practice the child has using both languages and the kind of practice. If a child who is learning more than one language has difficulty with language development, careful assessment by a specialist who understands development of skills in more than one language may be needed.

Treatment for Language or Speech Disorders and Delays

Children with language problems often need extra help and special instruction. Speech-language pathologists can work directly with children and their parents, caregivers, and teachers.

Having a language or speech delay or disorder can qualify a child for early intervention (for children up to three years of age) and special education services (for children three years of age and older). Schools can do their own testing for language or speech disorders to see if a child needs intervention. An evaluation by a healthcare professional is needed if there are other concerns about the child's hearing, behavior, or emotions. Parents, healthcare providers, and the school can work together to find the right referrals and treatment.

What Every Parent Should Know

Children with specific learning disabilities, including language or speech disorders, are eligible for special education services or accommodations at school under the Individuals with Disabilities in Education Act (IDEA) and Section 504, an antidiscrimination law.

The Role of Healthcare Providers

Healthcare providers can play an important part in collaborating with schools to help a child with speech or language disorders and delay or other disabilities get the special services they need. The American Academy of Pediatrics (AAP) has created a report that describes the roles that healthcare providers can have in helping children with disabilities, including language or speech disorders.

Section 13.4

Speech and Language Impairments in Children

This section includes text excerpted from "Speech and Language Impairments," Center for Parent Information and Resources (CPIR), U.S. Department of Education (ED), June 16, 2015. Reviewed April 2019.

There are many kinds of speech and language disorders that can affect children. In this section, four major areas in which these impairments occur are discussed. These are the areas of:

- **Articulation speech impairments,** where the child produces sounds incorrectly (e.g., lisp, difficulty articulating certain sounds, such as "l" or "r")

- **Fluency speech impairments,** where a child's flow of speech is disrupted by sounds, syllables, and words that are repeated, prolonged, or avoided and where there may be silent blocks or inappropriate inhalation, exhalation, or phonation patterns

- **Voice speech impairments,** where the child's voice has an abnormal quality to its pitch, resonance, or loudness

- **Language impairments,** where the child has problems expressing needs, ideas, or information, and/or in understanding what others say

These areas are reflected in how "speech or language impairment" is defined by the nation's special education law, the Individuals with Disabilities Education Act (IDEA), given below. The IDEA is the law that makes early intervention services available to infants and toddlers with disabilities and special education available to school-aged children with disabilities.

The Individuals with Disabilities Education Act defines the term "speech or language impairment" as follows:

Speech or language impairment means a communication disorder, such as stuttering, impaired articulation, a language impairment, or a voice impairment, that adversely affects a child's educational performance.

Development of Speech and Language Skills in Childhood

Speech and language skills develop in childhood according to fairly well-defined milestones. Parents and other caregivers may become concerned if a child's language seems noticeably behind (or different from) the language of same-aged peers. This may motivate parents to investigate further and, eventually, to have the child evaluated by a professional.

Having the child's hearing checked is a critical first step. The child may not have a speech or language impairment at all but, rather, a hearing impairment that is interfering with his or her development of language.

It is important to realize that a language delay is not the same thing as a speech or language impairment. Language delay is a very common developmental problem, in fact, the most common, affecting 5 to 10 percent of children in preschool. With language delay, children's language is developing in the expected sequence, only at a slower rate. In contrast, speech and language disorder refers to abnormal language development. Distinguishing between the two is most reliably done by a certified speech-language pathologist.

Characteristics of Speech or Language Impairments

The characteristics of speech or language impairments will vary depending upon the type of impairment involved. There may also be a combination of several problems.

119

When a child has an articulation disorder, she or he has difficulty making certain sounds. These sounds may be left off, added, changed, or distorted, which makes it hard for people to understand the child.

Leaving out or changing certain sounds is common when young children are learning to talk, of course. A good example of this is saying "wabbit" for "rabbit." The incorrect articulation is not necessarily a cause for concern unless it continues past the age where children are expected to produce such sounds correctly.

Fluency refers to the flow of speech. A fluency disorder means that something is disrupting the rhythmic and forward flow of speech—usually, a stutter. As a result, the child's speech contains an "abnormal number of repetitions, hesitations, prolongations, or disturbances. Tension may also be seen in the face, neck, shoulders, or fists."

Voice is the sound that is produced when air from the lungs pushes through the voice box in the throat (also called the "larnyx"), making the vocal folds within vibrate. From there, the sound generated travels up through the spaces of the throat, nose, and mouth, and emerges as our voice.

A voice disorder involves problems with the pitch, loudness, resonance, or quality of the voice. The voice may be hoarse, raspy, or harsh. For some, it may sound quite nasal; others might seem as if they are "stuffed up." People with voice problems often notice changes in pitch, loss of voice, loss of endurance, and sometimes a sharp or dull pain associated with voice use.

Language has to do with meanings, rather than sounds. A language disorder refers to an impaired ability to understand and/or use words in context. A child may have an expressive language disorder (difficulty in expressing ideas or needs), a receptive language disorder (difficulty in understanding what others are saying), or a mixed language disorder (which involves both).

Some characteristics of language disorders include:

- Improper use of words and their meanings

- Inability to express ideas

- Inappropriate grammatical patterns

- Reduced vocabulary

- Inability to follow directions

Children may hear or see a word but not be able to understand its meaning. They may have trouble getting others to understand what they are trying to communicate. These symptoms can easily be mistaken for other disabilities, such as autism or learning disabilities, so it is very important to ensure that the child receives a thorough evaluation by a certified speech-language pathologist.

What Causes Speech and Language Disorders

Some causes of speech and language disorders include hearing loss; neurological disorders; brain injury; intellectual disabilities; drug abuse; physical impairments, such as cleft lip or palate; and vocal abuse or misuse. Frequently, however, the cause is unknown.

Incidence

Of the 6.1 million children with disabilities who received special education under the IDEA in public schools in the 2005–2006 school year, more than 1.1 million were served under the category of speech or language impairment. This estimate does not include children who have speech/language problems secondary to other conditions, such as deafness, intellectual disability, autism, or cerebral palsy. Because many disabilities do impact the individual's ability to communicate, the actual incidence of children with speech-language impairment is undoubtedly much higher.

Finding Help

Because all communication disorders carry the potential to isolate individuals from their social and educational surroundings, it is essential to provide help and support as soon as a problem is identified. While many speech and language patterns can be called "baby talk" and are part of children's normal development, they can become problems if they are not outgrown as expected.

Therefore, it is important to take action if you suspect that your child has a speech or language impairment (or other disability or delay).

Chapter 14

Visual Processing Disorders

Visual processing disorders are weaknesses in the brain functions that process visual input. Although the eyes are the organs that actually receive visual images in the form of light, the brain must process these images and make sense of them. People with visual processing issues may have good eyesight, but their brains do not accurately receive or interpret the visual signals from their eyes. These weaknesses can create challenges in many areas of life, from recognizing letters and symbols, to distinguishing objects in space, to remembering things that have been seen.

Although visual processing issues are common in children with learning disabilities—and especially those with dyslexia—they are not considered learning disabilities by themselves. Nevertheless, they can have an impact on many areas of learning, such as reading, writing, vocabulary, verbal expression, memory, and attention. In addition to affecting learning, visual processing issues can impact socialization and self-esteem. Although medical research has not uncovered the cause of visual processing issues, the evidence suggests that preterm birth, low birth weight (LBW), and traumatic brain injury (TBI) may increase the likelihood of visual processing issues.

Symptoms of Visual Processing Disorders

Visual processing issues can be difficult to recognize, but there are some relatively common symptoms in children, including:

- Being clumsy, or bumping into things

- Experiencing difficulty writing or coloring within the lines

- Reversing or misreading letters, words, and numbers

- Difficulty remembering sequences or numbers or spelling of words

- Trouble paying attention to visual tasks or being distracted by visual information

- Showing a lack of interest in movies, television, or video presentations

- Having trouble with reading comprehension or remembering information when reading silently—especially when combined with strong verbal skills and oral comprehension

- Having trouble copying notes or recognizing changes in classroom displays, signs, or notices

- Skipping words or lines while reading

- Having weak math skills, confusing mathematical signs and symbols, or omitting steps in equations

- Frequently rubbing the eyes or complaining about eye strain

Diagnosis of Visual Processing Disorders

Diagnosing a visual processing disorder involves several steps. The first step is to take notes and keep records of the problems experienced by the child. The next step involves taking the child to a pediatrician or pediatric optometrist to conduct a basic vision test and look for health issues involving the eyes. If there are no significant problems with the child's eye health, the next step is to obtain a reference to a neuropsychologist.

Neuropsychologists are trained to diagnose visual processing issues and can perform tests to determine the extent to which these weaknesses may be affecting the child's development. Researchers have identified eight different types of visual processing disorders, each of which affects different skills and creates its own challenges. The types of visual processing issues include:

- **Visual discrimination.** People with this type of issue have trouble comparing similar items—such as letters, shapes, patterns, or objects—and telling the difference between them. They may mix up letters such as *d* and *b*, or *h* and *n*.

- **Visual sequencing.** People with this type of visual processing issue have difficulty distinguishing the order of letters, numbers, words, symbols, or images. They may misread letters or have trouble keeping their place on the page while reading.

- **Visual figure-ground discrimination.** This type of issue is characterized by difficulty seeing a shape or image against a background. People with this issue may not be able to locate a certain piece of information on a page or screen.

- **Visual memory.** People with this type of issue have difficulty remembering what they have seen or read, whether recently (short term) or some time ago (long term). They may struggle with reading comprehension, spelling familiar words, typing, using a calculator, or recalling a phone number.

- **Visual-spatial relationships.** People with this type of issue have trouble seeing where objects are positioned in space, whether in relation to themselves or to other objects. They may experience challenges in understanding distances, reading maps, judging time, or picturing the relationship of objects described in writing or in a spoken narrative.

- **Visual closure.** People with this type of issue have trouble recognizing familiar objects when only parts are visible. They may not be able to identify a face if the mouth is missing, for instance, or to recognize a familiar word if a letter is missing.

- **Letter and symbol reversal.** People with this issue tend to reverse letters or numbers when reading or writing. They may also struggle with letter formation.

- **Visual-motor processing.** People with this issue have difficulty coordinating bodily movements using feedback from the eyes. They may appear uncoordinated or clumsy and bump into things. They may also struggle to write within lines or copy from a blackboard.

Treatment of Visual Processing Disorders

Although there is no cure for visual processing disorders, there are many different strategies that can help people improve their skills and adapt to the challenges they face. Teachers and paraprofessionals at school may offer valuable assistance to children who are diagnosed with visual processing issues. Some of these children may qualify for special education services and receive an Individualized Education Program (IEP), which outlines the specific supports the school must provide. Schools also may provide informal supports to meet the children's needs, such as allowing them to use books with large print or have tests read aloud.

Parents and caregivers can also help children with visual processing disorders to improve their skills. Experts recommend writing out schedules and instructions in large print, with each step numbered clearly, and color-coding important points. It is also important to provide plenty of opportunities for children to practice visual processing skills through fun activities. Playing with jigsaw puzzles and games; reading "seek and find" books, such as *Where's Waldo?;* creating maps and travel logs; playing catch or rolling a ball back and forth; and estimating distances using a tape measure are all examples of activities that hone visual processing skills.

References

1. Arky, Beth. "Understanding Visual Processing Issues," Understood.org, 2016.

2. "Visual Processing Disorders—In Detail," LD Online, 2015.

3. "Visual Processing Issues: What You're Seeing," Understood. org, 2016.

Part Three

Other Disorders That Make Learning Difficult

Chapter 15

Aphasia and Apraxia of speech

Chapter Contents

Section 15.1

Aphasia

This section includes text excerpted from "Aphasia,"
National Institute on Deafness and Other Communication
Disorders (NIDCD), March 6, 2017.

What Is Aphasia?

Aphasia is a disorder that results from damage to portions of the brain that are responsible for language. For most people, these areas are on the left side of the brain. Aphasia usually occurs suddenly, often following a stroke or head injury, but it may also develop slowly, as the result of a brain tumor or a progressive neurological disease. The disorder impairs the expression and understanding of language, as well as reading and writing. Aphasia may co-occur with speech disorders, such as dysarthria or apraxia of speech, which also result from brain damage.

Who Can Acquire Aphasia?

Most people who have aphasia are middle-aged or older, but anyone can acquire it, including young children. About 1 million people in the United States currently have aphasia, and nearly 180,000 Americans acquire it each year, according to the National Aphasia Association (NAA).

What Causes Aphasia

Aphasia is caused by damage to one or more of the language areas of the brain. Most often, the cause of the brain injury is a stroke. A stroke occurs when a blood clot or a leaking or burst vessel cuts off blood flow to part of the brain. Brain cells die when they do not receive their normal supply of blood, which carries oxygen and important nutrients. Other causes of brain injury are severe blows to the head, brain tumors, gunshot wounds, brain infections, and progressive neurological disorders, such as Alzheimer disease (AD).

What Types of Aphasia Are There?

There are two broad categories of aphasia: fluent and nonfluent, and there are several types within these groups.

Damage to the temporal lobe of the brain may result in Wernicke aphasia, the most common type of fluent aphasia. People with Wernicke aphasia may speak in long, complete sentences that have no meaning, adding unnecessary words and even creating made-up words.

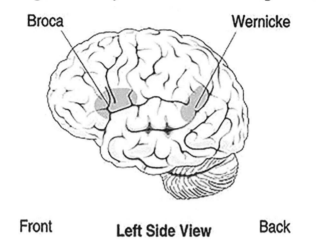

Figure 15.1. *Areas of the Brain Affected by Broca*

For example, someone with Wernicke aphasia may say, "You know that smoodle pinkered and that I want to get him round and take care of him like you want before."

As a result, it is often difficult to follow what the person is trying to say. People with Wernicke aphasia are often unaware of their spoken mistakes. Another hallmark of this type of aphasia is difficulty understanding speech.

The most common type of nonfluent aphasia is Broca's aphasia. People with Broca's aphasia have damage that primarily affects the frontal lobe of the brain. They often have right-sided weakness or paralysis of the arm and leg because the frontal lobe is also important for motor movements. People with Broca's aphasia may understand speech and know what they want to say, but they frequently speak in short phrases that are produced with great effort. They often omit small words, such as "is," "and," and "the."

For example, a person with Broca's aphasia may say, "Walk dog," meaning, "I will take the dog for a walk," or they may say "book two tables," for "There are two books on the table." People with Broca's aphasia typically understand the speech of others fairly well. Because of this, they are often aware of their difficulties and can become easily frustrated.

Another type of aphasia, global aphasia, results from damage to extensive portions of the language areas of the brain. Individuals with global aphasia have severe communication difficulties and may be extremely limited in their ability to speak or comprehend language. They may be unable to say even a few words or may repeat the same words or phrases over and over again. They may have trouble understanding even simple words and sentences.

There are other types of aphasia, each of which results from damage to different language areas in the brain. Some people may have difficulty repeating words and sentences even though they understand them and can speak fluently (conduction aphasia). Others may have difficulty naming objects even though they know what the object is and what it may be used for (anomic aphasia).

Sometimes, blood flow to the brain is temporarily interrupted and quickly restored. When this type of injury occurs, which is called a "transient ischemic attack," language abilities may return in a few hours or days.

How Is Aphasia Diagnosed?

Aphasia is usually first recognized by the physician who treats the person for his or her brain injury. Most individuals will undergo a magnetic resonance imaging (MRI) or a computed tomography (CT) scan to confirm the presence of a brain injury and to identify its precise location. The physician also typically tests the person's ability to understand and produce language, such as following commands, answering questions, naming objects, and carrying on a conversation.

If the physician suspects aphasia, the patient is usually referred to a speech-language pathologist, who performs a comprehensive examination of the person's communication abilities. The person's ability to speak, express ideas, converse socially, understand language, and read and write are all assessed in detail.

How Is Aphasia Treated?

Following a brain injury, tremendous changes occur in the brain, which help it to recover. As a result, people with aphasia often see dramatic improvements in their language and communication abilities in the first few months, even without treatment. But in many cases, some aphasia remains following this initial recovery period. In these instances, speech-language therapy is used to help patients regain their ability to communicate.

Research has shown that language and communication abilities can continue to improve for many years and are sometimes accompanied by new activity in brain tissue near the damaged area. Some of the factors that may influence the amount of improvement include the cause of the brain injury, the area of the brain that was damaged and its extent, and the age and health of the individual.

Aphasia therapy aims to improve a person's ability to communicate by helping her or him to use remaining language abilities; restore language abilities as much as possible; and learn other ways of communicating, such as gestures, pictures, or use of electronic devices. Individual therapy focuses on the specific needs of the person, while group therapy offers the opportunity to use new communication skills in a small-group setting.

Recent technologies have provided new tools for people with aphasia. "Virtual" speech pathologists provide patients with the flexibility and convenience of getting therapy in their homes through a computer. The use of speech-generating applications on mobile devices, such as tablets, can also provide an alternative way to communicate for people who have difficulty using spoken language.

Increasingly, patients with aphasia participate in activities, such as book clubs, technology groups, and art and drama clubs. Such experiences help patients regain their confidence and social self-esteem, in addition to improving their communication skills. Stroke clubs, regional support groups formed by people who have had a stroke, are available in most major cities. These clubs can help a person and his or her family adjust to the life changes that accompany stroke and aphasia.

Family involvement is often a crucial component of aphasia treatment because it enables family members to learn the best way to communicate with their loved one.

Family members are encouraged to:

- Participate in therapy sessions, if possible

- Simplify language by using short, uncomplicated sentences

- Repeat the content words or write down key words to clarify meaning as needed

- Maintain a natural conversational manner appropriate for an adult

- Minimize distractions, such as a loud radio or TV, whenever possible

- Include the person with aphasia in conversations

- Ask for and value the opinion of the person with aphasia, especially regarding family matters

- Encourage any type of communication, whether it is speech, gesture, pointing, or drawing

- Avoid correcting the person's speech

- Allow the person plenty of time to talk

- Help the person become involved outside the home and seek out support groups, such as stroke clubs

What Research Is Being Done for Aphasia?

Researchers are testing new types of speech-language therapy in people with both recent and chronic aphasia to see if new methods can better help them recover word retrieval, grammar, prosody (tone), and other aspects of speech.

Some of these new methods involve improving cognitive abilities that support the processing of language, such as short-term memory and attention. Others involve activities that stimulate the mental representations of sounds, words, and sentences, making them easier to access and retrieve.

Researchers are also exploring drug therapy as an experimental approach to treating aphasia. Some studies are testing whether drugs that affect the chemical neurotransmitters in the brain can be used in combination with speech-language therapy to improve recovery of various language functions.

Other research is focused on using advanced imaging methods, such as functional magnetic resonance imaging (fMRI), to explore how language is processed in the normal and damaged brain and to understand recovery processes. This type of research may advance our knowledge of how the areas involved in speech and understanding language reorganize after a brain injury. The results could have implications for the diagnosis and treatment of aphasia and other neurological disorders.

A relatively new area of interest in aphasia research is noninvasive brain stimulation in combination with speech-language therapy. Two such brain stimulation techniques, transcranial magnetic stimulation (TMS) and transcranial direct current stimulation (tDCS), temporarily alter normal brain activity in the region being stimulated.

Researchers originally used these techniques to help them understand the parts of the brain that played a role in language and recovery after a stroke. Recently, scientists are studying if this temporary alteration of brain activity might help people re-learn language use. Several clinical trials funded by the National Institute on Deafness and Other Communication Disorders (NIDCD) are currently testing these technologies.

Section 15.2

Apraxia of Speech

This section includes text excerpted from "Apraxia of Speech," National Institute on Deafness and Other Communication Disorders (NIDCD), October 31, 2017.

What Is Apraxia of Speech?

Apraxia of speech (AOS)—also known as "acquired apraxia of speech," "verbal apraxia," or "childhood apraxia of speech" (CAS) when diagnosed in children—is a speech sound disorder. Someone with AOS has trouble saying what she or he wants to say correctly and consistently. AOS is a neurological disorder that affects the brain pathways involved in planning the sequence of movements involved in producing speech. The brain knows what it wants to say but cannot properly plan and sequence the required speech sound movements.

AOS is not caused by weakness or paralysis of the speech muscles (the muscles of the jaw, tongue, or lips). Weakness or paralysis of the speech muscles results in a separate speech disorder, known as "dysarthria." Some people have both dysarthria and AOS, which can make diagnosis of the two conditions more difficult.

The severity of AOS varies from person to person. It can be so mild that it causes trouble with only a few speech sounds or with pronunciation of words that have many syllables. In the most severe cases, someone with AOS might not be able to communicate effectively by speaking, and may need the help of alternative communication methods.

135

What Are the Types and Causes of Apraxia of Speech?

There are two main types of AOS: acquired apraxia of speech and childhood apraxia of speech.

- **Acquired AOS** can affect someone at any age, although it most typically occurs in adults. Acquired AOS is caused by damage to the parts of the brain that are involved in speaking and involves the loss or impairment of existing speech abilities. It may result from a stroke, head injury, tumor, or other illness affecting the brain. Acquired AOS may occur together with other conditions that are caused by damage to the nervous system. One of these is dysarthria, as mentioned earlier. Another is aphasia, which is a language disorder.

- **Childhood AOS** is present from birth. This condition is also known as "developmental apraxia of speech," "developmental verbal apraxia," or "articulatory apraxia." Childhood AOS is not the same as developmental delays in speech, in which a child follows the typical path of speech development but does so more slowly than is typical. The causes of childhood AOS are not well understood. Imaging and other studies have not been able to find evidence of brain damage or differences in the brain structure of children with AOS. Children with AOS often have family members who have a history of a communication disorder or a learning disability. This observation and recent research findings suggest that genetic factors may play a role in the disorder. Childhood AOS appears to affect more boys than girls.

What Are the Symptoms of Apraxia of Speech?

People with either form of AOS may have a number of different speech characteristics, or symptoms:

- **Distorting sounds.** People with AOS may have difficulty pronouncing words correctly. Sounds, especially vowels, are often distorted. Because the speaker may not place the speech structures (e.g., tongue, jaw) quite in the right place, the sound comes out wrong. Longer or more complex words are usually harder to say than shorter or simpler words. Sound substitutions might also occur when AOS is accompanied by aphasia.

- **Making inconsistent errors in speech.** For example, someone with AOS may say a difficult word correctly but then have trouble repeating it, or they may be able to say a particular sound one day and have trouble with the same sound the next day.

- **Groping for sounds.** People with AOS often appear to be groping for the right sound or word, and may try saying a word several times before they say it correctly.

- **Making errors in tone, stress, or rhythm.** Another common characteristic of AOS is the incorrect use of prosody. Prosody is the rhythm and inflection of speech that we use to help express meaning. Someone who has trouble with prosody might use equal stress, segment syllables in a word, omit syllables in words and phrases, or pause inappropriately while speaking.

Children with AOS generally understand language much better than they are able to use it. Some children with the disorder may also have other speech problems, expressive language problems, or motor-skill problems.

How Is Apraxia of Speech Diagnosed?

Professionals known as "speech-language pathologists" play a key role in diagnosing and treating AOS. Because there is no single symptom or test that can be used to diagnose AOS, the person making the diagnosis generally looks for the presence of several of a group of symptoms, including those described earlier. Ruling out other conditions, such as muscle weakness or language production problems (e.g., aphasia), can help with the diagnostic process.

In formal testing for both acquired and childhood AOS, a speech-language pathologist may ask the patient to perform speech tasks, such as repeating a particular word several times or repeating a list of words of increasing length (for example, love, loving, lovingly). For acquired AOS, a speech-language pathologist may also examine the patient's ability to converse, read, write, and perform nonspeech movements. To diagnose childhood AOS, parents and professionals may need to observe a child's speech over a period of time.

How Is Apraxia of Speech Treated?

In some cases, people with acquired AOS recover some or all of their speech abilities on their own. This is called "spontaneous recovery."

Children with AOS will not outgrow the problem on their own. They also do not acquire the basics of speech just by being around other children, such as in a classroom. Therefore, speech-language therapy is necessary for children with AOS, as well as for people with acquired AOS who do not spontaneously recover all of their speech abilities.

Speech-language pathologists use different approaches to treat AOS, and no single approach has been proven to be the most effective. Therapy is tailored to the individual and is designed to treat other speech or language problems that may occur together with AOS. Frequent, intensive, one-on-one speech-language therapy sessions are needed for both children and adults with AOS. (The repetitive exercises and personal attention needed to improve AOS are difficult to deliver in group therapy.) Children with severe AOS may need intensive speech-language therapy for years, in parallel with normal schooling, to obtain adequate speech abilities.

In severe cases, adults and children with AOS may need to find other ways to express themselves. These might include formal or informal sign language; a notebook with pictures or written words that can be pointed to and shown to other people; or an electronic communication device—such as a smartphone, tablet, or laptop computer—that can be used to write or produce speech. Such assistive communication methods can also help children with AOS learn to read and better understand spoken language by stimulating areas of the brain involved in language and literacy.

Some adults and children will make more progress during treatment than others. Support and encouragement from family members and friends and extra practice in the home environment are important.

What Research Is Being Done to Better Understand Apraxia of Speech?

Researchers are searching for the causes of childhood AOS, including the possible role of abnormalities in the brain or other parts of the nervous system. They are also looking for genetic factors that may play a role in childhood AOS. Other research on childhood AOS aims to identify more specific criteria and new techniques to diagnose the disorder and to distinguish it from other communication disorders.

Research on acquired AOS includes studies to pinpoint the specific areas of the brain that are involved in the disorder. In addition, researchers are studying the effectiveness of various treatment approaches for both acquired and childhood AOS.

Chapter 16

Attention Deficit Hyperactivity Disorder

Chapter Contents

Section 16.1

What Is Attention Deficit Hyperactivity Disorder?

This section includes text excerpted from "Attention Deficit Hyperactivity Disorder," National Institute of Mental Health (NIMH), March 2016.

Attention deficit hyperactivity disorder (ADHD) is a brain disorder marked by an ongoing pattern of inattention and/or hyperactivity-impulsivity that interferes with functioning or development.

- **Inattention** means a person wanders off task, lacks persistence, has difficulty sustaining focus, and is disorganized; and these problems are not due to defiance or lack of comprehension.

- **Hyperactivity** means a person seems to move about constantly, including in situations in which it is not appropriate, or excessively fidgets, taps, or talks. In adults, it may be extreme restlessness or wearing others out with constant activity.

- **Impulsivity** means a person makes hasty actions that occur in the moment without first thinking about them, which may have high potential for harm, or a desire for immediate rewards or inability to delay gratification. An impulsive person may be socially intrusive and excessively interrupt others or make important decisions without considering the long-term consequences.

Signs and Symptoms of Attention Deficit Hyperactivity Disorder

Inattention and hyperactivity/impulsivity are the key behaviors of ADHD. Some people with ADHD only has problems with one of the behaviors, while others have both inattention and hyperactivity-impulsivity. Most children have the combined type of ADHD.

In preschool, the most common ADHD symptom is hyperactivity.

It is normal to have some inattention, unfocused motor activity and impulsivity, but for people with ADHD, these behaviors:

- Are more severe

140

- Occur more often

- Interfere with or reduce the quality of how they function socially, at school, or in a job

Inattention

People with symptoms of inattention may often:

- Overlook or miss details, make careless mistakes in schoolwork, at work, or during other activities

- Have problems sustaining attention in tasks or play, including conversations, lectures, or lengthy reading

- Not seem to listen when spoken to directly

- Not follow through on instructions and fail to finish schoolwork, chores, or duties in the workplace or start tasks but quickly lose focus and get easily sidetracked

- Have problems organizing tasks and activities, such as what to do in sequence, keeping materials and belongings in order, having messy work and poor time management, and failing to meet deadlines

- Avoid or dislike tasks that require sustained mental effort, such as schoolwork or homework, or for teens and older adults, preparing reports, completing forms, or reviewing lengthy papers

- Lose things necessary for tasks or activities, such as school supplies, pencils, books, tools, wallets, keys, paperwork, eyeglasses, and cell phones

- Be easily distracted by unrelated thoughts or stimuli

- Be forgetful in daily activities, such as chores, errands, returning calls, and keeping appointments

Hyperactivity-Impulsivity

People with symptoms of hyperactivity-impulsivity may often:

- Fidget and squirm in their seats

- Leave their seats in situations when staying seated is expected, such as in the classroom or in the office

- Run or dash around or climb in situations where it is inappropriate or, in teens and adults, often feel restless

- Be unable to play or engage in hobbies quietly

- Be constantly in motion or "on the go," or act as if "driven by a motor"

- Talk nonstop

- Blurt out an answer before a question has been completed, finish other people's sentences, or speak without waiting for a turn in conversation

- Have trouble waiting her or his turn

- Interrupt or intrude on others, for example in conversations, games, or activities

Diagnosis of ADHD requires a comprehensive evaluation by a licensed clinician, such as a pediatrician, psychologist, or psychiatrist with expertise in ADHD. For a person to receive a diagnosis of ADHD, the symptoms of inattention and/or hyperactivity-impulsivity must be chronic or long-lasting, impair the person's functioning, and cause the person to fall behind normal development for her or his age. The doctor will also ensure that any ADHD symptoms are not due to another medical or psychiatric condition. Most children with ADHD receive a diagnosis during the elementary school years. For an adolescent or adult to receive a diagnosis of ADHD, the symptoms need to have been present prior to the age of 12.

ADHD symptoms can appear as early as between the ages of 3 and 6 and can continue through adolescence and adulthood. Symptoms of ADHD can be mistaken for emotional or disciplinary problems or missed entirely in quiet, well-behaved children, leading to a delay in diagnosis. Adults with undiagnosed ADHD may have a history of poor academic performance, problems at work, or difficult or failed relationships.

ADHD symptoms can change over time as a person ages. In young children with ADHD, hyperactivity-impulsivity is the most predominant symptom. As a child reaches elementary school, the symptom of inattention may become more prominent and cause the child to struggle academically. In adolescence, hyperactivity seems to lessen and may show more often as feelings of restlessness or fidgeting, but inattention and impulsivity may remain. Many adolescents with ADHD also struggle with relationships and antisocial behaviors. Inattention, restlessness, and impulsivity tend to persist into adulthood.

Risk Factors for Attention Deficit Hyperactivity Disorder

Scientists are not sure what causes ADHD. As with other illnesses, a number of factors can contribute to ADHD, such as:

- Genes
- Cigarette smoking, alcohol use, or drug use during pregnancy
- Exposure to environmental toxins during pregnancy
- Exposure to environmental toxins, such as high levels of lead, at a young age
- Low birth weight
- Brain injuries

ADHD is more common in males than females, and females with ADHD are more likely to have problems primarily with inattention. Other conditions, such as learning disabilities, anxiety disorder, conduct disorder, depression, and substance abuse, are common in people with ADHD.

Treatment and Therapies for Attention Deficit Hyperactivity Disorder

While there is no cure for ADHD, currently available treatments can help reduce symptoms and improve functioning. Treatments include medication, psychotherapy, education or training, or a combination of treatments.

Medication

For many people, ADHD medications reduce hyperactivity and impulsivity and improve their ability to focus, work, and learn. Medication also may improve physical coordination. Sometimes, several different medications or dosages must be tried before finding the right one that works for a particular person. Anyone taking medications must be monitored closely and carefully by their prescribing doctor.

The most common type of medication used for treating ADHD is called a "stimulant." Although it may seem unusual to treat ADHD with a medication that is considered a stimulant, it works because it increases the brain chemicals dopamine and norepinephrine, which play essential roles in thinking and attention.

Under medical supervision, stimulant medications are considered safe. However, there are risks and side effects, especially when misused or taken in excess of the prescribed dose. For example, stimulants can raise blood pressure and heart rate and increase anxiety. Therefore, a person with other health problems, including high blood pressure, seizures, heart disease, glaucoma, liver or kidney disease, or an anxiety disorder, should tell their doctor before taking a stimulant.

Talk with a doctor if you see any of these side effects while taking stimulants:

- Decreased appetite

- Sleep problems

- Tics (sudden, repetitive movements or sounds)

- Personality changes

- Increased anxiety and irritability

- Stomachaches

- Headaches

A few other ADHD medications are nonstimulants. These medications take longer to start working than stimulants but can also improve focus, attention, and impulsivity in a person with ADHD. Doctors may prescribe a nonstimulant when a person has bothersome side effects from stimulants, when a stimulant was not effective, or in combination with a stimulant to increase effectiveness.

Although not approved by the U.S. Food and Drug Administration (FDA) specifically for the treatment of ADHD, some antidepressants are sometimes used alone or in combination with a stimulant to treat ADHD. Antidepressants may help all of the symptoms of ADHD and can be prescribed if a patient has bothersome side effects from stimulants. Antidepressants can be helpful in combination with stimulants if a patient also has another condition, such as an anxiety disorder, depression, or another mood disorder.

Doctors and patients can work together to find the best medication, dose, or medication combination.

Psychotherapy

Adding psychotherapy to treat ADHD can help patients and their families to better cope with everyday problems.

Behavioral therapy is a type of psychotherapy that aims to help a person change her or his behavior. It might involve practical assistance, such as help organizing tasks or completing schoolwork, or working through emotionally difficult events. Behavioral therapy also teaches a person how to:

- Monitor her or his own behavior

- Give oneself praise or rewards for acting in a desired way, such as controlling anger or thinking before acting

Parents, teachers, and family members also can give positive or negative feedback for certain behaviors and help establish clear rules, chore lists, and other structured routines to help a person control her or his behavior. Therapists may also teach children social skills, such as how to wait their turn, share toys, ask for help, or respond to teasing. Learning to read facial expressions and the tone of voice in others, and how to respond appropriately, can also be part of social skills training.

Cognitive behavioral therapy (CBT) can also teach a person mindfulness technique, or meditation. A person learns how to be aware and accepting of one's own thoughts and feelings to improve focus and concentration. The therapist also encourages the person with ADHD to adjust to the life changes that come with treatment, such as thinking before acting or resisting the urge to take unnecessary risks.

Family and marital therapy can help family members and spouses find better ways to handle disruptive behaviors, to encourage behavior changes, and improve interactions with the patient.

Education and Training

Children and adults with ADHD need guidance and understanding from their parents, families, and teachers to reach their full potential and to succeed. For school-age children, frustration, blame, and anger may have built up within a family before a child is diagnosed. Parents and children may need special help to overcome negative feelings. Mental-health professionals can educate parents about ADHD and how it affects a family. They also will help the child and her or his parents develop new skills, attitudes, and ways of relating to each other.

Parenting skills training (behavioral parent management training) teaches parents the skills they need to encourage and reward positive behaviors in their children. It helps parents learn how to use a system of rewards and consequences to change a child's behavior. Parents are taught to give immediate and positive feedback for behaviors they want to encourage, and ignore or redirect behaviors that they want to discourage. They may also learn to structure situations in ways that support desired behavior.

Stress management techniques can benefit parents of children with ADHD by increasing their ability to deal with frustration so that they can respond calmly to their child's behavior.

Support groups can help parents and families connect with others who have similar problems and concerns. Groups often meet regularly to share frustrations and successes, to exchange information about recommended specialists and strategies, and to talk with experts.

Tips to Help Kids and Adults with Attention Deficit Hyperactivity Disorder Stay Organized
For Kids

Parents and teachers can help kids with ADHD stay organized and follow directions with tools, such as:

- Keeping a routine and a schedule. Keep the same routine every day, from wake-up time to bedtime. Include time for homework, outdoor play, and indoor activities. Keep the schedule on the refrigerator or on a bulletin board in the kitchen. Write changes on the schedule as far in advance as possible.

- Organizing everyday items. Have a place for everything, and keep everything in its place. This includes clothing, backpacks, and toys.

- Using homework and notebook organizers. Use organizers for school material and supplies. Stress to your child the importance of writing down assignments and bringing home the necessary books.

- Being clear and consistent. Children with ADHD need consistent rules they can understand and follow.

- Giving praise or rewards when rules are followed. Children with ADHD often receive and expect criticism. Look for good behavior, and praise it.

For Adults

A professional counselor or therapist can help an adult with ADHD learn how to organize her or his life with tools, such as:

- Keeping routines

146

- Making lists for different tasks and activities

- Using a calendar for scheduling events

- Using reminder notes

- Assigning a special place for keys, bills, and paperwork

- Breaking down large tasks into more manageable, smaller steps so that completing each part of the task provides a sense of accomplishment.

Section 16.2

Attention Deficit Hyperactivity Disorder and Learning Disorder

This section includes text excerpted from "Other Concerns and Conditions with ADHD," Centers for Disease Control and Prevention (CDC), September 21, 2018.

Attention deficit hyperactivity disorder (ADHD) often occurs with other disorders. About two in three of children with ADHD referred to clinics have other disorders, as well as ADHD.

The combination of ADHD with other disorders often presents extra challenges for children, parents, educators, and healthcare providers. Therefore, it is important for doctors to screen every child with ADHD for other disorders and problems. This section provides an overview of the more common conditions and concerns that can occur with ADHD. Talk with your doctor if you have concerns about your child's symptoms.

Learning Disorder

Many children with ADHD also have a learning disorder (LD). This is in addition to other symptoms of ADHD, such as difficulties paying attention, staying on task, or being organized, which also keep a child from doing well in school.

Having a LD means that a child has a clear difficulty in one or more areas of learning, even when their intelligence is not affected. LDs include:

- Dyslexia: Difficulty with reading

- Dyscalculia: Difficulty with math

- Dysgraphia: Difficulty with writing

Data from the 2004–2006 National Health Interview Survey (NHIS) suggests that almost half of children between 6 and 17 years of age diagnosed with ADHD may also have a LD. The combination of problems caused by ADHD and LDs can make it particularly hard for a child to succeed in school. Properly diagnosing each disorder is crucial, so that the child can get the right kind of help for each.

Treatment for Learning Disorders

Children with LDs often need extra help and instruction that is specialized for them. Having a LD can qualify a child for special education services in school. Because children with ADHD often have difficulty in school, the first step is a careful evaluation to see if the problems are also caused by a LD. Schools usually do their own testing to see if a child needs intervention. Parents, healthcare providers, and the school can work together to find the right referrals and treatment.

Chapter 17

Cerebral Palsy

Cerebral palsy (CP) describes a group of neurological disorders that begin in infancy or early childhood and that primarily affect body movement but, in more severe cases, may also be associated with intellectual disabilities. These physical disabilities are permanent but do not usually get worse over time. The condition is caused by damage to parts of the brain that control movement, balance, and posture.

The *Eunice Kennedy Shriver* National Institute of Child Health and Human Development (NICHD) conducts and supports research relevant to CP, including studies of the mechanisms of brain injuries, of ways to prevent the condition, and of new treatments and rehabilitative approaches.

What Are the Types of Cerebral Palsy?

There are several types of CP, classified by the kind of movement affected, the body parts affected, and how severe the symptoms are. Some types involve intellectual and developmental disabilities (IDDs), as well as movement problems.

- **Spastic CP.** This type is the most common form of the disorder. People with spastic CP have stiff muscles, which cause jerky or repeated movements. There are different forms of spastic CP, depending on the body parts affected. These forms are:

This chapter includes text excerpted from "Cerebral Palsy," *Eunice Kennedy Shriver* National Institute of Child Health and Human Development (NICHD), December 1, 2016.

- Spastic hemiplegia or hemiparesis. This type affects the arm, the hand, and sometimes the leg on only one side of the body. Children with this form may have delays in learning to talk, but intelligence is usually normal.

- Spastic diplegia or diparesis. People with this form mostly have muscle stiffness in the legs, while the arms and face are less severely affected. Intelligence and language skills are usually normal.

- Spastic quadriplegia or quadriparesis. This is the most severe form of CP, involving severe stiffness of the arms and legs and a floppy, or weak, neck. People with spastic quadriplegia are usually unable to walk and often have trouble speaking. This form may involve moderate to severe IDD as well.

- **Dyskinetic CP.** This type involves slow and uncontrollable jerky movements of the hands, feet, arms, or legs. The face muscles and tongue may be overactive and cause some children to drool or make faces. People with this type often have trouble sitting straight or walking. People with dyskinetic CP do not usually have intellectual problems.

- **Ataxic CP.** This form of the disorder affects balance and depth perception. People with ataxic CP walk in an unsteady manner and have a hard time with quick or precise movements, such as writing, buttoning a shirt, or reaching for a book.

Mixed types. This kind of CP includes symptoms that are a mix of other types.

What Are the Symptoms of Cerebral Palsy?

Even though the symptoms of CP often differ from person to person, they can include:

- Ataxia, the loss of muscle coordination when making movements

- Spasticity, stiff or tight muscles; jerky, repeated movements; and stronger-than-normal reflexes (for example, the knee-jerk reflex)

- Weakness in arms or legs

- Walking on the toes

- Walking in a crouched position

- Muscle tone that is either too stiff or too floppy

- Drooling

- Trouble with swallowing or speaking

- Shaking (tremor) of arms, legs, hands, or feet

- Sudden, uncontrolled movements

- In infants and toddlers, delays in motor skills, (such as sitting, crawling, walking)

- Trouble with precise movements, such as writing or buttoning a shirt

It is important to note that many of these symptoms result from problems with muscles and not from problems with cognition or thinking. For example, a person with CP may have trouble speaking because she or he cannot control or move the muscles involved with speaking, not because of brain problems with language.

The symptoms of CP vary in type, can range from mild to severe, and can change over time. Symptoms are different for each person, depending on the areas of the brain that have been affected. All people with CP have movement and posture problems.

In addition to problems with muscle movement, symptoms occasionally include:

- Intellectual and developmental disabilities

- Seizures

- Feeling unusual physical sensations

- Vision problems

- Hearing problems

What Are the Early Signs of Cerebral Palsy?

The signs of CP usually appear in the first few months of life, but many children are not diagnosed until two years of age or later. In general, early signs of CP include:

- Developmental delays. The child is slow to reach milestones, such as rolling over, sitting, crawling, and walking. Developmental delays are the main clues that a child might have CP.

- Abnormal muscle tone. Body parts are floppy or too stiff.

- Abnormal posture. The child might also use one side of the body more than the other when reaching, crawling, or moving.

Children without CP may show some of these signs. If you notice any of these signs, you should talk to your child's healthcare provider. Some age-specific signs may include:

- Infants younger than six months of age:

  - Cannot hold up their head when picked up from lying on their back

  - May feel stiff or floppy

  - When picked up, their legs get stiff or cross

  - When held, they may overextend their back and neck, constantly acting as though they are pushing away from you

- Infants older than six months of age:

  - Cannot roll over

  - Cannot bring their hands to their mouth

  - Have a hard time bringing their hands together

  - Reach out with only one hand while holding the other in a fist

- Infants older than ten months of age:

  - Crawl in a lopsided way, pushing with one hand and leg while dragging the opposite hand and leg

  - Scoot around on their buttocks or hop on their knees, but do not crawl on all fours

  - Cannot stand, even when holding onto support

Children without CP may show some of these signs. If you notice any of these signs, you should talk to your child's healthcare provider.

What Causes Cerebral Palsy

Cerebral palsy is caused by damage or abnormal development in the parts of the brain that control movement. These events can happen before, during, or shortly after birth or in the first few years of life, when the brain is still developing. In many cases the exact cause of CP is not known.

The majority of children with CP were born with the condition, a situation called "congenital CP."

Causes of CP that occur before birth include:

- **Damage to the white matter of the brain.** The brain's white matter sends signals throughout the brain and the rest of the body. Damage to white matter can disrupt the signals between the brain and the body that control movement. The white matter in the fetus's brain is more sensitive to injury between 26 weeks and 34 weeks of pregnancy, but damage can happen at any time during pregnancy.

- **Abnormal brain development.** Disruptions in the normal growth process of the brain can cause abnormalities. These abnormalities affect the transmission of brain signals. Infections, fever, trauma, or gene changes (mutations) can cause the brain to develop abnormally.

- **Bleeding in the brain.** A fetus can have a stroke, which is a common cause of brain bleeding. Strokes occur when blood vessels in the brain become blocked or broken, leading to brain damage. Conditions, including blood clotting problems, abnormally formed blood vessels, heart defects, and sickle cell disease (SCD), can also cause bleeding in the brain.

- **Lack of oxygen in the brain.** The brain can become damaged if it does not get enough oxygen for a long time. Very low blood pressure in the mother, a torn uterus, detachment of the placenta, problems with the umbilical cord, or severe trauma to the infant's head during labor and delivery can prevent oxygen from getting to the brain.

A small number of children have what is called "acquired CP," which means the disorder begins more than 28 days after birth. Causes of acquired CP may include:

- Brain damage in the first few months or years of life

- Infections, such as meningitis or encephalitis

- Problems with blood flow to the brain due to stroke, blood clotting problems, abnormal blood vessels, a heart defect that was present at birth, or sickle cell disease (SCD)

- Head injury from a car accident, a fall, or child abuse

What Are the Risk Factors for Cerebral Palsy?

Some events or medical problems during pregnancy can increase the risk of congenital CP. These risk factors include:

- **Low birth weight or preterm birth.** Infants born preterm (defined as before 37 weeks of pregnancy) and infants who weigh less than 5.5 pounds at birth are at greater risk of CP than are early term (defined as 37 weeks to 38 weeks of pregnancy) and full-term (defined as 39 weeks to 40 weeks of pregnancy) infants and those who are heavier at birth. The earlier the birth and the lower the infant's birth weight, the greater the risk.

- **Multiple gestations.** Twins, triplets, and other multiple births are at higher risk of CP. The risk is also greater for an infant whose twin or triplet dies before or shortly after birth.

- **Infertility treatments.** Infants born from pregnancies resulting from the use of certain infertility treatments are at higher risk for CP than are infants born from pregnancies not related to infertility treatments. Much of this increased risk may be due to the fact that infertility treatments are more likely to result in preterm delivery and multiple gestations.

- **Infections during pregnancy.** Toxoplasmosis, rubella (German measles), cytomegalovirus (CMV), and herpes can infect the womb and placenta, leading to brain damage in the fetus.

- **Fever during pregnancy.** Sometimes, fever in the mother during pregnancy or delivery can lead to brain damage in the fetus, resulting in CP.

- **Blood factor between mother and fetus does not match.** Those who have a certain protein found on red blood cells (RBCs)—abbreviated Rh—are Rh positive; those who do not have the protein are Rh negative. If a mother's Rh factor is different from that of the fetus, her immune system may attack the blood cells of the fetus, including blood cells in the brain, which can lead to brain damage.

- **Exposure to toxic chemicals.** If a mother is exposed to a toxic substance, such as high levels of methyl mercury (found in some thermometers and in some seafood), during pregnancy, the fetus is at higher risk of CP.

- **Maternal medical conditions:**
  - Abnormal thyroid function
  - Intellectual and developmental disability
  - Too much protein in the urine
  - Seizures
- **Complicated labor and delivery.** Infant heart or breathing problems during labor and delivery and immediately after birth increase the risk of CP.
- **Jaundice.** Jaundice, which causes an infant's skin, eyes, and mouth to turn a yellowish color, can be a sign that the liver is not working normally. Jaundice occurs when a substance called "bilirubin" builds up faster than the liver can clear it from the body. This condition is common and is usually not serious. However, in cases of severe, untreated jaundice, the excess bilirubin can damage the brain and cause CP.
- **Seizures.** Infants who have seizures are more likely to be diagnosed with CP later in childhood.

Some risk factors for acquired CP are:

- **Infancy.** Infants are at greater risk than older children for an event that causes brain damage.
- **Preterm or low birth weight.** Children born preterm or at a low birth weight have a higher risk for acquired CP.
- **Not getting certain vaccinations.** Childhood vaccinations can prevent brain infections that can cause CP.
- **Injury.** Not taking certain safety precautions for infants or lack of adult supervision can lead to injury that can cause CP.

How Is Cerebral Palsy Diagnosed?

Most children with CP are diagnosed during their first two years of life. But if symptoms are mild, a healthcare provider may not be able to make a diagnosis before the age of four or five.

During regular well-baby and well-child visits, a child's healthcare provider will examine:

- Growth and development

- Muscle tone

- Control of movement

- Hearing and vision

- Posture

- Coordination and balance

If a healthcare provider finds signs of CP during an examination, she or he may then use one or more brain scanning methods to look for damage in the brain. These methods may include:

- **Ultrasound.** This method is used most commonly in high-risk preterm infants to take pictures of the brain. Ultrasound is not as good as other methods at taking images of the brain, but it is the safest way to look at the brains of preterm infants.

- **Computed tomography (CT).** CT uses X-rays to take pictures of the brain and can show areas that are damaged.

- **Magnetic resonance imaging (MRI).** MRI uses a computer, a magnetic field, and radio waves to create an image of the brain. It can show the location and type of damage in better detail than CT.

- **Electroencephalogram (EEG).** If a child has had seizures, a healthcare provider may order this test to rule out another disorder, such as epilepsy. Small disks called "electrodes" are placed on the scalp to measure the brain's activity.

If a healthcare provider thinks that your child has CP, she or he may then refer the child to specialists, such as a pediatric neurologist (doctor who specializes in the brain and nervous system), a developmental pediatrician (doctor who specializes in child development), an ophthalmologist (eye doctor), or an otologist (hearing doctor), depending on the specific symptoms. These healthcare providers can help give a more accurate diagnosis and create a treatment plan.

What Are Common Treatments for Cerebral Palsy?

A child may need one or several different types of treatment depending on how severe the symptoms are and what parts of the body are affected. The treatment differs from person to person, depending on each one's specific needs. Although the initial damage of CP in the brain cannot be reversed, earlier and aggressive treatments may help to improve function and adjustments for the young nervous system and musculoskeletal system.

Families may also work with their healthcare providers and, during the school years, school staff to develop individual care and treatment programs.

Common types of treatment for CP include:

- **Physical therapy and rehabilitation.** A child with CP usually starts these therapies in the first few years of life or soon after being diagnosed. Physical therapy is one of the most important parts of treatment. It involves exercises and activities that can maintain or improve muscle strength, balance, and movement. A physical therapist helps the child learn skills, such as sitting, walking, or using a wheelchair. Other types of therapy include:

  - **Occupational therapy.** This type of therapy helps a child learn to do everyday activities, such as dressing and going to school.

  - **Recreational therapy.** Participating in art programs, cultural activities, and sports can help improve a child's physical and intellectual skills.

  - **Speech and language therapy.** A speech therapist can help a child learn to speak more clearly, help with swallowing problems, and teach new ways to communicate, such as by using sign language or a special communication device.

- **Orthotic devices.** Braces, splints, and casts can be placed on the affected limbs and can improve movement and balance. Other devices that can help with movement and posture include wheelchairs, rolling walkers, and powered scooters.

- **Assistive devices and technologies.** These include special computer-based communication machines, Velcro-fastened shoes, or crutches, which can help make daily life easier.

- **Medication.** Certain medications can relax stiff or overactive muscles and reduce abnormal movement. They may be taken by mouth, injected into affected muscles, or infused into the fluid surrounding the spinal cord through a pump implanted near the spinal cord. For children who have CP and epilepsy (seizures), standard epileptic medications should be considered, but these medications may also have negative effects on the developing brain.

- **Surgery.** A child may need surgery if symptoms are severe. For instance, surgery can lengthen stiff, tightly contracted muscles. A surgeon can also place arms or legs in better positions or correct or improve an abnormally curved spine. Sometimes, if other treatments have not worked, a surgeon can cut certain nerves to treat abnormal, spastic movements. Before conducting surgery, it is important for a healthcare provider to assess the procedure's benefits by carefully analyzing biomechanics of the joints and muscles.

Not all therapies are appropriate for everyone with CP. It is important for parents, patients, and healthcare providers to work together to come up with the best treatment plan for the patient.

Cerebral Palsy: Other FAQs
Can Cerebral Palsy Be Prevented?

Because CP is associated with preterm and low-birth-weight infants, good prenatal care and perinatal support may reduce risks. This includes careful management of vaccines; for example, women can get a vaccine to prevent rubella before getting pregnant to reduce their risk for this infection that could cause CP. Acquired CP can sometimes be prevented by using common safety practices, such as correctly installed car seats for infants and toddlers and having children wear helmets during certain activities to prevent head injuries.

What Other Conditions Are Associated with Cerebral Palsy?

In addition to the main symptoms, people with CP sometimes have related conditions, which can include:

- **Intellectual and developmental disability (IDD).** Up to one-half of people with CP have IDD.

- **Seizures.** About half of all children with CP have one or more seizures during their lifetime.

- **Delayed growth.** Children with moderate to severe CP are often very small for their age.

- **Abnormally shaped spine.** The spine may curve in a way that makes sitting, standing, or walking more difficult.

- **Vision problems.**

- **Hearing loss.**

- **Infections and long-term illnesses.** Many people with CP have a higher risk of heart and lung disease and pneumonia (infection of the lungs).

- **Malnutrition.** Because people with CP can have trouble swallowing, sucking, or feeding, it can be hard to get the proper nutrition or eat enough to gain or maintain weight.

- **Dental problems.** Some people with CP may have movement problems that prevent them from being able to take care of their teeth.

Do Adults with Cerebral Palsy Face Special Health Challenges?

Adults with CP can experience:

- **Contractures.** Abnormal muscle and joint function in more severe CP can lead to degeneration and tightening of muscle tissue.

- **Musculoskeletal deformities.** Abnormal coordination and muscle function can lead to scoliosis or hip problems.

- **Early aging.** Because CP places extra stress and strain on the body, many adults begin to have age-related problems when they reach their forties. In people with CP, the heart, veins, arteries, and lungs must work harder throughout life and may wear out sooner.

- **Arthritis.** Over a person's life, constant pressure from limbs and joints that are not properly aligned may cause painful swelling in the joints.

- **Depression.** People with disabilities, such as CP, are three to four times as likely to have depression as people in the general population.

- **Post-impairment syndrome.** This syndrome can result from the muscle and bone abnormalities and arthritis related to CP. It can cause pain, extreme tiredness, and weakness.

- **Pain.** Adults with CP often have pain in their hips, knees, ankles, and back. The pain is caused by the constant stress and strain from muscle problems over a lifetime.

- **Other medical conditions.** Adults with CP are more likely to have high blood pressure (HBP), bladder problems, problems swallowing, and broken bones.

Chapter 18

Chromosomal Disorders

Chapter Contents

Section 18.1

What Are Chromosomal Disorders?

This section includes text excerpted from "FAQs about Chromosome Disorders," Genetic and Rare Diseases Information Center (GARD), National Center for Advancing Translational Sciences (NCATS), October 25, 2017

What Are Chromosomes?

Chromosomes are organized packages of deoxyribonucleic acid (DNA) found inside your body's cells. Your DNA contains genes that tell your body how to develop and function. Humans have 23 pairs of chromosomes (46 in total). You inherit one of each chromosome pair from your mother and the other from your father. Chromosomes vary in size. Each chromosome has a centromere, which divides the chromosome into 2 uneven sections. The shorter section is called the "p arm," and the longer section is called the "q arm."

Are There Different Types of Chromosomes?

Yes, there are two different types of chromosomes; sex chromosomes and autosomal chromosomes. The sex chromosomes are the X and Y chromosomes. They determine your gender (male or female). Females have two X chromosomes, XX, one X from their father and one X from their mother. Males have one X chromosome from their mother and one Y chromosome, from their father, XY. Mothers always contribute an X chromosome (to either their son or daughter). Fathers can contribute either an X or a Y, which determines the gender of the child. The remaining chromosomes (pairs 1 through 22) are called "autosomal chromosomes." They contain the rest of your genetic information.

What Are the Different Types of Chromosomal Disorders?

Chromosome disorders can be classified into 2 main types: numerical and structural. Numerical disorders occur when there is a change in the number of chromosomes (more or fewer than 46). Examples of numerical disorders include trisomy, monosomy, and triploidy. Probably one of the most well-known numerical disorders is Down syndrome (trisomy 21). Other common types of numerical disorders include trisomy 13, trisomy 18, Klinefelter syndrome, and Turner syndrome.

Structural chromosome disorders result from breakages within a chromosome. In these types of disorders, there may be more or less than two copies of any gene. This difference in number of copies of genes may lead to clinical differences in affected individuals. Types of structural disorders include the following:

- Chromosomal deletions, sometimes known as "partial monosomies," occur when a piece or section of chromosomal material is missing. Deletions can occur in any part of any chromosome. When there is just one break in the chromosome, the deletion is called a "terminal deletion" because the end (or terminus) of the chromosome is missing. When there are two breaks in the chromosome, the deletion is called an "interstitial deletion" because a piece of chromosome material is lost from within the chromosome. Deletions that are too small to be detected under a microscope are called "microdeletions." A person with a deletion has only one copy of a particular chromosome segment instead of the usual two copies. Some examples of more common chromosome deletion syndromes include cri-du-chat syndrome and 22q11.2 deletion syndrome.

- Chromosomal duplications, sometimes known as "partial trisomies," occur when there is an extra copy of a segment of a chromosome. A person with a duplication has three copies of a particular chromosome segment instead of the usual two copies. Similar to deletions, duplications can happen anywhere along the chromosome. Examples of duplication syndromes include 22q11.2 duplication syndrome and MECP2 duplication syndrome.

- Balanced translocations occur when a chromosome segment is moved from one chromosome to another. In balanced translocations, there is no detectable net gain or loss of DNA.

- Unbalanced translocations occur when a chromosome segment is moved from one chromosome to another. In unbalanced translocations, the overall amount of DNA has been altered (some genetic material has been gained or lost).

- Inversions occur when a chromosome breaks in two places and the resulting piece of DNA is reversed and re-inserted into the chromosome. Inversions that involve the centromere are called "pericentric inversions;" inversions that do not involve the centromere are called "paracentric inversions."

- Isochromosomes are abnormal chromosomes with identical arms—either two short (p) arms or two long (q) arms. Both arms are from the same side of the centromere, are of equal length, and possess identical genes. Pallister-Killian syndrome is an example of a condition resulting from the presence of an isochromosome.

- Dicentric chromosomes result from the abnormal fusion of two chromosome pieces, each of which includes a centromere.

Ring chromosomes form when the ends of both arms of the same chromosome are deleted, which causes the remaining broken ends of the chromosome to be "sticky." These sticky ends then join together to make a ring shape. The deletion at the end of both arms of the chromosome results in missing DNA, which may cause a chromosome disorder. An example of a ring condition is ring chromosome 14 syndrome.

What Causes Chromosomal Disorders

The exact cause is unknown, but we know that chromosome abnormalities usually occur when a cell divides in 2 (a normal process that a cell goes through). Sometimes chromosome abnormalities happen during the development of an egg or sperm cell (called "germline"), and other times they happen after conception (called "somatic"). In the process of cell division, the correct number of chromosomes is supposed to end up in the resulting cells. However, errors in cell division, called "nondisjunction," can result in cells with too few or too many copies of a whole chromosome or a piece of a chromosome. Some factors, such as when a mother is of advanced maternal age (older than 35 years of age), can increase the risk for chromosome abnormalities in a pregnancy.

What Is Mosaicism?

Mosaicism is when a person has a chromosome abnormality in some, but not all, of their cells. It is often difficult to predict the effects of mosaicism because the signs and symptoms depend on which cells of the body have the chromosome abnormality.

How Are Chromosomal Disorders Diagnosed?

Chromosome disorders may be suspected in people who have developmental delays, intellectual disabilities, and/or physical abnormalities. Several types of genetic tests can identify chromosome disorders:

- Karyotyping

- Microarray (also called "array CGH")

- Fluorescence in situ hybridization (FISH)

What Signs and Symptoms Are Associated with Rare Chromosomal Disorders?

In general, the effects of rare chromosome disorders vary. With a loss or gain of chromosomal material, symptoms might include a combination of physical problems, health problems, learning difficulties, and challenging behavior. The symptoms depend on which parts of which chromosomes are involved. The loss of a segment of a chromosome is usually more serious than having an extra copy of the same segment. This is because when you lose a segment of a chromosome, you may be losing one copy of an important gene that your body needs to function.

There are general characteristics of rare chromosomal disorders that occur to varying degrees in most affected people. For instance, some degree of learning disability and/or developmental delay will occur in most people with any loss or gain of material from chromosomes 1 through 22. This is because there are many genes located across all of these chromosomes that provide instructions for normal development and function of the brain. Health providers can examine the chromosome to see where there is a break (a breakpoint). Then, they can look at what genes may be involved at the site of the break. Knowing the gene(s) involved can sometimes, but not always, help to predict signs and symptoms.

Can Chromosomal Disorders Be Inherited?

Although it is possible to inherit some types of chromosomal disorders, many chromosomal disorders are not passed from one generation to the next. Chromosome disorders that are not inherited are called "de novo," which means "new." You will need to speak with genetics professional about how (and if) a specific chromosome disorder might be inherited in your family.

Section 18.2

47, XYY Syndrome

This section includes text excerpted from "47,
XYY Syndrome," Genetic and Rare Diseases
Information Center (GARD), National Center for
Advancing Translational Sciences (NCATS), October 25, 2017.

What Is 47, XYY Syndrome?

47, XYY syndrome is a syndrome (a group of signs and symptoms) that affects males. For some males with this syndrome, signs and symptoms are barely noticeable. For others, signs and symptoms may include learning disabilities, speech delay, low muscle tone (hypotonia), and being taller than expected.

47, XYY syndrome is caused by having an extra copy of the Y chromosome in every cell of the body. The syndrome is usually not inherited. Diagnosis can be made based on prenatal tests, or it may occur during childhood or adulthood if a male has signs or symptoms of the disease. Management may include special education, as well as intervention or therapies for developmental delays.

Symptoms of 47, XYY Syndrome

The signs and symptoms of 47, XYY syndrome can range from barely noticeable to more severe. It is thought that some males with 47, XYY syndrome may never be diagnosed because the signs and symptoms may not be noticeable. For other males, signs and symptoms, such as hypotonia and/or speech delay, may begin in late infancy or early childhood. Some boys with 47, XYY syndrome may have difficulty in certain subjects in school, such as reading and writing. However, boys with this syndrome do not typically have an intellectual disability.

Other signs and symptoms of 47, XYY syndrome may include asthma, dental problems, and acne. Boys with the syndrome do not typically have physical features different from most people, but they may be taller than expected. These boys are not expected to have differences in the appearance of the sex organs (genitalia). Some males with 47, XYY syndrome have behavioral differences, such as autism spectrum disorder (ASD) (usually on the milder end) or attention deficit hyperactivity disorder (ADHD). Boys with 47, XYY syndrome are also at an increased risk to have anxiety or mood disorders.

Most boys with 47, XYY syndrome go through normal sexual development, and fertility is expected to be normal. However, some boys with the syndrome may develop testicular failure (when the testes cannot produce sperm or testosterone), which can lead to problems with fertility.

Cause of 47, XYY Syndrome

47, XYY syndrome is caused by having an extra copy of the Y chromosome in each cell of the body. The Y chromosome is one of the sex chromosomes, and the other sex chromosome is called the "X chromosome." Most people have two sex chromosomes, with girls having two X chromosomes, and boys having one X and one Y chromosome.

Boys with 47, XYY syndrome have one X chromosome and two Y chromosomes in each cell of the body. This typically happens due to a random event when a sperm cell is formed that causes the sperm cell to have two Y chromosomes. When a sperm that has two Y chromosomes fertilizes an egg (which has an X chromosome), the resulting baby will be a male with two Y chromosomes and one X chromosome. It is also possible that a similar random event could occur very early in an embryo's development. This can produce a boy who has some cells that have two sex chromosomes and some cells that have an extra Y chromosome.

It is not fully understood why an extra copy of the Y chromosome causes the features associated with 47, XYY syndrome. It is thought that the tall stature seen in some males with the syndrome is caused by having an extra copy of a gene that is located on the sex chromosomes called the "SHOX gene." This gene provides instructions to the body to control the growth of the bones. People who have an extra copy of the Y chromosome also have an extra copy of the SHOX gene, which could explain why they may be taller than expected. Another gene that is thought to cause the signs and symptoms of 47, XYY syndrome is called "NLGN4Y." This gene is located on the Y chromosome and provides instructions to the body that helps form connections between the cells in the brain. It is thought that having an extra copy of this gene may cause the learning problems associated with 47, XYY syndrome.

Inheritance of 47, XYY Syndrome

47, XYY syndrome is usually not inherited from a parent. Instead, it is typically caused by a random event that happens during the formation of a sperm cell before conception (when the sperm fertilizes the egg). Even though this random event occurs in the sperm cell of the father of a person with 47, XYY syndrome, the syndrome is not inherited from the father because the father himself typically does not have the syndrome.

It is uncommon for more than one person in a family to have 47, XYY syndrome. If a couple has a child with 47, XYY syndrome, the chances for the couple or family members to have another child with the syndrome are not increased. Men who have 47, XYY syndrome themselves are also not thought to be at an increased risk to have a child with chromosome differences. Some sperm cells of a man with 47, XYY syndrome will have an extra Y chromosome. However, it is thought that these cells are less likely to be able to survive to fertilize an egg. Therefore, the chances for a man with 47, XYY syndrome to have a child with a sex chromosome abnormality are not thought to be increased.

People with questions about their chance of having a child with a chromosome abnormality are encouraged to speak with genetic counselor or other genetics professional.

Diagnosis of 47, XYY Syndrome

47, XYY syndrome may be suspected when a doctor observes signs and symptoms that can be associated with the syndrome, such as hypotonia, speech delay, or learning problems in school. A doctor may then order testing to see if there is a genetic explanation for the signs and symptoms. Tests that may be ordered include:

- **Karyotype:** a test that is used to view all the chromosomes in a cell

- **Chromosomal microarray:** a test that looks for extra or missing chromosomes or pieces of chromosomes

In some cases, 47, XYY syndrome may be suspected prenatally based on routine screening tests. A diagnosis can be confirmed with prenatal tests, such as an amniocentesis or chorionic villus sampling (CVS).

It is thought that some people who have 47, XYY syndrome are never diagnosed because they do not have severe signs or symptoms of the syndrome.

Treatment for 47, XYY Syndrome

The signs and symptoms of 47, XYY syndrome can be managed with a variety of therapies. Occupational therapy may be recommended for infants and young boys who have hypotonia, and speech therapy may be recommended for boys who have a speech delay. Boys with 47, XYY syndrome may be in special education at school, or they may have extra help in some classes.

Other management options for boys with 47, XYY syndrome may include behavioral therapy or medications for boys with ADHD or behavioral problems. If autism spectrum disorder is present, applied behavioral analysis (ABA) therapy may be recommended. In some cases, hormonal therapy may be used.

Prognosis for 47, XYY Syndrome

The long-term outlook for people with 47, XYY is typically good. Boys with this syndrome can do well both in school and in building social relationships. Men with 47, XYY syndrome can also have successful careers and families of their own. Therapies and other management for the syndrome can be important in allowing affected males to reach their full potentials.

Section 18.3

Down Syndrome

This section includes text excerpted from "Facts about Down Syndrome," Centers for Disease Control and Prevention (CDC), February 15, 2018.

What Is Down Syndrome?

Down syndrome is a condition in which a person has an extra chromosome. Chromosomes are small "packages" of genes in the body. They determine how a fetus's body forms during pregnancy and how the baby's body functions as it grows in the womb and after birth. Typically, a baby is born with 46 chromosomes. Babies with Down syndrome have an extra copy of 1 of these chromosomes, chromosome 21. A medical term for having an extra copy of a chromosome is "trisomy." Down syndrome is also referred to as "Trisomy 21." This extra copy changes how the baby's body and brain develop, which can cause both mental and physical challenges for the baby.

Even though people with Down syndrome might act and look similar, each person has different abilities. People with Down syndrome usually have an intelligence quotient (IQ) (a measure of intelligence) in the mildly-to-moderately low range and are slower to speak than other children.

Some common physical features of Down syndrome include:

- A flattened face, especially the bridge of the nose

- Almond-shaped eyes that slant up

- A short neck

- Small ears

- A tongue that tends to stick out of the mouth

- Tiny white spots on the iris (colored part) of the eye

- Small hands and feet

- A single line across the palm of the hand (palmar crease)

- Small pinky fingers that sometimes curve toward the thumb

- Poor muscle tone or loose joints

- Shorter in height as children and adults

Occurrence

Down syndrome remains the most common chromosomal condition diagnosed in the United States. Each year, about 6,000 babies born in the United States have Down syndrome. This means that Down syndrome occurs in about 1 out of every 700 babies.

Types of Down Syndrome

There are three types of Down syndrome. People often cannot tell the difference between each type without looking at the chromosomes because the physical features and behaviors are similar.

- **Trisomy 21:** About 95 percent of people with Down syndrome have Trisomy 21. With this type of Down syndrome, each cell in the body has three separate copies of chromosome 21 instead of the usual two copies.

- **Translocation Down syndrome:** This type accounts for a small percentage of people with Down syndrome (about 3%). This occurs when an extra part or a whole extra chromosome 21 is present, but it is attached or "translocated" to a different chromosome rather than being a separate chromosome 21.

- **Mosaic Down syndrome:** This type affects about two percent of the people with Down syndrome. "Mosaic" means mixture or combination. For children with mosaic Down syndrome, some of their cells have three copies of chromosome 21, but other cells have the typical two copies of chromosome 21. Children with mosaic Down syndrome may have the same features as other children with Down syndrome. However, they may have fewer features of the condition due to the presence of some (or many) cells with a typical number of chromosomes.

Causes and Risk Factors of Down Syndrome

The extra chromosome 21 leads to the physical features and developmental challenges that can occur among people with Down syndrome. Researchers know that Down syndrome is caused by an extra chromosome, but no one knows for sure why Down syndrome occurs or how many different factors play a role.

One factor that increases the risk for having a baby with Down syndrome is the mother's age. Women who are 35 years of age or older when they become pregnant are more likely to have a pregnancy affected by Down syndrome than women who become pregnant at a younger age. However, the majority of babies with Down syndrome are born to mothers less than 35 years of age because there are many more births among younger women.

Diagnosis of Down Syndrome

There are two basic types of tests available to detect Down syndrome during pregnancy: screening tests and diagnostic tests. A screening test can tell a woman and her healthcare provider whether her pregnancy has a lower or higher chance of having Down syndrome. Screening tests do not provide an absolute diagnosis, but they are safer for the mother and the developing fetus. Diagnostic tests can typically detect whether or not a fetus will have Down syndrome, but they can be risky for the mother and developing fetus. Neither screening nor diagnostic tests can predict the full impact of Down syndrome on a baby; no one can predict this.

Screening Tests for Down Syndrome

Screening tests often include a combination of a blood test, which measures the amount of various substances in the mother's blood (e.g., maternal serum alpha-fetoprotein screening (MSAFP), triple screen, quad screen), and an ultrasound, which creates a picture of the fetus. During an ultrasound, one of the things the technician looks at is the fluid behind the fetus's neck. Extra fluid in this region could indicate a genetic problem. These screening tests can help determine the fetus's risk of Down syndrome. Rarely, screening tests can give an abnormal result even when there is nothing wrong with the fetus. Sometimes, the test results are normal, and yet, they miss a problem that does exist.

Diagnostic Tests for Down Syndrome

Diagnostic tests are usually performed after a positive screening test in order to confirm a Down syndrome diagnosis. Types of diagnostic tests include:

- **Chorionic villus sampling (CVS)**—examines material from the placenta

- **Amniocentesis**—examines the amniotic fluid (the fluid from the sac surrounding the fetus)

- **Percutaneous umbilical blood sampling (PUBS)**—examines blood from the umbilical cord

These tests look for changes in the chromosomes that would indicate a Down syndrome diagnosis.

Health Problems Associated with Down Syndrome

Many people with Down syndrome have the common facial features and no other major birth defects. However, some people with Down syndrome might have one or more major birth defects or other medical problems. Some of the more common health problems among children with Down syndrome are listed below.

- Hearing loss

- Obstructive sleep apnea, which is a condition where the person's breathing temporarily stops while asleep

- Ear infections

- Eye diseases

- Heart defects present at birth

Healthcare providers routinely monitor children with Down syndrome for these conditions.

Treatments for Down Syndrome

Down syndrome is a lifelong condition. Services early in life will often help babies and children with Down syndrome to improve their physical and intellectual abilities. Most of these services focus on helping children with Down syndrome develop to their full potential. These services include speech, occupational, and physical therapy, and they are typically offered through early intervention programs in each state. Children with Down syndrome may also need extra help or attention in school, although many children are included in regular classes.

Section 18.4

Fragile X Syndrome

This section includes text excerpted from "Fragile X Syndrome: Condition Information," *Eunice Kennedy Shriver* National Institute of Child Health and Human Development (NICHD), December 1, 2016.

What Is Fragile X Syndrome?

Fragile X syndrome is a genetic disorder that affects a person's development, especially that person's behavior and ability to learn. In addition, fragile X can affect:

- Communication skills

- Physical appearance

- Sensitivity to noise, light, or other sensory information

Fragile X syndrome is the most common form of inherited intellectual and developmental disability (IDD).

People with fragile X syndrome may not have noticeable symptoms, or they can have more serious symptoms that range from learning disabilities to cognitive and behavioral problems.

How Is the Fragile X Mental Retardation 1 Mutation Related to Fragile X-Associated Disorders?

Fragile X syndrome and its associated conditions are caused by changes (mutations) in the fragile X mental retardation 1 (*FMR1*) gene found on the X chromosome. This mutation affects how the body makes the fragile X mental retardation protein (FMRP). The mutation causes the body to make only a little bit or none of the protein, which can cause the symptoms of fragile X.

In a gene, the information for making a protein has two parts: the introduction and the instructions for making the protein itself. Researchers call the introduction the "promoter" because of how it helps to start the process of building the protein.

The promoter part of the *FMR1* gene includes many repeats—repeated instances of a specific deoxyribonucleic acid (DNA) sequence called the "CGG sequence." A normal *FMR1* gene has between 6 and 40 repeats in the promoter; the average is 30 repeats.

People with between 55 and 200 repeats have a premutation of the gene. The premutation may cause the gene to not work properly, but it does not cause IDD. The premutation is linked to the disorders fragile X-associated primary ovarian insufficiency (FXPOI) and fragile X-associated tremor/ataxia syndrome (FXTAS). However, not all people with the premutation show symptoms of FXPOI or FXTAS.

People with 200 or more repeats in the promoter part of the gene have a full mutation, meaning the gene might not work at all. People with a full mutation often have fragile X syndrome.

The number of repeats, also called the "size of the mutation," affects the type of symptoms and how serious the symptoms of fragile X syndrome will be.

Inheriting Fragile X Syndrome

Fragile X syndrome is inherited, which means it is passed down from parents to children. Anyone with the *FMR1* gene mutation can pass it to their children. However, a person who inherits the gene mutation may not develop fragile X syndrome. Males will pass it down to all of their daughters and not their sons. Females have a 50/50 chance to pass it along to both their sons and daughters. In some cases, an *FMR1* premutation can change to a full mutation when it is passed from parent to child.

What Causes Fragile X Syndrome

Fragile X results from a change or mutation in the fragile X mental retardation 1 *(FMR1) gene*, which is found on the X chromosome. The gene normally makes a protein called "fragile X mental retardation protein," or "FMRP." This protein is important for creating and maintaining connections between cells in the brain and nervous system. The mutation causes the body to make only a little bit or none of the protein, which often causes the symptoms of fragile X.

Not everyone with the mutated *FMR1* gene has symptoms of fragile X syndrome, because the body may still be able to make FMRP. A few things affect how much FMRP the body can make:

- **The size of the mutation.** Some people have a smaller mutation (a lower number of repeats) in their *FMR1* gene, while others have big mutations (a large number of repeats) in the gene. If the mutation is small, the body may be able to make some of the protein. Having the protein available makes the symptoms milder.

- **The number of cells that have the mutation.** Because not every cell in the body is exactly the same, some cells might have the *FMR1* mutation, while others do not. This situation is called "mosaicism." If the mutation is in most of the body's cells, the person will probably have symptoms of fragile X syndrome. If the mutation is in only some of the cells, the person might not have any symptoms at all or only mild symptoms.

- **Being female.** Females have two X chromosomes (XX), while males have only one. In females, if the *FMR1* gene on one X chromosome has the mutation, the *FMR1* gene on the other X chromosome might not have the mutation. Even if one of the female's genes has a very large mutation, the body can usually make at least some FMRP, leading to milder symptoms.

What Are Common Symptoms of Fragile X Syndrome?

People with fragile X do not all have the same signs and symptoms, but they do have some things in common. Symptoms are often milder in females than in males.

- **Intelligence and learning.** Many people with fragile X have problems with intellectual functioning.

  - These problems can range from mild, such as learning disorders or problems with mathematics, to severe, such as an intellectual or developmental disability.

  - The syndrome may affect the ability to think, reason, and learn.

  - Because many people with fragile X also have attention disorders, hyperactivity, anxiety, and language-processing problems, a person with fragile X may have more capabilities than her or his IQ (intelligence quotient) score suggests.

- **Physical.** Most infants and younger children with fragile X do not have any specific physical features of this syndrome. When these children start to go through puberty, however, many will begin to develop certain features that are typical of those with fragile X.

  - These features include a narrow face, large head, large ears, flexible joints, flat feet, and a prominent forehead.

  - These physical signs become more obvious with age.

- **Behavioral, social, and emotional.** Most children with fragile X have some behavioral challenges.

  - They may be afraid or anxious in new situations.

  - They may have trouble making eye contact with other people.

  - Boys, especially, may have trouble paying attention or be aggressive.

  - Girls may be shy around new people. They may also have attention disorders and problems with hyperactivity.

- **Speech and language.** Most boys with fragile X have some problems with speech and language.

  - They may have trouble speaking clearly, may stutter, or may leave out parts of words. They may also have problems understanding other people's social cues, such as tone of voice or specific types of body language.

- Girls usually do not have severe problems with speech or language.

- Some children with fragile X begin talking later than typically developing children. Most will talk eventually, but a few might stay nonverbal throughout their lives.

- **Sensory**. Many children with fragile X are bothered by certain sensations, such as bright light, loud noises, or the way certain clothing feels on their bodies.

  - These sensory issues might cause them to act out or display behavior problems.

How Is It Diagnosed?

Healthcare providers often use a blood sample to diagnose fragile X. The healthcare provider will take a sample of blood and send it to a laboratory, which will determine what form of the *FMR1* gene is present.

Prenatal Testing (During Pregnancy)

Pregnant women who have an *FMR1* premutation or full mutation may pass that mutated gene on to their children. A prenatal test allows healthcare providers to detect the mutated gene in the developing fetus. This important information helps families and providers to prepare for fragile X syndrome and to intervene as early as possible.

Possible types of prenatal tests include:

- **Amniocentesis.** A healthcare provider takes a sample of amniotic fluid, which is then tested for the *FMR1* mutation.

- **Chorionic villus sampling (CVS).** A healthcare provider takes a sample of cells from the placenta, which is then tested for the *FMR1* mutation.

Because prenatal testing involves some risk to the mother and fetus, if you or a family member is considering prenatal testing for fragile X, discuss all the risks and benefits with your healthcare provider.

Prenatal testing is not very common, and many parents do not know they carry the mutation. Therefore, parents usually start to notice symptoms in their children when they are infants or toddlers. The average age at diagnosis is 36 months for boys and 42 months for girls.

Diagnosis of Children

Many parents first notice symptoms of delayed development in their infants or toddlers. These symptoms may include delays in speech and language skills, social and emotional difficulties, and being sensitive to certain sensations. Children may also be delayed in or have problems with motor skills, such as learning to walk.

A healthcare provider can perform developmental screening to determine the nature of delays in a child. If a healthcare provider suspects the child has fragile X syndrome, she or he can refer parents to a clinical geneticist, who can perform a genetic test for fragile X syndrome.

What Are the Treatments?

There is no single treatment for fragile X syndrome, but there are treatments that help minimize the symptoms of the condition. Individuals with fragile X who receive appropriate education, therapy services, and medications have the best chance of using all of their individual capabilities and skills. Even those with an intellectual or developmental disability can learn to master many self-help skills.

Early intervention is important. Because a young child's brain is still forming, early intervention gives children the best start possible and the greatest chance of developing a full range of skills. The sooner a child with fragile X syndrome gets treatment, the more opportunity there is for learning.

Educational Treatments

Most children with fragile X can benefit from special education services that are tailored to their particular strengths and weaknesses. Educational treatments should take the child's specific symptoms of fragile X into account to promote the best learning environment.

Eligibility for Special Education

Most children with fragile X are eligible for free, appropriate public education under federal law. Although a medical diagnosis does not guarantee access to special education services, most children with fragile X will have certain cognitive or learning deficits that make them eligible for services. Parents can contact a local school principal or special education coordinator to learn how to have a child examined to see if she or he qualifies for services under the Individuals with Disabilities Education Act (IDEA).

Suggestions for Working with Individuals with Fragile X

Everyone with fragile X is unique. However, those with this disorder often share some particular behaviors and intellectual characteristics. For example, children with fragile X can easily become overwhelmed by crowds, noise, and touch. Other common characteristics include weak abstract thinking skills and poor quantitative (measuring and counting) skills. However, these children often have unique strengths as well, including visual memory. By taking these unique strengths and weaknesses into account, teachers can promote the best learning for these children.

Suggestions:

- Know the learning style of the individual.

- Develop a consistent daily schedule or routine.

- Use visual signs (pictures, sign language, logos, words) and concrete examples or materials to present ideas, concepts, steps, etc.

- Prepare the individual for any changes in routine by explaining these changes ahead of time, possibly by using visual signs.

- Include functional goals with academic goals; for instance, teach the individual the names of different pieces of clothing, as well as how to dress herself or himself.

- Provide opportunities for the child to be active and move around.

- Use computers and interactive educational software.

- Provide a quiet place where the child can first retreat and then regroup.

Teachers can use the National Fragile X Foundation's lesson planning guide for fragile X to learn more about the best strategies for teaching children with fragile X.

Classroom for Children with Fragile X Syndrome

In general, there are three options for the classroom placement of a child with fragile X, based on that child's specific abilities and needs.

- Full inclusion in a regular classroom

- Inclusion with "pull-out" services

- Full-time special education classroom

Placement decisions should be based on each child's needs and abilities.

The Individualized Educational Plan

If a child with fragile X syndrome qualifies for special services, a team of people will work together to design an Individualized Educational Plan (IEP) for the child. The team may include parents or caregivers, teachers, a school psychologist, and other specialists in child development or education. The IEP includes specific learning goals for that child, based on her or his needs and capabilities. The team also decides how best to carry out the IEP. It reaches a consensus on classroom placement for the child, determines any devices or special assistance the child needs, and identifies the specialists who will work with the child.

The special services team should evaluate the child on a regular basis. The team can chart progress and decide whether changes in treatment are needed (for instance, changes to the IEP, in classroom placement, or in the services provided).

Therapy Treatments

A variety of professionals can help individuals with fragile X syndrome and their families manage the symptoms of the disorder. Those with fragile X might benefit from services provided by several different specialists:

- **Speech-language therapists** can help people with fragile X syndrome improve their pronunciation of words and sentences, slow down their speech, and use language more effectively.

- **Occupational therapists** help find ways to adjust tasks and conditions to match a person's needs and abilities.

- **Physical therapists** design activities and exercises that help build motor control and improve posture and balance.

- **Behavioral therapists** try to understand why someone with fragile X acts out, and they create ways and strategies for avoiding or preventing these situations from occurring, while also teaching better or more positive ways to respond to situations.

Medication Treatments

To this point, the U.S. Food and Drug Administration (FDA) has not approved any drugs specifically for the treatment of fragile X or its symptoms. But in many cases, medications are used to treat certain symptoms of fragile X syndrome, as shown in the chart below. The *Eunice Kennedy Shriver* National Institute of Child Health and Human Development (NICHD) does not endorse or support the use of any of these medications in treating the symptoms of fragile X syndrome, or for other conditions for which the medications are not FDA-approved.

Medication is most effective when paired with therapy designed to teach new coping or behavioral skills. Not every medication helps every child.

Please note that some of these medications carry serious risks. Others may make symptoms worse at first, or they may take several weeks to become effective. Doctors may have to try different dosages or combinations of medications to find the most effective plan. Families, caregivers, and doctors need to work together to ensure that a medication is working and that the medication plan is safe.

The following table is meant for reference only and should not take the place of a healthcare provider's advice. Discuss any questions about medication with a healthcare provider.

Table 18.1. Fragile X Syndrome Symptoms and Generic Medications

Symptom	Generic Medication (Brand Name in Parentheses)
Seizures Mood instability	• Carbamazepine (Tegretol) • Valproic acid or Divalproex (Depakote) • Lithium carbonate • Gabapentin (Neurontin) • Lamotrigine (Lamictal) • Topiramate (Topamax), Tiagabine (Gabitril), and Vigabatrin (Sabril) • Phenobarbital and Primidone (Mysoline) • Phenytoin (Dilantin)

Table 18.1. Continued

Symptom	Generic Medication (Brand Name in Parentheses)
Attention deficit (with or without hyperactivity)	• Methylphenidate (Ritalin, Concerta) and Dextroamphetamine (Adderall, Dexedrine) • L-acetylcarnitine • Venlafaxine (Effexor) and Nefazodone (Serzone) • Amantadine (Symmetrel) • Folic acid
Hyperarousal Sensory overstimulation (often occurs with ADD/ADHD)	• Clonidine (Catapres TTS patches) • Guanfacine (Tenex)
Aggression Intermittent explosive disorder Obsessive-compulsive disorder (often occurs with anxiety and/or depression)	• Fluoxetine (Prozac) • Sertraline (Zoloft) and Citalopram (Celexa) • Paroxetine (Paxil) • Fluvoxamine (Luvox) • Risperidone (Risperdal) • Quetiapine (Seroquel) • Olanzapine (Zyprexa)
Sleep disturbances	• Trazodone • Melatonin

ADD: attention deficit disorder; ADHD: attention deficit hyperactivity disorder; TTS: transdermal therapeutic system.

Other FAQs

Are There Specific Disorders or Conditions Associated with Fragile X Syndrome?

Other conditions associated with fragile X syndrome are as follows:

- **Autism spectrum disorder (ASD).** Up to one-half of people with fragile X also meet the criteria for ASD.

- **Mitral valve prolapse.** In mitral valve prolapse, a heart condition, the valve that separates the upper and lower left chambers of the heart does not work properly. This condition is usually not life-threatening, but in severe cases, surgery might be required to correct the problem.

- **Seizures.** Up to one-fifth of children with fragile X syndrome also have seizures. Seizures associated with the syndrome are more common in boys than in girls.

How Is Fragile X Syndrome Inherited?

The gene for fragile X is carried on the X chromosome. Because both males (XY) and females (XX) have at least one X chromosome, both can pass on the mutated gene to their children.

- A father with the altered gene for fragile X on his X chromosome will pass that gene on only to his daughters. To his sons, he will pass on a Y chromosome, which does not transmit fragile X syndrome. Therefore, a father with the altered gene on his X chromosome and a mother with normal X chromosomes would have daughters with the altered gene for fragile X, while none of their sons would have the mutated gene.

- A father can pass on the premutation form of the *FMR1* gene to his daughters but not the full mutation. Even if the father himself has a full mutation of this gene, it appears that sperm can carry only the premutation. Scientists do not understand how or why fathers can pass on only the milder form of fragile X to their daughters. This remains an area of focused research.

- Mothers pass on only X chromosomes to their children, so if a mother has the altered gene for fragile X, she can pass that gene to either her sons or her daughters. If a mother has the mutated gene on one X chromosome and has one normal X chromosome, and the father has no mutations, all the children have a 50-50 chance of inheriting the mutated gene.

- These 50-50 odds apply for each child the parents have. Having one child with the *FMR1* mutation does not increase or decrease the chances of having another child with the mutated *FMR1* gene. This is also true for the severity of the symptoms. Having one child with mild symptoms does not mean that the other children will have severe symptoms, and having a child with severe symptoms does not mean that the other children will have mild symptoms.

How Does the **FMR1** *Gene Change as It Is Passed from Parent to Child?*

The repeats in the promoter part of the *FMR1* gene are unstable, and sometimes the number of repeats increases from one generation to the next.

A premutation gene is less stable than a full mutation gene. So, as it passes from parent to child, a premutation gene might expand to become a full mutation gene. The chances of expansion depend on the number of repeats in the promoter of the premutation gene.

Normal

FMR1 genes that have 5 to 44 cytosine-guanine-guanine (CGG) repeats in the promoter are considered normal. When these genes are passed from parent to child, the number of repeats does not increase or decrease.

Intermediate

FMR1 genes with 45 to 54 CGG repeats in the promoter are considered intermediate, or borderline. An intermediate gene may expand from one generation to the next, depending on which parent has the gene.

Mother to Child

Sometimes, when a mother passes an intermediate gene to her child, the CGG repeats increase to a number seen with permutations. Research shows that an intermediate gene will not become a full mutation gene in one generation, and so a mother with an intermediate gene will not have a child with a full mutation.

Father to Child

When intermediate genes are transmitted from father to child, they are generally stable and do not increase to permutations.

Permutations

Premutation (55 to 199 CGG repeats) *FMR1* genes can expand to a full mutation from one generation to the next. The risk of expansion depends on which parent has the gene and the number of repeats in that gene.

Mother to Child

An *FMR1* gene from the mother with 100 CGG repeats is very likely to expand to a full mutation when passed to the child. About one-third of the time, an *FMR1* gene from the mother with 70 to 79 CGG repeats expands to a full mutation in one generation.

Father to Child

Permutations passed from father to child have almost no chance of expanding to full mutations.

Section 18.5

Klinefelter Syndrome

This section includes text excerpted from "Klinefelter Syndrome (KS): Condition Information," *Eunice Kennedy Shriver* National Institute of Child Health and Human Development (NICHD), December 1, 2016.

What Is Klinefelter Syndrome?

The term "Klinefelter syndrome," or "KS," describes a set of features that can occur in a male who is born with an extra X chromosome in his cells. It is named after Dr. Henry Klinefelter, who identified the condition in the 1940s.

Usually, every cell in a male's body, except sperm and red blood cells, contains 46 chromosomes. The 45th and 46th chromosomes—the X and Y chromosomes—are sometimes called "sex chromosomes" because they determine a person's sex. Normally, males have one X and one Y chromosome, making them XY. Males with KS have an extra X chromosome, making them XXY.

KS is sometimes called "47, XXY" (47 refers to total chromosomes) or the "XXY condition." Those with KS are sometimes called "XXY males."

Some males with KS may have both XY cells and XXY cells in their bodies. This is called "mosaic." Mosaic males may have fewer symptoms of KS, depending on the number of XY cells they have in their bodies and where these cells are located. For example, males who have normal XY cells in their testes may be fertile.

In very rare cases, males might have two or more extra X chromosomes in their cells, for instance, XXXY or XXXXY, or an extra Y, such as XXYY. This is called "poly-X Klinefelter syndrome," and it causes more severe symptoms.

What Causes Klinefelter Syndrome

The extra chromosome results from a random error that occurs when a sperm or egg is formed; this error causes an extra X cell to be included each time the cell divides to form new cells. In very rare cases, more than one extra X or an extra Y is included.

How Many People Are Affected by or at Risk for Klinefelter Syndrome?

Researchers estimate that 1 male in about 500 newborn males has an extra X chromosome, making KS among the most common chromosomal disorders seen in all newborns. The likelihood of a third or fourth X is much rarer:

Table 18.2. Prevalence of Klinefelter Syndrome Variants

Number of Extra X Chromosomes	One (XXY)	Two (XXXY)	Three (XXXXY)
Number of newborn males with the condition	1 in 500	1 in 50,000	1 in 85,000 to 100,000

Scientists are not sure what factors increase the risk of KS. The error that produces the extra chromosome occurs at random, meaning the error is not hereditary or passed down from parent to child. Research suggests that older mothers might be slightly more likely to have a son with KS. However, the extra X chromosome in KS comes from the father about one-half of the time.

What Are Common Symptoms of Klinefelter Syndrome?

Because XXY males do not really appear different from other males and because they may not have any or have mild symptoms, XXY males often do not know they have KS.

In other cases, males with KS may have mild or severe symptoms. Whether or not a male with KS has visible symptoms depends on many factors, including how much testosterone his body makes, if he is mosaic (with both XY and XXY cells), and his age when the condition is diagnosed and treated.

KS symptoms fall into these main categories:

- Physical symptoms

- Language and learning symptoms

- Social and behavioral symptoms

- Symptoms of poly-X KS

Physical Symptoms

Many physical symptoms of KS result from low testosterone levels in the body. The degree of symptoms differs based on the amount of testosterone needed for a specific age or developmental stage and the amount of testosterone the body makes or has available.

During the first few years of life, when the need for testosterone is low, most XXY males do not show any obvious differences from typical male infants and young boys. Some may have slightly weaker muscles, meaning they might sit up, crawl, and walk slightly later than average. For example, on average, baby boys with KS do not start walking until the age of 18 months.

After five years of age, when compared to typically developing boys, boys with KS may be slightly:

- Taller

- Fatter around the belly

- Clumsier

- Slower in developing motor skills, coordination, speed, and muscle strength

Puberty for boys with KS usually starts normally. But because their bodies make less testosterone than non-KS boys, their pubertal development may be disrupted or slow. In addition to being tall, KS boys may have:

- Smaller testes and penis

- Breast growth (about one-third of teens with KS have breast growth)

- Less facial and body hair

- Reduced muscle tone

- Narrower shoulders and wider hips

- Weaker bones, greater risk for bone fractures

- Decreased sexual interest

- Lower energy

- Reduced sperm production

An adult male with KS may have these features:

- Infertility. Nearly all men with KS are unable to father a biologically related child without help from a fertility specialist.

- Small testes, with the possibility of testes shrinking slightly after the teen years

- Lower testosterone levels, which lead to less muscle, hair, and sexual interest and function

- Breasts or breast growth (called "gynecomastia")

In some cases, breast growth can be permanent, and about 10 percent of XXY males need breast reduction surgery.

Language and Learning Symptoms

Most males with KS have normal intelligence quotients (IQs) and successfully complete education at all levels. (IQ is a frequently used intelligence measure, but it does not include emotional, creative, or other types of intelligence.) Between 25 percent and 85 percent of all males with KS have some kind of learning or language-related problem, which makes it more likely that they will need some extra help in school. Without this help or intervention, KS males might fall behind their classmates as schoolwork becomes harder.

KS males may experience some of the following learning and language-related challenges:

- **A delay in learning to talk.** Infants with KS tend to make only a few different vocal sounds. As they grow older, they may have difficulty saying words clearly. It might be hard for them to distinguish differences between similar sounds.

- **Trouble using language to express their thoughts and needs.** Boys with KS might have problems putting their thoughts, ideas, and emotions into words. Some may find it hard to learn and remember some words, such as the names of common objects.

- **Trouble processing what they hear.** Although most boys with KS can understand what is being said to them, they might take longer to process multiple or complex sentences. In some cases, they might fidget or "tune out" because they take longer to process the information. It might also be difficult for KS males to concentrate in noisy settings. They might also be less able to understand a speaker's feelings from just speech alone.

- **Reading difficulties.** Many boys with KS have difficulty understanding what they read (called "poor reading comprehension"). They might also read more slowly than other boys.

By adulthood, most males with KS learn to speak and converse normally, although they may have a harder time doing work that involves extensive reading and writing.

Social and Behavioral Symptoms

Many of the social and behavioral symptoms in KS may result from the language and learning difficulties. For instance, boys with KS who have language difficulties might hold back socially and could use help building social relationships.

Boys with KS, compared to typically developing boys, tend to be:

- Quieter

- Less assertive or self-confident

- More anxious or restless

- Less physically active

- More helpful and eager to please

- More obedient or more ready to follow directions

In the teenage years, boys with KS may feel their differences more strongly. As a result, these teen boys are at higher risk of depression, substance abuse, and behavioral disorders. Some teens might withdraw, feel sad, or act out their frustration and anger.

As adults, most men with KS have lives similar to those of men without KS. They successfully complete high school, college, and other levels of education. They have successful and meaningful careers and professions. They have friends and families.

Contrary to research findings published several decades ago, males with KS are no more likely to have serious psychiatric disorders or to get into trouble with the law.

Symptoms of Poly-X Klinefelter Syndrome

Males with poly-X Klinefelter syndrome have more than one extra X chromosome, so their symptoms might be more pronounced than in males with KS. In childhood, they may also have seizures, crossed eyes, constipation, and recurrent ear infections. Poly-KS males might also show slight differences in other physical features.

Some common additional symptoms for several poly-X Klinefelter syndromes are listed below.

48, XXYY

- Long legs
- Little body hair
- Lower IQ, average of 60 to 80 (normal IQ is 90 to 110)
- Leg ulcers and other vascular disease symptoms
- Extreme shyness, but also occasional aggression and impulsiveness

48, XXXY (Or Tetrasomy)

- Eyes set further apart
- Flat nose bridge
- Arm bones connected to each other in an unusual way
- Short
- Fifth (smallest) fingers curve inward (clinodactyly)
- Lower IQ, average of 40 to 60
- Immature behavior

49, XXXXY (Or Pentasomy)

- Low IQ, usually between 20 and 60
- Small head
- Short

- Upward-slanted eyes

- Heart defects, such as when the chambers do not form properly

- High feet arches

- Shy, but friendly

- Difficulty with changing routines

What Treatment Options Are Available for Klinefelter Syndrome?

It is important to remember that because symptoms can be mild, many males with KS are never diagnosed or treated.

The earlier in life that KS symptoms are recognized and treated, the more likely it is that the symptoms can be reduced or eliminated. It is especially helpful to begin treatment by early puberty. Puberty is a time of rapid physical and psychological change, and treatment can successfully limit symptoms. However, treatment can bring benefits at any age.

The type of treatment needed depends on the type of symptoms being treated.

Treating Physical Symptoms
Treatment for Low Testosterone

About one-half of XXY males' chromosomes have low testosterone levels. These levels can be raised by taking supplemental testosterone. Testosterone treatment can:

- Improve muscle mass

- Deepen the voice

- Promote the growth of facial and body hair

- Help the reproductive organs to mature

- Build and maintain bone strength and help prevent osteoporosis in later years

- Produce a more masculine appearance, which can also help relieve anxiety and depression

- Increase focus and attention

There are various ways to take testosterone:

- Injections or shots, every two to three weeks
- Pills
- Through the skin, also called "transdermal;" current methods include wearing a testosterone patch or rubbing testosterone gel on the skin

Males taking testosterone treatment should work closely with an endocrinologist, a doctor who specializes in hormones and their functions, to ensure the best outcome from testosterone therapy.

Males and testosterone therapy. Not all males with XXY condition benefit from testosterone therapy. For males whose testosterone level is low to normal, the benefits of taking testosterone are less clear than for when testosterone is very low.

Side effects, although generally mild, can include acne, skin rashes from patches or gels, breathing problems (especially during sleep), and higher risk of an enlarged prostate gland or prostate cancer in older age. In addition, testosterone supplementation will not increase testicular size, decrease breast growth, or correct infertility.

Although the majority of boys with KS grow up to live as males, some develop atypical gender identities. For these males, supplemental testostcrone may not be suitable. Gender identity should be discussed with healthcare specialists before starting treatment.

Treatment for Enlarged Breasts

No approved drug treatment exists for this condition of overdeveloped breast tissue, termed gynecomastia. Some healthcare providers recommend surgery—called "mastectomy"—to remove or reduce the breasts of XXY males.

When adult men have breasts, they are at higher risk for breast cancer than other men and need to be checked for this condition regularly. The mastectomy lowers the risk of cancer and can reduce the social stress associated with XXY males having enlarged breasts.

Because it is a surgical procedure, mastectomy carries a variety of risks. XXY males who are thinking about mastectomy should discuss all the risks and benefits with their healthcare provider.

Treatment for Infertility

Between 95 percent and 99 percent of XXY men are infertile because they do not produce enough sperm to fertilize an egg naturally. However, sperm are found in more than 50 percent of men with KS.

Advances in assistive reproductive technology (ART) have made it possible for some men with KS to conceive. One type of ART, called "testicular sperm extraction with intracytoplasmic sperm injection" (TESE-ICSI), has shown success for XXY males. For this procedure, a surgeon removes sperm from the testes and places one sperm into an egg.

Similar to all ARTs, TESE-ICSI carries both risks and benefits. For instance, it is possible that the resulting child might have the XXY condition. In addition, the procedure is expensive and often not covered by health insurance plans. Importantly, there is no guarantee the procedure will work.

Studies suggest that collecting sperm from adolescent XXY males and freezing the sperm until later might result in more pregnancies during subsequent fertility treatments. This is because although XXY males may make some healthy sperm during puberty, this becomes more difficult as they leave adolescence and enter adulthood.

Treating Language and Learning Symptoms

Some, but not all, children with KS have language development and learning delays. They might be slow to learn to talk, read, and write, and they might have difficulty processing what they hear. But various interventions, such as speech therapy and educational assistance, can help to reduce and even eliminate these difficulties. The earlier treatment begins, the better the outcomes.

Parents might need to bring these types of problems to the teacher's attention. Because these boys can be quiet and cooperative in the classroom, teachers may not notice the need for help.

Boys and men with KS can benefit by visiting therapists who are experts in areas such as coordination, social skills, and coping. XXY males might benefit from any or all of the following:

- **Physical therapists** design activities and exercises to build motor skills and strength and to improve muscle control, posture, and balance.

- **Occupational therapists** help build skills needed for daily functioning, such as social and play skills, interaction and conversation skills, and job or career skills that match interests and abilities.

- **Behavioral therapists** help with specific social skills, such as asking other kids to play and starting conversations. They can also teach productive ways of handling frustration, shyness, anger, and other emotions that can arise from feeling "different."

- **Mental-health therapists or counselors** help males with KS find ways to cope with feelings of sadness, depression, self-doubt, and low self-esteem. They can also help with substance-abuse problems. These professionals can also help families deal with the emotions of having a son with KS.

- **Family therapists** provide counseling to a man with KS, his spouse, partner, or family. They can help identify relationship problems and help patients develop communication skills and understand other people's needs.

Parents of XXY males have also mentioned that taking part in physical activities at low-key levels, such as karate, swimming, tennis, and golf, were helpful in improving motor skills, coordination, and confidence.

With regard to education, some boys with KS will qualify to receive state-sponsored special needs services to address their developmental and learning symptoms. But, because these symptoms may be mild, many XXY males will not be eligible for these services. Families can contact a local school district official or special education coordinator to learn more about whether XXY males can receive the following free services:

- The early intervention program for infants and toddlers with disabilities is required by two national laws; the Individuals with Disabilities and Education Improvement Act (IDEIA) and the Individuals with Disabilities Education Act (IDEA). Every state operates special programs for children from birth to the age of three, helping them develop in areas such as behavior, development, communication, and social play.

- An Individualized Education Plan (IEP) for school is created and administered by a team of people, starting with parents and including teachers and school psychologists. The team works together to design an IEP with specific academic, communication, motor, learning, functional, and socialization goals, based on the child's educational needs and specific symptoms.

Treating Social and Behavioral Symptoms

Many of the professionals and methods for treating learning and language symptoms of the XXY condition are similar to or the same as the ones used to address social and behavioral symptoms.

For instance, boys with KS may need help with social skills and interacting in groups. Occupational or behavioral therapists might be able to assist with these skills. Some school districts and health centers might also offer these types of skill-building programs or classes.

In adolescence, symptoms such as lack of body hair could make XXY males uncomfortable in school or other social settings, and this discomfort can lead to depression, substance abuse, and behavioral problems or "acting out." They might also have questions about their masculinity or gender identity. In these instances, consulting a psychologist, counselor, or psychiatrist may be helpful.

Contrary to research results released decades ago, current research shows that XXY males are no more likely than other males to have serious psychiatric disorders or to get into trouble with the law.

How Do Healthcare Providers Diagnose Klinefelter Syndrome?

The only way to confirm the presence of an extra chromosome is by a karyotype test. A healthcare provider will take a small blood or skin sample and send it to a laboratory, where a technician inspects the cells under a microscope to find the extra chromosome. A karyotype test shows the same results at any time in a person's life.

Tests for chromosome disorders, including KS, may be done before birth. To obtain tissue or liquid for this test, a pregnant woman undergoes chorionic villus sampling (CVS) or amniocentesis. These types of prenatal testing carry a small risk for miscarriage and are not routinely conducted unless the woman has a family history of chromosomal disorders, has other medical problems, or is above 35 years of age.

Factors That Influence When Klinefelter Syndrome Is Diagnosed

Because symptoms can be mild, some males with KS are never diagnosed.

Several factors affect whether and when a diagnosis occurs:

- Few newborns and boys are tested for or diagnosed with KS.

  - Although newborns in the United States are screened for some conditions, they are not screened for XXY or other sex chromosome differences.

- In childhood, symptoms can be subtle and overlooked easily. Only about 1 in 10 males with KS is diagnosed before puberty.

- Sometimes, visiting a healthcare provider will not produce a diagnosis. Some symptoms, such as delayed early speech, might be treated successfully without further testing for KS.

- Most XXY diagnoses occur at puberty or in adulthood.

  - Puberty brings a surge in diagnoses as some males (or their parents) become concerned about slow testes growth or breast development and consult a healthcare provider.

  - Many men are diagnosed for the first time in fertility clinics. Among men seeking help for infertility, about 15 percent have KS.

Is There a Cure for Klinefelter Syndrome?

There is no way to remove chromosomes from cells to cure the XXY condition.

But many symptoms can be successfully treated, minimizing the impact the condition has on length and quality of life (QOL). Most adult XXY men have full independence and have friends, families, and normal social relationships. They live about as long as other men, on average.

Klinefelter Syndrome: Other FAQs
Are There Disorders or Conditions Associated with Klinefelter Syndrome?

Males with KS are at higher risk for some other health conditions, for reasons that are not fully understood. However, these risks can be minimized by paying attention to symptoms and treating them appropriately.

Associated conditions include:

- **Autoimmune disorders,** such as type 1 diabetes, rheumatoid arthritis, hypothyroidism, and lupus. In these disorders, the immune cells attack parts of the body instead of protecting them.

- **Breast cancer.** Males with KS have a higher risk of developing this cancer, although they still have a lower risk than females. XXY males should pay attention to any changes in their breasts, such as lumps or any leakage from the nipple, and should see their healthcare provider right away if they have any concerns.

- **Venous disease,** or diseases of the arteries and veins. Some of these include:

  - Varicose veins

  - Deep vein thrombosis (DVT), a blood clot in a deep vein

  - Pulmonary embolism, a blockage of an artery in the lungs

  - To reduce their risk, males can keep a normal body weight; get regular, moderate physical activity; quit smoking; and avoid sitting or standing in the same position for long periods of time. If venous diseases develop, they can be treated in different ways, depending on their severity. For instance, some treatments include wearing compression socks and others require taking blood-thinner medications.

- **Tooth decay.** Almost one-half of men with KS have taurodontism, a dental problem in which the teeth have larger-than-normal chambers for holding pulp (the soft tissue that contains nerve endings and blood vessels) and shorter-than-normal tooth roots, both of which make it easier for tooth decay to develop. Regular dental check-ups and good oral hygiene habits will help prevent, catch, and treat problems.

- **Osteoporosis,** in which bones lose calcium, become brittle, and break more easily, may develop over time in KS males who have low testosterone levels for long periods of time. Testosterone treatment; regular, moderate physical activity; and eating a healthy diet can decrease the risk of osteoporosis. If the disease develops, medications can help limit its severity.

Can Klinefelter Syndrome Lead to Cancer?

Compared with the general male population, men with KS may have a higher chance over time of getting breast cancer, non-Hodgkin lymphoma, and lung cancer. There are ways to reduce this risk, such as removing the breasts and avoiding the use of tobacco products. In general, XXY males are also at lower risk for prostate cancer.

If I Have Klinefelter Syndrome, Will I Be Able to Get a Woman Pregnant?

It is possible that an XXY male could get a woman pregnant naturally. Although sperm is found in more than 50 percent of men with KS, low sperm production could make conception very difficult.

A few men with KS have recently been able to father a biologically related child by undergoing assisted fertility services, specifically TESE-ICSI. TESE-ICSI carries a slightly higher risk of chromosomal disorders in the child, including having an extra X.

If My Son, Family Member, Partner, or Spouse Is Diagnosed with XXY Condition, How Can I Help Him and the Family?

If someone you know is diagnosed with KS:

- **Recognize your feelings.** It is natural for parents or family members to feel that they have done something to cause KS. But, remember it is a genetic disorder that occurs at random—there is nothing you could have done or not done to prevent it from happening. Allow yourself and your family time to deal with your feelings. Talk with your healthcare provider about your concerns.

- **Educate yourself about the disorder.** It is common to fear the unknown. Educate yourself about the XXY condition and its symptoms so you know how you can help your son, family member, or partner/spouse.

- **Support your son, family member, or partner/spouse.** Provide appropriate education about KS, and give him the emotional support and encouragement he needs. Remember, most XXY males go through life with few problems, and many never find out they have the condition.

- **Be actively involved in your son's, family member's, or partner's/spouse's care.** Talk with your healthcare provider and his healthcare provider about his treatment. If counseling for behavioral problems is needed, or if special learning environments or methods are needed, get help from qualified professionals who have experience working with XXY males.

- **Encourage your son, family member, partner/spouse to do activities** to improve his physical motor skills, such as karate or swimming.

- **Work with your teachers/educators and supervisors/ coworkers.**

  - Contact these people regularly to compare how he is doing at home and at school/work.

  - When appropriate, encourage him to talk with his teachers, educators, supervisor, and coworkers. Suggest using brief notes, telephone calls, and meetings to identify problems and propose solutions.

- **Encourage your son's, family member's, partner's/ spouse's independence.** Although it is important to be supportive, realize that watching over too much can send the message that you think he is not able to do things on his own.

- **Share the following information with healthcare providers about XXY problems:**

Table 18.3. Problems and Problem-Solving Recommendations

XXY Males May Have	Consider Recommending
Delayed early expressive language and speech milestones	Early speech therapy and language evaluation
Difficulty during transition from elementary school to middle school or high school	Re-testing to identify learning areas that require extra attention at or before entrance to middle/high school
Difficulty with math at all ages	Testing to identify problem areas and remediation for math disabilities
Difficulty with complex language processing, specifically with understanding and creating spoken language	Language evaluation, increased opportunities to communicate through written language, possibly getting written notes from lectures/discussions
Decreased running speed, agility, and overall strength in childhood	Physical therapy, occupational therapy, activities that build strength

What Is the Best Way to Teach or Communicate with Males Who Have Klinefelter Syndrome?

Research has identified some ways in which educators and parents can improve learning and communication among XXY males, including:

- Using images and visual clues

- Teaching them new words

- Encouraging conversation

- Using examples in the language

- Minimizing distractions

- Breaking tasks into small steps

- Creating opportunities for social interaction and understanding

- Reminding them to stay focused

Section 18.6

Prader-Willi Syndrome

This section includes text excerpted from "Prader-Willi Syndrome
(PWS): Condition Information," *Eunice Kennedy Shriver*
National Institute of Child Health and Human
Development (NICHD), December 1, 2016.

What Is Prader-Willi Syndrome?

The term "Prader-Willi syndrome" (PWS) refers to a genetic disorder that affects many parts of the body. Genetic testing can successfully diagnose nearly all infants with PWS.

The syndrome usually results from deletions or partial deletions on chromosome 15 that affect the regulation of gene expression, or how genes turn on and off. Andrea Prader and Heinrich Willi first described the syndrome in the 1950s.

One of the main symptoms of PWS is the inability to control eating. In fact, PWS is the leading genetic cause of life-threatening obesity. Other symptoms include low muscle tone and poor feeding as an infant, delays in intellectual development, and difficulty controlling emotions.

There is no cure for PWS, but people with the disorder can benefit from a variety of treatments to improve their symptoms. These treatments depend on the individual's needs, but they often include strict dietary supervision, physical therapy, behavioral therapy, and treatment with growth hormone, among others. As adults, people with PWS usually do best in special group homes for people with this disorder. Some can work in sheltered environments.

Scientists do not know what increases the risk for PWS. The genetic error that leads to Prader-Willi syndrome occurs randomly, usually very early in fetal development. The syndrome is usually not hereditary.

What Are Common Symptoms of Prader-Willi Syndrome?

Scientists think that the symptoms of PWS may be caused by a problem in a portion of the brain called the "hypothalamus." The hypothalamus lies in the base of the brain. When it works normally, it controls hunger or thirst, body temperature, pain, and when it is time to awaken and to sleep. Problems with the hypothalamus can affect various body functions and pathways, leading to a variety of symptoms.

Individuals with PWS may have mild to severe symptoms, which often include:

- Feeding and metabolic symptoms

- Physical symptoms

- Intellectual symptoms

- Behavioral and psychiatric symptoms

- Stages of PWS symptoms

Feeding and Metabolic Symptoms

An important early symptom of PWS is an infant's inability to suck, which affects the ability to feed. Nearly all infants with PWS need help with feeding. Infants may require feeding support for several months. Without assistance, they will not grow. Nursing systems with one-way valves and manual sucking assistive devices, similar to those used with cleft palate (such as bottles with special nipples for babies who do not have the sucking reflex), often are needed. Occasionally, feeding tubes are required, but generally for no more than the first six months after birth. The infants may need fewer calories because of the reduced metabolism associated with PWS and may not demand feeding on their own. Frequent weight checks will help in adjusting the infant's diet to maintain a suitable weight gain.

As the infants grow into toddlers and children, compulsive overeating replaces the need for feeding support. Because the metabolic rate of individuals with PWS is lower than normal, their caloric intake must be restricted to maintain a healthy weight, often to 60 percent of the caloric requirement of comparably sized children without the syndrome.

Feeding and metabolic symptoms persist into adulthood. Unless individuals with PWS live in environments that limit access to food (such as locked cabinets and a locked refrigerator), they will eat uncontrollably, even food that is rotten or sitting in the garbage. Uncontrollable eating can cause choking, a ruptured esophagus, and blockages in the digestive system. It can also lead to extreme weight gain and morbid obesity. Because of their inability to stop eating, people with PWS are at increased risk for diabetes, trouble breathing during sleep, and other health risks. For these reasons, people with PWS need to be monitored by a healthcare professional their entire lives.

Physical Symptoms

Many physical symptoms of PWS arise from poor regulation of various hormones, including growth hormone, thyroid hormone, and possibly adrenalin. Individuals with PWS grow slowly and experience delays in reaching physical activity milestones (e.g., standing, walking).

Children with PWS tend to be substantially shorter than other children of similar age. They may have small hands and feet and a curvature of the back called "scoliosis." In addition, they frequently have difficulty making their eyes work together to focus, a condition called "strabismus."

Infants with PWS are often born with underdeveloped sex organs, including a small penis and scrotum or a small clitoris and vaginal lips. Most individuals with PWS are infertile.

Intellectual Symptoms

Individuals with PWS have varying levels of intellectual disabilities. Learning disabilities are common, as are delays in starting to talk and in the development of language.

Behavioral and Psychiatric Symptoms

Imbalances in hormone levels may contribute to behavioral and psychiatric problems. Behavioral problems may include temper tantrums, extreme stubbornness, obsessive-compulsive symptoms, picking the skin, and general trouble in controlling emotions. The individual will often repeat questions or statements. Sleep disturbances may include excessive daytime sleepiness and disruptions of sleep. Many individuals with PWS have a high pain threshold.

Stages of Prader-Willi Syndrome Symptoms

The appearance of PWS symptoms occurs in two recognized stages:

Stage 1 (Infancy to Two Years of Age)

- "Floppiness" and poor muscle tone
- Weak cries and a weak sucking reflex
- Inability to breastfeed, which may require feeding support, such as tube feeding
- Developmental delays
- Small genital organs

Stage 2 (Between Two and Eight Years of Age)

- Unable to feel satisfied with the normal intake of food
- Inability to control eating, which can lead to overeating if not monitored
- Food-seeking behaviors
- Low metabolism
- Weight gain and obesity
- Daytime sleepiness and sleep problems
- Intellectual disabilities
- Small hands and feet
- Short stature
- Scoliosis
- High pain threshold
- Behavioral problems, including the display of obsessive-compulsive symptoms, picking the skin, and difficulty controlling emotions
- Small genitals, often resulting in infertility in later life

What Causes Prader-Willi Syndrome

PWS is caused by genetic changes on an "unstable" region of chromosome 15 that affects the regulation of gene expression, or how genes turn on and off. This part of the chromosome is called "unstable" because it is prone to being shuffled around by the cell's genetic machinery before the chromosome is passed on from parent to child.

The genetic changes that cause PWS occur in a portion of the chromosome, referred to as the "Prader-Willi critical region" (PWCR), around the time of conception or during early fetal development. This region was identified in 1990 using genetic deoxyribonucleic acid (DNA) probes. Although Prader-Willi syndrome is genetic, it usually is not inherited and generally develops due to deletions or partial deletions on chromosome 15.

Specific changes to the chromosome can include the following:

- **Deletions.** A section of a chromosome may be lost or deleted, along with the functions that this section supported. A majority of PWS cases result from a deletion in one region of the father's chromosome 15 that leads to a loss of function of several genes. The corresponding mother's genes on chromosome 15 are always inactive and thus cannot make up for the deletion on the father's chromosome 15. The missing paternal genes normally play a fundamental role in regulating hunger and fullness.

- **Maternal uniparental disomy.** A cell usually contains one set of chromosomes from the father and another set from the mother. In ordinary cases, a child has two chromosome 15s, one from each parent. In around one-fourth of PWS cases, the child has two copies of chromosome 15 from the mother and none from the father. Because genes located in the PWCR are normally inactive in the chromosome that comes from the mother, the child's lack of active genes in this region leads to PWS.

- **An imprinting center defect.** Genes in the PWCR on the chromosome that came from the mother are normally inactivated, due to a process known as "imprinting" that affects whether the cell is able to "read" a gene or not. In a small percentage of PWS cases, the chromosome 15 inherited from the father is imprinted in the same way as the mother. This can be caused by a small deletion in a region of the father's chromosome that controls the imprinting process, called the "imprinting center." In these cases, both of the child's copies of chromosome 15 have inactive PWCRs, leading to PWS.

How Is Prader-Willi Syndrome Diagnosed?

In many cases of PWS, diagnosis is prompted by physical symptoms in the newborn.

If a newborn is unable to suck or feed for a few days and has a "floppy" body and weak muscle tone, a healthcare provider may conduct genetic testing for PWS. Formal diagnostic criteria for recognizing PWS depend on the age of the individual-specifically, whether the third birthday has been reached. Before the age of three, the most important symptom is extremely poor muscle tone, called "hypotonia," which makes infants feel floppy. In affected children three years of age and older, other symptoms become apparent, such as obesity, intellectual delays, learning disabilities, or behavior problems, especially connected with food and eating.

- **Children younger than three years** of age must have at least four major criteria and at least one minor criterion for a PWS diagnosis.

- **Those older than three years** of age must have at least five major criteria and at least three minor criteria for a diagnosis of PWS.

Major Clinical Criteria of Prader-Willi Syndrome

- Extremely weak muscles in the body's torso

- Difficulty sucking, which improves after the first few months

- Feeding difficulties and/or failure to grow, requiring feeding assistance, such as feeding tubes or special nipples to aid in sucking

- Beginning of rapid weight gain, between the ages of one and six, resulting in severe obesity

- Excessive, uncontrollable overeating

- Specific facial features, including narrow forehead and downturned mouth

- Reduced development of the genital organs, including small genitalia (vaginal lips and clitoris in females and small scrotum and penis in males); incomplete and delayed puberty; and infertility

- Developmental delays, mild-to-moderate intellectual disability, and multiple learning disabilities

Minor Clinical Criteria of Prader-Willi Syndrome

- Decreased movement and noticeable fatigue during infancy

- Behavioral problems—specifically, temper tantrums, obsessive-compulsive behavior, stubbornness, rigidity, stealing, and lying (especially related to food)

- Sleep problems, including daytime sleepiness and sleep disruption

- Short stature, compared with other members of the family, noticeable by the age of 15

- Light color of skin, eyes, and hair

- Small hands and feet in comparison to standards for height and age

- Narrow hands

- Nearsightedness and/or difficulty focusing both eyes at the same time

- Thick saliva

- Poor pronunciation

- Picking of the skin

Additional Findings

- High pain threshold

- Inability to vomit

- Scoliosis

- Earlier-than-usual activity in the adrenal glands, which can lead to early puberty

- Especially brittle bones (called "osteoporosis")

Genetic testing must confirm the PWS diagnosis. Almost all individuals with PWS have an abnormality within a specific area of chromosome 15. Early diagnosis is best because it enables affected individuals to begin early intervention/special needs programs and treatment specifically for PWS symptoms.

Genetic testing can confirm the chance that a sibling might be born with PWS. Prenatal diagnosis also is available for at-risk pregnancies—that is pregnancies among women with a family history of PWS abnormalities.

Genetic Counseling and Testing of At-Risk Relatives

Genetic counseling and testing provide individuals and families with information about the nature, inheritance, and implications of genetic disorders so that they can make informed medical and personal decisions about having children. Genetic counseling helps people understand their risks. The risk of occurrence in siblings of patients with PWS depends on what caused the disorder to occur.

Is There a Cure for Prader-Willi Syndrome?

PWS has no cure. However, early diagnosis and treatment may help prevent or reduce the number of challenges that individuals with PWS may experience, which may be more of a problem if diagnosis or treatment is delayed.

What Treatment Options Are Available for Prader-Willi Syndrome?

Parents can enroll infants with PWS in early intervention programs. However, even if a PWS diagnosis is delayed, treatments are valuable at any age.

The types of treatment depend on the individual's symptoms. The healthcare provider may recommend the following:

- **Use of special nipples or tubes for feeding difficulties.** Difficulty in sucking is one of the most common symptoms of newborns with PWS. Special nipples or tubes are used for several months to feed newborns and infants who are unable to suck properly, to make sure that the infant is fed adequately and grows. To ensure that the child is growing properly, the healthcare provider will monitor height, weight, and body mass index (BMI) monthly during infancy.

- **Strict supervision of daily food intake.** Once overeating starts between two and four years of age, supervision will help to minimize food hoarding and stealing and prevent rapid weight gain and severe obesity. Parents should lock refrigerators and all cabinets containing food. No medications have proven beneficial in reducing food-seeking behavior.

A well-balanced, low-calorie diet and regular exercise are essential and must be maintained for the rest of the individual's life. People with PWS rarely need more than 1,000 to 1,200 calories per day. Height, weight, and BMI should be monitored every 6 months during the first 10 years of life after infancy and once a year after the age of 10 for the rest of the person's life to make sure she or he is maintaining a healthy weight. Ongoing consultation with a dietitian to guarantee adequate vitamin and mineral intake, including calcium and vitamin D, might be needed.

- **Growth hormone (GH) therapy.** GH therapy has been demonstrated to increase height, lean body mass, and mobility; decrease fat mass; and improve movement and flexibility in individuals with PWS from infancy through adulthood. When given early in life, it also may prevent or reduce behavioral difficulties. Additionally, GH therapy can help improve speech, improve abstract reasoning, and often allow information to be processed more quickly. It also has been shown to improve sleep quality and resting energy expenditure. GH therapy usually is started during infancy or at diagnosis with PWS. This therapy often continues during adulthood at 20 to 25 percent of the recommended dose for children.

- **Treatment of eye problems by a pediatric ophthalmologist.** Many infants have trouble getting their eyes to focus together. These infants should be referred to a pediatric ophthalmologist who has expertise in working with infants with disabilities.

- **Treatment of curvature of the spine by an orthopedist.** An orthopedist should evaluate and treat, if necessary, scoliosis. Treatment will be the same as that for people with scoliosis who do not have PWS.

- **Sleep studies and treatment.** Sleep disorders are common with PWS. Treating a sleep disorder can help improve the quality of sleep. The same treatments that healthcare providers use with the general population can apply to individuals with PWS.

- **Physical therapy.** Muscle weakness is a serious problem among individuals with PWS. For children younger than the age of three, physical therapy may increase muscular strength and help such children achieve developmental milestones. For older children, daily exercise will help build lean body mass.

- **Behavioral therapy.** People with PWS have difficulty controlling their emotions. Using behavioral therapy can help. Stubbornness; anger; and obsessive-compulsive behavior, including obsession with food, should be handled with behavioral management programs using firm limit-setting strategies. Structure and routines also are advised.

- **Medications.** Medications, especially serotonin reuptake inhibitors (SRIs), may reduce obsessive-compulsive symptoms. SRIs also may help manage psychosis.

- **Early interventions/special needs programs.** Individuals with PWS have varying degrees of intellectual difficulty and learning disabilities. Early intervention programs, including speech therapy for delays in acquiring language and for difficulties with pronunciation, should begin as early as possible and continue throughout childhood.

Special education is almost always necessary for school-age children. Groups that offer training in social skills may also prove beneficial. An individual aide is often useful in helping PWS children focus on schoolwork.

- **Sex hormone treatments and/or corrective surgery.** These treatments are used to treat small genitals (penis, scrotum, clitoris).

- **Replacement of sex hormones.** Replacement of sex hormones during puberty may result in the development of adequate secondary sex characteristics (e.g., breasts, pubic hair, a deeper voice).

Placement in group homes during adulthood. Group homes offer necessary structure and supervision for adults with PWS, helping them avoid compulsive eating, severe obesity, and other health problems.

Other FAQs
Are There Disorders or Conditions Associated with Prader-Willi Syndrome?

Several other disorders and conditions are associated with PWS:

- Obesity and secondary problems due to extreme obesity
- Diabetes

- Sleep apnea
- Obsessive-compulsive disorder (OCD)
- Infertility
- Autism spectrum disorder (ASD)

Does Prader-Willi Syndrome Affect Pregnancy?

Until recently, experts believed that people with PWS were infertile. However, because several pregnancies have occurred in women with PWS, birth control should be considered.

Inheritance of Prader-Willi Syndrome and Angelman Syndrome

PWS could affect the offspring of someone with the syndrome, depending on how the individual developed the disorder and the individual's sex. The offspring could be at risk of being born with PWS or with Angelman syndrome. Angelman syndrome, similar to PWS, results from defects in one region of chromosome 15. The two syndromes both involve missing or silenced genes in the PWCR. This section of the chromosome is "imprinted," and the genes involved in Angelman syndrome and PWS have different sex-specific imprinting patterns. This is the reason why the sex of the parent with PWS affects which disorder the offspring is at risk to inherit.

Deletion

If a mother with PWS developed the syndrome because of the deletion of a section of 1 of her 2 copies of chromosome 15, her child will have a 50 percent risk of being born with Angelman syndrome. That is, if the mother with PWS passes on her chromosome 15 with the deletion, the child will have Angelman syndrome. This is because the father's genes in this region that are linked to Angelman syndrome are normally inactivated; thus, the child will have no active copies of these genes, causing Angelman syndrome. If the mother passes on her normal copy of chromosome 15, the child will not be born with Angelman syndrome or PWS.

In the case of a father with PWS who has a deletion in chromosome 15, there is a 50 percent chance that he will pass on the affected chromosome to his child, leading to PWS. This is because a mother's genes that are linked to PWS are normally inactivated; thus, the child will have no active copies of these genes.

Because fertility is so rare in individuals with PWS, only one case of a mother with a deletion passing on Angelman syndrome to her child has been reported. No cases have been reported of a father who had PWS because of a deletion passing on PWS to his child, but it is possible.

Uniparental Disomy

No case of either syndrome in the child of an individual with PWS through uniparental disomy (two copies of chromosome 15 from the mother and none from the father) has ever been reported, but they are theoretically possible. Inheritance could happen in three different ways, but all require the parent with PWS passing on both copies of her or his chromosome 15, which is unlikely.

- If the offspring also receives a copy of chromosome 15 from the other parent and none of these three copies is lost, this condition will be fatal before birth.

- If the parent with PWS is the mother and the offspring end up with only two copies of chromosome 15 during development, the child will probably be born with PWS because she or he has inherited two inactivated copies of the genes in the PWCR.

- If the parent with PWS is the father and the offspring end up with only two copies of chromosome 15 during development, the child will probably be born with Angelman syndrome. This is because the genes related to Angelman syndrome in the chromosome inherited from the mother are inactivated, and thus the child does not have any working copies of these genes, causing Angelman syndrome.

Imprinting Center Defect

No cases have been reported of a parent who has PWS because of an imprinting center defect passing on PWS to her or his child. However, there is a theoretical possibility of this happening.

Section 18.7

Turner Syndrome

This section includes text excerpted from "Turner
Syndrome: Condition Information," *Eunice Kennedy Shriver*
National Institute of Child Health and Human
Development (NICHD), December 1, 2016.

Turner syndrome is a disorder caused by a partially or completely
missing X chromosome. This condition affects only females.

Most people have 46 chromosomes in each cell—23 from their
mother and 23 from their father. The twenty third of chromosomes
are called the "sex chromosomes"—X and Y—because they determine
whether a person is male or female. Females have two X chromosomes
(XX) in most of their cells, and males have one X chromosome and
one Y chromosome (XY) in most of their cells. A female with all of her
chromosomes is referred to as "46, XX." A male is 46, XY.

Turner syndrome most often occurs when a female has one normal
X chromosome, but the other X chromosome is missing (45, X). Other
forms of Turner syndrome result when one of the two chromosomes is
partially missing or altered in some way.

What Are Common Symptoms of Turner Syndrome?

Turner syndrome causes a variety of symptoms in girls and women.
For some people, symptoms are mild, but for others, Turner syndrome can
cause serious health problems. In general, women with Turner syndrome
have female sex characteristics, but these characteristics are underdeveloped compared to the typical female. Turner syndrome can affect:

- **Appearance.** Features of Turner syndrome may include a short
  neck with a webbed appearance, low hairline at the back of the
  neck, low-set ears, hands and feet that are swollen or puffy at
  birth, and soft nails that turn upward.

- **Stature.** Girls with Turner syndrome grow more slowly than
  other children. Without treatment, they tend to have short
  stature (around four feet, eight inches) as adults.

- **Puberty.** Most girls with Turner syndrome do not start puberty
  naturally.

- **Reproduction.** In most girls with Turner syndrome, the ovaries
  are missing or do not function properly. Without the estrogen

made by their ovaries, girls with Turner syndrome will not develop breasts. Most women with Turner syndrome cannot become pregnant without assistive technology.

- **Cardiovascular.** Turner syndrome can cause problems with the heart or major blood vessels. In addition, some women and girls with Turner syndrome have high blood pressure.

- **Kidney.** Kidney function is usually normal in Turner syndrome, but some people with this condition have kidneys that look abnormal.

- **Osteoporosis.** Women with Turner syndrome often have low levels of the hormone estrogen, which can put them at risk for osteoporosis. Osteoporosis can cause height loss and bone fractures.

- **Diabetes.** People with Turner syndrome are at higher risk for type 2 diabetes.

- **Thyroid.** Many people with Turner syndrome have thyroid problems. The most common one is hypothyroidism, or an underactive thyroid gland.

- **Cognitive.** People with Turner syndrome have normal intelligence. Some, however, have problems learning mathematics and can have trouble with visual-spatial coordination (such as determining the relative positions of objects in space).

How Many People Are Affected with Turner Syndrome?

Turner syndrome affects about 1 of every 2,500 female live births worldwide.

This disorder affects all races and regions of the world equally. There are no known environmental risks for Turner syndrome. Parents who have had many unaffected children can still have a child with Turner syndrome later on.

Generally, Turner syndrome is not passed on from mother to child. In most cases, women with Turner syndrome are infertile.

What Causes Turner Syndrome

Turner syndrome occurs when part or all of an X chromosome is missing from most or all of the cells in a girl's body. A girl normally receives one X chromosome from each parent. The error that leads to the missing chromosome appears to happen during the formation of the egg or sperm.

Most commonly, a girl with Turner syndrome has only one X chromosome. Occasionally, she may have a partial second X chromosome. Because she is missing part or all of a chromosome, certain genes are missing. The loss of these genes leads to the symptoms of Turner syndrome.

Sometimes, girls with Turner syndrome have some cells that are missing one X chromosome (45, X) and some that are normal. This is because not every cell in the body is exactly the same, so some cells might have the chromosome, while others might not. This condition is called "mosaicism." If the second sex chromosome is lost from most of a girl's cells, then it is likely that she will have symptoms of Turner syndrome. If the chromosome is missing from only some of her cells, she may have no symptoms or only mild symptoms.

How Is Turner Syndrome Diagnosed?

Healthcare providers use a combination of physical symptoms and the results of a genetic blood test, called a "karyotype," to determine the chromosomal characteristics of the cells in a female's body. The test will show if one of the X chromosomes is partially or completely missing.

Turner syndrome also can be diagnosed during pregnancy by testing the cells in the amniotic fluid. Newborns may be diagnosed after heart problems are detected or after certain physical features, such as swollen hands and feet or webbed skin on the neck, are noticed. Other characteristics, such as widely spaced nipples or low-set ears, also may lead to a suspicion of Turner syndrome. Some girls may be diagnosed as teenagers because of a slow growth rate or a lack of puberty-related changes. Still, others may be diagnosed as adults when they have difficulty becoming pregnant.

What Are Common Treatments for Turner Syndrome?

Although there is no cure for Turner syndrome, some treatments can help minimize its symptoms. These include:

- **Human growth hormone.** If given in early childhood, hormone injections can often increase adult height by a few inches.

- **Estrogen replacement therapy (ERT).** ERT can help start the secondary sexual development that normally begins at puberty (around the age of 12). This includes breast development and the development of wider hips. Healthcare providers may prescribe a combination of estrogen and progesterone to girls who have not started menstruating by 15 years of age. ERT also provides protection against bone loss.

Regular health checks and access to a wide variety of specialists are important to care for the various health problems that can result from Turner syndrome. These include ear infections, high blood pressure, and thyroid problems.

Other FAQs on Turner Syndrome
Is Turner Syndrome Inherited?

Turner syndrome is usually not inherited, but it is genetic. It is caused by a random error that leads to a missing X chromosome in the sperm or egg of a parent.

Very few pregnancies in which the fetus has Turner Syndrome result in live births. Most end in early pregnancy loss.

Most women with Turner syndrome cannot get pregnant naturally. In one study, as many as 40 percent of women with Turner syndrome got pregnant using donated eggs. However, pregnant women with Turner syndrome are at increased risk for high blood pressure during pregnancy, which can result in complications, including preterm birth and fetal growth restriction.

Women with Turner syndrome also are at risk for aortic dissection during pregnancy. This happens about two percent of the time. An aortic dissection is a tear in or damage to the inner wall of the aorta, the major artery carrying blood to the heart. Damage to the aorta's inner wall causes blood to flow rapidly into the lining of the aorta. This can restrict the main flow of blood through the aorta or cause the aorta to balloon—a condition called an "aneurysm." An aneurysm can rupture, which can be life-threatening.

Can Turner Syndrome Be Prevented?

Turner syndrome cannot be prevented. It is a genetic problem that is caused by a random error that leads to a missing X chromosome in the sperm or egg of a parent. There is nothing the father or mother can do to prevent the error from occurring. However, there are many options for treatment.

What Health Complications Can Occur with Turner Syndrome?

Some of the health complications that can occur in people with Turner syndrome include:

Hearing problems. Ear malformations and hearing problems are common in people with Turner syndrome. They may need hearing aids as children or adults. Girls with Turner syndrome may be prone to ear infections.

Heart. Some girls with Turner syndrome have a constriction, or narrowing, of the aorta. Many girls with Turner syndrome have an abnormal valve between the heart and the aorta. The abnormal valve usually does not cause symptoms, but it can lead to infection of the valve or damage to the aorta. Heart defects are the major cause of premature death in people with Turner syndrome.

Kidneys. Many people with Turner syndrome have abnormalities in their kidneys. However, these usually do not cause problems. The only reported effect has been an increased risk for urinary tract infections.

Diabetes. People with Turner syndrome are at high risk for type 2 diabetes. Researchers are not sure why this is so, but because diabetes can cause many medical complications, women with Turner syndrome should be checked regularly for diabetes.

Osteoporosis. Many women with Turner syndrome have osteoporosis, a condition that causes bone fractures. Women with Turner syndrome are at higher risk for osteoporosis because their bodies do not make enough estrogen. Estrogen is a hormone that helps to maintain bone density. Women who are given estrogen can lower their risk of osteoporosis.

Thyroid conditions. Many women with Turner syndrome also have a thyroid disorder. The most common is hypothyroidism, an underactive thyroid. Symptoms include decreased energy, intolerance to cold, and dry skin. This condition is easily treated with medication.

Gluten intolerance. Some people with Turner syndrome have gluten intolerance, also called "celiac disease."

Is Turner Syndrome Considered a Disability?

Turner syndrome is not considered a disability, although it can cause certain learning challenges, including problems learning mathematics and with memory. Most girls and women with Turner syndrome lead a normal, healthy, productive life with proper medical care.

My Daughter Has Been Diagnosed with Turner Syndrome. Now What?

If your daughter has been diagnosed with Turner syndrome, you may be wondering what to expect as she grows up. A few of these questions, with answers, are listed here.

- Will she mature normally?
  - Most girls with Turner syndrome do not mature typically. They may not develop breasts or start getting a period. Estrogen treatment can replace hormones that the body does not naturally produce, spurring development and preventing osteoporosis.
- Will she have problems in school?
  - Some girls with Turner syndrome have difficulty with arithmetic, visual memory, and visio-spatial skills (such as determining the relative positions of objects in space). They may also have some trouble understanding nonverbal communication (body language, facial expression) and interacting with peers.
- What care will she need as she grows up?
  - Girls and women with Turner syndrome usually require care from a variety of specialists throughout their lives.
- Will she be able to have a normal sex life as an adult?
  - Women with Turner syndrome can enjoy normal sex lives.
- Will she be able to have children?
  - Most women with Turner syndrome cannot get pregnant naturally. Those who can are at risk for blood pressure-related complications, which can lead to premature birth or fetal growth restriction. Pregnancy also is associated with increased risk for maternal complications, including aortic dissection and rupture.

Section 18.8

Velocardiofacial Syndrome

This section includes text excerpted from "Learning about
Velocardiofacial Syndrome," National Human Genome
Research Institute (NHGRI), June 29, 2017.

What Is Velocardiofacial Syndrome?

Velocardiofacial syndrome (VCFS) is a genetic condition that is some-times hereditary. VCFS is characterized by a combination of medical problems that vary from child to child. These medical problems include cleft palate, or an opening in the roof of the mouth, and other differences in the palate; heart defects; problems fighting infection; low calcium levels; differences in the way the kidneys are formed or work; a characteristic facial appearance; learning problems; and speech and feeding problems.

The name "velocardiofacial" syndrome comes from the Latin words; "velum" meaning palate, "cardia" meaning heart and "facies" having to do with the face. Not all of these identifying features are found in each child who is born with VCFS. The most common features are palatal differences (~75%), heart defects (75%), problems fighting infection (77%), low calcium levels (50%), differences in the kidney (35%), characteristic facial appearance (numbers vary depending on the individual's ethnic and racial background), learning problems (~90%), and speech (~75%) and feeding problems (35%).

Two genes—*COMT* and *TBX1*—are associated with VCFS. How-ever, not all of the genes that cause VCFS have been identified. Most children who have been diagnosed with this syndrome are missing a small part of chromosome 22. Chromosomes are thread-like structures found in every cell of the body. Each chromosome contains hundreds of genes. A human cell normally contains 46 chromosomes (23 from each parent). The specific location or address of the missing segment in individuals with VCFS is 22q11.2.

VCFS is also called the "22q11.2 deletion syndrome." It also has other clinical names, such as "DiGeorge syndrome," "conotruncal anomaly face syndrome" (CTAF), "autosomal dominant Opitz G/BBB syndrome," or "Cayler cardiofacial syndrome." As a result of this dele-tion, about 30 genes are generally absent from this chromosome.

VCFS affects about 1 in 4,000 newborns. VCFS may affect more individuals, however, because some people who have the 22q11.2 dele-tion may not be diagnosed as they have very few signs and symptoms.

What Are the Symptoms of Velocardiofacial Syndrome?

Despite the involvement of a very specific portion of chromosome 22, there is great variation in the symptoms of this syndrome. At least 30 different symptoms have been associated with the 22q11 deletion. Most of these symptoms are not present in all individuals who have VCFS.

Symptoms include cleft palate, usually of the soft palate (the roof of the mouth nearest the throat which is behind the bony palate); heart problems; similar faces (elongated face, almond-shaped eyes, wide nose, small ears); eye problems; feeding problems that include food coming through the nose (nasal regurgitation) because of the palatal differences; middle-ear infections (otitis media); low calcium due to hypoparathyroidism (low levels of the parathyroid hormone that can result in seizures); immune system problems which make it difficult for the body to fight infections; differences in the way the kidneys are formed or how they work; weak muscles; differences in the spine, such as curvature of the spine (scoliosis) or bony abnormalities in the neck or upper back; and tapered fingers. Children are born with these features.

Children who have VCFS also often have learning difficulties and developmental delays. About 65 percent of individuals with 22q11.2 deletion, are found to have a nonverbal learning disability. When tested, their verbal intelligence quotient (IQ) scores are greater than 10 points higher than their performance IQ scores. This combination of test scores brings down the full-scale IQ scores, but they would not represent the abilities of the individual accurately. As a result of this type of learning disability, students will have relative strengths in reading and rote memorization but will struggle with math and abstract reasoning. These individuals may also have communication and social interaction problems, such as autism. As adults, these individuals have an increased risk for developing mental illness, such as depression, anxiety, and schizophrenia.

How Is Velocardiofacial Syndrome Diagnosed?

VCFS is suspected as a diagnosis based on clinical examination and the presence of the signs and symptoms of the syndrome.

A special blood test called "fluorescence in situ hybridization" (FISH) is then done to look for the deletion in chromosome 22q11.2. More than 95 percent of individuals who have VCFS have a deletion in chromosome 22q11.2.

Those individuals who do not have the 22q11.2 deletion by standard FISH testing may have a smaller deletion that may only be found using more sophisticated lab studies, such as comparative genomic hybridization, multiplex ligation-dependent probe amplification (MLPA), additional FISH studies performed in a research laboratory, or using specific gene studies to look for mutations in the genes known to be in this region. Again, these studies may only be available through a research lab.

What Is the Treatment for Velocardiofacial Syndrome?

Treatment is based on the type of symptoms that are present. For example, heart defects are treated as they would normally be via surgical interventions in the newborn period. Individuals who have low calcium levels are given calcium supplements and, frequently, vitamin D to help them absorb the calcium. Palate problems are treated by a team of specialists called a "cleft palate team" or "craniofacial team" and again often require surgical interventions and intensive speech therapy. Infections are generally treated aggressively with antibiotics in infants and children with immune problems.

Early intervention and speech therapies are started when possible at one year of age to assess and treat developmental delays.

Is Velocardiofacial Syndrome Inherited?

VCFS is due to a 22q11.2 deletion. Most often, neither parent has the deletion; so, it is new in the child (93%), and the chance for the couple to have another child with VCFS is quite low (close to zero). However, once the deletion is present in a person, she or he has a 50 percent chance for having children who also have the deletion. The 22q11 deletion happens as an accident when either the egg or sperm are being formed or early in fetal development.

In less than 10 percent of cases, a person with VCFS inherits the deletion in chromosome 22 from a parent. When VCFS is inherited in families, this means that other family members may be affected as well.

Since some people with the 22q11.2 deletion are very mildly affected, it is suggested that all parents of children with the deletion have testing. Furthermore, some people with the deletion have no symptoms, but they have the deletion in some of their cells, not all. This is called "mosaicism." Even other people have the deletion only in their egg cells or sperm cells but not in their blood cells. It is recommended that all parents of a child with a 22q11.2 deletion seek genetic counseling before or during a subsequent pregnancy to learn more about their chances of having another child with VCFS.

Section 18.9

Williams Syndrome

This section contains text excerpted from the following sources:
Text in this section begins with excerpts from "Williams Syndrome Information Page," National Institute of Neurological Disorders and Stroke (NINDS), March 27, 2019; Text beginning with the heading "What Are the Signs and Symptoms of Williams Syndrome?" is excerpted from "Williams Syndrome," Genetic and Rare Diseases Information Center (GARD), National Center for Advancing Translational Sciences (NCATS), March 27, 2017.

Williams syndrome (WS) is a rare genetic disorder characterized by mild to moderate delays in cognitive development or learning difficulties, a distinctive facial appearance, and a unique personality that combines overfriendliness and high levels of empathy with anxiety. The most significant medical problem associated with WS is cardiovascular disease caused by narrowed arteries. WS is also associated with elevated blood calcium levels in infancy. A random genetic mutation (deletion of a small piece of chromosome 7), rather than inheritance, most often causes the disorder. However, individuals who have WS have a 50 percent chance of passing it on if they decide to have children. The characteristic facial features of WS include puffiness around the eyes, a short nose with a broad nasal tip, wide mouth, full cheeks, full lips, and a small chin. People with WS are also likely to have a long neck, sloping shoulders, short stature, limited mobility in their joints, and curvature of the spine. Some individuals with WS have a star-like pattern in the iris of their eyes. Infants with WS are often irritable and colicky, with feeding problems that keep them from gaining weight. Chronic abdominal pain is common in adolescents and adults. By 30 years of age, the majority of individuals with WS have diabetes or prediabetes and mild to moderate sensorineural hearing loss (a form of deafness due to disturbed function of the auditory nerve). For some people, hearing loss may begin as early as late childhood. WS also is associated with a characteristic "cognitive profile" of mental strengths and weaknesses composed of strengths in verbal short-term memory and language, combined with severe weakness in visuospatial construction (the skills used to copy patterns, draw, or write). Within language, the strongest skills are typically in concrete, practical vocabulary, which in many cases is in the low-average to average range for the general population. Abstract or conceptual-relational vocabulary is much more limited. Most older children and adults with WS speak fluently and use good grammar. More than 50 percent of children with WS have attention deficit disorders (ADD) or attention deficit hyperactivity disorder (ADHD), and about 50 percent have specific phobias, such as a fear of loud noises. The majority of individuals with WS worry excessively.

What Are the Signs and Symptoms of Williams Syndrome?

The signs and symptoms of WS can vary, but generally include:

- Mild to moderate intellectual disability

- A distinctive facial appearance

- A unique personality that combines overfriendliness and high levels of empathy with anxiety

People with WS typically have difficulty with tasks such as drawing and assembling puzzles. They tend to do well on tasks that involve spoken language, music, and learning by repetition.

Facial features common in young children with WS include a broad forehead, a short nose with a broad tip, full cheeks, and a wide mouth with full lips. In older children and adults, the face appears longer and gaunt. Dental problems are common and may include small, widely spaced teeth and teeth that are crooked or missing.

People with WS often have outgoing, engaging personalities and tend to take an extreme interest in other people. ADD, problems with anxiety, and phobias are common.

The most significant medical problem associated with WS is a form of heart disease called "supravalvular aortic stenosis" (SVAS). SVAS is a narrowing of the large blood vessel that carries blood from the heart to the rest of the body (the aorta). If this condition is not treated, it can lead to shortness of breath, chest pain, and heart failure. The presence of other heart and blood vessel problems has also been reported.

Additional signs and symptoms of WS may include:

- Abnormalities of connective tissue (tissue that supports the body's joints and organs), such as joint problems and soft, loose skin
- Increased calcium levels in the blood (hypercalcemia) in infancy
- Developmental delays
- Problems with coordination
- Short stature
- Vision and eye problems
- Digestive problems
- Urinary problems

What Causes Williams Syndrome

WS is caused by a missing piece (deletion) of genetic material from a specific region of chromosome 7. The deleted region includes more than 25 genes.

CLIP2, *ELN*, *GTF2I*, *GTF2IRD1*, and *LIMK1* are among the genes that are typically deleted in people with WS. Researchers have found that the loss of the *ELN* gene is associated with the connective tissue abnormalities and heart disease in many people with this condition. Studies suggest that deletions of *CLIP2*, *GTF2I*, *GTF2IRD1*, *LIMK1*, and perhaps other genes, may help explain many of the unique behavioral characteristics and cognitive difficulties. Loss of the *GTF2IRD1* gene may also contribute to the distinctive facial features often present. The relationship between some of the other deleted genes and the features of WS is not yet known.

Is Williams Syndrome Inherited?

Most cases of WS are not inherited. The condition typically occurs due to random events during the formation of egg or sperm cells in a parent. Therefore, it most often occurs in people with no family history of WS.

In a small portion of cases, people with WS inherit the chromosome deletion from a parent with the condition. In these cases, it is inherited in an autosomal dominant manner. This is because having only one changed copy of chromosome 7 in each cell is enough to cause signs and symptoms.

Regardless of whether WS occurs randomly or is inherited from a parent, each child of a person with WS has a 50 percent chance of inheriting the condition.

Can Williams Syndrome Be Prevented?

There is no known way to prevent the genetic problem that causes WS. Prenatal testing is available for couples with a family history of WS who wish to conceive. For instance, for pregnancies at 50 percent risk of WS, fluorescence in situ hybridization, or FISH, testing may be used to detect the microdeletion of the Williams-Beuren syndrome critical region (WBSCR) in fetal cells obtained by chorionic villus sampling (CVS) at about 10 to 12 weeks' gestation or amniocentesis usually performed at about 15 to 18 weeks' gestation. Prenatal testing may also be offered to unaffected parents who have had a child with WS (and perhaps other family members) because of the recurrence risk associated with the possibility of germline mosaicism or inversion polymorphism or in cases of parental anxiety. Prenatal testing for pregnancies not known to be at increased risk for WS is available but is rarely used because most cases are a single occurrence in a family.

Chapter 19

Emotional Disturbance

The term "emotional disturbance" has been used in the nation's special education law, the Individuals with Disabilities Education Act (IDEA).

The IDEA defines "emotional disturbance" as the following:

A condition exhibiting one or more of the following characteristics over a long period of time and to a marked degree that adversely affects a child's educational performance:

- An inability to learn that cannot be explained by intellectual, sensory, or health factors.

- An inability to build or maintain satisfactory interpersonal relationships with peers and teachers.

- Inappropriate types of behavior or feelings under normal circumstances.

- A general pervasive mood of unhappiness or depression.

- A tendency to develop physical symptoms or fears associated with personal or school problems.

As defined by the IDEA, emotional disturbance includes schizophrenia but does not apply to children who are socially maladjusted, unless it is determined that they have an emotional disturbance.

This chapter includes text excerpted from "Emotional Disturbance," Center for Parent Information & Resources (CPIR), U.S. Department of Education (ED), December 6, 2017.

Characteristics

As is evident in the IDEA's definition, emotional disturbances can affect an individual in areas beyond the emotional. Depending on the specific mental disorder involved, a person's physical, social, or cognitive skills may also be affected. The National Alliance on Mental Illness (NAMI) of Southern Arizona puts this very well:

Mental illnesses are medical conditions that disrupt a person's thinking, feeling, mood, ability to relate to others, and daily functioning. Just as diabetes is a disorder of the pancreas, mental illnesses are medical conditions that often result in a diminished capacity for coping with the ordinary demands of life.

Some of the characteristics and behaviors seen in children who have an emotional disturbance include:

- Hyperactivity (short attention span, impulsiveness)

- Aggression or self-injurious behavior (acting out, fighting)

- Withdrawal (not interacting socially with others, excessive fear or anxiety)

- Immaturity (inappropriate crying, temper tantrums, poor coping skills)

- Learning difficulties (academically performing below grade level)

Children with the most serious emotional disturbances may exhibit distorted thinking, excessive anxiety, bizarre motor acts, and abnormal mood swings.

Many children, who do not have emotional disturbance, may display some of these same behaviors at various times during their development. However, when children have an emotional disturbance, these behaviors continue over long periods of time. Their behavior signals that they are not coping with their environment or peers.

Causes

No one knows the actual cause or causes of emotional disturbance, although several factors—heredity, brain disorder, diet, stress, and family functioning—have been suggested and vigorously researched. A great deal of research goes on every day, but to date, researchers have not found that any of these factors are the direct cause of behavioral or emotional problems.

According to NAMI, mental illnesses can affect persons of any age, race, religion, or income. Further:

Mental illnesses are not the result of personal weakness, lack of character, or poor upbringing. Mental illnesses are treatable. Most people diagnosed with a serious mental illness can experience relief from their symptoms by actively participating in an individual treatment plan.

Frequency

Of the 74.5 million children in the United States, an estimated 17.1 million have or have had a psychiatric disorder. Half of all psychiatric illness occurs before the age of 14, and 75 percent by the age of 24. The most common psychiatric disorders in childhood are anxiety disorders, attention deficit hyperactivity disorder (ADHD), disruptive behavior, depression and bipolar disorders, and eating disorders.

Help for School-Aged Children

The IDEA requires that special education and related services be made available free of charge to every eligible child with a disability, including preschoolers (between the ages of 3 and 21). These services are specially designed to address the child's individual needs associated with the disability—in this case, emotional disturbance, as defined by the IDEA (and further specified by states). In the 2013 to 2014 school year, more than 354,000 children and youth with emotional disturbance received these services to address their individual needs related to emotional disturbance.

Determining a child's eligibility for special education and related services begins with a full and individual evaluation of the child. Under the IDEA, this evaluation is provided free of charge in public schools.

More about School

As mentioned, emotional disturbance is one of the categories of disability specified in IDEA. This means that a child with an emotional disturbance may be eligible for special education and related services in public school. These services can be of tremendous help to students who have an emotional disturbance.

Typically, educational programs for children with an emotional disturbance need to include attention to providing emotional and behavioral support, as well as helping them to master academics, develop social skills, and increase self-awareness, self-control, and self-esteem. A large body of research exists regarding methods of providing students with positive behavioral support (PBS) in the school environment, so that problem behaviors are minimized and positive, appropriate behaviors are fostered. It is also important to know that, within the school setting:

For a child whose behavior impedes learning (including the learning of others), the team developing the child's Individualized Education Program (IEP) needs to consider, if appropriate, strategies to address that behavior, including positive behavioral interventions, strategies, and supports.

Students eligible for special education services under the category of emotional disturbance may have IEPs that include psychological or counseling services. These are important related services available under the IDEA and are to be provided by a qualified social worker, psychologist, guidance counselor, or other qualified personnel.

The Importance of Support

Families often need help in understanding their child's disability and how to address the needs that arise from the disability. Help is available from psychiatrists, psychologists, and other mental-health professionals that work in the public or private sector. There is also a network of mental-health support operating in every state, as well as locally.

To locate systems of support in your community or state, different organizations can connect you with local resources, including support groups that provide connection and understanding, information, referral, and advocacy for those living with emotional disturbance.

Chapter 20

Epilepsy

Epilepsy versus Seizure

Epilepsy, which is sometimes called a "seizure disorder," is a disorder of the brain. A person is diagnosed with epilepsy when they have had two or more seizures.

A seizure is a short change in normal brain activity.

Seizures are the main sign of epilepsy. Some seizures can look like staring spells. Other seizures cause a person to fall, shake, and lose awareness of what is going on around them.

How Long Do Seizures Usually Last?

Usually, a seizure lasts from a few seconds to a few minutes. It depends on the type of seizure.

What Are the Major Types of Seizures?

Sometimes, it is hard to tell when a person is having a seizure. A person having a seizure may seem confused or look as if they are staring at something that is not there. Other seizures can cause a person to fall, shake, and become unaware of what is going on around them.

Seizures are classified into two groups.

This chapter includes text excerpted from "Frequently Asked Questions about Epilepsy," Centers for Disease Control and Prevention (CDC), January 4, 2019.

1. Generalized seizures affect both sides of the brain.

2. Focal seizures affect just one area of the brain. These seizures are also called "partial seizures."

A person with epilepsy can have more than one kind of seizure.

If You Have a Seizure, Does That Mean You Have Epilepsy?

Not always. Seizures can also happen because of other medical problems. These problems include:

- A high fever

- Low blood sugar

- Alcohol or drug withdrawal

What Causes Epilepsy

Epilepsy can be caused by different conditions that affect a person's brain. Some known causes include:

- Stroke

- Brain tumor

- Brain infection from parasites (malaria, neurocysticercosis), viruses (influenza, dengue, Zika), and bacteria

- Traumatic brain injury (TBI) or head injury

- Loss of oxygen to the brain (for example, during birth)

- Some genetic disorders (such as Down syndrome)

- Other neurologic diseases (such as Alzheimer disease (AD))

For two in three people, the cause of epilepsy is unknown. This type of epilepsy is called "cryptogenic" or "idiopathic."

Is Epilepsy Common?

Epilepsy is one of the most common conditions affecting the brain. When counting both children and adults in the United States:

- About 5.1 million people in the United States have a history of epilepsy.

- About 3.4 million people in the United States have active epilepsy.

How Can You Prevent Epilepsy?

Sometimes epilepsy be prevented. These are some of the most common ways to reduce your risk of developing epilepsy:

- Have a healthy pregnancy. Some problems during pregnancy and childbirth may lead to epilepsy. Follow a prenatal care plan with your healthcare provider to keep you and the fetus healthy.

- Prevent brain injuries.

- Lower the chances of stroke and heart disease.

- Stay up-to-date on your vaccinations.

- Wash your hands and prepare food safely to prevent infections, such as cysticercosis.

How Is Epilepsy Diagnosed?

A person who has a seizure for the first time should talk to a healthcare provider, such as a doctor or nurse practitioner. The provider will talk to the person about what happened, and look for the cause of the seizure. Many people who have seizures take tests, such as brain scans, for a closer look at what is going on. These tests do not hurt.

How Is Epilepsy Treated?

There are many things a provider and person with epilepsy can do to stop or lessen seizures.

The most common treatments for epilepsy are:

- **Medicine.** Anti-seizure drugs are medicines that limit the spread of seizures in the brain. A healthcare provider will change the amount of the medicine or prescribe a new drug, if needed, to find the best treatment plan. Medicines work for about two in three people with epilepsy.

- **Surgery.** When seizures come from a single area of the brain (focal seizures), surgery to remove that area may stop future seizures or make them easier to control with medicine. Epilepsy surgery is mostly used when the seizure focus is located in the temporal lobe of the brain.

- **Other treatments.** When medicines do not work and surgery is not possible, other treatments can help. These include vagus nerve stimulation, where an electrical device is placed, or implanted, under the skin on the upper chest to send signals to a large nerve in the neck. Another option is the ketogenic diet, a high fat, low carbohydrate diet with limited calories.

Who Treats Epilepsy

Many kinds of healthcare providers treat people with epilepsy. Primary care providers, such as family physicians, pediatricians, and nurse practitioners, are often the first people to see a person with epilepsy who has new seizures. These providers may make the diagnosis of epilepsy, or they may talk with a neurologist or epileptologist.

A neurologist is a doctor who specializes in the brain and nervous system. An epileptologist is a neurologist who specializes in epilepsy. When problems occur such as seizures or side effects of medicine, the primary-health provider may send the patient to a neurologist or epileptologists for specialized care.

People who have seizures that are difficult to control or who need advanced care for epilepsy may be referred to an epilepsy center. Epilepsy centers are staffed by providers who specialize in epilepsy care, such as:

- Epileptologists and neurologists
- Nurses
- Psychologists
- Technicians

Many epilepsy centers work with university hospitals and researchers.

How Do You Find an Epilepsy Specialist?

There are several ways you can find a neurologist or an epileptologist near you. Your primary care or family provider can tell you about types of specialists. The American Academy of Neurology (AAN) and the American Epilepsy Society (AES) provide a listing of its member neurologists and epilepsy specialists, including epileptologists. The National Association of Epilepsy Centers (NAEC) also provides a list of its member centers, organized by state.

What Can You Do to Manage Epilepsy?

Self-management is what you do to take care of yourself. You can learn how to manage seizures and keep an active and full life. Begin with these tips:

- Take your medicine.
- Talk with your doctor or nurse when you have questions.
- Recognize seizure triggers (such as flashing or bright lights).
- Keep a record of your seizures.
- Get enough sleep.
- Lower stress.

Chapter 21

Fetal Alcohol Spectrum Disorders

Chapter Contents

Section 21.1

Facts about Fetal Alcohol Spectrum Disorders

This section includes text excerpted from "Basics about FASDs,"
Centers for Disease Control and Prevention (CDC), May 10, 2018.

Fetal alcohol spectrum disorders (FASDs) are a group of conditions that can occur in a person whose mother drank alcohol during pregnancy. These effects can include physical problems and problems with behavior and learning. Often, a person with an FASD has a mix of these problems.

Fetal Alcohol Spectrum Disorders: Cause and Prevention

FASDs are caused by a woman drinking alcohol during pregnancy. Alcohol in the mother's blood passes to the fetus through the umbilical cord. When a woman drinks alcohol, so does the fetus.

There is no known safe amount of alcohol during pregnancy or when trying to get pregnant. There is also no safe time to drink during pregnancy. Alcohol can cause problems for a developing fetus throughout pregnancy, including before a woman knows she is pregnant. All types of alcohol are equally harmful, including all wines and beer.

To prevent FASDs, a woman should not drink alcohol while she is pregnant or when she might get pregnant. This is because a woman could get pregnant and not know for up to four to six weeks. In the United States, nearly half of pregnancies are unplanned.

If a woman is drinking alcohol during pregnancy, it is never too late to stop drinking. Because brain growth takes place throughout pregnancy, the sooner a woman stops drinking the safer it will be for her and the fetus.

FASDs are completely preventable if a woman does not drink alcohol during pregnancy—so why take the risk?

Fetal Alcohol Spectrum Disorders: Signs and Symptoms

FASDs refer to the whole range of effects that can happen to a person whose mother drank alcohol during pregnancy. These conditions can affect each person in different ways and can range from mild to severe.

A person with an FASD might have:

- Abnormal facial features, such as a smooth ridge between the nose and upper lip (this ridge is called the "philtrum")
- Small head size
- Shorter-than-average height
- Low body weight
- Poor coordination
- Hyperactive behavior
- Difficulty with attention
- Poor memory
- Difficulty in school (especially with math)
- Learning disabilities
- Speech and language delays
- Intellectual disability or low intelligence quotient (IQ)
- Poor reasoning and judgment skills
- Sleep and sucking problems as a baby
- Vision or hearing problems
- Problems with the heart, kidneys, or bones

Types of Fetal Alcohol Spectrum Disorders

Different terms are used to describe FASDs, depending on the type of symptoms.

Fetal alcohol syndrome (FAS) is the most involved end of the FASD spectrum. Fetal death is the most extreme outcome from drinking alcohol during pregnancy. People with FAS might have abnormal facial features, growth problems, and central nervous system (CNS) problems. People with FAS can have problems with learning, memory, attention span, communication, vision, or hearing. They might have a mix of these problems. People with FAS often have a hard time in school and trouble getting along with others.

Alcohol-related neurodevelopmental disorder (ARND). People with ARND might have intellectual disabilities and problems with behavior and learning. They might do poorly in school and have difficulties with math, memory, attention, judgment, and poor impulse control.

Alcohol-related birth defects (ARBD). People with ARBD might have problems with the heart, kidneys, or bones, or with hearing. They might have a mix of these.

Neurobehavioral disorder associated with prenatal alcohol exposure (ND-PAE): ND-PAE was first included as a recognized condition in the *Diagnostic and Statistical Manual 5* of the American Psychiatric Association (APA) in 2013. A child or youth with ND-PAE will have problems in three areas:

1. **Thinking and memory,** where the child may have trouble planning or may forget material, she or he has already learned

2. **Behavior problems,** such as severe tantrums, mood issues (for example, irritability), and difficulty shifting attention from one task to another

3. **Trouble with day-to-day living,** which can include problems with bathing, dressing for the weather, and playing with other children. In addition, to be diagnosed with ND-PAE, the mother of the child must have consumed more than minimal levels of alcohol before the child's birth, which APA defines as more than 13 alcoholic drinks per month of pregnancy (that is, any 30-day period of pregnancy) or more than 2 alcoholic drinks in one sitting.

Fetal Alcohol Spectrum Disorders: Diagnosis

The term "FASDs" is not meant for use as a clinical diagnosis. The Centers for Disease Control and Prevention (CDC) worked with a group of experts and organizations to review the research and develop guidelines for diagnosing FAS. The guidelines were developed for FAS only. The CDC and its partners are working to put together diagnostic criteria for other FASDs, such as ARND.

Diagnosing FAS can be hard because there is no medical test, such as a blood test, for it. And other disorders, such as attention deficit hyperactivity disorder (ADHD) and Williams syndrome (WS), have some symptoms similar to FAS.

To diagnose FAS, doctors look for:

- Abnormal facial features (e.g., smooth ridge between nose and upper lip)

238

- Lower-than-average height, weight, or both
- Central nervous system problems (e.g., small head size, problems with attention and hyperactivity, poor coordination)
- Prenatal alcohol exposure; although confirmation is not required to make a diagnosis.

Fetal Alcohol Spectrum Disorders: Treatment

FASDs last a lifetime. There is no cure for FASDs, but research shows that early intervention treatment services can improve a child's development.

There are many types of treatment options, including medication to help with some symptoms, behavior and education therapy, parent training, and other alternative approaches. No one treatment is right for every child. Good treatment plans will include close monitoring, follow-ups, and changes as needed along the way.

Also, "protective factors" can help reduce the effects of FASDs and help people with these conditions reach their full potential.

Protective factors include:

- Diagnosis before six years of age
- Loving, nurturing, and stable home environment during the school years
- Absence of violence
- Involvement in special education and social services

Get Help

If you or the doctor thinks there could be a problem, ask the doctor for a referral to a specialist (someone who knows about FASDs), such as a developmental pediatrician, child psychologist, or clinical geneticist. In some cities, there are clinics whose staffs have special training in diagnosing and treating children with FASDs. To find doctors and clinics in your area, visit the National and State Resource Directory (www.nofas.org) from the National Organization on Fetal Alcohol Syndrome (NOFAS).

At the same time as you ask the doctor for a referral to a specialist, call your state or territory's early intervention program to request a free evaluation to find out if your child can get services to help. This is sometimes called a "child find evaluation." You do not need to wait for a doctor's referral or a medical diagnosis to make this call.

Where to call for a free evaluation from the state depends on your child's age; if your child is younger than three years of age, call your state or territory's early intervention program and say: "I have concerns about my child's development, and I would like to have my child evaluated to find out if she or he is eligible for early intervention services."

If your child is three years of age or older, contact your local public-school system.

Even if your child is not old enough for kindergarten or enrolled in a public school, call your local elementary school or board of education and ask to speak with someone who can help you have your child evaluated (www.parentcenterhub.org.).

Section 21.2

Alcohol Use and Pregnancy

This section includes text excerpted from "Alcohol and Pregnancy," Centers for Disease Control and Prevention (CDC), February 2, 2016.

Alcohol use during pregnancy can cause fetal alcohol spectrum disorders (FASDs), which are physical, behavioral, and intellectual disabilities that last a lifetime. More than three million United States women are at risk of exposing a fetus to alcohol because they are drinking, having sex, and not using birth control to prevent pregnancy. About half of all United States pregnancies are unplanned, and even if planned, most women do not know they are pregnant until they are four to six weeks into the pregnancy. This means a woman might be drinking and exposing the fetus to alcohol without knowing it. Alcohol screening and counseling help people who are drinking too much to drink less. It is recommended that women who are pregnant or might be pregnant not drink alcohol at all. FASDs does not occur if the fetus is not exposed to alcohol before birth.

Women can:

- Talk with their healthcare provider about their plans for pregnancy, their alcohol use, and ways to prevent pregnancy if they are not planning to get pregnant.

- Stop drinking alcohol if they are trying to get pregnant or could get pregnant.
- Ask their partner, family, and friends to support their choice not to drink during pregnancy or while trying to get pregnant.
- Ask their healthcare provider or another trusted person about resources for help if they cannot stop drinking on their own.

Problem

Alcohol can harm a fetus before a woman knows she is pregnant.

Why Take the Risk

- Women who are pregnant or who might be pregnant should be aware that any level of alcohol use could harm the fetus.
- All types of alcohol can be harmful, including all wine and beer.
- The fetuses' brain, body, and organs are developing throughout pregnancy and can be affected by alcohol at any time.
- Drinking while pregnant can also increase the risk of miscarriage, stillbirth, prematurity, and sudden infant death syndrome (SIDS).

Doctors, nurses, or other health professionals can help prevent alcohol use during pregnancy in the following ways:

- Provide alcohol screening and brief counseling to all women.
- Recommend birth control to women who are having sex (if appropriate), not planning to get pregnant, and drinking alcohol.
- Advise women who are trying to get pregnant to stop drinking alcohol.
- Refer for additional services for women who cannot stop drinking on their own.
- Follow up yearly or more often, as needed.

What Can Be Done

What the government can do:

- The federal government is requiring most health insurance plans to cover recommended alcohol screening and counseling services without cost to the patient.

- Requiring most health insurance plans to cover the U.S. Food and Drug Administration (FDA)-approved methods of birth control and patient education and counseling as prescribed by a healthcare provider for women of reproductive age without cost to the patient

- Adopting clinical guidelines to carry out alcohol screening and counseling in community health centers

- Working with partner organizations to promote alcohol screening and counseling

What women can do:

- Women can talk with their healthcare provider about their plans for pregnancy, their alcohol use, and ways to prevent pregnancy if they are not planning to get pregnant.

- Stop drinking alcohol if they are trying to get pregnant or could get pregnant.

- Ask their partner, family, and friends to support their choice not to drink during pregnancy or while trying to get pregnant.

- Ask their healthcare provider or another trusted person about resources for help if they cannot stop drinking on their own.

What healthcare providers can do:

- Screen all adult patients for alcohol use at least yearly

- Advise women not to drink at all if there is any chance, they could be pregnant

- Counsel, refer and follow-up with patients who need more help

- Use the correct billing codes so that alcohol screening and counseling is reimbursable

State and local governments can:

- Work with their Medicaid programs to make sure alcohol screening and counseling services are reimbursable

- Encourage health insurance plans and provider organizations to support alcohol screening and counseling

- Monitor how many adults are receiving these services in communities

- Support proven policies and programs that work to prevent drinking too much

Chapter 22

Gerstmann Syndrome

What Is Gerstmann Syndrome?

Gerstmann syndrome (GS) is a cognitive impairment that results from damage to a specific area of the brain—the left parietal lobe in the region of the angular gyrus. It may occur after a stroke or in association with damage to the parietal lobe.

The disorder should not be confused with Gerstmann-Sträussler-Scheinker disease (GSS), a type of transmissible spongiform encephalopathy (TSEs).

What Are the Symptoms of Gerstmann Syndrome?

GS is characterized by four primary symptoms:

- A writing disability (agraphia or dysgraphia)
- A lack of understanding of the rules for calculation or arithmetic (acalculia or dyscalculia)
- An inability to distinguish right from left
- An inability to identify fingers (finger agnosia)

This chapter includes text excerpted from "Gerstmann's Syndrome Information Page," National Institute of Neurological Disorders and Stroke (NINDS), November 2, 2018.

In addition to exhibiting the above symptoms, many adults also experience aphasia, which is a difficulty in expressing oneself when speaking, in understanding speech, or in reading and writing.

What Is Developmental Gerstmann Syndrome?

There are few reports of the syndrome, sometimes called "developmental Gerstmann syndrome," in children. The cause is not known. Most cases are identified when children reach school age, a time when they are challenged with writing and math exercises. Generally, children with the disorder exhibit poor handwriting and spelling skills, and difficulty with math functions, including adding, subtracting, multiplying, and dividing. An inability to differentiate right from left and to discriminate among individual fingers may also be apparent.

In addition to the four primary symptoms, many children also suffer from constructional apraxia, an inability to copy simple drawings. Frequently, there is also an impairment in reading. Children with a high level of intellectual functioning, as well as those with brain damage, may be affected with the disorder.

What Treatment Is Available for Gerstmann Syndrome?

There is no cure for GS. Treatment is symptomatic and supportive. Occupational and speech therapies may help diminish the dysgraphia and apraxia. In addition, calculators and word processors may help school children cope with the symptoms of the disorder.

What Is the Prognosis for Gerstmann Syndrome?

In adults, many of the symptoms diminish over time. Although it has been suggested that children symptoms may diminish over time, it appears likely that most children probably do not overcome their deficits, but rather, they learn to adjust to them.

Chapter 23

Hearing Disabilities

Chapter Contents

Section 23.1

Facts about Hearing Disabilities

This section contains text excerpted from the following sources:
Text in this section begins with excerpts from "How Do We Hear?"
National Institute on Deafness and Other Communication Disorders
(NIDCD), January 3, 2018; Text beginning with the heading
"Hearing Loss in Children?" is excerpted from "What Is Hearing
Loss in Children?" Centers for Disease Control and
Prevention (CDC), April 11, 2018.

Hearing depends on a series of complex steps that change sound waves in the air into electrical signals. Our auditory nerve then carries these signals to the brain.

1. Sound waves enter the outer ear and travel through a narrow passageway called the "ear canal," which leads to the eardrum.

2. The eardrum vibrates from the incoming sound waves and sends these vibrations to three tiny bones in the middle ear. These bones are called the "malleus," "incus," and "stapes."

3. The bones in the middle ear amplify, or increase, the sound vibrations and send them to the cochlea, a snail-shaped structure filled with fluid, in the inner ear. An elastic partition runs from the beginning to the end of the cochlea, splitting it into an upper and lower part. This partition is called the "basilar membrane" because it serves as the base, or ground floor, on which key hearing structures sit.

4. Once the vibrations cause the fluid inside the cochlea to ripple, a traveling wave forms along the basilar membrane. Hair cells—sensory cells sitting on top of the basilar membrane—ride the wave. Hair cells near the wide end of the snail-shaped cochlea detect higher-pitched sounds, such as an infant crying. Those closer to the center detect lower-pitched sounds, such as a large dog barking.

5. As the hair cells move up and down, microscopic hair-like projections (known as "stereocilia") that perch on top of the hair cells bump against an overlying structure and bend. Bending causes pore-like channels, which are at the tips of the stereocilia, to open up. When that happens, chemicals rush into the cells, creating an electrical signal.

6. The auditory nerve carries this electrical signal to the brain, which turns it into a sound that we recognize and understand.

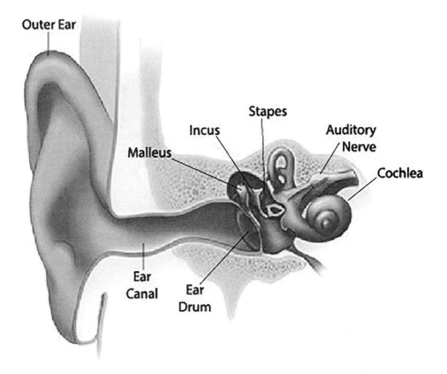

Figure 23.1. *How Do We Hear* (Source: National Institutes of Health (NIH) Medical Arts.)

Hearing Loss in Children

Hearing loss can affect a child's ability to develop speech, language, and social skills. The earlier children with hearing loss start getting services, the more likely they are to reach their full potential. If you think that a child might have hearing loss, ask the child's doctor for a hearing screening as soon as possible. Do not wait.

What Is Hearing Loss?

Hearing loss can happen when any part of the ear is not working in the usual way. This includes the outer ear, middle ear, inner ear, hearing (acoustic) nerve, and auditory system.

Signs and Symptoms of Hearing Loss

The signs and symptoms of hearing loss are different for each child. If you think that your child might have hearing loss, ask the child's doctor for a hearing screening as soon as possible. Do not wait.

Even if a child has passed a hearing screening before, it is important to look out for the following signs.

Signs in Babies

- Does not startle at loud noises

- Does not turn to the source of a sound after 6 months of age

- Does not say single words, such as "dada" or "mama" by one year of age

- Turns head when she or he sees you but not if you only call out her or his name. This sometimes is mistaken for not paying attention or just ignoring, but it could be the result of a partial or complete hearing loss.

- Seems to hear some sounds but not others

Signs in Children

- Speech is delayed.

- Speech is not clear.

- Does not follow directions. This sometimes is mistaken for not paying attention or just ignoring, but it could be the result of a partial or complete hearing loss.

- Often says, "Huh?"

- Turns the TV volume up too high

Babies and children should reach milestones in how they play, learn, communicate, and act. A delay in any of these milestones could be a sign of hearing loss or other developmental problem.

Causes and Risk Factors for Hearing Loss

Hearing loss can happen any time during life—from before birth to adulthood.

The following are some of the things that can increase the chance that a child will have hearing loss:

- **A genetic cause.** About one out of two cases of hearing loss in babies is due to genetic causes. Some babies with a genetic cause for their hearing loss might have family members who also have a hearing loss. About one out of three babies with genetic hearing loss have a "syndrome." This means they have other conditions in addition to the hearing loss, such as Down syndrome or Usher syndrome.

- **Maternal infection during pregnancy.** One out of four cases of hearing loss in babies is due to maternal infections during pregnancy, complications after birth, and head trauma. For example, the child:

  - Was exposed to infection before birth

  - Spent five days or more in a hospital neonatal intensive care unit (NICU) or had complications while in the NICU

  - Needed a special procedure, such as a blood transfusion to treat bad jaundice

  - Has head, face or ears shaped or formed in a different way than usual

  - Has a condition, such as a neurological disorder, that may be associated with hearing loss

  - Had an infection around the brain and spinal cord called "meningitis"

  - Suffered a bad head injury that required a hospital stay

- For about one out of four babies born with hearing loss, the cause is unknown.

Screening and Diagnosis for Hearing Loss

Hearing screening can tell if a child might have hearing loss. Hearing screening is easy and is not painful. In fact, babies are often asleep while being screened. It takes a very short time—usually only a few minutes.

Babies

All babies should have a hearing screening no later than one month of age. Most babies have their hearing screened while still in the hospital. If a baby does not pass a hearing screening, it is very important to get a full hearing test as soon as possible, but no later than three months of age.

Children

Children should have their hearing tested before they enter school or any time there is a concern about the child's hearing. Children who do not pass the hearing screening need to get a full hearing test as soon as possible.

Treatments and Intervention Services for Hearing Loss

No single treatment or intervention is the answer for every person or family. Good treatment plans will include close monitoring, follow-ups, and any changes needed along the way. There are many different types of communication options for children with hearing loss and for their families. Some of these options include:

- Learning other ways to communicate, such as sign language
- Technology to help with communication, such as hearing aids and cochlear implants
- Medicine and surgery to correct some types of hearing loss
- Family support services

How to Prevent Hearing Loss

The following are tips for parents to help prevent hearing loss in their children.

- Have a healthy pregnancy.
- Make sure your child gets all the regular childhood vaccines.
- Keep your child away from high noise levels, such as from very loud toys.

Get Help

Hearing loss can affect a child's ability to develop speech, language, and social skills. The earlier children with hearing loss start getting services, the more likely they are to reach their full potential. If you are a parent and you suspect your child has hearing loss, trust your instincts and speak with your child's doctor.

- If you think that your child might have hearing loss, ask the child's doctor for a hearing screening as soon as possible. Do not wait.

- If your child does not pass a hearing screening, ask the child's doctor for a full hearing test as soon as possible.

- If your child has hearing loss, talk to the child's doctor about treatment and intervention services.

Section 23.2

Hearing Loss Treatment and Intervention Services

This section includes text excerpted from "Hearing Loss Treatment and Intervention Services," Centers for Disease Control and Prevention (CDC), April 11, 2018.

No single treatment or intervention is the answer for every child or family. Good intervention plans will include close monitoring, follow-ups, and any changes needed along the way. There are many different options for children with hearing loss and their families.

Some of the treatment and intervention options include:

- Working with a professional (or team) who can help a child and family learn to communicate

- Getting a hearing device, such as a hearing aid

- Joining support groups

- Taking advantage of other resources available to children with a hearing loss and their families

Early Intervention and Special Education
Early Intervention (0 to 3 Years of Age)

Hearing loss can affect a child's ability to develop speech, language, and social skills. The earlier a child who is deaf or hard-of-hearing starts getting services, the more likely the child's speech, language, and social skills will reach their full potential.

Early intervention program services help young children with hearing loss learn language skills and other important skills. Research shows that early intervention services can greatly improve a child's development.

Babies that are diagnosed with hearing loss should begin to get intervention services as soon as possible, but no later than 6 months of age.

There are many services available through the Individuals with Disabilities Education Improvement Act 2004 (IDEA 2004). External Services for children from birth through 36 months of age are called "early intervention" or "part C services." Even if your child has not been diagnosed with a hearing loss, she or he may be eligible for early intervention treatment services. The IDEA 2004 says that children under the age of 3 (36 months) who are at risk of having developmental delays may be eligible for services. These services are provided through an early intervention system in your state. Through this system, you can ask for an evaluation.

Special Education (3 to 22 Years of Age)

Special education is instruction specifically designed to address the educational and related developmental needs of older children with disabilities, or those who are experiencing developmental delays. Services for these children are provided through the public-school system. These services are available through the IDEA 2004, Part B.

Early Hearing Detection and Intervention Program

Every state has an Early Hearing Detection and Intervention (EHDI) program. EHDI works to identify infants and children with hearing loss. EHDI also promotes timely follow-up testing and services or interventions for any family whose child has a hearing loss.

Technology

Many people who are deaf or hard-of-hearing have some hearing. The amount of hearing a deaf or hard-of-hearing person has is called "residual hearing." Technology does not cure hearing loss, but may help a child with hearing loss to make the most of their residual hearing. For parents who choose to have their child use technology, there are many options. Some of them are discussed below.

Hearing Aids

Hearing aids make sounds louder. They can be worn by people of any age, including infants. Babies with hearing loss may understand sounds better when using hearing aids. This may give them the chance to learn speech skills at a young age.

There are many styles of hearing aids. They can help many types of hearing losses. A young child is usually fitted with behind-the-ear style hearing aids because they are better suited to growing ears.

Cochlear Implants

A cochlear implant may help many children with severe to profound hearing loss—even very young children. It gives that child a way to hear when a hearing aid is not enough. Unlike a hearing aid, cochlear implants do not make sounds louder. A cochlear implant sends sound signals directly to the hearing nerve.

A cochlear implant has two main parts—the parts that are placed inside the ear during surgery and the parts that are worn outside the ear after surgery. The parts outside the ear send sounds to the parts inside the ear.

The Centers for Disease Control and Prevention (CDC) and the U.S. Food and Drug Administration (FDA) carried out studies in 2002 and 2006 to learn more about a possible link between cochlear implants and bacterial meningitis in children with cochlear implants.

Bone-Anchored Hearing Aids

This type of hearing aid can be considered when a child has either a conductive, mixed, or unilateral hearing loss and is specifically suitable for children who cannot otherwise wear in-the-ear or behind-the-ear hearing aids.

Other Assistive Devices

Besides hearing aids, there are other devices that help people with hearing loss. The following are some examples of other assistive devices:

- **Frequency modulation (FM) system.** An FM system is a kind of device that helps people with hearing loss hear in background noise. FM stands for frequency modulation. It is the same type of signal used for radios. FM systems send sound from a microphone used by someone speaking to a person wearing the receiver. This system is sometimes used with hearing aids. An extra piece is attached to the hearing aid that works with the FM system.

- **Captioning.** Many television programs, videos, and digital video discs (DVDs) are captioned. Television sets made after 1993 are made to show the captioning. You do not have to buy anything special. Captions show the conversation spoken in soundtrack of a program on the bottom of the television screen.

- **Other devices.** There are many other devices available for children with hearing loss. Some of these include:

  - Text messaging
  - Telephone amplifiers
  - Flashing and vibrating alarms
  - Audio loop systems
  - Infrared listening devices
  - Portable sound amplifiers
  - TTY (Text telephone or teletypewriter)

Medical and Surgical

Medications or surgery may also help make the most of a person's hearing. This is especially true for a conductive hearing loss, or one that involves a part of the outer or middle ear that is not working in the usual way.

One type of conductive hearing loss can be caused by a chronic ear infection. A chronic ear infection is a buildup of fluid behind the eardrum in the middle ear space. Most ear infections are managed with medication or careful monitoring. Infections that do not go away with medication can be treated with a simple surgery that involves putting a tiny tube into the eardrum to drain the fluid out.

Another type of conductive hearing loss is caused by either the outer and or middle ear not forming correctly while the fetus was growing in the mother's womb. Both the outer and middle ear need to work together in order for sound to be sent correctly to the inner ear. If any of these parts did not form correctly, there might be hearing loss in that ear. This problem may be improved, and perhaps even corrected, with surgery. An ear, nose, and throat doctor (otolaryngologist) is the healthcare professional who usually takes care of this problem.

Placing a cochlear implant or bone-anchored hearing aid will also require a surgery.

Learning Language

Without extra help, children with hearing loss have problems learning language. These children can then be at risk for other delays. Families who have children with hearing loss often need to change their communication habits or learn special skills (such as sign language) to help their children learn language. These skills can be used together with hearing aids, cochlear implants, and other devices that help children hear.

Family Support Services

For many parents, their child's hearing loss is unexpected. Parents sometimes need time and support to adapt to the child's hearing loss.

Parents of children with recently identified hearing loss can seek different kinds of support. Support is anything that helps a family and may include advice, information, having the chance to get to know other parents that have a child with hearing loss, locating a deaf mentor, finding child care or transportation, giving parents time for personal relaxation, or just a supportive listener.

Chapter 24

Pervasive Developmental Disorders

Chapter Contents

257

Section 24.1

What Are Pervasive Developmental Disorders?

This section includes text excerpted from "Pervasive Developmental Disorders Information Page," National Institute of Neurological Disorders and Stroke (NINDS), July 2, 2018.

The diagnostic category of pervasive developmental disorders (PDD) refers to a group of disorders characterized by delays in the development of socialization and communication skills. Parents may note symptoms as early as infancy; although the typical age of onset is before three years of age. Symptoms may include problems with using and understanding language; difficulty relating to people, objects, and events; unusual play with toys and other objects; difficulty with changes in routine or familiar surroundings, and repetitive body movements or behavior patterns. Autism (a developmental brain disorder characterized by impaired social interaction and communication skills and a limited range of activities and interests) is the most characteristic and best studied PDD. Other types of PDD include Asperger Syndrome (AS), Childhood Disintegrative Disorder (CDD), and Rett Syndrome (RTT). Children with PDD vary widely in abilities, intelligence, and behaviors. Some children do not speak at all, others speak in limited phrases or conversations, and some have relatively normal language development. Repetitive play skills and limited social skills are generally evident. Unusual responses to sensory information, such as loud noises and lights, are also common.

What Are the Treatment Options for Pervasive Developmental Disorders?

There is no known cure for PDD. Medications are used to address specific behavioral problems; therapy for children with PDD should be specialized according to need. Some children with PDD benefit from specialized classrooms in which the class size is small, and instruction is given on a one-on-one basis. Others function well in standard special education classes or regular classes with additional support.

What Is the Prognosis for Pervasive Developmental Disorders?

Early intervention (EI), including appropriate and specialized educational programs and support services, plays a critical role in improving the outcome of individuals with PDD. PDD is not fatal and does not affect normal life expectancy.

Section 24.2

Autism

This section includes text excerpted from "About Autism," *Eunice Kennedy Shriver* National Institute of Child Health and Human Development (NICHD), January 31, 2017.

Autism spectrum disorder (ASD) is a complex neurological and developmental disorder that begins early in life and affects how a person acts and interacts with others, communicates and learns. ASD affects the structure and function of the brain and nervous system. Because it affects development, ASD is called a "developmental disorder." ASD can last throughout a person's life.

People with this disorder experience:

- Difficulties with communication and interaction with other people

- Restricted interests and repetitive behaviors

Different people with autism can have different symptoms. For this reason, autism is known as a "spectrum disorder," which means that there is a range of similar features in different people with the disorder.

In giving a diagnosis of ASD, a healthcare provider will also specify whether the person also has:

- Intellectual problems, including problems with reasoning or memory

- Language problems, such as problems with speech

- Another medical or genetic condition that is related to or contributes to autism, such as seizures or fragile X syndrome (FXS)

In May 2013, a revised version of the *Diagnostic and Statistical Manual of Mental Disorders* (DSM-5), the main resource healthcare providers use to diagnose different mental-health conditions, was released. The DSM-5 made significant changes to how autism is classified and diagnosed.

Now: Under the DSM-5, someone with more severe autism symptoms and someone with less severe autism symptoms both have the same disorder: ASD.

Then: In the previous version of the DSM, ASD was a category and there were four types of autism within the category. These were autistic disorder ("classic" autism); AS, which usually involved milder symptoms that are mostly related to social behaviors; childhood disintegrative disorder (CDD), in which a child develops normally for several months or years and then loses skills related to language, movement, coordination, and other brain functions;), and pervasive developmental disorder not otherwise specified (PDD-NOS, or "atypical" autism), which included some, but not all, of the features of classic autism or AS.

Healthcare providers no longer use these terms to describe someone with ASD.

What Are the Symptoms of Autism?

The symptoms of one person with autism can be very different from the symptoms of another person with autism. Healthcare providers think of autism as a spectrum disorder—which means that there is a range of similar features in different people with the disorder.

One person with autism may have mild symptoms, while another may have more serious symptoms, but they both have ASD.

Despite the range of possible symptoms, there are certain actions and behaviors that are common in ASD and could signal that a child is on the autism spectrum. Parents and caregivers who notice these "red flags" should speak to their child's healthcare provider about autism and screening the child for ASD.

In general, the main signs and symptoms of ASD relate to:

- Communication and interactions with other people

- Routines or repetitive behaviors, sometimes called "stereotyped behaviors"

Healthcare providers organize some noticeable symptoms of autism into "red flags" to help parents and caregivers know what to look for as children grow and develop. These red flags are listed below.

Red Flags for Autism Spectrum Disorder
Communication

- Does not respond to her or his name by 12 months of age
- Cannot explain what she or he wants
- Does not follow directions
- Seems to hear sometimes, but not other times
- Does not point or wave "bye-bye"
- Used to say a few words or babble, but now does not

Social Behavior

- Does not smile when smiled at
- Has poor eye contact
- Seems to prefer to play alone
- Gets things for her- or himself only
- Is very independent for her or his age
- Seems to be in her or his "own world"
- Seems to tune people out
- Is not interested in other children
- Does not point out interesting objects by 14 months of age
- Does not like to play "peek-a-boo"
- Does not try to attract her or his parent's attention

Stereotyped Behavior

- Gets "stuck" doing the same things over and over and cannot move on to other things
- Shows unusual attachments to toys, objects, or routines (for example, always holding a string or having to put on socks before pants)

- Spends a lot of time lining things up or putting things in a certain order

- Repeats words or phrases (sometimes called "echolalia")

Other Behavior

You can find age-specific milestones on the Centers for Disease Control and Prevention (CDC) website (www.cdc.gov). If your child does not meet developmental milestones, talk to her or his healthcare provider about screening for ASD.

Note about these red flags:

- Some of these red flags apply only at certain ages, so consider what is typical for other children your child's age.

- Some red flags are more strongly associated with autism than others.

- If your child shows any red flags for autism, talk to her or his healthcare provider.

When Do Children Usually Show Symptoms of Autism?

The behavioral symptoms of ASD often appear early in development. Many children show symptoms of autism by 12 to 18 months of age or earlier. Some early signs of autism include:

- Problems with eye contact

- No response to her or his name

- Problems following another person's gaze or pointed finger to an object (or "joint attention")

- Poor skills in pretend play and imitation

- Problems with nonverbal communication

Many parents are not aware of these "early" signs of autism and do not start thinking about autism until their children do not start talking at a typical age.

Most children with autism are not diagnosed until after the age of three, even though healthcare providers can often see developmental problems before that age.

Regression

Some children with autism regress, meaning they stop using language, play, or social skills that they have already learned. This regression may happen between one and two years of age. It might happen earlier for some social behaviors, such as looking at faces and sharing a smile.

Other Early Signs

There also may be early biological signs of ASD. Studies have shown that:

- People with autism have unique brain activity, structures, and connections, even at very young ages.
- There are differences in brain growth in ASD as early as six months of age.

What Causes Autism

Scientists do not know exactly what causes ASD.

Autism was first described in the 1940s, but very little was known about it until the last few decades. Even nowadays, there is a great deal that we do not know about autism.

Because the disorder is so complex and no two people with autism are exactly alike, there are probably many causes for autism. It is also likely that there is not a single cause for autism, but rather that it results from a combination of causes.

Scientists are studying some of the following as possible causes of or contributors to ASD.

Genes and Autism Spectrum Disorder

A great deal of evidence supports the idea that genes are one of the main causes of or a major contributor to ASD. More than 100 genes on different chromosomes may be involved in causing ASD, to different degrees.

Many people with autism have slight changes, called "mutations," in many of these genes. However, the link between genetic mutations and autism is complex:

- Most people with autism have different mutations and combinations of mutations. Not everyone with autism has changed in every gene that scientists have linked to ASD.

- Many people without autism or autism symptoms also have some of these genetic mutations that scientists have linked to autism.

This evidence means that different genetic mutations probably play different roles in ASD. For example, certain mutations or combinations of mutations might:

- Cause-specific symptoms of ASD

- Control how mild or severe those symptoms are

- Increase susceptibility to autism. This means someone with one of these gene mutations is at greater risk for autism than someone without the mutation.

Interaction between the Genes and the Environment

If someone is susceptible to ASD because of genetic mutations, then certain situations might cause autism in that person.

For instance, an infection or contact with chemicals in the environment could cause autism in someone who is susceptible because of genetic mutations. However, someone who is genetically susceptible might not get an ASD even if she or he has the same experiences.

Other Biological Causes

Researchers are also looking into biological factors other than genes that might be involved in ASD. Some of these include:

- Problems with brain connections

- Problems with growth or overgrowth in certain areas of the brain

- Problems with metabolism (the body's energy production system)

- Problems in the body's immune system, which protects against infections

How Do Healthcare Providers Diagnose Autism?

Healthcare providers look for certain symptoms or groups of symptoms to diagnose ASD. If you have concerns about your child's development, talk to her or his healthcare provider right away. The provider then can examine the child and check for specific problems, such as autism.

Routine Developmental Screening

Your child's healthcare provider will check for problems with your child's development at every well-baby and well-child visit, even if you do not report any of the signs of autism or other problems. In addition, the American Academy of Pediatrics (AAP) recommends that healthcare providers administer an ASD-specific tool to assess development at the 18-month and 24-month visits, regardless of whether the child has risk factors for ASD.

During these developmental screenings, the healthcare provider may:

- Ask you specific questions about your child's actions and behavior

- Ask you to fill out a questionnaire about your child's behavior

- Speak directly to the child

Specialized Screening for Autism Spectrum Disorder

The healthcare provider might use a screening test specifically for ASD. This test might be the Checklist of Autism in Toddlers (CHAT), the Modified Checklist for Autism in Toddlers (M-CHAT), or another test.

In addition, the healthcare provider may also recommend that your child have a blood test to help rule out some other conditions and problems.

Depending on the results of the blood test and the developmental and other screenings, your child's healthcare provider will either:

- Rule out autism

- Refer your child to a specialist in child development or another specialized field to diagnose the child with autism. The specialist will then do a number of tests to figure out whether your child has autism or another condition. These will include tests of your child's communication abilities and observation of the child's behaviors.

Because the diagnostic criteria for ASD changed in 2013, ongoing research will help ensure that these screening tests are accurately identifying children who meet the new criteria for ASD.

Diagnosing Autism Spectrum Disorder

The American Psychiatric Association, a professional society of psychiatrists, updated the criteria for an autism diagnosis in May 2013. The criteria are published in the *Diagnostic and Statistical Manual of Mental Disorders, Fifth Edition (*DSM-5*)*.

According to the DSM-5 criteria, a person has ASD if she or he:

- Has problems with communication and social interactions, namely:

  - Does not respond appropriately to social and emotional cues

  - Has deficits in nonverbal communication during social interactions

  - Has trouble developing friendships, keeping friends, and understanding relationships

- Has at least two types of repetitive behavioral patterns. These might include repetitive movements, inflexible routines, very restricted interests, or unusual responses to certain sensory inputs, such as the way a particular object feels.

There are various tools that specialists commonly use to diagnose autism. The only tool that currently fits the revised DSM-5 criteria is the Autism Diagnostic Observation Schedule (ADOS-2). However, it alone is not enough to make a diagnosis of ASD. Existing diagnostic tools are being modified to better fit the DSM-5 criteria.

During an ADOS-2 assessment, the specialist interacts directly with your child in social and play activities. For example, the specialist will see whether your child responds to her or his name and how she or he performs in pretend play, such as with dolls. The specialist is looking for specific characteristics that are hallmarks of ASD. To be diagnosed with ASD, a child must have had symptoms since an early age.

As part of the diagnosis, the specialist will also note whether your child has:

- Any genetic disorder that is known to cause ASD or its symptoms, including fragile X syndrome or Rett syndrome; your child might receive a genetic test to detect these types of disorders.

- A language disability and the level of disability

- Intellectual disability and the level of disability

- Any medical conditions common among those with ASD, such as seizures, anxiety, depression, or problems with the digestive system

Depending on your child's unique symptoms and needs, the team of specialists may also want to give your child a range of other tests. If your child shows symptoms of seizures, a brain specialist, or neurologist, might use electrical sensors to observe your child's brain activity.

Your child may need other tests to determine how best to treat the symptoms of ASD. A hearing specialist, or audiologist, might test your child's hearing, which can sometimes seem poor in children with ASD. Other tests might include tests of muscle strength and tests of your child's ability to control movement.

What Are the Treatments for Autism?

There is currently no one standard treatment for ASD.

Many people with ASD benefit from treatment, no matter how old they are when they are diagnosed. People of all ages, at all levels of ability, can often improve after well-designed interventions.

But there are many ways to help minimize the symptoms and maximize abilities. People who have ASD have the best chance of using all of their abilities and skills if they receive appropriate therapies and interventions.

The most effective therapies and interventions are often different for each person. However, most people with ASD respond best to highly structured and specialized programs. In some cases, treatment can help people with autism to function at near-normal levels.

Research shows that early diagnosis and interventions, such as during preschool or before, are more likely to have major positive effects on symptoms and later skills.

Because there can be overlap in symptoms between ASD and other disorders, such as attention deficit hyperactivity disorder (ADHD), it is important that treatment focuses on a person's specific needs, rather than the diagnostic label.

Section 24.3

Asperger Syndrome

This section includes text excerpted from "Asperger Syndrome Information Page," National Institute of Neurological Disorders and Stroke (NINDS), June 20, 2018.

Asperger syndrome (AS) is a developmental disorder. It is an autism spectrum disorder (ASD), one of a distinct group of neurological conditions characterized by a greater or lesser degree of impairment in language and communication skills, as well as repetitive or restrictive patterns of thought and behavior. Other ASDs include classic autism, Rett syndrome, childhood disintegrative disorder (CDD), and pervasive developmental disorder not otherwise specified (usually referred to as PDD-NOS). Unlike children with autism, children with AS retain their early language skills.

The most distinguishing symptom of AS is a child's obsessive interest in a single object or topic to the exclusion of any other. Children with AS want to know everything about their topic of interest and their conversations with others will be about little else. Their expertise, high level of vocabulary, and formal speech patterns make them seem as if they are little professors. Other characteristics of AS include repetitive routines or rituals, peculiarities in speech and language, socially and emotionally inappropriate behavior and the inability to interact successfully with peers, problems with nonverbal communication, and clumsy and uncoordinated motor movements.

Children with AS are isolated because of their poor social skills and narrow interests. They may approach other people but make normal conversation impossible by inappropriate or eccentric behavior, or by wanting only to talk about their singular interest. Children with AS usually have a history of developmental delays in motor skills, such as pedaling a bike, catching a ball, or climbing outdoor play equipment. They are often awkward and poorly coordinated with a walk that can appear either stilted or bouncy.

Treatment for Asperger Syndrome

The ideal treatment for AS coordinates therapies that address the three core symptoms of the disorder: poor communication skills, obsessive or repetitive routines, and physical clumsiness. There is no single best treatment package for all children with AS, but most professionals agree that the earlier the intervention, the better.

An effective treatment program builds on the child's interests, offers a predictable schedule, teaches tasks as a series of simple steps, actively engages the child's attention in highly structured activities, and provides regular reinforcement of behavior. It may include social skills training (SST), cognitive behavioral therapy (CBT), medication for co-existing conditions, and other measures.

Prognosis for Asperger Syndrome

With effective treatment, children with AS can learn to cope with their disabilities, but they may still find social situations and personal relationships challenging. Many adults with AS are able to work successfully in mainstream jobs, although they may continue to need encouragement and moral support to maintain an independent life.

Chapter 25

Specific Language Impairment

What Is Specific Language Impairment?

Specific language impairment (SLI) is a language disorder that delays the mastery of language skills in children who have no hearing loss or other developmental delays. SLI is also called "developmental language disorder" (DLD), "language delay," or "developmental dysphasia." It is one of the most common childhood learning disabilities, affecting approximately seven to eight percent of children in kindergarten. The impact of SLI persists into adulthood.

What Causes Specific Language Impairment

The cause of SLI is unknown, but discoveries suggest it has a strong genetic link. Children with SLI are more likely than those without SLI to have parents and siblings who also have had difficulties and delays in speaking. In fact, 50 to 70 percent of children with SLI have at least 1 other family member with the disorder.

This chapter includes text excerpted from "Specific Language Impairment," National Institute on Deafness and Other Communication Disorders (NIDCD), March 6, 2017.

What Are the Symptoms of Specific Language Impairment?

Children with SLI are often late to talk and may not produce any words until they are two years of age. At three years of age, they may talk but may not be understood. As they grow older, children with SLI will struggle to learn new words and make conversation. Having difficulty using verbs is a hallmark of SLI. Typical errors that a five-year-old child with SLI would make include dropping the "s" from the end of present-tense verbs, dropping past tense, and asking questions without the usual "be" or "do" verbs. For example, instead of saying "She rides the horse," a child with SLI will say, "She ride the horse." Instead of saying "He ate the cookie," a child with SLI will say, "He eat the cookie." Instead of saying "Why does he like me?" a child with SLI will ask, "Why he like me?"

How Is Specific Language Impairment Diagnosed in Children?

The first person to suspect a child might have SLI is often a parent or preschool or school teacher. A number of speech-language professionals might be involved in the diagnosis, including a speech-language pathologist (a health professional trained to evaluate and treat children with speech or language problems). Language skills are tested using assessment tools that evaluate how well the child constructs sentences and keeps words in their proper order, the number of words in her or his vocabulary, and the quality of her or his spoken language. There are a number of tests commercially available that can specifically diagnose SLI. Some of the tests use interactions between the child and puppets and other toys to focus on specific rules of grammar, especially the misuse of verb tenses. These tests can be used with children between three and eight years of age and are especially useful for identifying children with SLI once they enter school.

What Treatments Are Available for Specific Language Impairment?

Because SLI affects reading, it also affects learning. If it is not treated early, it can affect a child's performance in school. Since the early signs of SLI are often present in children as young as three years of age, the preschool years can be used to prepare them for kindergarten with special programs designed to enrich language development.

This kind of classroom program might enlist normally developing children to act as role models for children with SLI and feature activities that encourage role-playing and sharing time, as well as hands-on lessons to explore new, interesting vocabulary. Some parents also might want their child to see a speech-language pathologist, who can assess their child's needs, engage her or him in structured activities, and recommend home materials for at-home enrichment.

What Kinds of Research Are Being Conducted?

The National Institute on Deafness and Other Communication Disorders (NIDCD) supports a wide variety of research to understand the genetic underpinnings of SLI, the nature of the language deficits that cause it, and better ways to diagnose and treat children with it.

- **Genetic research.** An NIDCD-supported investigator has recently identified a common variant in a gene on chromosome 6, called the "KIAA0319 gene," that appears to play a key role in SLI. The genetic variant plays a supporting role in other learning disabilities, such as dyslexia, some cases of autism, and speech sound disorders (conditions in which speech sounds are either not produced or produced or used incorrectly). This finding lends support to the idea that difficulties in learning language may be coming from the same genes that influence difficulties with reading and understanding printed text. Other potentially influential genes also are being explored.

- **Bilingual research**. The standardized tests that speech-language pathologists use in schools to screen for language impairments are based on typical language development milestones in English. Because bilingual children are more likely to score in the at-risk range on these tests, it becomes difficult to distinguish between children who are struggling to learn a new language and children with true language impairments. After studying a large group of Hispanic children who speak English as a second language, NIDCD-funded researchers have developed a dual language diagnostic test to identify bilingual children with language impairments. It is now being tested in a group of children between four and six years of age, and will eventually be expanded to children between seven and nine years of age. The same research team is also trying out an intervention program with a small group of bilingual first graders with SLI to find techniques and strategies to help them succeed academically.

- **Diagnostic research.** Children with SLI have significant communication problems, which are also characteristic of most children with autism spectrum disorders (ASD). Impairments in understanding and the onset of spoken language are common in both groups. No one knows yet if there are early developmental signs that could signal or predict language difficulties and might potentially allow for early identification and intervention with these children. The NIDCD is currently funding researchers looking for risk markers associated with SLI and ASD that could signal later problems in speech and communication. In a group of children between six months to one year of age who, because of family history, are at risk for SLI or ASD, the investigators are collecting data using behavioral, eye-tracking, and neurophysiological measures, as well as general measures of cognitive and brain development. They will then follow these children until they are three years of age to see if there are indicators that are specific to SLI or ASD or that could predict the development of either disorder.

Chapter 26

Tourette Syndrome

Chapter Contents

Section 26.1

About Tourette Syndrome

This section includes text excerpted from "What Is
Tourette Syndrome?" Centers for Disease Control and
Prevention (CDC), April 13, 2018.

Tourette syndrome (TS) is a condition of the nervous system. TS
causes people to have "tics."

Tics are sudden twitches, movements, or sounds that people do
repeatedly. People who have tics cannot stop their body from doing
these things. For example, a person might keep blinking over and over
again, or a person might make a grunting sound unwillingly.

Having tics is a little bit like having hiccups. Even though you
might not want to hiccup, your body does it anyway. Sometimes people
can stop themselves from doing a certain tic for a while, but it is hard.
Eventually, the person has to do the tic.

Types of Tics

There are two types of tics—motor and vocal.

Motor Tics

Motor tics are movements of the body. Examples of motor tics
include blinking, shrugging the shoulders, or jerking an arm.

Vocal Tics

Vocal tics are sounds that a person makes with her or his voice.
Examples of vocal tics include humming, clearing the throat, or yelling
out a word or phrase.

Tics can be either simple or complex:

Simple Tics

Simple tics involve just a few parts of the body. Examples of simple
tics include squinting the eyes or sniffing.

Complex Tics

Complex tics usually involve several different parts of the body and
can have a pattern. An example of a complex tic is bobbing the head
while jerking an arm and then jumping up.

Symptoms of Tourette Syndrome

The main symptoms of TS are tics. Symptoms usually begin when a child is between 5 and 10 years of age. The first symptoms often are motor tics that occur in the head and neck area. Tics usually are worse during times that are stressful or exciting. They tend to improve when a person is calm or focused on an activity.

The types of tics and how often a person has tics changes a lot over time. Even though the symptoms might appear, disappear, and reappear, these conditions are considered chronic.

In most cases, tics decrease during adolescence and early adulthood and sometimes disappear entirely. However, many people with TS experience tics into adulthood, and, in some cases, tics can become worse during adulthood.

Although the media often portrays people with TS as involuntarily shouting out swear words (called "coprolalia") or constantly repeating the words of other people (called "echolalia"), these symptoms are rare and are not required for a diagnosis of TS.

Diagnosis of Tourette Syndrome

There is no single test, such as a blood test, to diagnose TS. Health professionals look at the person's symptoms to diagnose TS and other tic disorders. The tic disorders differ from each other in terms of the type of tic present (motor, vocal, or combination of them both), and how long the symptoms have lasted. TS can be diagnosed if a person has both motor and vocal tics and has had tic symptoms for at least a year.

Treatments of Tourette Syndrome

Although there is no cure for TS, there are treatments available to help manage the tics. Many people with TS have tics that do not get in the way of their daily life and, therefore, do not need any treatment. However, medication and behavioral treatments are available if tics cause pain or injury; interfere with school, work, or social life; or cause stress.

Risk Factors and Causes of Tourette Syndrome

Doctors and scientists do not know the exact cause of TS. Research suggests that it is an inherited genetic condition. That means it is passed on from parent to child through genes.

Who Is Affected with Tourette Syndrome?

In the United States, 1 of every 360 children between 6 and 17 years of age has been diagnosed with TS. Other studies that also included children with undiagnosed TS have estimated that 1 of every 162 children has TS. This suggests that about half of children with TS are not diagnosed.

TS can affect people of all racial and ethnic groups. Boys are affected three to five times more often than girls.

Section 26.2

Other Concerns and Conditions of Tourette Syndrome

This section includes text excerpted from "Other Concerns and Conditions of Tourette Syndrome" Centers for Disease Control and Prevention (CDC), April 13, 2018.

Tourette syndrome (TS) often occurs with other related conditions (also called "co-occurring conditions"). These conditions can include attention deficit hyperactivity disorder (ADHD), obsessive-compulsive disorder (OCD), and other behavioral or conduct problems. People with TS and related conditions can be at higher risk for learning, behavioral, and social problems.

The symptoms of other disorders can complicate the diagnosis and treatment of TS and create extra challenges for people with TS and their families, educators, and health professionals.

Findings from Center for Disease Control and Prevention (CDC) study indicated that 86 percent of children who had been diagnosed with TS also had been diagnosed with at least one additional mental-health, behavioral, or developmental condition based on parent report.

Among children with TS:

- 63 percent had ADHD

- 26 percent had behavioral problems, such as oppositional defiant disorder (ODD) or conduct disorder (CD)

- 49 percent had anxiety problems

- 25 percent had depression

- 35 percent had an autism spectrum disorder (ASD)

- 47 percent had a learning disability

- 29 percent had a speech or language problem

- 30 percent had a developmental delay

- 12 percent had an intellectual disability

Because co-occurring conditions are so common among people with TS, it is important for doctors to assess every child with TS for other conditions and problems.

Attention Deficit Hyperactivity Disorder

ADHD was the most common co-occurring condition among children with TS.

Children with ADHD have trouble paying attention and controlling impulsive behaviors. They might act without thinking about what the result will be, and in some cases, they are also overly active. It is normal for children to have trouble focusing and behaving at one time or another. However, for children with ADHD, symptoms can continue, can be severe, and cause difficulty at school, at home, or with friends.

Educational Concerns

As a group, people with TS have levels of intelligence similar to those of people without TS. However, people with TS might be more likely to have learning differences, a learning disability, or a developmental delay that affects their ability to learn.

Many people with TS have problems with writing, organizing, and paying attention. People with TS might have problems processing what they hear or see. This can affect a person's ability to learn by listening to or watching a teacher. Or, the person might have problems with their other senses (such as how things feel, smell, taste, and movement) that affects learning and behavior. Children with TS might have trouble with social skills that affect their ability to interact with others.

As a result of these challenges, children with TS might need extra help in school. Many times, these concerns can be addressed with accommodations and behavioral interventions (for example, help with social skills).

Accommodations can include things such as providing a different testing location or extra testing time, providing tips on how to be more organized, giving the child less homework, or letting the child use a computer to take notes in class. Children also might need behavioral interventions, therapy, or they may need to learn strategies to help with stress, paying attention, or other symptoms.

Section 26.3

Tourette Syndrome, Other Conditions, and School Measures

This section includes text excerpted from "Key Findings: Tourette Syndrome, Other Conditions, and School Measures" Centers for Disease Control and Prevention (CDC), May 23, 2018.

The Journal of Developmental and Behavioral Pediatrics has published findings about how having Tourette syndrome (TS) and other conditions affect how children do in school, such as repeating a grade, school problems, or needing special services. The other conditions included mental, behavioral, or emotional disorders, as well as learning and language disorders.

Researchers from the Centers for Disease Control and Prevention (CDC) and the Tourette Association of America used parent-reported data from national studies in 2007 and 2011 and found that having another condition was a major concern for children with Tourette's. Having other conditions along with Tourette's was related to having difficulty in school and needing educational services. Children with severe Tourette's symptoms were also more likely to experience these problems compared to children with milder symptoms. Children with Tourette's were more likely to receive special education services than those without Tourette's.

This is important information for healthcare providers, teachers, and parents. Being aware of the potential challenges related to both TS and other conditions can help them to best support the child's education.

Main Findings

- Most children with TS had other mental, behavioral, or emotional disorders or learning and language disorders.

- Compared to children without Tourette's, children with Tourette's were more likely to:

  - Have an individualized education program (IEP)

  - Have a parent contacted about school problems

  - Not complete homework

- Once the presence of other disorders was taken into account, children with Tourette's were still more likely to have an IEP, compared to children without Tourette's.

About This Study

Data on children between the ages of 6 and 17 were pooled from the 2007 and 2011 to 12 National Survey of Children's Health (NSCH), a nationally representative telephone-based survey of parents in the United States.

Parents reported on their child's conditions:

- Whether a healthcare provider had told them their child currently has Tourette syndrome

- How severe it was

- Mental, emotional, and behavioral conditions:

  - Attention deficit hyperactivity disorder (ADHD)

  - Behavior or conduct problems

  - Depression

  - Anxiety

- Learning and language conditions:

  - Developmental delay

  - Speech and language problems

  - Learning disability

  - Autism spectrum disorder (ASD)

  - Intellectual disability

Parents reported on the following school measures:

- Type of school attended (public, private, home)
- Number of school days missed for illness or injury
- The number of times parents were contacted about school problems
- Whether the child cared about doing well in school
- Whether the child does all required homework
- Whether the child had repeated a grade
- Whether the child had an individualized education program

Chapter 27

Traumatic Brain Injury

What Is Traumatic Brain Injury?

A traumatic brain injury (TBI) is an injury to the brain caused by the head being hit by something or shaken violently. This injury can change how the person acts, moves, and thinks. A TBI can also change how a student learns and acts in school. The term "TBI" is used for head injuries that can cause changes in one or more areas, such as:

- Thinking and reasoning
- Understanding words
- Remembering things
- Paying attention
- Solving problems
- Thinking abstractly
- Talking
- Behaving
- Walking and other physical activities
- Seeing and/or hearing

This chapter includes text excerpted from "Traumatic Brain Injury," Center for Parent Information and Resources (CPIR), U.S. Department of Education (ED), June 16, 2015. Reviewed April 2019.

- Learning

The term "TBI" is not used for a person who is born with a brain injury. It also is not used for brain injuries that happen during birth.

How Is Traumatic Brain Injury Defined?

The definition of "TBI" below comes from the Individuals with Disabilities Education Act (IDEA). The IDEA is the federal law that guides how schools provide special education and related services to children and youth with disabilities.

Individuals with Disabilities Education Act's Definition of "Traumatic Brain Injury"

Our nation's special education law, the IDEA defines "TBI" as "an acquired injury to the brain caused by an external physical force, resulting in total or partial functional disability or psychosocial impairment, or both, that adversely affects a child's educational performance. The term applies to open or closed head injuries resulting in impairments in one or more areas, such as cognition; language; memory; attention; reasoning; abstract thinking; judgment; problem-solving; sensory, perceptual, and motor abilities; psycho-social behavior; physical functions; information processing; and speech. The term does not apply to brain injuries that are congenital or degenerative, or to brain injuries induced by birth trauma."

How Common Is Traumatic Brain Injury?

Approximately 1.7 million people receive TBIs every year. Of children between birth and 19 years of age, TBI results in 631,146 trips to the emergency room annually, 35,994 hospitalizations, and nearly 6,169 deaths.

What Are the Signs of Traumatic Brain Injury?

The signs of brain injury can be very different depending on where the brain is injured and how severely. Children with TBI may have one or more difficulties, including:

- **Physical disabilities.** Individuals with TBI may have problems speaking, seeing, hearing, and using their other senses. They may have headaches and feel tired a lot. They may also have trouble with skills, such as writing or drawing. Their muscles may suddenly contract or tighten (this is called "spasticity"). They may also have seizures. Their balance and walking may also be affected. They may be partly or completely paralyzed on one side of the body or both sides.

- **Difficulties with thinking.** Because the brain has been injured, it is common that the person's ability to use the brain changes. For example, children with TBI may have trouble with short-term memory (being able to remember something from one minute to the next, such as what the teacher just said). They may also have trouble with their long-term memory. People with TBI may have trouble concentrating and only be able to focus their attention for a short time. They may think slowly. They may have trouble talking and listening to others. They may also have difficulty with reading and writing, planning, understanding the order in which events happen (called "sequencing"), and judgment.

- **Social, behavioral, or emotional problems.** These difficulties may include sudden changes in mood, anxiety, and depression. Children with TBI may have trouble relating to others. They may be restless and may laugh or cry a lot. They may not have much motivation or much control over their emotions.

A child with TBI may not have all of the above difficulties. Brain injuries can range from mild to severe, and so can the changes that result from the injury. This means that it is hard to predict how an individual will recover from the injury. Early and ongoing help can make a big difference in how the child recovers. This help can include physical or occupational therapy, counseling, and special education.

It is also important to know that, as the child grows and develops, parents and teachers may notice new problems. This is because, as students grow, they are expected to use their brain in new and different ways. The damage to the brain from the earlier injury can make it hard for the student to learn new skills that come with getting older. Sometimes, parents and educators may not even realize that the student's difficulty comes from the earlier injury.

Is There Help Available?

Yes, there is a lot of help available, beginning with the free evaluation of the child. The nation's special education law, IDEA, requires that all children suspected of having a disability be evaluated without cost to their parents to determine if they do have a disability and, because of the disability, need special services under the IDEA. Those special services are:

- **Early intervention (EI).** A system of services to support infants and toddlers with disabilities (before their third birthday) and their families.

- **Special education and related services.** Services available through the public-school system for school-aged children, including preschoolers (between 3 and 21 years of age).

  - **To access early intervention.** To identify the early intervention program (EIP) in your neighborhood, ask your child's pediatrician for a referral. You can also call the local hospital's maternity ward or pediatric ward, and ask for the contact information of the local early intervention program. There, you can have your child evaluated free of charge, and, if found eligible, your child can begin receiving early intervention services.

  - **To access special education and related services.** It is recommended that you get in touch with your local public-school system. Calling the elementary school in your neighborhood is an excellent place to start. The school should be able to tell you the next steps to having your child evaluated, free of charge. If found eligible, she or he can begin receiving services specially designed to address your child's needs.

In the fall of 2011, nearly 26,000 school-aged children (between the ages of 3 and 21) received special education and related services in our public schools under the category of "traumatic brain injury."

What about School

Although TBI is very common, many medical and education professionals may not realize that some difficulties can be caused by a childhood brain injury. Often, students with TBI are thought to have a learning disability, emotional disturbance, or an intellectual disability. As a result, they do not receive the type of educational help and support they really need.

When children with TBI return to school, their educational and emotional needs are often very different than before the injury. Their disability has happened suddenly and traumatically. They can often remember how they were before the brain injury. This can bring on many emotional and social changes. The child's family, friends, and teachers also recall what the child was like before the injury. These other people in the child's life may have trouble changing or adjusting their expectations of the child.

Therefore, it is extremely important to plan carefully for the child's return to school. Parents will want to find out ahead of time about special education services at the school. This information is usually available from the school's principal or special education teacher. The school will need to evaluate the child thoroughly. This evaluation will let the school and parents know what the student's educational needs are. The school and parents will then develop an Individualized Education Program (IEP) that addresses those educational needs.

It is important to remember that the IEP is a flexible plan. It can be changed as the parents, the school, and the student learns more about what the student needs at school.

Tips for Parents

- Learn about TBI. The more you know, the more you can help yourself and your child.

- Work with the medical team to understand your child's injury and treatment plan. Do not be shy about asking questions. Tell them what you know or think. Make suggestions.

- Keep track of your child's treatment. A three-ring binder or a box can help you store this history. As your child recovers, you may meet with many doctors, nurses, and others. Write down what they say. Put any paperwork they give you in the notebook or throw it in the box. You cannot remember all of this. Also, if you need to share any of this paperwork with someone else, make a copy. Do not give away your original.

- Talk to other parents whose children have TBI. There are parent groups all over the United States. Parents can share practical advice and emotional support.

- If your child was in school before the injury, plan for her or his return to school. Get in touch with the school. Ask the principal about special education services. Have the medical team share information with the school.

- When your child returns to school, ask the school to test your child as soon as possible to identify her or his special education needs. Meet with the school and help develop an IEP for your child.

- Keep in touch with your child's teacher. Tell the teacher about how your child is doing at home. Ask how your child is doing in school.

Tips for Teachers

- Find out as much as you can about the child's injury and her or his present needs.

- Give the student more time to finish schoolwork and tests.

- Give directions one step at a time. For tasks with many steps, it helps to give the student written directions.

- Show the student how to perform new tasks. Give examples to go with new ideas and concepts.

- Have consistent routines. This helps the student know what to expect. If the routine is going to change, let the student know ahead of time.

- Check to make sure that the student has actually learned the new skill. Give the student lots of opportunities to practice the new skill.

- Show the student how to use an assignment book and a daily schedule. This helps the student get organized.

- Realize that the student may get tired quickly. Let the student rest as needed. Reduce distractions.

- Keep in touch with the student's parents. Share information about how the student is doing at home and at school.

- Be flexible about expectations. Be patient. Maximize the student's chances for success.

Chapter 28

Visual Impairment

Visual Impairments in Children

Vision is one of our five senses. Being able to see gives us tremendous access to learning about the world around us—people's faces and the subtleties of expression, what different things look like and how big they are, and the physical environments where we live and move, including approaching hazards.

When a child has a visual impairment, it is cause for immediate attention. That is because so much learning typically occurs visually. When vision loss goes undetected, children are delayed in developing a wide range of skills. While they can do virtually all the activities and tasks that sighted children take for granted, children who are visually impaired often need to learn to do them in a different way or using different tools or materials. Central to their learning will be touching, listening, smelling, tasting, moving, and using whatever vision they have. The assistance of parents, family members, friends, caregivers, and educators can be indispensable in that process.

Types of Visual Impairment

Not all visual impairments are the same, although the umbrella term "visual impairment" may be used to generally describe the consequence of an eye condition or disorder.

This chapter includes text excerpted from "Visual Impairment, Including Blindness," Center for Parent Information & Resources (CPIR), U.S. Department of Education (ED), March 31, 2017.

The eye has different parts that work together to create our ability to see. When a part of the eye does not work right or communicate well with the brain, vision is impaired.

Most of us are familiar with visual impairments, such as nearsightedness and farsightedness. Less familiar visual impairments include:

- **Strabismus,** where the eyes look in different directions and do not focus simultaneously on a single point

- **Congenital cataracts,** where the lens of the eye is cloudy

- **Retinopathy of prematurity (ROP),** which may occur in premature babies when the light-sensitive retina has not developed sufficiently before birth

- **Retinitis pigmentosa (RP),** a rare inherited disease that slowly destroys the retina

- **Coloboma,** where a portion of the structure of the eye is missing

- **Optic nerve hypoplasia (ONH),** which is caused by underdeveloped fibers in the optic nerve and which affects depth perception, sensitivity to light, and acuity of vision

- **Cortical visual impairment (CVI),** which is caused by damage to the part of the brain related to vision, not to the eyes themselves

There are also numerous other eye conditions that can cause visual impairment.

Because there are many different causes of visual impairment, the degree of impairment a child experiences can range from mild to severe (up to, and including, blindness). The degree of impairment will depend on:

- The particular eye condition a child has

- What aspect of the visual system is affected (e.g., ability to detect light, shape, or color; ability to see things at a distance, up close, or peripherally)

- How much correction is possible through glasses, contacts, medicine, or surgery

The term "blindness" does not necessarily mean that a child cannot see anything at all. A child who is considered legally blind may very well be able to see light, shapes, colors, and objects (albeit indistinctly).

Having such a residual vision can be a valuable asset for the child in learning, movement, and life.

Signs of a Visual Impairment

It is very important to diagnose and address visual impairment in children as soon as possible. Some vision screening may occur at birth, especially if the baby is born prematurely or there is a family history of vision problems, but baby-wellness visits as early as six months should also include basic vision screening to ensure that a little one's eyes are developing and functioning as might be expected.

That said, common signs that a child may have a visual impairment include the following:

- Eyes that do not move together when following an object or a face

- Crossed eyes, eyes that turn out or in, eyes that flutter from side to side or up and down, or eyes that do not seem to focus

- Eyes that bulge, dance, or bounce in rapid rhythmic movements

- Pupils that are unequal in size or that appear white instead of black

- Repeated shutting or covering of one eye

- Unusual degree of clumsiness, such as frequent bumping into things or knocking things over

- Frequent squinting, blinking, eye-rubbing, or face crunching, especially when there is no bright light present

- Sitting too close to the TV or holding toys and books too close to the face

- Avoiding tasks and activities that require good vision

If any of these symptoms are present, parents will want to have their child's eyes professionally examined. Early detection and treatment are very important to the child's development.

How Common Are Visual Impairments?

Very common, especially as we grow older. However, there are many causes of visual impairments that have nothing to do with the aging process, and children certainly can be—and are—affected. In the United States there are approximately:

- 455,462 children with vision difficulty (the term "vision difficulty" refers only to children who have serious difficulty seeing, even when wearing glasses and those who are blind.)

- 42,000 children with a severe vision impairment (unable to see words and letters in ordinary newsprint)

- 61,739 children in educational settings who are legally blind

Each year states must report to the U.S. Department of Education (ED or DoED) how many children with visual impairments received special education and related services in their schools under the Individuals with Disabilities Education Act (IDEA), the nation's special education law. Data for the 2015–16 school year indicate that the following numbers of children were served in the U.S. and its outlying areas:

- 2,799 children (between the ages of 3 and 5) with visual impairment

- 24,944 children (between the ages of 6 and 21) with visual impairment

Understanding How Children with Visual Impairments Learn

Children with visual impairments can certainly learn and do learn well, but they lack the easy access to visual learning that sighted children have. The enormous amount of learning that takes place via vision must now be achieved using other senses and methods.

Hands are a primary information-gathering tool for children with visual impairments. So are the senses of smell, touch, taste, and hearing. Until the child holds the "thing" to be learned and explores its dimensions—let us say, a stuffed animal, a dog, a salt shaker, or a CD player—she or he cannot grasp its details. That is why sensory learning is so powerful for children with visual impairment and why they need to have as many opportunities as possible to experience objects directly and sensorially.

- Families, friends, and others can support sensorial learning in many ways.

- "Mmmm. Do you smell dinner?" appeals to the child's sense of smell.

- "Listen to that bird singing outside" calls to the child's hearing. You might also say, "That is a robin," which gives the child a name for the bird that sings the song she or he is hearing.

- "Your clothes are so soft today" speaks to the child's sense of touch and helps the child build a picture of the "whole" from the many details.

Being able to see enables us to capture the "whole" of an object immediately. This is not so for children with a visual impairment. They cannot see the "whole;" they have to work from the details up to build an understanding of the whole.

The Help Available under Individuals with Disabilities Education Act

If you suspect (or know) that your child has a visual impairment, you will be pleased to know there is a lot of help available under the IDEA—beginning with a free evaluation of your child. The IDEA requires that all children suspected of having a disability be evaluated without cost to their parents to determine if they do have a disability and, because of the disability, need special services under the IDEA. Those special services are:

- **Early intervention.** A system of services to support infants and toddlers with disabilities (before their third birthday) and their families.

- **Special education and related services:** Services available through the public-school system for school-aged children, including preschoolers (between the ages of 3 and 21).

Visual impairment, including blindness, is one of the disabilities specifically mentioned and defined in IDEA. If a child meets the definition of visual impairment in IDEA, as well as the state's criteria (if any), then she or he is eligible to receive early intervention services or special education and related services under IDEA (depending on her or his age).

To identify the early intervention program in your neighborhood. Ask your child's pediatrician for a referral. You can also call the local hospital's maternity ward or pediatric ward, and ask for the contact information of the local early intervention program.

Accessing special education and related services. If your child is between 3 and 21 years of age, it is recommended that you get in touch with your local public-school system. Calling the public school in your neighborhood is an excellent place to start. The school should be able to tell you the next steps of having your child evaluated, free of charge. If found eligible, your child can begin receiving services specially designed to address her or his educational needs and other needs associated with the disability.

Developing a written plan of services. In both cases—in early intervention for a baby or toddler with a visual impairment and in special education for a school-aged child—parents work together with program professionals to develop a plan of services the child will receive based on her or his needs. In early intervention, that plan is called the "individualized family service plan" (IFSP). In special education, the plan is called the "individualized education program" (IEP). Parents are part of the team that develops their child's IFSP or IEP.

There is a lot to know about early intervention for infants and toddlers with disabilities and about special education and related services for school-aged children.

How Individuals with Disabilities Education Act Defines Visual Impairment

The IDEA provides the nation with definitions of many disabilities that can make children eligible for special education and related services in schools. Visual impairment is one such disability the law defines and is as follows:

Visual impairment, including blindness, means an impairment in vision that, even with correction, adversely affects a child's educational performance. The term includes both partial sight and blindness.

Working with the Medical Community

If you have a child with a visual impairment, you will probably find yourself dealing with a variety of eye care professionals who become involved to diagnose and address your child's specific disability or eye condition. Wondering who these professionals might be, what qualifications they should have, and what kind of expertise they can bring to your child's care?

Family Connect is an excellent source of information. Family Connect is an online, multimedia community created by the American

Foundation for the Blind (AFB) and the National Association for Parents of Children with Visual Impairments (NAPVI).

Adapting the Environment

Making adaptations to the environment where a child with a visual impairment lives, works, or plays makes evident sense, but it may be difficult for families, day care providers, or school personnel to decide what kinds of adaptations are necessary to ensure the child's safety while also encouraging her or his ability to do things independently.

Educational Considerations

Children with visual impairments need to learn the same subjects and academic skills as their sighted peers, although they will probably do so in adapted ways. They must also learn an expanded set of skills that are distinctly vision-related, including learning how to:

- Move about safely and independently, which is known as "orientation and mobility" (O&M)

- Use assistive technologies designed for children with visual impairments

- Use what residual vision they have effectively and efficiently

- Read and write in Braille, if determined appropriate by the IEP team of the child after a thorough evaluation

These are just some of the skills that need to be discussed by the student's IEP team and included in the IEP if the team decides that it is appropriate. Each of the above skill areas—and more—can be addressed under the umbrella of special education and related services for a child with a visual impairment.

Tips for Teachers

Learn as much as you can about the student's specific visual impairment. What aspects of vision are affected, and how does that affect the student's ability to move about the classroom, see the board, or read a textbook? Parents (and the student!) can be an excellent source of this information.

- Learn about the many instructional and classroom accommodations that truly help students with visual impairments learn. Strongly support the student by making sure that needed accommodations are provided for classwork, homework, and testing. These will help the student learn successfully.

- If you are not part of the student's IEP team, ask for a copy of her or his IEP. The student's educational goals will be listed there, as well as the services and classroom accommodations she or he is to receive.

- Consult with others (e.g., special educators, the O&M specialist) who can help you identify strategies for teaching and supporting this student, ways to adapt the curriculum, and how to address the student's IEP goals in your classroom.

- Find out if your state or school district has materials or resources available to help educators address the learning needs of children with visual impairments.

- Communicate with the student's parents. Regularly share information about how the student is doing at school and at home.

Tips for Parents

- Learn as much as you can about your child's specific visual impairment. The more you know, the more you can help yourself and your child.

- Understand that your child is receiving small bits of information at a time, not all at once through vision. Help your child explore new things with her or his senses and build up a concept of the "whole." For example, your child might need to be shown a banana, help you peel it, feel the banana without its skin, have a bite of it, and then help you mash it in her or his bowl to understand the qualities of bananas and that bananas can be eaten in different ways.

- Encourage curiosity, and explore new things and places often with your child. Give lots of opportunities to touch and investigate objects, ask questions, and hear explanations of what something is, where it comes from, and so on.

- Learn how to adapt your home, given the range and degree of your child's visual impairment. Help your son or daughter explore the house and learn to navigate it safely.

- Encourage your child's independence by letting her or him do things, rather than you do them. Teach how to do a chore by using hands-on guidance, give lots of practice opportunities with feedback. Now, your child knows the skill too.

- Work with the early interventionists or school staff (depending on your child's age) to build a solid individualized plan of services and supports that address your child's unique developmental and educational needs.

- Talk to other parents of children who have visual impairments similar to your child's. They can be a great source of support and insight in the challenges and joys of raising a child with vision problems.

- Keep in touch with the professionals working with your child. Offer support. Demonstrate any assistive technology your child uses, and provide any information teachers will need. Find out how you can augment your child's learning at home.

Part Four

Learning Disabilities and the Educational Process

Chapter 29

Decoding Learning Disabilities

Children with learning disabilities can face significant academic and emotional challenges as they struggle to master reading, writing, and doing basic mathematics. Learning disabilities are caused by differences in brain function that affect how a person's brain processes information. They are not an indication of a person's intelligence; people with learning disabilities are just as bright as other people. While learning disabilities are present throughout an individual's life, they may be lessened with the right educational supports.

Learning disabilities are one of the most prevalent disabilities. It is estimated that between 12 and 20 percent of individuals have some type of learning disability. Dyslexia is the most common learning disability.

This chapter aims to understand how children learn to read, write, and do math; why some children heavily struggle to acquire these skills; and what can be done to help them.

This chapter includes text excerpted from "Decoding Learning Disabilities," *Eunice Kennedy Shriver* National Institute of Child Health and Human Development (NICHD), December 30, 2017.

Teaching Children with Learning Disabilities

Research funded by the *Eunice Kennedy Shriver* National Institute of Child Health and Human Development (NICHD) followed students at the end of fifth grade who were more than one year behind in their reading level. They were given explicit, systematic, and direct instruction in reading for one, two, or three years. The children were directly and explicitly taught reading skills—including the rules of phonics—building their skills from the ground up. They also were given plenty of opportunity to practice their reading and to generally enhance their understanding of the text. Children who made good progress within the first year transitioned to less intensive interventions. Those who continued to struggle received a second year of even more intensive intervention with smaller group instruction and more direct and explicit instruction. Those who continued to have difficulty went into a third year of intervention that was even more intensive than the first two years.

It was found that the children who had three years of intensive intervention showed robust growth in reading comprehension and in word-level reading. However, the research could not succeed in reducing the gap between the reading levels of these children and their peers. Their peers also continued to develop their reading skill, and so the gap remained.

What the Research Suggests

This and other studies suggest that children with learning disabilities need direct, explicit, and systematic instruction, whether you are talking about reading or mathematics. These children will likely need more time to build their skills and receive instruction in smaller groups so that they get more focused attention; it can be a small group or it can be one on one, depending upon the needs of the child and how significant their learning challenges are.

The most efficient and effective interventions are for young learners. Intervening at a young age helps reduce the impact the disability has on a student's broader academic development.

When Should These Interventions Begin?

Even before the start of kindergarten, there are certain risk factors that children may face. For instance, if a parent has a learning disability, the child then has an increased risk for having a learning disability.

A child that is going into preschool or kindergarten who has a higher risk of having reading difficulties needs to be monitored to see how they perform and given explicit, direct, and systematic instruction early on. Fortunately, this type of instruction not only benefits those who struggle, but it also benefits those who do not, so it is effective for all kids.

The Science of Learning Disabilities
What Do Brain Imaging Studies Tell Us?

Reading requires coordinated activity that draws on several different parts of the brain.

Brain imaging studies provides a window into understanding reading and reading disabilities. For the kids who develop typically with reading compared to those who do not, it is observed that more focal activation in areas on the left hemisphere of the brain and activation of parts of the left hemisphere relate to improved word reading.

Kids who struggle with reading show more disperse activation in the left hemisphere. But if they successfully respond to a reading intervention, they show a brain activation pattern that looks similar to the patterns of individuals who do not struggle to read. This is a remarkable example of neuroplasticity; that is, you give an intervention in the classroom, and when the intervention is successful, you see changes in the structure and function of the brain.

Are There Genes Associated with Learning Disabilities?

Learning disabilities are complex conditions, and there is no single gene that causes a learning disability or a reading disability. At this point, about nine dyslexia susceptibility genes has been identified. If you have one of these genes, it does not mean that you will have dyslexia; it means that you are at higher risk for having dyslexia. This is one piece of information that could help ascertain who would be at risk for problems.

Are There New Technologies to Help People with Learning Disabilities?

There are a number of resources available for individuals with learning disabilities to help support their learning. For example, there is software that reads a book to you. Recorded books have the benefit of reading that sounds more natural and with appropriate intonation, as opposed to the reading software. But it is not practical to record every book, so reading will still be a necessary skill.

For individuals who have problems with writing, there are tools to help structure sentences and organize paragraphs and longer papers.

Tips for Parents to Help Their Children

If you are a parent of a younger child, you can create a language-rich environment by talking with and reading with your child. This can help your child understand language structure—where to pause, how to allow someone else to talk—and improve her or his vocabulary.

You should read books to your child every day, giving them the story, vocabulary, background; an understanding of how text is structured; how reading flows from left to right; and how the pages are turned. You can ask children questions to encourage them to think about what you have been reading and what is coming next in the story.

For children with a math disability (dyscalculia), you can point out numbers in your environment. When you are going to the grocery store or doing everyday tasks, you can incorporate opportunities to learn about numbers. For example, where you see three apples, you can count them. You are taking advantage of these opportunities to immerse your child in language- and mathematical reasoning–rich environments.

For children in school, create a positive environment where you celebrate successes and work with the challenges. It is important for parents to be role models who read and are engaged in their own lifelong learning. You can show children the calculations or measurements that you are doing, such as showing them how you do the bills or measuring length of objects with a tape measure. You can have writing activities, such as keeping a diary, blog, or other activities, that are engaging and fun for your children.

Chapter 30

Early Intervention Strategies

Chapter Contents

Section 30.1

Early Intervention: An Overview

This section includes text excerpted from "Overview of Early
Intervention," Center for Parent Information & Resources (CPIR),
U.S. Department of Education (ED), September 1, 2017.

If you are concerned about the development of an infant or toddler,
or you suspect that a little one has a disability, this section will sum-
marize one terrific source of help—the early intervention system in
your state. Early intervention (EI) services can help infants and toddlers with disabilities or delays to learn many key skills and catch up
in their development. There is a lot to know about early intervention.
This section presents the "basics" to get you started.

What Is Early Intervention?

Early intervention is a system of services that helps babies and
toddlers with developmental delays or disabilities. Early intervention
focuses on helping eligible babies and toddlers learn the basic and
brand-new skills that typically develop during the first three years
of life, such as:

- Physical (reaching, rolling, crawling, and walking)

- Cognitive (thinking, learning, solving problems)

- Communication (talking, listening, understanding)

- Social/emotional (playing, feeling secure and happy)

- Self-help (eating, dressing)

Examples of Early Intervention Services

If an infant or toddler has a disability or a developmental delay
in one or more of these developmental areas, that child will likely be
eligible for early intervention services. Those services will be tailored
to meet the child's individual needs and may include:

- Assistive technology (devices a child might need)

- Audiology or hearing services

- Speech and language services

- Counseling and training for a family

- Medical services

- Nursing services

- Nutrition services

- Occupational therapy

- Physical therapy

- Psychological services

Services may also be provided to address the needs and priorities of the child's family. Family-directed services are meant to help family members understand the special needs of their child and how to enhance her or his development.

Authorized by Law

Early intervention is available in every state and territory of the United States. The Individuals with Disabilities Education Act (IDEA) requires it—Part C of IDEA, to be precise. That is why you will sometimes hear early intervention referred to as "Part C."

Who Is Eligible for Early Intervention?

Early intervention is intended for infants and toddlers who have a developmental delay or disability. Eligibility is determined by evaluating the child (with parents' consent) to see if the child does, in fact, have a delay in development or a disability. Eligible children can receive early intervention services from birth through the third birthday (and sometimes beyond).

- **For some children, from birth.** Sometimes, it is known from the moment a child is born that early intervention services will be essential in helping the child grow and develop. Often, this is so for children who are diagnosed at birth with a specific condition or who experience significant prematurity, very low birth weight, illness, or surgery soon after being born. Even before heading home from the hospital, this child's parents may be given a referral to their local early intervention office.

- **For others, because of delays in development.** Some children have a relatively routine entry into the world, but may develop more slowly than others, experience setbacks, or develop in ways that seem very different from other children.

For these children, a visit with a developmental pediatrician and a thorough evaluation may lead to an early intervention referral.

Parents do not have to wait for a referral to early intervention, however. If you are concerned about your child's development, you may contact your local program directly and ask to have your child evaluated. That evaluation is provided free of charge. If you are not sure how to locate the early intervention program in your community—keep reading.

However, a child comes to be referred, evaluated, and determined eligible, early intervention services provide vital support so that children with developmental needs can thrive and grow.

What Is a Developmental Delay?

The term "developmental delay" is an important one in early intervention. Broadly speaking, it means that a child is delayed in some areas of development. There are five areas in which development may be affected:

- Cognitive development

- Physical development, including vision and hearing

- Communication development

- Social or emotional development

- Adaptive development

Developmental Milestones

Think of all the baby skills that can fall under any one of those developmental areas. Babies and toddlers have a lot of new skills to learn, so it is always of concern when a child's development seems slow or more difficult than would normally be expected.

Definition of Developmental Delay

Part C of the IDEA broadly defines the term "developmental delay." But, the exact meaning of the term varies from state to state because each state defines the term for itself, including:

- Describing the evaluation and assessment procedures that will be used to measure a child's development in each of the five developmental areas

- Specifying the level of delay in functioning (or other comparable criteria) that constitutes a developmental delay in each of the five developmental areas

If You Are Concerned about a Baby or Toddler's Development

It is not uncommon for parents and family members to become concerned when their growing baby or toddler does not seem to be developing according to the normal schedule of "baby" milestones.

"He has not rolled over yet."

"The little girl next door is already sitting up on her own!"

"She should be saying a few words by now."

Sound familiar? While it is true that children develop differently, at their own pace, and that the range of what is "normal" development is quite broad, it is hard not to worry and wonder.

What to Do

If you think that your child is not developing at the same pace or in the same way as most children her or his age, it is often a good idea to talk first to your child's pediatrician. Explain your concerns. Tell the doctor what you have observed with your child. Your child may have a disability or a developmental delay, or she or he may be at risk of having a disability or delay.

You can also get in touch with your community's early intervention program and ask to have your child evaluated to see if she or he has a developmental delay or disability. This evaluation is free of charge, will not hurt your child, and looks at her or his basic skills. Based on that evaluation, your child may be eligible for early intervention services, which will be designed to address your child's special needs or delays.

How to Get in Touch with Your Community's Early Intervention Program

There are several ways to connect with the EI program in your community. Try any of these suggestions:

- Contact the pediatrics branch in a local hospital, and ask where you should call to find out about early intervention services in your area.

- Ask your pediatrician for a referral to the local early intervention system.

- Visit the Early Childhood Technical Assistance (ECTA) Center's early intervention "contacts" page, at (ectacenter.org)

What to Say to the Early Intervention's Contact Person

Explain that you are concerned about your child's development. Say that you think your child may need early intervention services. Explain that you would like to have your child evaluated under Part C of the IDEA.

The Evaluation and Assessment Process
Service Coordinator

Once connected with either Child Find or your community's early intervention program, you will be assigned a service coordinator who will explain the early intervention process and help you through the next steps in that process. The service coordinator will serve as your single point of contact with the early intervention system.

Screening and / or Evaluation

One of the first things that will happen is that your child will be evaluated to see if, indeed, she or he has a developmental delay or disability. (In some states, there may be a preliminary step called "screening" to see if there is cause to suspect that a baby or toddler has a disability or developmental delay.) The family's service coordinator will explain what is involved in the screening and/or evaluation and ask for your permission to proceed. You must provide your written consent before screening and/or evaluation may take place.

The evaluation group will be made up of qualified people who have different areas of training and experience. Together, they know about children's speech and language skills, physical abilities, hearing and vision, and other important areas of development. They know how to work with children, even very young ones, to discover if a child has a problem or is developing within normal ranges. Group members may evaluate your child together or individually. As part of the evaluation, the team will observe your child, ask your child to do things, talk to you and your child, and use other methods to gather information. These procedures will help the team find out how your child functions in the five areas of development.

Exceptions for Diagnosed Physical or Mental Conditions

It is important to note that an evaluation of your child will not be necessary if she or he is automatically eligible due to a diagnosed physical or mental condition that has a high probability of resulting in a developmental delay. Such conditions include, but are not limited to, chromosomal abnormalities; genetic or congenital disorders; sensory impairments; inborn errors of metabolism; disorders reflecting disturbance of the development of the nervous system; congenital infections; severe attachment disorders; and disorders secondary to exposure to toxic substances, including fetal alcohol syndrome (FAS). Many states have policies that further specify what conditions automatically qualify an infant or toddler for early intervention (e.g., Down syndrome (DS), fragile X syndrome).

Determining Eligibility

The results of the evaluation will be used to determine your child's eligibility for early intervention services. You and a team of professionals will meet and review all of the data, results, and reports. The people on the team will talk with you about whether your child meets the criteria under the IDEA and state policy for having a developmental delay, a diagnosed physical or mental condition, or being at risk for having a substantial delay. If so, your child is generally found to be eligible for services.

Initial Assessment of the Child

With parental consent, the in-depth assessment must now be conducted to determine your child's unique needs and the early intervention services appropriate to address those needs. Initial assessment will include reviewing the results of the evaluation, personal observation of your child, and identifying her or his needs in each developmental area.

Initial Assessment of the Family

With the approval of the family members involved, assessments of family members are also conducted to identify the resources, concerns, and priorities of the family related to enhancing the development of your child. The family-directed assessment is voluntary on the part of each family member participating in the assessment and is based on information gathered through an assessment tool and an interview with the family members who elect to participate.

Who Pays for All This

Under the IDEA, evaluations and assessments are provided at no cost to parents. They are funded by state and federal monies.

Writing the Individualized Family Service Plan

Having collected a great deal of information about your child and family, it is now possible for the team (including you as parents) to sit down and write an individualized plan of action for your child and family. This plan is called the "Individualized Family Service Plan," or IFSP. It is a very important document, and you are important members of the team that develops it. Each state has specific guidelines for the IFSP. Your service coordinator can explain what the IFSP guidelines are in your state.

Guiding Principles

The IFSP is a written document that, among other things, outlines the early intervention services that your child and family will receive. One guiding principle of the IFSP is that the family is a child's greatest resource, that a young child's needs are closely tied to the needs of her or his family. The best way to support children and meet their needs is to support and build upon the individual strengths of their family. So, the IFSP is a whole family plan with the parents as major contributors in its development. Involvement of other team members will depend on what the child needs. These other team members could come from several agencies and may include medical personnel, therapists, child-development specialists, social workers, and others.

What Info Is Included in an Individualized Family Service Plan

Your child's IFSP must include the following:

- Your child's present physical, cognitive, communication, social/ emotional, and adaptive development levels and needs

- Family information (with your agreement), including the resources, priorities, and concerns of you, as parents, and other family members closely involved with the child

- The major results or outcomes expected to be achieved for your child and family

- The specific services your child will be receiving

- Where in the natural environment (e.g., home, community) the services will be provided (if the services will not be provided in the natural environment, the IFSP must include a statement justifying why not)

- When and where your son or daughter will receive services

- The number of days or sessions she or he will receive each service and how long each session will last

- Who will pay for the services

- The name of the service coordinator overseeing the implementation of the IFSP

- The steps to be taken to support your child's transition out of early intervention and into another program when the time comes.

- The IFSP may also identify services your family may be interested in, such as financial information or information about raising a child with a disability.

Informed Parental Consent

The IFSP must be fully explained to you, the parents, and your suggestions must be considered. You must give written consent for each service to be provided. If you do not give your consent in writing, your child will not receive that service.

Reviewing and Updating the Individualized Family Service Plan

The IFSP is reviewed every six months and is updated at least once a year. This takes into account that children can learn, grow, and change quickly in just a short period of time.

Timeframes for All This

When the early intervention system receives a referral about a child with a suspected disability or developmental delay, a time clock starts running. Within 45 days, the early intervention system must complete the critical steps discussed thus far:

- Screening (if used in the state)
- Initial evaluation of the child
- Initial assessments of the child and family
- Writing the IFSP (if the child has been found eligible)

That is a tall order, but important, given how quickly children grow and change. When a baby or toddler has developmental issues, they need to be addressed as soon as possible. So, 45 days is the timeframe from referral to completion of the IFSP for an eligible child.

Who Pays for the Services

Whether or not you, as parents, will have to pay for any services for your child depends on the policies of your state. Check with your service coordinator. Your state's system of payments must be available in writing and given to you, so there are no surprises or unexpected bills later.

What Is Free to Families?

Under Part C of the IDEA, the following services must be provided at no cost to families:

- Child Find services
- Evaluations and assessments
- The development and review of the IFSP
- Service coordination

When Services Are Not Free

Depending on your state's policies, you may have to pay for certain other services. You may be charged a "sliding-scale" fee, meaning the fees are based on what you earn. Some services may be covered by your health insurance, by Medicaid, or by Indian Health Services (IHS). The Part C system may ask for your permission to access your public or private insurance in order to pay for the early intervention services your child receives. In most cases, the early intervention system may not use your healthcare insurance (private or public) without your expressed, written consent. If you do not give such consent, the system may not limit or deny you or your child services.

Every effort is made to provide services to all infants and toddlers who need help, regardless of family income. Services cannot be denied to a child just because her or his family is not able to pay for them.

Section 30.2

Parent Notification and Consent in Early Intervention

This section includes text excerpted from "Parent Notification and Consent in Early Intervention," Center for Parent Information and Resources (CPIR), U.S. Department of Education (ED), November 3, 2017.

Parents are essential partners in early intervention. They have the right to be deeply involved at every step along the way, from evaluation of their child, to the writing of the individualized family service plan (IFSP), to helping to determine the early intervention services their child receives. Not surprisingly, Part C of the Individuals with Disabilities Education Act (IDEA) includes specific provisions to support the informed involvement of parents in their child's early intervention program. Two notable requirements are:

- **Prior written notice**, which the early intervention system must provide to parents at key points in time

- **Parental consent**, which must be obtained from parents, also at key points in time

The right to be informed and the right to give or refuse consent for pivotal activities are important procedural safeguards for parents, and it recognizes their authority and responsibility in making decisions about both their child's involvement in early intervention and the family's.

315

Prior Written Notice: Parents' Right to Be Fully Informed

Prior written notice refers to the notification that must be provided to parents a reasonable time before the lead agency or an early intervention services (EIS) provider proposes (or refuses) to "initiate or change the identification, evaluation, or placement of their infant or toddler, or the provision of early intervention services to the infant or toddler with a disability" and his or her family.

Purpose of Prior Written Notice

The purpose of prior written notice is always the same—to ensure that parents are fully informed regarding whatever action the lead agency or EIS provider is proposing to take (or not take) with their infant or toddler or with the family. Parental consent is often needed before the lead agency or EIS provider may proceed, and that consent must be informed. Even if parental consent is not required, parents still have the right to know when something about their child's (or family's) involvement in early intervention is being proposed, refused, about to start, or about to change.

Content of the Notice

The notice must be in sufficient detail to inform parents about:

- The action that is being proposed or refused

- The reasons for taking (or refusing to take) the action

- All procedural safeguards that are available to parents, should they disagree with the early intervention system (e.g., mediation, filing a state complaint or a due process complaint, relevant timelines)

Prior written notice to parents is required in circumstances such as the following:

- The early intervention system wants to evaluate their infant or toddler and is seeking parental consent for the evaluation.

- The early intervention system refuses to evaluate an infant or toddler when parents have requested an evaluation.

- The early intervention system intends to change the child's identification as an eligible "infant or toddler with a disability."

- The early intervention system wants to begin providing early intervention services to the infant or toddler and family.

- A service provider wants to change the services being provided to an infant or toddler with a disability.

Native Language

To ensure that a parent can understand the notice, it must be written in a language understandable to the general public and provided in the parent's native language (or other mode of communication), unless it is clearly not feasible to do so. If the parent's language is not a written one, the lead agency or EIS provider must ensure that:

- The prior written notice is translated orally to the parent

- The parent understands the notice

- There is written evidence that these requirements have been met

Parental Consent

Consent within the IDEA has a very specific meaning that is closely tied to prior written notice. Consent, in the IDEA, means informed written consent. The notice that is provided to parents informs them by completely describing a proposed or refused action and the reasons for it. This builds the foundation of understanding upon which informed consent may then be given (or not). The term "consent" is defined in the Part C regulations as follows:

§303.7. Consent. Consent means that:

a) The parent has been fully informed of all information relevant to the activity for which consent is sought, in the parent's native language, as defined in §303.25

b) The parent understands and agrees in writing to the carrying out of the activity for which the parent's consent is sought, and the consent form describes that activity and lists the early intervention records (if any) that will be released and to whom they will be released

C) i. The parent understands that the granting of consent is voluntary on the part of the parent and may be revoked at any time.

ii. If a parent revokes consent, that revocation is not retroactive (i.e., it does not apply to an action that occurred before the consent was revoked)

This definition makes it clear that:

- The early intervention system must use the parents' native language (or other mode of communication) when seeking their consent for an activity.

- Consent must be given by parents in writing.

- There is a consent form and it describes the activity for which consent is sought.

- The consent form also lists the early intervention records that will be released (if any) and to whom.

- Giving consent is voluntary on the part of parents.

- Parents may revoke their consent at any time.

Consent during Evaluation Process

It will come as no surprise that both prior written notice and parental consent are required repeatedly throughout the evaluation process. These times are:

- Before administering screening procedures to see if an infant or toddler is suspected of having a disability

- Before conducting evaluation of the infant or toddler to determine eligibility for Part C

- Before conducting all assessments of the infant or toddler

Consent before Services Are Provided

Parental consent is also required before the early intervention services listed in the child's IFSP may be provided. In order to ensure that parents understand what they are being asked to consent to, the Part C regulations require that the contents of the IFSP be fully explained to the parents. The Part C regulations also make it clear that parents have the right to give or refuse consent for each service (one by one) and to revoke consent at any time for any service. Those regulations read:

d. The parents of an infant or toddler with a disability:

   i. Determine whether they, their infant or toddler with a disability, or other family members will accept or decline any early intervention service under this part at any time, in accordance with state law

ii. May decline a service after first accepting it, without jeopardizing other early intervention services under this part. Each early intervention service must be provided as soon as possible after the parent provides consent for that service.

Other Times When Consent Is Required

There are other times when parental consent may be required, but these depend on state policy. Two are mentioned in §303.420

a) And stipulate that parental consent must be obtained before the lead agency:

i. May use the family's public benefits or insurance or private insurance, if such consent is required under §303.520

ii. Discloses personally identifiable information

May the Lead Agency Challenge or Try to Override a Parent's Refusal to Give Consent?

No. The lead agency may not challenge a parent's refusal to provide consent, not even through using the due process procedures that Part C and Part B provide for resolving disputes.

Section 30.3

Writing the Individualized Family Service Plan for Your Child

This section includes text excerpted from "Writing the IFSP for Your Child," Center for Parent Information & Resources (CPIR), U.S. Department of Education (ED), September 8, 2017.

After your young child's evaluation is complete and she or he is found eligible for early intervention services, you, as parents, and a team will meet to develop a written plan for providing early intervention services to your child and, as necessary, to your family. This plan is called the "Individualized Family Service Plan," or "IFSP."

The IFSP is a very important document, and parents are important members of the team that develops it. This section focuses on the IFSP–both the process of writing it and what type of information it will contain.

What Is an Individualized Family Service Plan?

The IFSP is a written document that, among other things, outlines the early intervention services that your child and family will receive.

One guiding principle of the IFSP is that the family is a child's greatest resource, meaning that a young child's needs are closely tied to the needs of his or her family. The best way to support children and meet their needs is to support and build upon the individual strengths of their family. So, the IFSP is a whole family plan with the parents as major contributors in its development. Involvement of other team members will depend on what the child needs. These other team members could come from several agencies and may include medical personnel, therapists, child development specialists, social workers, and others.

Each state has specific guidelines for the IFSP. Your service coordinator can explain what the IFSP guidelines are in your state.

What Is Included in the Individualized Family Service Plan?

Your child's IFSP must include the following:

- Your child's present levels of functioning and need in the areas of his or her physical, cognitive, communication, social/emotional, and adaptive development

- Family information (with your agreement), including the resources, priorities, and your concerns, as parents, and other family members closely involved with the child

- The major results or outcomes expected to be achieved for your child and family

- The specific early intervention services your child will be receiving

- Where in the natural environment (e.g., home, community) the services will be provided (if the services will not be provided in the natural environment, the IFSP must include a statement justifying why not)

- When and where your daughter or son will receive services

- The number of days or sessions she or he will receive each service and how long each session will last

- Who will pay for the service

- The name of the service coordinator overseeing the implementation of the IFSP

- The steps to be taken to support your child's transition out of early intervention and into another program when the time comes.

The IFSP may also identify services your family may be interested in, such as financial information or information about raising a child with a disability.

The IFSP must be fully explained to you, the parents, and your suggestions must be considered. You must give written consent before services can start. If you do not give your consent in writing, your child will not receive services.

Who Develops the Individualized Family Service Plan

The meeting to develop the child's first IFSP (and each annual meeting thereafter to review the IFSP) must include the following participants:

- The parent or parents of the child

- Other family members, as requested by the parent, if feasible to do so

- An advocate or person outside of the family, if the parent requests that the person participate

- The service coordinator designated by the system to be responsible for implementing the IFSP

- A person or persons directly involved in conducting the evaluations and assessments of the child and family

- Persons who will be providing early intervention services under this part to the child or family (as appropriate)

What Happens Next

With your written consent, the IFSP is then implemented, meaning that the services described in the IFSP are provided to your child in the manner described in the IFSP. In other words, all that information you included in the IFSP now serves as a roadmap for the early intervention system as it provides services to your child and family.

You, as parents, have the right to decline any early intervention service without jeopardizing your child's eligibility for other early intervention services. Parents may also revoke their consent for one or more services at any time.

The IFSP is reviewed every six months and is updated at least once a year. Parents are a part of that review and revision process. Together, you and the team will look at your child's progress and decide how (or if) the IFSP needs to be changed to reflect your child's growth toward the goals you have set, the family's current situation, and so on.

Resources of Additional Info on the Individualized Family Service Plan

The Individualized Family Service Plan (IFSP) is the cornerstone of family involvement and early intervention services provided to infants and toddlers with disabilities. Find out the basics and more about the IFSP below.

IFSPweb. This online self-paced tutorial is designed to help families and professionals develop better IFSPs for young children with disabilities. It is specifically for Nebraska families and professionals, but we all can learn here, too. See ifspweb.org.

The ECTA Center. The ECTA Center is the Early Childhood Technical Assistance Center. The ECTA offers lots of information about early intervention, including info on the IFSP. Definitely visit the ECTA's Resources for Writing Good IFSP Outcomes. See all ECTA offers at ectacenter.org.

IFSPs in your state. It is amazing how many states have online modules and explanations for parents and professionals with respect to the state's approach to IFSPs and service delivery. Your state's agency responsible for early intervention can prove to be a valuable resource. Connect with your state's early intervention website through the ECTA Center's list at ectacenter.org.

Your state's parent center. Every state has at least one parent center funded to provide information and guidance to families of children with disabilities. Visit your parent center's website or call to find out what IFSP trainings they offer in your area and about the entire early intervention process. They will know your state's policies too and are an excellent resource for families to consult. Find your parent center at www.parentcenterhub.org.

Section 30.4

Providing Early Intervention Services in Natural Environments

This section includes text excerpted from "Providing Early Intervention Services in Natural Environments," Center for Parent Information & Resources (CPIR), U.S. Department of Education (ED), September 3, 2017.

Early intervention (EI) services are to be provided in natural environments to the maximum extent appropriate for the child and for the EI service itself. So, what is considered a natural environment? What is not?

Individuals with Disabilities Education Act Definition of "Natural Environment"

Part C of the Individuals with Disabilities Education Act (IDEA) requires that eligible infants and toddlers with disabilities receive needed early intervention services in natural environments to the maximum extent appropriate. The 2011 regulations for Part C define the term as follows:

§303.26 Natural environments. Natural environment means settings that are natural or typical for a same-aged infant or toddler without a disability, may include the home or community settings, and must be consistent with the provisions of §303.126.

That is a straightforward, easily understood definition—with the exception of how it ends ("must be consistent with the provisions of §303.126"). What might the provisions of §303.126 require? The provisions are as follows:

§303.126 Early intervention services in natural environments. Each system must include policies and procedures to ensure, consistent with §§303.13(a)(8) (early intervention services), 303.26 (natural environments), and 303.344(d)(1)(ii) (content of an IFSP), that early intervention services for infants and toddlers with disabilities are provided—

a) To the maximum extent appropriate, in natural environments

b) In settings other than the natural environment that are most appropriate, as determined by the parent and the IFSP team, only when early intervention services cannot be achieved satisfactorily in a natural environment

Combining these two sets of provisions makes it clear that early intervention services:

- Must be provided in settings that are natural or typical for a same-aged infant or toddler without a disability to the maximum extent appropriate

- May be provided in other settings only when the services cannot be achieved satisfactorily in a natural environment

Who Decides Where Services Will Be Provided

The Part C regulations also make it clear that the IFSP team determines the appropriate setting for providing early intervention services to a child or toddler. The IFSP team may determine that a service will not be provided in a natural environment only "when early intervention services cannot be achieved satisfactorily in a natural environment."

The term "IFSP team" refers broadly to the group of people who write the child's individualized family service plan (IFSP). More specifically, as described in the Part C regulations:

- The child's parents are members of the IFSP team. They may invite other family members to participate on the team as well (if it is feasible to do so). They may also request an advocate or person from outside the family to participate on the team.

- The IFSP team must include two or more individuals from separate disciplines or professions, one of which must be the family's service coordinator.

- The IFSP team must also include a person or persons directly involved in conducting the evaluations and assessments of the child and family.

- As appropriate, people who will be providing early intervention services to the child may also serve on the IFSP team. (§303.343)

This, then, is the group of well-informed individuals that makes the decision as to where early intervention services will be provided to the baby or toddler.

On What Basis Does the Team Decide the Setting?

The short answer: The IFSP team decides where each EI service will be provided based on the measurable results or measurable outcomes expected to be achieved by the child. Those results or outcomes have been identified by the IFSP team and listed in the IFSP.

The longer answer: Again, the Part C regulations provide the necessary guidance. At §303.344(d)(1)(ii)(B), the regulations state:

(B) The determination of the appropriate setting for providing early intervention services to an infant or toddler with a disability, including any justification for not providing a particular early intervention service in the natural environment for that infant or toddler with a disability and service, must be—

1. Made by the IFSP Team (which includes the parent and other team members)

2. Consistent with the provisions in §§303.13(a)(8), 303.26, and 303.126

3. Based on the child's outcomes that are identified by the IFSP Team in paragraph (c) of this section (emphasis added)

An example: The Department of Education (ED) provides an example of how it may not always be practicable or appropriate for an infant or toddler with a disability to receive an early intervention service in the natural environment based either on the nature of the service or the child's specific outcomes. The ED states:

For example, the IFSP team may determine that an eligible child needs to receive speech services in a clinical setting that serves only children with disabilities in order to meet a specific IFSP outcome. When the natural environment is not chosen with regard to an early intervention service, the IFSP Team must provide, in the IFSP, an appropriate justification for that decision. (76 Fed. Reg. at 60205)

What Must Be Included about Natural Environments in the Child's Individualized Family Service Plan?

The Part C regulations indicate that the IFSP must include:

- A statement that each early intervention service is provided in the natural environment for that child or service to the maximum extent appropriate.

Or:

- A justification as to why an early intervention service will not be provided in the natural environment. (§303.344(d)(1)(ii)(A)) If the IFSP team determines that an early intervention service will not be provided in the natural environment, it must document in the IFSP the justification for why not—in other words, "why the alternative service setting is needed for the child to meet the developmental outcomes identified for the child in her or his IFSP" (76 Fed. Reg. at 60205).

Two Points from the Department of Education

When the Department of Education released the 2011 Part C implementing regulations, it included the often-fascinating Analysis of Comments and Changes. The ED's discussion of "natural environments" includes two very interesting and illuminating observations.

Why not include a list of settings considered "natural environments" and those not considered "natural environments?" The ED declined to add a fuller list of settings that may be considered (or would not be considered) "natural environments." The current regulations only mention that natural environments "may include home and community settings."

"It would not be appropriate or practicable to include a list of every setting that may be the natural environment for a particular child or those settings that may not be natural environments in these regulations. In some circumstances, a setting that is natural for one eligible child based on that child's outcomes, family routines, or the nature of the service may not be natural for another child. The decision about whether an environment is the natural environment is an individualized decision made by an infant's or toddler's IFSP team, which includes the parent." (76 Fed. Reg. at 60157–60158)

Are clinics, hospitals, or a service provider's office considered "natural environments?"

Natural environments mean settings that are natural or typical for an infant or toddler without a disability. A clinic, hospital or service provider's office is not a natural environment for an infant or toddler without a disability; therefore, such a setting would not be natural for an infant or toddler with a disability.

However, §303.344(d)(1) requires that the identification of the early intervention service needed, as well as the appropriate setting for providing each service to an infant or toddler with a disability, be individualized decisions made by the IFSP team based on that child's unique needs, family routines, and developmental outcomes. If a determination is made by the IFSP Team that, based on a review of all relevant information regarding the unique needs of the child, the child cannot satisfactorily achieve the identified early intervention outcomes in natural environments, then services could be provided in another environment (e.g., clinic, hospital, service provider's office). In such cases, a justification must be included in the IFSP. (76 Fed. Reg. at 60158)

Section 30.5

Response to Intervention

This section includes text excerpted from "Response to Intervention (RTI)," Center for Parent Information & Resources (CPIR), U.S. Department of Education (ED), August 2012. Reviewed April 2019.

What Is Response to Intervention?

There is no single, absolute definition of response to intervention (RTI). A quick and descriptive summary, though, comes from the National Center on RTI and reads:

> With RTI, schools identify students at risk for poor learning outcomes, monitor student progress, provide evidence-based interventions and adjust the intensity and nature of those interventions depending on a student's responsiveness, and identify students with learning disabilities or other disabilities.

These elements of RTI can be observed readily in almost any RTI implementation. Struggling children are identified through a poor performance on a classwide, schoolwide, or districtwide screening intended to indicate which children may be at risk of academic or behavioral problems. A child may also be identified through other means, such as teacher observation. The school provides the child with research-based interventions while the child is still in the general education environment and closely monitors the student's progress (or response to the interventions) and adjusts their intensity or nature, given the student's progress. RTI can also be instrumental in identifying students who have learning disabilities.

Response to Intervention Typically Has Different Levels of Intensity

Tier 1. At-risk children who have been identified through a screening process receive research-based instruction, sometimes in small groups, sometimes as part of a classwide intervention. A certain amount of time (generally not more than six or eight weeks) is allocated to see if the child responds to the intervention—hence, the name RTI. Each student's progress is monitored closely. If the child does, indeed, respond to the research-based intervention, then this indicates that perhaps her or his difficulties have resulted from less appropriate or insufficiently targeted instruction.

Tier 2. If, however, the child does not respond to the first level of group-oriented interventions, she or he typically moves to the next RTI level. The length of time in Tier 2 is generally a bit longer than in Tier 1, and the level of intensity of the interventions is greater. They may also be more closely targeted to the areas in which the child is having difficulty. Again, child progress is closely monitored. The time allotted to see if the child responds to interventions in this more intensive level may be longer than in the first level—a marking period, for instance, rather than six weeks—but the overall process is much the same. If the child shows adequate progress, then the intervention has been successful, and a "match" has been found as to what type of instruction works with that child. It is quite possible that, if the problem is caught early enough and addressed via appropriate instruction, the child learns the skills necessary to continue in general education without further intervention.

Tier 3. On the other hand, if the child does not respond adequately to the intervention(s) in Tier 2, then a third level becomes an option for continued and yet more intensive intervention. This third level is typically more individualized as well. If the child does not respond to instruction in this level, then she or he is likely to be referred for a full and individual evaluation under the IDEA.

The data gathered on the child's response to interventions in Tiers 1, 2, and 3 become part of the information available during the evaluation process and afterward, when a determination must be made as to disability and the child's possible eligibility for special education and related services. Considering the amount of data typically collected in a RTI approach, thanks to its monitoring of student progress all along the way, the information that will now be available should be very helpful to the team of individuals involved in evaluating the child and determining his or her eligibility for special education services.

At any point in this multileveled process, a child may be referred for evaluation under the IDEA to determine if she or he is a "child with a disability" as the IDEA 2004's regulation defines that term at §300.8. Becoming involved in RTI does not mean that a child has to complete a level, or all levels, of a RTI approach before she or he may be evaluated for eligibility for special education and related services. The IDEA 2004's regulation is very clear about this. RTI may not be used as a means of delaying or refusing to conduct such an evaluation if the school suspects that the child has a disability or if the parents request that the school system evaluate the child

Essential Elements of Response to Interventions

Although there is no specific definition of RTI, essential elements can be found when we take a look at how states, schools, and districts fit RTI into their work. In general, RTI includes:

- Screening children within the general curriculum

- Tiered instruction of increasing intensity

- Evidence-based instruction

- Close monitoring of student progress

- Informed decision-making regarding next steps for individual students

Universal screening means all students are involved in an initial assessment of knowledge and skills. From this universal screening, it is possible to identify which students appear to be struggling or lacking specific knowledge or skills in a given area. Assessment of early reading skills has received particular attention as screening tools have been developed.

Tiered instruction. The tiered instruction was mentioned above, and this is certainly a central concept of RTI. Students identified through the universal screening as "at risk" or "struggling" then move through the general education curriculum with adapted and individualized interventions that increase in intensity (the tiers) for specific students who do not show sufficient learning or skill development. RTI models vary with respect to the number of tiers involved in the process. There is no "official" recommendation as to the most effective number of tiers. Three tiers of instructional intervention is a common practice.

Evidenced-based interventions are a cornerstone of instruction within a RTI process. Within a RTI process, instructional strategies and interventions are based on what research has shown to be effective with students. Using evidence-based practices ensures better results for students—the thinking goes, "it has been proven to work before for other students, therefore, it may likely work with my students as well."

Progress monitoring is very much what it sounds like. It is a constant checking of student progress with whatever evidence-based instruction is being used. Progress monitoring helps pinpoint where each individual student is having difficulties. Speece, writing for the National Center on Child Progress Monitoring (a former Office of

330

Special Education Programs (OSEP)-funded project), summarizes the role of progress monitoring within RTI as follows:

> Progress monitoring is a method of keeping track of children's academic development. Progress monitoring requires frequent data collection (i.e., weekly) with technically adequate measures, interpretation of the data at regular intervals, and changes to instruction based on the interpretation of child progress. The approach requires a different way of thinking about children's learning but is a powerful method of judging responsiveness.

The information gathered through progress monitoring directly informs decision making for individual students. Is the student making progress in this approach? Where? Where not? Is moving to the next tier of RTI appropriate, given that evidence? Does the student need to be referred for special education evaluation?

Informed decision-making for individual students. When used as part of a tiered instructional process, progress monitoring can provide the information by which informed judgments can be made about the student's development. This includes the need to move to the next tier of instructional intensity, or perhaps be referred for a comprehensive and individualized evaluation under the IDEA.

Models of Response to Interventions

Two predominant RTI program models include the problem-solving and the standard protocol.

- The problem-solving model, which evolved out of the school problem-solving team approach, uses individually designed prevention interventions with students who have academic and/or behavioral challenges.

- The standard protocol model uses specific, predetermined, instructional techniques that have been demonstrated to improve student achievement in research studies.

As state and local education agencies have learned about the unique needs of their districts and schools, hybrids of the models have also evolved.

Response to Interventions and Families

Communication with parents and family plays a key role in a RTI process. Certainly, parents need to be informed when their child is not making expected academic or behavioral progress, the very reasons that a public agency might involve a child in a RTI approach. The sticky issue is that RTI is typically used before a child is evaluated under the IDEA, before the public agency is even proposing to evaluate the child, so many of the IDEA's provisions for parent notification have not yet come into play.

What is clear from practice in the field—and, indeed, from the long-time underpinnings of the IDEA—is that informing parents along the way is important, valuable, and good policy. In practice, parents are generally informed when the child is unsuccessful in Tier 1 and moves on to Tier 2. Interventions here are typically more intensive, with the instructional intervention delivered to small groups of children, not the entire class. It is at this point that parents may meet with school staff to discuss their child's lack of progress and hear what the school has in mind. This would include:

- What type of performance data will be collected, and how much

- What general education services are planned

- What strategies the school will use to increase the child's rate of learning

Parents would also be informed that they have the right to request that their child be evaluated under the IDEA—a full and individual evaluation. If they do request such an evaluation, the school must promptly ask for parents' written consent and conduct the evaluation in keeping with the IDEA's time frame requirements (60 days from receiving parental permission, or within the timeframe designated by the state).

Response to Interventions and Specific Learning Disabilities

The role of RTI is to address the needs of children who are not succeeding within the general instructional approach by identifying and implementing research-based interventions that will work with those children. The probability exists that some of those children will have learning disabilities and will not respond in the same way to these interventions as children without learning disabilities. This is where the intersection of RTI and learning disabilities occurs and why RTI is seen as a promising component in identifying learning disabilities.

Learning disability determinations in the past. To date, the "severe discrepancy" model has been the prevailing tool for determining learning disabilities. This is because many children with learning disabilities manifest a "severe discrepancy" between intellectual ability and academic achievement. This approach has been faulted in several areas, including the lack of agreement on how severe a discrepancy has to be in order for a learning disability to be determined. Another genuine concern has been the amount of time needed to establish the "discrepancy "between achievement and ability. A child might literally fail year after year before a disability determination would be made.

Current determinations of learning disabilities. Under the IDEA 2004, states may no longer require the use of a severe discrepancy between intellectual ability and achievement for determining whether a child has a specific learning disability. Additionally, states must allow school systems to include a child's response to scientific, research-based intervention as part of determining whether or not that child has a specific learning disability (SLD). Not responding or making sufficient progress within that intervention is an indication that learning disabilities may lie at the root of the child's academic difficulties.

As a result of these changes in law, RTI has become an important part in many states' criteria for how specific learning disabilities are to be identified.

Chapter 31

Understanding the Special Education Process: An Overview

When a child is having trouble in school, it is important to find out why. The child may have a disability. By law, schools must provide special help to eligible children with disabilities. This help is called "special education and related services."

There is a lot to know about the process by which children are identified as having a disability and in need of special education and related services. This chapter is devoted to helping you learn about that process.

Ten Basic Steps in Special Education
Step 1. Child Is Identified as Possibly Needing Special Education and Related Services

There are two primary ways in which children are identified as possibly needing special education and related services: the system known as Child Find (which operates in each state) and by referral of parent or school personnel.

This chapter includes text excerpted from "10 Basic Steps in Special Education," Center for Parent Information & Resources (CPIR), U.S. Department of Education (ED), April 9, 2017.

- Child Find. Each state is required by the Individuals with Disabilities Education Act (IDEA) to identify, locate, and evaluate all children with disabilities in the state who need special education and related services. To do so, states conduct what are known as "Child Find activities."

- When a child is identified by Child Find as possibly having a disability and as needing special education, parents may be asked for permission to evaluate their child. Parents can also call the Child Find office and ask that their child is evaluated.

- Referral or request for evaluation. A school professional may ask that a child is evaluated to see if she or he has a disability. Parents may also contact the child's teacher or other school professionals to ask that their child is evaluated. This request may be verbal, but it is best to put it in writing.

Parental consent is needed before a child may be evaluated. Under the federal IDEA regulations, evaluation needs to be completed within 60 days after the parent gives consent. However, if a state's IDEA regulations give a different timeline for completion of the evaluation, the state's timeline is applied.

Step 2. Child Is Evaluated

Evaluation is an essential early step in the special education process for a child. It is intended to answer these questions:

- Does the child have a disability that requires the provision of special education and related services?

- What are the child's specific educational needs?

- What special education services and related services, then, are appropriate for addressing those needs?

By law, the initial evaluation of the child must be "full and individual"—which is to say, focused on that child and that child alone. The evaluation must assess the child in all areas related to the child's suspected disability.

The evaluation results will be used to decide the child's eligibility for special education and related services and to make decisions about an appropriate educational program for the child.

If the parents disagree with the evaluation, they have the right to take their child for an Independent Educational Evaluation (IEE). They can ask that the school system pays for this IEE.

Step 3. Eligibility Is Decided

A group of qualified professionals and the parents look at the child's evaluation results. Together, they decide if the child is a "child with a disability," as defined by the IDEA. If the parents do not agree with the eligibility decision, they may ask for a hearing to challenge the decision.

Step 4. Child Is Found Eligible for Services

If the child is found to be a "child with a disability," as defined by the IDEA, she or he is eligible for special education and related services. Within 30 calendar days after a child is determined eligible, a team of school professionals and the parents must meet to write an individualized education program (IEP) for the child.

Step 5. Individualized Education Program Meeting Is Scheduled

The school system schedules and conducts the IEP meeting. School staff must:

- Contact the participants, including the parents
- Notify parents early enough to make sure they have an opportunity to attend
- Schedule the meeting at a time and place agreeable to parents and the school
- Tell the parents the purpose, time, and location of the meeting
- Tell the parents who will be attending
- Tell the parents that they may invite people to the meeting who have knowledge or special expertise about the child

Step 6. Individualized Education Program Meeting Is Held and the Individualized Education Program Is Written

The IEP team gathers to talk about the child's needs and to write the student's IEP. Parents and the student (when appropriate) are full participating members of the team. If the child's placement (meaning, where the child will receive her or his special education and related services) is decided by a different group, the parents must be part of that group as well.

Before the school system may provide special education and related services to the child for the first time, the parents must give consent. The child begins to receive services as soon as possible after the IEP is written and this consent is given.

If the parents do not agree with the IEP and placement, they may discuss their concerns with other members of the IEP team and try to work out an agreement. If they still disagree, parents can ask for mediation, or the school may offer mediation. Parents may file a state complaint with the state education agency or a due process complaint, which is the first step in requesting a due process hearing, at which time mediation must be available.

Step 7. After the Individualized Education Program Is Written, Services Are Provided

The school makes sure that the child's IEP is carried out as it was written. Parents are given a copy of the IEP. Each of the child's teachers and service providers has access to the IEP and knows her or his specific responsibilities for carrying out the IEP. This includes the accommodations, modifications, and supports that must be provided to the child, in keeping with the IEP.

Step 8. Progress Is Measured and Reported to Parents

The child's progress toward the annual goals is measured, as stated in the IEP. Her or his parents are regularly informed of their child's progress and whether that progress is enough for the child to achieve the goals by the end of the year. These progress reports must be given to parents at least as often as parents are informed of their nondisabled children's progress.

Step 9. Individualized Education Program is reviewed

The child's IEP is reviewed by the IEP team at least once a year or more often if the parents or school ask for a review. If necessary, the IEP is revised. Parents, as team members, must be invited to participate in these meetings. Parents can make suggestions for changes, can agree or disagree with the IEP, and agree or disagree with the placement.

If parents do not agree with the IEP and placement, they may discuss their concerns with other members of the IEP team and try to work out an agreement. There are several options, including additional testing, an independent evaluation, or asking for mediation, or a due process hearing. They may also file a complaint with the state education agency.

Step 10. Child Is Reevaluated

The child must be reevaluated every three years, at least. This evaluation is sometimes called a "triennial." Its purpose is to find out if the child continues to be "a child with a disability," as defined by the IDEA, and what the child's educational needs are. However, the child must be reevaluated more often if conditions warrant or if the child's parent or teacher asks for a new evaluation.

Chapter 32

Understanding Your Child's Right to Special Education Services

Chapter Contents

Section 32.1

Section 504

This section contains text excerpted from the following sources:
Text in this section begins with excerpts from "Discrimination on the
Basis of Disability," U.S. Department of Health and Human Services
(HHS), June 16, 2017; Text under the heading "What Is Section
504 and How Does It Relate to Section 508?" is excerpted from
"What Is Section 504 and How Does It Relate to Section 508?" U.S.
Department of Health and Human Services (HHS),
August 19, 2015. Reviewed April 2019.

As they apply to entities under the jurisdiction of the Office for Civil
Rights (OCR), the OCR enforces:

- Section 504 of the Rehabilitation Act of 1973, including
  programs and activities that are conducted by the U.S.
  Department of Health and Human Services (HHS) or receiving
  federal financial assistance from HHS

- Section 508 of the Rehabilitation Act of 1973, covering access to
  electronic and information technology provided by HHS

- Title II of the Americans with Disabilities Act (ADA) of 1990,
  covering all healthcare and social services programs and
  activities of public entities

- Section 1557 of the Patient Protection and Affordable Care
  Act (ACA), ensuring that an individual is not excluded from
  participating in, denied benefits because of, or subjected
  to discrimination as prohibited under Section 504 of the
  Rehabilitation Act of 1973 (disability), under any health
  program or activity, any part of which is receiving federal
  financial assistance, or under any program or activity that is
  administered by an executive agency or any entity established
  under Title I of the Affordable Care Act or its amendments.

Rights and Responsibilities under Section 504 and the Americans with Disabilities Act

Section 504 and the ADA protect qualified individuals with disabilities from discrimination on the basis of disability in the provision of benefits and services.

Covered entities must not, on the basis of disability:

342

- Exclude a person with a disability from a program or activity

- Deny a person with a disability the benefits of a program or activity

- Afford a person with a disability an opportunity to participate in or benefit from a benefit or service that is not equal to what is afforded others

- Provide a benefit or service to a person with a disability that is not as effective as what is provided others

- Provide different or separate benefits or services to a person with a disability, unless necessary to provide benefits or services that are as effective as what is provided others

- Apply eligibility criteria that tend to screen out persons with disabilities, unless necessary for the provision of the service, program, or activity

Covered entities must:

- Provide services and programs in the most integrated setting appropriate to the needs of the qualified individual with a disability

- Ensure that programs, services, activities, and facilities are accessible

- Make reasonable modifications in their policies, practices, and procedures to avoid discrimination on the basis of disability, unless it would result in a fundamental alteration of the program

- Provide auxiliary aids to persons with disabilities, at no additional cost, where necessary, to afford an equal opportunity to participate in or benefit from a program or activity

- Designate a responsible employee to coordinate their efforts to comply with Section 504 and the ADA

- Adopt grievance procedures to handle complaints of disability discrimination in their programs and activities

- Provide notice that indicates:

  - That the covered entity does not discriminate on the basis of disability

- How to contact the employee who coordinates the covered entity's efforts to comply with the law

- Information about the grievance procedures

Section 508 of the Rehabilitation Act

Section 508 requires that any electronic and information technology used, maintained, developed, or procured by the federal government allow persons with disabilities comparable access to information and technology. This applies to persons with disabilities who use assistive technology to read and navigate electronic materials.

What Is Section 504 and How Does It Relate to Section 508?

Responsibilities under Section 504 and Section 508 can overlap. Both statutes impose different but somewhat related, obligations on the HHS operating and staff divisions (OPDIVs/STAFFDIVs) that are intended to protect individuals with disabilities from discrimination based on their disabilities. Agencies must comply with both provisions when they distribute information.

Section 508 requires federal agencies to ensure that persons with disabilities (both employees and members of the public) have comparable access to and use of electronic information technology. That means that any electronic and information technology used, maintained, developed, or procured by the HHS must be accessible to persons with disabilities.

Section 504 requires agencies to provide individuals with disabilities an equal opportunity to participate in their programs and benefit from their services, including the provision of information to employees and members of the public. Agencies must provide appropriate auxiliary aids where necessary to ensure an equal opportunity. Types of auxiliary aids may include braille or large print versions of materials, electronic diskettes, audiotapes, qualified interpreters or readers, telecommunications devices for deaf persons (TDDs), captioning of video, and other methods of making information available and accessible to persons with disabilities. In considering what type of auxiliary aid to provide, agencies must give primary consideration to the request of the individual with a disability and shall honor that request, unless it can demonstrate that another effective means of communication exists.

Section 32.2

The Individuals with Disabilities Education Act

This section includes text excerpted from "About IDEA,"
U.S. Department of Education (ED), December 15, 2015.
Reviewed April 2019.

The Individuals with Disabilities Education Act (IDEA) is a law
that makes free appropriate public education available to eligible
children with disabilities throughout the nation and ensures special
education and related services to those children.

The IDEA governs how states and public agencies provide early
intervention (EI), special education, and related services to more
than 6.5 million eligible infants, toddlers, children, and youth with
disabilities.

Infants and toddlers with disabilities, between birth and 2 years
of age, and their families receive early intervention services under
the IDEA Part C. Children and youth between the ages of 3 and 21
receive special education and related services under the IDEA Part
B.

Additionally, the IDEA authorizes:

- Formula grants to states to support special education and
  related services and early intervention services

- Discretionary grants to state educational agencies, institutions
  of higher education, and other nonprofit organizations to
  support research, demonstrations, technical assistance and
  dissemination, technology development, personnel preparation
  and development, and parent-training and information
  centers.

Congress reauthorized the IDEA in 2004 and amended the IDEA
through Public Law 114–95, Every Student Succeeds Act (ESSA), in
December 2015.

In the law, Congress states: "Disability is a natural part of the
human experience and in no way diminishes the right of individuals to participate in or contribute to society. Improving educational
results for children with disabilities is an essential element of our
national policy of ensuring equality of opportunity, full participation,
independent living, and economic self-sufficiency for individuals with
disabilities."

The Individuals with Disabilities Education Act's Purpose

The stated purpose of the IDEA is:

- To ensure that all children with disabilities have free appropriate public education available to them that emphasizes special education and related services designed to meet their unique needs and prepare them for further education, employment, and independent living

- To ensure that the rights of children with disabilities and parents of such children are protected

- To assist states, localities, educational service agencies, and federal agencies to provide for the education of all children with disabilities

- To assist states in the implementation of a statewide, comprehensive, coordinated, multidisciplinary, interagency system of early intervention services for infants and toddlers with disabilities and their families

- To ensure that educators and parents have the necessary tools to improve educational results for children with disabilities by supporting system improvement activities; coordinated research and personnel preparation; coordinated technical assistance, dissemination, and support; and technology development and media services

- To assess, and ensure the effectiveness of, efforts to educate children with disabilities

History of the Individuals with Disabilities Education Act

On November 29, 1975, President Gerald Ford signed into law the Education for All Handicapped Children Act (Public Law 94–142), now known as the "Individuals with Disabilities Education Act" (IDEA). In adopting this landmark civil rights measure, Congress opened public school doors for millions of children with disabilities and laid the foundation of the country's commitment to ensuring that children with disabilities have opportunities to develop their talents, share their gifts, and contribute to their communities.

The law guaranteed access to free appropriate public education (FAPE) in the least restrictive environment (LRE) to every child with a disability. Subsequent amendments, as reflected in the IDEA, have led to an increased emphasis on access to the general education curriculum, the provision of services for young children from birth to the age of five, transition planning, and accountability for the achievement of students with disabilities. The IDEA upholds and protects the rights of infants, toddlers, children, and youth with disabilities and their families.

In the last 40+ years, we have advanced our expectations for all children, including children with disabilities. Classrooms have become more inclusive, and the future of children with disabilities is brighter. Significant progress has been made toward protecting the rights of, meeting the individual needs of, and improving educational results and outcomes for infants, toddlers, children, and youths with disabilities.

Since 1975, we have progressed from excluding nearly 1.8 million children with disabilities from public schools to providing more than 6.9 million children with disabilities special education and related services designed to meet their individual needs.

Nowadays, more than 62 percent of children with disabilities are in general education classrooms 80 percent or more of their school day, and early intervention services are being provided to more than 340,000 infants and toddlers with disabilities and their families.

Section 32.3

Every Student Succeeds Act

This section includes text excerpted from "Every Student
Succeeds Act (ESSA)," U.S. Department of Education (ED),
December 10, 2015. Reviewed April 2019.

A New Education Law

The Every Student Succeeds Act (ESSA) was signed by President Obama on December 10, 2015 and represents good news for schools. This bipartisan measure reauthorizes the 50-year-old Elementary and Secondary Education Act (ESEA), the nation's national education law and longstanding commitment to equal opportunity for all students.

The new law builds on key areas of progress, made possible by the efforts of educators, communities, parents, and students across the country. For example, nowadays, high-school graduation rates are at all-time highs. Dropout rates are at historic lows. And more students are going to college than ever before. These achievements provide a firm foundation for further work to expand educational opportunity and improve student outcomes under ESSA.

The previous version of the law, the No Child Left Behind (NCLB) Act, was enacted in 2002. NCLB represented a significant step forward for nation's children in many respects, particularly as it shined a light on where students were making progress and where they needed additional support, regardless of race, income, zip code, disability, home language, or background. The law was scheduled for revision in 2007, and, over time, NCLB's prescriptive requirements became increasingly unworkable for schools and educators. Recognizing this fact, in 2010, the Obama administration joined a call from educators and families to create a better law that focused on the clear goal of fully preparing all students for success in college and careers.

Congress responded to that call.

Every Student Succeeds Act Highlights

ESSA includes provisions that helps ensure success for students and schools. Below are just a few. The law:

- Advances equity by upholding critical protections for America's disadvantaged and high-need students

- Requires—for the first time—that all students in America be taught to high academic standards that will prepare them to succeed in college and careers

- Ensures that vital information is provided to educators, families, students, and communities through annual statewide assessments that measure students' progress toward those high standards

- Helps to support and grow local innovations—including evidence-based and place-based interventions developed by local leaders and educators—consistent with our Investing in Innovation and Promise Neighborhoods

- Sustains and expands this administration's historic investments in increasing access to high-quality preschool

- Maintains an expectation that there will be accountability and action to effect positive change in our lowest-performing schools, where groups of students are not making progress, and where graduation rates are low over extended periods of time

President Barack Obama signed the Every Student Succeeds Act into law on December 10, 2015.

History of Elementary and Secondary Education Act

The Elementary and Secondary Education Act (ESEA) was signed into law in 1965 by President Lyndon Baines Johnson, who believed that "full educational opportunity" should be "our first national goal." From its inception, ESEA was a civil rights law.

ESEA offered new grants to districts serving low-income students, federal grants for textbooks and library books, funding for special education centers, and scholarships for low-income college students. Additionally, the law provided federal grants to state educational agencies to improve the quality of elementary and secondary education.

No Child Left Behind and Accountability

No Child Left Behind (NCLB) put in place measures that exposed achievement gaps among traditionally underserved students and their peers and spurred an important national dialogue on education improvement. This focus on accountability has been critical in ensuring a quality education for all children, yet also revealed challenges in the effective implementation of this goal.

Parents, educators, and elected officials across the country recognized that a strong, updated law was necessary to expand opportunity to all students; support schools, teachers, and principals; and to strengthen our education system and economy.

In 2012, the Obama administration began granting flexibility to states regarding specific requirements of NCLB in exchange for rigorous and comprehensive state-developed plans designed to close achievement gaps, increase equity, improve the quality of instruction, and increase outcomes for all students.

Chapter 33

Individualized Education Programs

An Individualized Education Program (IEP) is a written statement of the educational program designed to meet a child's individual needs. Every child who receives special education services must have an IEP. That is why the process of developing this vital document is of great interest and importance to educators, administrators, and families alike. Here is a crash course on the IEP.

What Are the Purposes of Individualized Education Programs?

The IEP has two general purposes:

- To set reasonable learning goals for a child

- To state the services that the school district will provide for the child

Who Develops the Individualized Education Program

The IEP is developed by a team of individuals that includes key school staff and the child's parents. The team meets, reviews the assessment information available about the child, and designs an

This chapter includes text excerpted from "The Short-and-Sweet IEP Overview," Center for Parent Information & Resources (CPIR), U.S. Department of Education (ED), August 1, 2017.

educational program to address the child's educational needs that result from her or his disability.

When Is the Individualized Education Program Developed?

An IEP meeting must be held within 30 calendar days after it is determined, through a full and individual evaluation, that a child has one of the disabilities listed in the Individuals with Disabilities Education Act (IDEA) and needs special education and related services. A child's IEP must also be reviewed at least annually thereafter to determine whether the annual goals are being achieved and must be revised as appropriate.

What Is in an Individualized Education Program?

Each child's IEP must contain specific information, as listed within the IDEA, our nation's special education law. This includes (but is not limited to):

- The child's present levels of academic achievement and functional performance, describing how the child is currently doing in school and how the child's disability affects her or his involvement and progress in the general curriculum

- Annual goals for the child, meaning what parents and the school team think she or he can reasonably accomplish in a year

- The special education and related services to be provided to the child, including supplementary aids and services (such as a communication device) and changes to the program or supports for school personnel

- How much of the school day the child will be educated separately from nondisabled children or not participate in extracurricular or other nonacademic activities, such as lunch or clubs

- How (and if) the child is to participate in state- and district-wide assessments, including what modifications to tests the child needs

- When services and modifications will begin, how often they will be provided, where they will be provided, and how long they will last

- How school personnel will measure the child's progress toward the annual goals

Can Students Be Involved in Developing Their Own Individualized Education Programs?

Yes, they certainly can be. The IDEA actually requires that the student be invited to any IEP meeting where transition services will be discussed. These are services designed to help the student plan for her or his transition to adulthood and life after high school.

Chapter 34

Supports, Modifications, and Accommodations for Students with Disabilities

You might wonder if the terms "supports," "modifications," and "adaptations" all mean the same thing. The simple answer is: No, not completely, but yes, for the most part. People tend to use the terms interchangeably for ease of reading, but distinctions can be made between the terms.

Sometimes people get confused about what it means to have a modification and what it means to have an accommodation. Usually, a modification means a change in what is being taught to or expected from the student. Making an assignment easier so the student is not doing the same level of work as other students is an example of a modification.

An accommodation is a change that helps a student overcome or work around the disability. Allowing a student who has trouble writing to give her or his answers orally is an example of an accommodation. This student is still expected to know the same material and answer the same questions as fully as the other students, but she or he does

This chapter includes text excerpted from "Supports, Modifications, and Accommodations for Students," Center for Parent Information & Resources (CPIR), U.S. Department of Education (ED), February 8, 2017.

not have to write her or his answers to show that she or he knows the information.

What is most important to know about modifications and accommodations is that both are meant to help a child to learn.

Different Types of Supports
Special Education

By definition, "special education" is "specially designed instruction" (§300.39). And the Individuals with Disabilities Education Act (IDEA) defines that term as follows:

"Specially designed instruction means adapting, as appropriate, to the needs of an eligible child under this part, the content, methodology, or delivery of instruction:

- To address the unique needs of the child that result from the child's disability

- To ensure access of the child to the general curriculum, so that the child can meet the educational standards within the jurisdiction of the public agency that apply to all children (§300.39(b)(3))"

Thus, special education involves adapting the "content, methodology, or delivery of instruction." In fact, the special education field can take pride in the knowledge base and expertise it is developed in the past 30+ years of individualizing instruction to meet the needs of students with disabilities.

Adapting Instruction

Sometimes a student may need to have changes made in class work or routines because of her or his disability. Modifications can be made to:

- *What* a child is taught
- *How* a child works at school

For example:

Jack is an eighth-grade student who has learning disabilities in reading and writing. He is in a regular eighth-grade class that is team-taught by a general education teacher and a special education teacher. Modifications and accommodations provided for Jack's daily school routine (and when he takes state or district-wide tests) include the following:

- Jack will have shorter reading and writing assignments.

- Jack's textbooks will be based upon the eighth-grade curriculum but at his independent reading level (fourth grade).

- Jack will have test questions read/explained to him, when he asks.

- Jack will give his answers to essay-type questions by speaking, rather than writing them down.

Modifications or accommodations are most often made in the following areas:

Scheduling. For example,

- Giving the student extra time to complete assignments or tests

- Breaking up testing over several days

Setting. For example,

- Working in a small group

- Working one-on-one with the teacher

Materials. For example,

- Providing audiotaped lectures or books

- Giving copies of teacher's lecture notes

- Using large print books, Braille, or books on CD (digital text)

Instruction. For example,

- Reducing the difficulty of assignments

- Reducing the reading level

- Using a student/peer tutor

Student Response. For example,

- Allowing answers to be given orally or dictated

- Using a word processor for written work

- Using sign language, a communication device, Braille, or native language if it is not English.

Because adapting the content, methodology, and/or delivery of instruction is an essential element in special education and an extremely valuable support for students, it is equally essential to know as much as possible about how instruction can be adapted to address the needs of an individual student with a disability. The special education teacher who serves on the Individualized Education Program (IEP) team can contribute her or his expertise in this area, which is the essence of special education.

Related Services

One look at the IDEA's definition of related services at §300.34, and it is clear that these services are supportive in nature, although not in the same way that adapting the curriculum is. Related services support children's special education and are provided when necessary to help students benefit from special education. Thus, related services must be included in the treasure chest of accommodations and supports. That definition begins:

General. Related services refer to transportation and such developmental, corrective, and other supportive services as are required to assist a child with a disability to benefit from special education, and includes:

- Speech-language pathology and audiology services
- Interpreting services
- Psychological services
- Physical and occupational therapy
- Recreation, including therapeutic recreation
- Early identification and assessment of disabilities in children
- Counseling services, including rehabilitation counseling
- Orientation and mobility services
- Medical services for diagnostic or evaluation purposes
- School-health services and school nurse services
- Social work services in schools

This is not an exhaustive list of possible related services. There are others (not named here or in the law) that states and schools routinely make available under the umbrella of related services. The IEP team decides which related services a child needs and specifies them in the child's IEP.

Supplementary Aids and Services

One of the most powerful types of supports available to children with disabilities are the other kinds of supports or services (other than special education and related services) that a child needs to be educated with nondisabled children to the maximum extent appropriate. Some examples of these additional services and supports, called "supplementary aids and services" in the IDEA, are:

- Adapted equipment—such as a special seat or a cut-out cup for drinking

- Assistive technology—such as a word processor, special software, or a communication system

- Training for staff, student, and/or parents

- Peer tutors

- A one-on-one aide

- Adapted materials—such as books on tape, large print, or highlighted notes

- Collaboration/consultation among staff, parents, and/or other professionals

The IEP team, which includes the parents, is the group that decides which supplementary aids and services a child needs to support her or his access to and participation in the school environment. The IEP team must really work together to make sure that a child gets the supplementary aids and services that she or he needs to be successful. Team members talk about the child's needs, the curriculum, and school routine, and openly explore all options to make sure the right supports for the specific child are included.

Program Modifications or Supports for School Staff

If the IEP team decides that a child needs a particular modification or accommodation, this information must be included in the IEP. Supports are also available for those who work with the child, to help them help that child be successful. Supports for school staff must also be written into the IEP. Some of these supports might include:

- Attending a conference or training related to the child's needs

- Getting help from another staff member or administrative person

- Having an aide in the classroom

- Getting special equipment or teaching materials

Accommodations in Large Assessments

The IDEA requires that students with disabilities take part in state or district-wide assessments. These are tests that are periodically given to all students to measure achievement. It is one way that schools determine how well and how much students are learning. The IDEA now states that students with disabilities should have as much involvement in the general curriculum as possible. This means that, if a child is receiving instruction in the general curriculum, she or he could take the same standardized test that the school district or state gives to nondisabled children. Accordingly, a child's IEP must include all modifications or accommodations that the child needs so that she or he can participate in state- or district-wide assessments.

The IEP team can decide that a particular test is not appropriate for a child. In this case, the IEP must include:

- An explanation of why that test is not suitable for the child

- How the child will be assessed instead (often called "alternate assessment")

Ask your state and/or local school district for a copy of their guidelines on the types of accommodations, modifications, and alternate assessments available to students.

Conclusion

Even a child with many needs should be involved with nondisabled peers to the maximum extent appropriate. Just because a child has severe disabilities or needs modifications to the general curriculum does not mean that she or he may be removed from the general education class. If a child is removed from the general education class for any part of the school day, the IEP team must include in the IEP an explanation for the child's nonparticipation.

Because accommodations can be so vital to helping children with disabilities access the general curriculum, participate in school (including extracurricular and nonacademic activities), and be educated alongside their peers without disabilities, the IDEA reinforces their use again and again, in its requirements, definitions, and principles. The wealth of experience that the special education field has gained over the years since the IDEA was first passed by Congress is the very resource you will want to tap for more information on what accommodations are appropriate for students, given their disability, and how to make those adaptations to support their learning.

Chapter 35

Specialized Teaching Techniques

Chapter Contents

Section 35.1

Differentiated Instruction

This section includes text excerpted from "TEAL Center
Fact Sheet No. 5: Differentiated Instruction," Literacy
Information and Communication System (LINCS),
October 29, 2011. Reviewed April 2019.

Differentiated instruction is an approach that enables instructors to plan strategically to meet the needs of every learner. It is rooted in the belief that there is variability among any group of learners and that instructors should adjust instruction accordingly. The approach encompasses the planning and delivery of instruction, classroom management techniques, and expectations of learners' performance that take into consideration the diversity and varied levels of readiness, interests, and learning profiles of the learners.

Differentiated instruction can be looked at as an instructor's response to learner differences by adapting curriculum and instruction on six dimensions, including how the instructor approaches the:

- Content (the what of the lesson)

- Process (the how of the lesson

- Expected product (the learner-produced result), and takes into consideration the learner's interest

- Profile (learning strengths, weaknesses, and gaps)

- Readiness

These adaptations can be planned to happen simultaneously, in sequence, or as needed, depending on the circumstance and goals of instruction. Teaching small groups of learners, grouped based on instructional approach and learner profile, is a cornerstone of differentiated instruction.

How Can Technology Help?

Technology tools can help make this coordination more efficient by providing productivity support for instructors, providing support for learners at varying levels of readiness, and offering learners options for demonstrating their understanding and mastery of the material.

Managing Differentiated Instruction

Classroom management to coordinate flexible groupings and projects is a key component of applying differentiated instruction. The following are some ideas for creating and coordinating groups in a multi-level, differentiated class:

- Set up stations in the classroom where different learning groups can work simultaneously. Such stations naturally invite flexible grouping.
  - Encourage peer-to-peer learning and mentoring, and help learners learn to be tutors.
  - Ask volunteers to lead small-group instruction stations.
- Structure problem-based learning (PBL) to have learners actively solve problems, either individually or in small groups.
  - Use WebQuests (webquest.org) as PBL for teams of learners; these inquiry-based projects are prearranged, and many have teaching supports (lesson plans, tips, handouts, and additional materials) linked to them.
  - Share reflections with other instructors leading problem-based learning at www.Edutopia.org.
- Assign tiered activities to allow learners to work on the same concepts but with varying degrees of complexity.
  - Find texts on a single, encompassing topic (for example, climate change) in various levels of complexity and readability.
  - Encourage learners to find audio books and digital text at their interest level rather than their independent reading level.
- Employ compacting: assess learners' knowledge and skills before beginning a unit of study and allow learners to move to advanced work based on their preassessment.
  - Find ways to give credit for independent study and advancement if a learner is particularly motivated or interested in a topic.
  - Help learners supplement class instruction with online classes or learning opportunities, such as webinars, online chats, blogs, social networks, or daily content blasts (e-mails, such as a word of the day or this day in history, can be a boost to vocabulary and content knowledge).

- Institute chunking, or breaking assignments and activities into smaller, more manageable parts, and providing more structured directions for each part.

  - Have learners make personalized lists of tasks to complete the chunks in a specified but flexible time frame.

  - Encourage self-study, especially when learners have to "stop out" of regular attendance.

- Model differentiation by keeping grades and scores in a variety of ways.

  - Use portfolios as a means for reflecting on learner growth over time, and encourage learners to critique their growth.

  - Keep scores and observations in a spreadsheet that can be sorted flexibly to reveal natural groups.

Section 35.2

Speech-Language Therapy

This section contains text excerpted from the following sources: Text in this section begins with excerpts from "Speech-Language Therapy for Autism," *Eunice Kennedy Shriver* National Institute of Child Health and Human Development (NICHD), January 31, 2017; Text under the heading "Tips for Parents" is excerpted from "Speech and Language Impairments," Center for Parent Information & Resources (CPIR), U.S. Department of Education (ED), June 16, 2015. Reviewed April 2019.

Speech-language therapy can help people with autism spectrum disorder (ASD) improve their abilities to communicate and interact with others.

Verbal Skills

This type of therapy can help some people improve their spoken or verbal skills, such as:

- Correctly naming people and things
- Better explaining feelings and emotions
- Using words and sentences better
- Improving the rate and rhythm of speech

Nonverbal Communication

Speech-language therapy can also teach nonverbal communication skills, such as:

- Using hand signals or sign language
- Using picture symbols to communicate (Picture Exchange Communication System)

Speech-language therapy activities can also include social skills and normal social behaviors. For example, a child might learn how to make eye contact or to stand at a comfortable distance from another person. These skills make it a little easier to interact with others.

Tips for Parents

Learn the specifics of your child's speech or language impairment. The more you know, the more you can help yourself and your child.

Be patient. Your child, like every child, has a whole lifetime to learn and grow.

Meet with the school and develop an IEP to address your child's needs. Be your child's advocate. You know your son or daughter best, so share what you know.

Be well informed about the speech-language therapy your daughter or son is receiving. Talk with the speech-language pathologist (SLP), find out how to augment and enrich the therapy at home and in other environments. Also, find out what not to do.

Give your child chores. Chores build confidence and ability. Keep your child's age, attention span, and abilities in mind. Break down jobs into smaller steps. Explain what to do, step by step, until the job is done. Demonstrate. Provide help when it is needed. Praise a job (or part of a job) well done.

Listen to your child. Do not rush to fill gaps or make corrections. Conversely, do not force your child to speak. Be aware of the other ways in which communication takes place between people.

Talk to other parents whose children have a similar speech or language impairment. Parents can share practical advice and emotional support. See if there is a parent nearby by visiting the Parent to Parent USA program and using the interactive map.

Keep in touch with your child's teachers. Offer support. Demonstrate any assistive technology your child uses, and provide any information teachers will need. Find out how you can augment your child's school learning at home.

Chapter 36

Coping with School-Related Challenges

Chapter Contents

Section 36.1

Building a Good Relationship with Your Child's Teacher

This section includes text excerpted from "Tips for Developing a Strong Relationship with Your Child's Teacher," U.S. Department of Education (ED), August 25, 2014. Reviewed April 2019.

The start of the school year is the perfect time to build a positive relationship with your child's teacher.

It is a good idea to let your child's educator know you want to partner with her or him and share the responsibility for your child's academic growth.

Here are some tips to bear in mind:

- **Keep in touch.** Make sure your child's teacher has multiple ways and times of day to contact you. Provide as many ways as possible—which might include a work, cell, and home phone number and email address if possible.

- **Mark your calendar.** Ask your child's teacher about the best ways and times to contact her or him. Keep in mind that most teachers are in the classroom all day, so after school may be the best time to call or to make an appointment to meet with her or him.

- **Reach out.** Let the teacher know that you as a parent are there to help. Volunteer to assist with school trips or functions at school that might require additional adult supervision.

- **Stay informed.** Within the first few weeks after school starts, find out from the teacher if your child needs any assistance in one or more subject areas. Find out what resources are available at the school and what resources the teacher would recommend to help your child keep improving.

- **Team up.** Remember, you and the teacher have the exact same goals. You are both working to ensure the academic development and progress of your child. So, sit down together and figure out what you can do at home to reinforce what your child's teacher is doing in the classroom. That way, your child can keep learning long after the school day ends.

Section 36.2

Parental Involvement in Child's Success in School and Life

This section includes text excerpted from "Intellectual Disability,"
Center for Parent Information & Resources (CPIR), U.S.
Department of Education (ED), June 16, 2017.

A child with an intellectual disability can do well in school but is likely to need the individualized help that is available as special education and related services. The level of help and support that is needed will depend upon the degree of intellectual disability involved.

General education. It is important that students with intellectual disabilities be involved in, and make progress in, the general education curriculum. That is the same curriculum that is learned by those without disabilities. Be aware that the Individuals with Disabilities Education Act (IDEA) does not permit a student to be removed from education in age-appropriate general education classrooms solely because she or he needs modifications to be made in the general education curriculum.

Supplementary aids and services. Given that intellectual disabilities affect learning, it is often crucial to provide supports to students with intellectual disabilities (ID) in the classroom. This includes making accommodations appropriate to the needs of the student. It also includes providing what the IDEA calls "supplementary aids and services." Supplementary aids and services are supports that may include instruction, personnel, equipment, or other accommodations that enable children with disabilities to be educated with nondisabled children to the maximum extent appropriate.

Thus, for families and teachers alike, it is important to know what changes and accommodations are helpful to students with intellectual disabilities. These need to be discussed by the individualized education programs (IEP) team and included in the IEP, if appropriate.

Adaptive skills. Many children with intellectual disabilities need help with adaptive skills, which are skills needed to live, work, and play in the community. Teachers and parents can help a child work on these skills at both school and home. Some of these skills include:

- Communicating with others

- Taking care of personal needs (dressing, bathing, going to the bathroom)

- Health and safety

- Home living (helping to set the table, cleaning the house, or cooking dinner)

- Social skills (manners, knowing the rules of conversation, getting along in a group, playing a game)

- Reading, writing, and basic math

- As they get older, skills that will help them in the workplace

Transition planning. It is extremely important for families and schools to begin planning early for the student's transition into the world of adulthood. Because intellectual disability affects how quickly and how well an individual learns new information and skills, the sooner transition planning begins, the more can be accomplished before the student leaves secondary school.

The IDEA requires that, at the latest, transition planning for students with disabilities must begin no later than the first IEP to be in effect when they turn 16 years of age. The IEP teams of many students with intellectual disabilities feel that it is important for these students to begin earlier than that. And they do.

Tips for Teachers

Recognize that you can make an enormous difference in this student's life. Find out what the student's strengths and interests are, and emphasize them. Create opportunities for success.

If you are not part of the student's IEP team, ask for a copy of her or his IEP. The student's educational goals will be listed there, as well as the services and classroom accommodations she or he is to receive. Talk to others in your school (e.g., special educators), as necessary. They can help you identify effective methods of teaching this student, ways to adapt the curriculum, and how to address the student's IEP goals in your classroom.

Be as concrete as possible. Demonstrate what you mean rather than giving verbal directions. Rather than just relating new information verbally, show a picture. And rather than just showing a picture, provide the student with hands-on materials and experiences and the opportunity to try things out.

Break longer, new tasks into small steps. Demonstrate the steps. Have the student do the steps, one at a time. Provide assistance as necessary.

Offer feedback. Give the student immediate feedback.

Teach life skills. Teach the student life skills, such as daily living, social skills, and occupational awareness and exploration, as appropriate. Involve the student in group activities or clubs.

Include parents in your plan. Work together with the student's parents and other school personnel to create and implement an IEP tailored to meet the student's needs. Regularly share information about how the student is doing at school and at home.

Tips for Parents

Be patient, be hopeful. Your child, as with every child, has a whole lifetime to learn and grow.

Encourage independence in your child. For example, help your child learn daily care skills, such as dressing, feeding her- or himself, using the bathroom, and grooming.

Give your child chores. Keep her or his age, attention span, and abilities in mind. Break down jobs into smaller steps. For example, if your child's job is to set the table, first ask her or him to get the right number of napkins. Then have her or him put one at each family member's place at the table. Do the same with the utensils, going one at a time. Tell her or him what to do, step by step, until the job is done. Demonstrate how to do the job. Help her or him when she or he needs assistance.

Give your child frequent feedback. Praise your child when she or he does something well. Build your child's abilities.

Find out what skills your child is learning at school. Find ways for your child to apply those skills at home. For example, if the teacher is going over a lesson about money, take your child to the supermarket with you. Help her or him count out the money to pay for your groceries. Help her or him count the change.

Find opportunities in your community for social activities, such as scouts, recreation center activities, sports, and

so on. These will help your child build social skills, as well as to have fun.

Talk to other parents whose children have an intellectual disability. Parents can share practical advice and emotional support. Find out more about and connect with parent groups.

Meet with the school and develop an IEP to address your child's needs. Keep in touch with your child's teachers. Offer support. Find out how you can support your child's school learning at home.

Take pleasure in your child. Learn from your child, too. Those with intellectual disabilities have a special light within—let it shine.

Chapter 37

Alternative
Educational Options

Chapter Contents

Section 37.1

Homeschooling

This section includes text excerpted from "Beyond the Brick Walls: Homeschooling Students with Special Needs," Education Resources Information Center (ERIC), U.S. Department of Education (ED), March 2013. Reviewed April 2019.

History of Homeschooling in the United States

Throughout history, children have been educated at home. However, the industrial revolution of the late 1800s and early 1900s resulted in compulsory U.S. public school attendance legislation, and, thus, homeschooling was no longer considered an option for most U.S. families for more than a half-century. Homeschooling, however, made a resurgence in the 1960s. The rise in homeschools during that time was influenced by many different social and political influences. The number of children being homeschooled steadily increased from the 1960s onward, and by 1993, homeschooling was legal in all 50 states. Today's compulsory attendance laws stipulate attendance in public or nonpublic schools—including homeschools—and all K-12 programs must be approved by the state. In 2007, the National Household Education Surveys Program estimated that 1.5 million U.S. children, or almost 3% of school-aged children, are homeschooled.

Laws and Regulations

The U.S. Congress first passed legislation to provide funding for the education of students with disabilities in the 1970s. This legislation has been reauthorized several times over the years and is currently known as the "Individuals with Disabilities Education Act" (IDEA). Although making a distinction between public and private schools in the disbursement of funds, the IDEA did not define what constitutes a private school nor did it specifically address funding for students in homeschools. Therefore, decisions on whether to provide funding for special education services to students in homeschools were left to individual states, and many states considered the IDEA rights to be forfeited for homeschool students. The U.S. Supreme Court has supported the power of the individual states to make decisions about support of children with disabilities in homeschools. For example, in Hooks v. Clark County School District (1998), the U.S. Supreme Court upheld a Nevada school system's denial of speech therapy services for a homeschooled child (as cited in Knickerbocker, 2001). The Supreme Court ruled that individual states have the power to treat a home-school as either a private school or as a nonschool; if categorized as a nonschool, a student in a homeschool is not eligible for the IDEA services. However, some states, such as Arizona, Iowa, North Dakota, and Pennsylvania, have homeschool laws that include provisions for students with disabilities. The state of Washington allows funding for special services for homeschool students who also attend public schools part time; other states or local education agencies provide special ser-vices for homeschool students on a case-by-case basis. Several authors argued that the IDEA should be amended to define homeschools as private schools so that services will be available for homeschool stu-dents with disabilities.

It is notable that the U.S. Office of Special Education Programs has interpreted the IDEA's Child Find provisions to be inclusive of children who are being homeschooled, even though services may not be available to eligible children who remain homeschooled. In states that do allow the IDEA funds to be used for homeschool students, two additional factors are typically in play: (a) in order to receive services, the parents must also agree to submit to evaluations for their children and work with a team to develop educational plans, thereby giving up some control of their children's educational management; and (b) the IDEA funding for all eligible students in nonpublic schools is not guaranteed. Whether or not a homeschool student has a disability, the homeschool must comply with its state's compulsory attendance laws. Homeschool regulations vary from state-to-state, but most states stipu-late that homeschools document some or all of the following: (a) specific qualifications of the home educator, (b) curriculum choices, (c) required number of hours per day and days per year of instructional time, (d) standardized testing, and (e) reports to local school systems. The burden for compliance with state homeschool laws and regulations rests on the parents. In sum, parents need to know the local homeschool regulations and the accessibility of special education services for homeschools; a good place to start searching for information is the local school board.

Reasons for Homeschooling

Two main philosophical perspectives for homeschooling have tra-ditionally been described as ideological and pedagogical. Parents with deep philosophical differences with public education may choose to homeschool, regardless of the services their children with disabil-ities could be offered in public school. However, other reasons for homeschooling, frequently rooted in pedagogy, include the perception that the public school has failed to meet a child's needs. That is, the main motivation for many parents to homeschool was that their children's special education needs simply were not being met. For example, a chief concern of parents of children with autism spectrum disorder (ASD) was that schools were either unwilling or unable to provide therapies or treatments that parents considered effective. In addition, parents also attributed negative experiences with public schools as a deciding factor in choosing to homeschool. Other reasons for homeschooling included escape from bullying and avoiding the stigma of a labeled disability. The salient point is that some parents, frustrated with their child's services, choose to homeschool and to figure out how to deliver those services on their own. These findings suggest that, especially in school systems that do not have official policies and programs to support homeschool families, public schools could do a better job of outreach, connection, and communication with families to prevent much of the dissatisfaction that has led many parents to choose homeschooling over public schools.

Benefits and Challenges of Homeschooling

A majority of parents across several studies reported satisfaction with their children's progress in homeschools. Parents specified the benefits of freedom in selecting curriculum, pace of instruction, and daily routines that met their family's and individual children's needs. In this era of increased access to technology, many parents reported reliance on Internet sources for instructional support. In addition, educational consultants were often used at some point in the homeschool planning process, especially when the child had special needs. Some students were unschooled, meaning they had an unstructured schedule guided by the student's day-to-day learning interests.

However, researchers found that most of the families followed a structured daily routine for their children with disabilities. Furthermore, parents of children with disabilities were significantly more likely to use traditional teaching methods (i.e., parent directed) in homeschooling rather than more loosely structured instruction. Although there has been some indication that homeschool families shift from original values and attitudes over time, becoming more nontraditional the longer they homeschooled, it is unclear whether families whose children have special needs follow this progression. However, no matter the degree of structure or the method of instruction, parents reported enjoying much more control over their children's education when they homeschooled. Even though parents tended to give high ratings to the overall homeschool experience, many reported challenges with homeschooling students with disabilities. Some families described a lack of emotional, social, and moral support from outside sources. When support was found, it was more likely to be from other homeschool families and organized homeschool groups than from public schools. In interviews with two parents who homeschooled their children with severe multiple health problems, researchers found that parents did not receive enough professional and social support, and as a result, the parents were feeling overwhelmed with sadness and frustration. While many other factors may influence the intensity of homeschooling challenges, certainly the severity of the child's needs and the amount of support available to the family are two major components that will affect the success of the homeschool program. Despite the fact that a commonly stated concern related to homeschooling was that students might have limited social interactions, most parents reported feeling satisfied with the socialization opportunities afforded their children from homeschool groups, sports, and religious services. However, very few researchers gathered information directly from the homeschool students with disabilities about their perspectives on socialization. In one study that included interviews with homeschool adolescent females with a learning disability, all three participants reported feeling uncomfortable in social situations. The first participant, an adolescent girl who also had a physical disability, reported struggling to make friends even though she had plenty of opportunities to socialize. The second adolescent reported not feeling a part of her peer group because of her learning deficits, and the third adolescent reported feelings of peer isolation because her family lived in a rural area. While it is possible that these teens would have felt the same awkwardness or isolation in a public-school setting, socialization might remain an area of legitimate concern for many homeschool students and their parents.

Section 37.2

Choosing a Tutor

"Choosing a Tutor," © 2016 Omnigraphics. Reviewed April 2019.

A tutor is a teacher who offers private or small-group instruction to help students who have trouble keeping up in a regular school classroom. Tutors can teach specific skills that support learning or reinforce subjects that are taught in school. They can assist children who fall behind their grade level due to motivational problems, psychiatric disorders, or learning disabilities. In many cases, tutoring leads to increased self-confidence and improved academic performance.

Signs a Tutor May Be Needed

Some of the common signs that may indicate a child would benefit from the services of a tutor include:

- Receiving poor grades in school

- Struggling to master basic grade-level skills

- Falling behind in certain subjects

- Having problems with organization, time management, and study skills

- Experiencing severe test anxiety

- Exhibiting a pattern of disruptive behavior

- Showing a lack of motivation

- Making constant excuses for not doing homework

- Experiencing medical, social, emotional, or family problems

- Having a learning disability that makes it challenging to master material and impedes progress in school

Types of Tutors

There are several different types of tutors available to assist children with learning disabilities or attention disorders.

- **Remediation tutoring** is appropriate for children who need extra instruction and practice to master specific skills or subject areas, such as math or reading, in order to catch up to their grade level.

- **Maintenance tutoring** is useful for children who work at their grade level but need help with time management, organization, or study skills in order to manage their workload and meet their academic goals.

- **Support tutoring** includes elements of both remediation and maintenance tutoring, as needed, to help students who struggle in some areas but not others.

- **Test preparation tutoring** is available to teach students techniques for taking tests and help eliminate text anxiety.

- **Enrichment tutoring** offers activities designed to strengthen existing skills or enhance knowledge in areas of special interest.

Finding a Tutor

Tutoring is available from a wide variety of sources, including learning centers, educational therapists, private tutors, and online programs. To find a qualified tutor, parents can ask friends, acquaintances, or teachers for recommendations. The public library may also have information to help parents locate tutors and educational resources. Organizations that are dedicated to serving children with learning disabilities may also be able to provide assistance in finding a qualified tutor.

After compiling a list of possibilities, experts recommend interviewing several tutors in order to find one whose qualifications, approach, schedule, and fees provide the best fit with the family's needs. Ideally, the student should be involved in the interview process to ensure that they feel comfortable with the tutor and support the choice. Interviews with prospective tutors should cover the following main areas:

- **Experience.** Parents need to find out how much experience the tutor has in teaching the specific skills or subject areas of concern. Five or more years of experience is desirable. Parents should also ask whether the tutor has experience working with students at their child's grade level and with similar learning disabilities or attention issues.

- **Qualifications.** Parents should also inquire about prospective tutors' training and qualifications. Ideally, the tutor should be a certified teacher in the subject area being taught. If the child has learning disabilities, the tutor should be trained to use appropriate multisensory techniques to address the child's special needs. The tutor should also be willing to provide references to verify their qualifications.

- **Approach.** Parents should gather information about prospective tutors' teaching philosophy and approach. A tutor should be able to provide a clear explanation of how they will go about identifying the child's skill deficits and what strategies they plan to use in order to improve those skills.

- **Scheduling.** The next area for parents to address involves establishing a schedule for tutoring sessions. Since students with learning disabilities need practice and repetition to master skills, experts recommend scheduling a minimum of two lessons per week, with each lesson lasting one hour. It is important to schedule tutoring sessions for a time of day when the student is fresh, engaged, and ready to learn. Many tutoring programs take place immediately after school, but students tend to be tired and distracted at this time. It may take a while to see results, so parents should plan on continuing the tutoring sessions for three to four months. Finally, parents need to figure out logistical details like where the lessons will be held and how long each session will last.

- **Fees.** Tutoring can be very expensive, so parents need to ask how much each prospective tutor charges per lesson. It may also be helpful to inquire about additional fees for materials or assessments, and the tutor's policies regarding cancellations and make-up sessions. In some cases, tutoring programs may qualify as "supplemental educational services" under the federal No Child Left Behind Act. Students from low-income families who attend Title I schools that fail to meet state standards for at least three years may be eligible to receive free tutoring under this program.

- **Goals.** Parents should work closely with the tutor to establish clear goals for the tutoring sessions. The tutor should provide a written plan for accomplishing the goals. Ideally, the child's classroom teacher should participate in setting the goals so that they support school work. Experts suggest that parents avoid setting unrealistic goals or trying to accomplish too much. Instead, they should focus on specific skills or subject areas that need improvement and expect to see gradual progress rather than instant results.

- **Fit.** The personal relationship between the child and the tutor is an important factor in achieving results. Ideally, the tutor should establish a good rapport with the student, and tutoring sessions should include a mix of directed teaching, guided practice, and interactive, hands-on learning. Parents should observe some tutoring sessions to see how the relationship develops, and consider changing tutors if the child is not responding well after about eight lessons.

- **Communication.** Communication between parents and the tutor is vital in supporting the child's learning. Parents should request periodic updates from the tutor, as well as reports on academic progress from the child's teacher. Parents should also reinforce what the tutor is doing by scheduling time for the child to do homework, providing a quiet place to study, being available to help, checking homework daily, and placing a high value on education.

References

1. Shanley, Judy. "How to Choose a Tutor," LD Online, 2005.

2. Morin, Amanda. "How Different Types of Tutoring Can Help Kids with Learning and Attention Issues," Understood.org, 2014.

Chapter 38

Transition to High School

Chapter Contents

Section 38.1

Transition to High School: An Overview

This section includes text excerpted from "Transition of Students
with Disabilities to Postsecondary Education: A Guide for High
School Educators," U.S. Department of Education (ED),
March 2011. Reviewed April 2019.

For students with disabilities, a big factor in their successful transition from high school to postsecondary education is accurate knowledge about their civil rights. The purpose of this section is to provide high-school educators with answers to questions students with disabilities may have as they get ready to move to the postsecondary education environment.

The Office for Civil Rights (OCR) has enforcement responsibilities under Section 504 of the Rehabilitation Act of 1973 (Section 504), as amended, and Title II of the Americans with Disabilities Act (ADA) of 1990, as amended, (Title II), which prohibit discrimination on the basis of disability. Every school district and nearly every college and university in the United States is subject to one or both of these laws, which have similar requirements. Private postsecondary institutions that do not receive federal financial assistance are not subject to Section 504 or Title II. They are, however, subject to Title III of the Americans with Disabilities Act, which is enforced by the U.S. Department of Justice (DOJ) and which prohibits discrimination on the basis of disability by private entities that are not private clubs or religious entities.

This guide also makes reference to Part B of the Individuals with Disabilities Education Act (IDEA), which provides funds to states to assist in making free appropriate public education (FAPE) available to eligible children with disabilities. The IDEA requirements apply to state education agencies, school districts, and other public agencies that serve IDEA-eligible children. Institutions of postsecondary education have no legal obligations under the IDEA.

Similarly, this guide references the state Vocational Rehabilitation (VR) Services Program, authorized by the Rehabilitation Act, which provides funds to state VR agencies to assist eligible individuals with disabilities in obtaining employment. State VR agencies provide a wide range of employment-related services, including services designed to facilitate the transition of eligible students with disabilities from school to postschool activities.

In preparing this guide, the OCR has highlighted the significant differences between the rights and responsibilities of students with disabilities in the high school setting and the rights and responsibilities these students will have once they are in the postsecondary education setting. Following a set of frequently asked questions, the OCR has provided some practical suggestions that high-school educators can share with students to facilitate their successful transition to postsecondary education.

Section 38.2

Frequently Asked Questions about Transition to High School

This section includes text excerpted from "Transition of Students with Disabilities to Postsecondary Education: A Guide for High School Educators," U.S. Department of Education (ED), March 2011. Reviewed April 2019.

The Admissions Process
Are Students with Disabilities Entitled to Changes in Standardized Testing Conditions on Entrance Exams for Institutions of Postsecondary Education?

It depends. In general, tests may not be selected or administered in a way that tests the disability rather than the achievement or aptitude of the individual. In addition, federal law requires changes to the testing conditions that are necessary to allow a student with a disability to participate, as long as the changes do not fundamentally alter the examination or create undue financial or administrative burdens. Although some institutions of postsecondary education may have their own entrance exams, many use a student's score on commercially available tests. In general, in order to request one or more changes in standardized testing conditions, which test administrators may also refer to as "testing accommodations," the student will need to contact the institution of postsecondary education or the entity that administers the exam and provide documentation of a disability and the need for a change in testing conditions. The issue of documentation is discussed below. Examples of changes in testing conditions that may be available include, but are not limited to:

- Braille
- Large print
- Fewer items on each page
- Tape recorded responses
- Responses on the test booklet
- Frequent breaks
- Extended testing time
- Testing over several sessions
- Small group setting
- Private room
- Preferential seating
- The use of a sign language interpreter for spoken directions

Are Institutions of Postsecondary Education Permitted to Ask an Applicant If She or He Has a Disability before an Admission Decision Is Made?

Generally, institutions of postsecondary education are not permitted to make what is known as a "preadmission inquiry" about an applicant's disability status. Preadmission inquiries are permitted only if the institution of postsecondary education is taking remedial action to correct the effects of past discrimination or taking voluntary action to overcome the effects of conditions that limited the participation of individuals with disabilities.

Examples of impermissible preadmission inquiries include:

- Are you in good health?
- Have you been hospitalized for a medical condition in the past five years?

Institutions of postsecondary education may inquire about an applicant's ability to meet essential program requirements provided that such inquiries are not designed to reveal disability status. For example, if physical lifting is an essential requirement for a degree program in physical therapy, an acceptable question that could be asked is, "With or without reasonable accommodation, can you lift 25 pounds?" After admission, in response to a student's request for "academic adjustments," reasonable modifications or auxiliary aids and services, institutions of postsecondary education may ask for documentation regarding disability status.

May Institutions of Postsecondary Education Deny an Applicant Admission Because She or He Has a Disability?

No. If an applicant meets the essential requirements for admission, an institution may not deny that applicant admission simply because she or he has a disability, nor may an institution categorically exclude an applicant with a particular disability as not being qualified for its program. For instance, an institution may not automatically assume that all applicants with hearing or visual impairments would be unable to meet the essential eligibility requirements of its music program. An institution may, however, require an applicant to meet any essential technical or academic standards for admission to, or participation in, the institution and its program. An institution may deny admission to any student, disabled or not, who does not meet essential requirements for admission or participation.

Are Institutions Obligated to Identify Students with Disabilities?

No. Institutions do not have a duty to identify students with disabilities. Students in institutions of postsecondary education are responsible for notifying institution staff of their disability should they need academic adjustments. High schools, in contrast, have an obligation to identify students within their jurisdiction who have a disability and who may be entitled to services.

Are Students Obligated to Inform Institutions That They Have a Disability?

No. A student has no obligation to inform an institution of postsecondary education that she or he has a disability; however, if the student wants an institution to provide an academic adjustment or assign the student to accessible housing or other facilities, or if a student wants other disability-related services, the student must identify herself or himself as having a disability. The disclosure of a disability is always voluntary. For example, a student who has a disability that does not require services may choose not to disclose her or his disability.

Post-Admission: Documentation of a Disability
What Are Academic Adjustments and Auxiliary Aids and Services?

"Academic adjustments" are defined in the Section 504 regulations at 34 C.F.R. § 104.44(a) as:

> Such modifications to the academic requirements as are necessary to ensure that such requirements do not discriminate or have the effect of discriminating, on the basis of disability against a qualified applicant or student with a disability. Academic requirements that the recipient can demonstrate are essential to the instruction being pursued by such student or to any directly related licensing requirement will not be regarded as discriminatory within the meaning of this section. Modifications may include changes in the length of time permitted for the completion of degree requirements, substitution of specific courses required for the completion of degree requirements, and adaptation of the manner in which specific courses are conducted.

Academic adjustments also may include a reduced course load, extended time on tests, and the provision of auxiliary aids and services. Auxiliary aids and services are defined in the Section 504 regulations at 34 C.F.R. § 104.44(d), and in the Title II regulations at 28 C.F.R. § 35.104. They include note-takers, readers, recording devices, sign language interpreters, screen-readers, voice recognition and other adaptive software or hardware for computers, and other devices designed to ensure the participation of students with impaired sensory, manual, or speaking skills in an institution's programs and activities. Institutions are not required to provide personal devices and services, such as attendants; individually prescribed devices, such as eyeglasses; readers for personal use or study; or other services of a personal nature, such as tutoring. If institutions offer tutoring to the general student population, however, they must ensure that tutoring services also are available to students with disabilities. In some instances, a state VR agency may provide auxiliary aids and services to support an individual's postsecondary education and training once that individual has been determined eligible to receive services under the VR program.

In General, What Kind of Documentation Is Necessary for Students with Disabilities to Receive Academic Adjustments from Institutions of Postsecondary Education?

Institutions may set their own requirements for documentation so long as they are reasonable and comply with Section 504 and Title II. It is not uncommon for documentation standards to vary from institution to institution; thus, students with disabilities should research documentation standards at those institutions that interest them. A student must provide documentation, upon request, that she or he has a disability, that is, an impairment that substantially limits a major life activity and that supports the need for an academic adjustment. The documentation should identify how a student's ability to function is limited as a result of his or her disability. The primary purpose of the documentation is to establish a disability in order to help the institution work interactively with the student to identify appropriate services. The focus should be on whether the information adequately documents the existence of a current disability and need for an academic adjustment.

Who Is Responsible for Obtaining Necessary Testing to Document the Existence of a Disability?

The student. Institutions of postsecondary education are not required to conduct or pay for an evaluation to document a student's disability and need for an academic adjustment, although some institutions do so. If a student with a disability is eligible for services through the state VR Services program, she or he may qualify for an evaluation at no cost. High-school educators can assist students with disabilities in locating their state VR agency at (rsa.ed.gov). If students with disabilities are unable to find other funding sources to pay for necessary evaluation or testing for postsecondary education, they are responsible for paying for it themselves.

At the elementary and secondary school levels, a school district's duty to provide a free appropriate public education (FAPE) encompasses the responsibility to provide, at no cost to the parents, an evaluation of suspected areas of disability for any of the district's students who are believed to be in need of special education or related aids and services. School districts are not required under Section 504 or Title II to conduct evaluations that are for the purpose of obtaining academic adjustments once a student graduates and goes on to postsecondary education.

391

Is a Student's Most Recent Individualized Education Program or Section 504 Plan Sufficient Documentation to Support the Existence of a Disability and the Need for an Academic Adjustment in a Postsecondary Setting?

Generally, no. Although an IEP or Section 504 plan may help identify services that have been used by the student in the past, they generally are not sufficient documentation to support the existence of a current disability and need for an academic adjustment from an institution of postsecondary education. Assessment information and other material used to develop an IEP or Section 504 plan may be helpful to document a current disability or the need for an academic adjustment or auxiliary aids and services. In addition, a student receiving services under Part B of the IDEA must be provided with a summary of his or her academic achievements and functional performance that includes recommendations on how to assist in meeting the student's postsecondary goals.

What Can High-School Personnel, Such as School Psychologists and Counselors, Transition Specialists, Special Education Staff, and Others, Do to Assist Students with Disabilities with Documentation Requirements?

By the time most students with disabilities are accepted into a postsecondary institution, they are likely to have a transition plan and/ or to be receiving transition services, which may include evaluations and services provided by the state VR agency. High-school personnel can help a student with disabilities to identify and address the specific documentation requirements of the postsecondary institution that the student will be attending. This may include assisting the student to identify existing documentation in his or her education records that would satisfy the institution's criteria, such as evaluation reports and the summary of the student's academic achievement and functional performance. School personnel should be aware that institutions of postsecondary education typically do not accept brief conclusory statements for which no supporting evidence is offered as sufficient documentation of a disability and the need for an academic adjustment. School personnel should also be aware that some colleges may delay or deny services if the diagnosis or the documentation is unclear.

Will a Medical Diagnosis from a Treating Physician Help to Document Disability?

A diagnosis of impairment alone does not establish that an individual has a disability within the meaning of Section 504 or Title II. Rather, the impairment must substantially limit a major life activity, or the individual must have a record of such an impairment or be regarded as having such an impairment. A diagnosis from a treating physician, along with information about how the disability affects the student, may suffice. As noted above, institutions of postsecondary education may set their own requirements for documentation so long as they are reasonable and comply with Section 504 and Title II.

If It Is Clear That a Student Has a Disability, Why Does an Institution Need Documentation?

Students who have the same disability may not necessarily require the same academic adjustment. Section 504 and Title II require that institutions of postsecondary education make individualized determinations regarding appropriate academic adjustments for each individual student. If the student's disability and need for an academic adjustment are obvious, less documentation may be necessary.

If an Institution Thinks That the Documentation Is Insufficient, How Will the Student Know?

If the documentation a student submitted for the institution's consideration does not meet the institution's requirements, an official should notify the student in a timely manner of what additional documentation the student needs to provide. As noted above, a student may need a new evaluation in order to provide documentation of a current disability.

Post-Admission: Obtaining Services
Must Institutions Provide Every Academic Adjustment a Student with a Disability Wants?

It depends. Institutions are not required to provide an academic adjustment that would alter or waive essential academic requirements. They also do not have to provide an academic adjustment that would fundamentally alter the nature of a service, program or activity, or result in undue financial or administrative burdens considering the institution's resources as a whole. For example, an appropriate academic adjustment may be to extend the time a student with a disability is allotted to take tests, but an institution is not required to change the substantive content of the tests. In addition, an institution is not required to make modifications that would result in undue financial or administrative burdens. Public institutions are required to give primary consideration to the auxiliary aid or service that the student requests but can opt to provide alternative aids or services if they are effective. They can also opt to provide an effective alternative if the requested auxiliary aid or service would fundamentally alter the nature of a service, program or activity or result in undue financial or administrative burdens. For example, if it would be a fundamental alteration or undue burden to provide a student with a disability with a note-taker for oral classroom presentations and discussions and a tape recorder would be an effective alternative, a postsecondary institution may provide the student with a tape recorder instead of a note-taker.

If Students Want to Request Academic Adjustments, What Must They Do?

Institutions may establish reasonable procedures for requesting academic adjustments; students are responsible for knowing these procedures and following them. Institutions usually include information on the procedures and contacts for requesting an academic adjustment in their general information publications and websites. If students are unable to locate the procedures, they should contact an institution official, such as an admissions officer or counselor.

What Should Students Expect in Working with a Disability Coordinator at an Institution of Postsecondary Education?

A high-school counselor, a special education teacher, or a VR counselor may meet with high-school students with disabilities to provide services or monitor their progress under their education plans on a periodic basis. The role of the disability coordinator at an institution of postsecondary education is very different. At many institutions, there may be only one or two staff members to address the needs of all students with disabilities attending the institution. The disability coordinator evaluates documentation, works with students to determine appropriate services, assists students in arranging services or testing modifications, and deals with problems as they arise. A disability coordinator may have contact with a student with a disability only two or three times a semester. Disability coordinators usually will not directly provide educational services, tutoring or counseling, or help students plan or manage their time or schedules. Students with disabilities are, in general, expected to be responsible for their own academic programs and progress in the same ways that nondisabled students are responsible for them.

When Should Students Notify the Institution of Their Intention to Request an Academic Adjustment?

As soon as possible. Although students may request academic adjustments at any time, students needing services should be advised to notify the institution as early as possible to ensure that the institution has enough time to review their request and provide an appropriate academic adjustment. Some academic adjustments, such as interpreters, may take time to arrange. In addition, students should not wait until after completing a course or activity or receiving a poor grade to request services and then expect the grade to be changed or to be able to retake the course.

How Do Institutions Determine What Academic Adjustments Are Appropriate?

Once a student has identified her- or himself as an individual with a disability, requested an academic adjustment, and provided appropriate documentation upon request, institution staff should discuss with the student what academic adjustments are appropriate in light of the student's individual needs and the nature of the institution's program. Students with disabilities possess unique knowledge of their individual disabilities and should be prepared to discuss the functional challenges they face and, if applicable, what has or has not worked for them in the past. Institution staff should be prepared to describe the barriers students may face in individual classes that may affect their full participation, as well as academic adjustments that might enable students to overcome those barriers.

Who Pays for Auxiliary Aids?

Once the needed auxiliary aids and services have been identified, institutions may not require students with disabilities to pay part or all of the costs of such aids and services, nor may institutions charge students with disabilities more for participating in programs or activities than they charge students who do not have disabilities. Institutions generally may not condition their provision of academic adjustments on the availability of funds, refuse to spend more than a certain amount to provide academic adjustments, or refuse to provide academic adjustments because they believe other providers of such services exist. In many cases, institutions may meet their obligation to provide auxiliary aids and services by assisting students in either obtaining them or obtaining reimbursement for their cost from an outside agency or organization, such as a state VR agency. Such assistance notwithstanding, institutions retain ultimate responsibility for providing necessary auxiliary aids and services and for any costs associated with providing such aids and services or utilizing outside sources. However, as noted above, if the institution can demonstrate that providing a specific auxiliary aid or service would result in undue financial or administrative burdens, considering the institution's resources as a whole, it can opt to provide another effective one.

What If the Academic Adjustments the Institution Provides Are Not Working?

If the academic adjustments provided are not meeting the student's needs, it is the student's responsibility to notify the institution as soon as possible. It may be too late to correct the problem if the student waits until the course or activity is completed. The student and the institution should work together to resolve the problem.

Chapter 39

Transition to College and Vocational Programs

As a student approaches the time to leave high school, it is important that preparations for adult life are well underway. For early transition planning and active participation in decision-making to occur for students with disabilities, members of the planning team need to be well-informed about the student's abilities, needs, and available services. This chapter highlights educational opportunities, credentials, and employment strategies designed to assist students with disabilities while in school to prepare for a meaningful postsecondary education and thriving career.

Transition Planning

"A truly successful transition process is the result of comprehensive team planning that is driven by the dreams, desires, and abilities of youth. A transition plan provides the basic structure for preparing an individual to live, work, and play in the community, as fully and independently as possible." Local educational agencies (LEAs) and state vocational rehabilitation (VR) agencies participate in planning meetings to assist students and family members to make critical decisions about this stage of the student's life and her or his future postschool

---

This chapter includes text excerpted from "Transition Planning: Opportunities and Programs to Prepare Students with Disabilities for Success," U.S. Department of Education (ED), May 2017.

goals. During the planning process, schools and VR agencies work together to identify the transition needs of students with disabilities, such as the need for assistive or rehabilitation technology, orientation and mobility services or travel training, and career exploration through vocational assessments or work experience opportunities. The individualized education program (IEP), as developed under the Individuals with Disabilities Education Act (IDEA), for each student with a disability, must address transition services requirements, beginning no later than the first IEP to be in effect when the child turns 16 years of age or younger if determined appropriate by the IEP Team, and must be updated annually thereafter. The IEP must include:

- Appropriate, measurable postsecondary goals based upon age-appropriate transition assessments related to training, education, employment, and, where appropriate, independent living skills

- The transition services (including courses of study) needed to assist the student with a disability in reaching those goals. While the IDEA statute and regulations refer to courses of study, they are but one example of appropriate transition services. Examples of independent living skills to consider when developing postsecondary goals include self-advocacy, management of the home and personal finances, and the use of public information.

Education and Training Opportunities

There are a number of opportunities and programs available for students preparing to exit secondary school. Many of these education and training opportunities involve formal or informal connections between educational, VR, employment, training, social services, and health-services agencies. Specifically, high schools, career centers, community colleges, four-year colleges and universities, and state technical colleges are key partners. These partners offer federal, state, and local funds to assist a student preparing for postsecondary education.

Further, research suggests that enrollment in more rigorous, academically intense programs (e.g., Advanced Placement (AP), International Baccalaureate (IB), or dual enrollment) in high school prepares students, including those with low achievement levels, to enroll and persist in postsecondary education at higher rates than similar students who pursue less challenging courses of study.

The following are examples of exiting options, programs, and activities that may be available as IEP teams develop IEPs to prepare the student for the transition to adult life:

Regular High School Diploma

The term "regular high school diploma:"

1. Means the standard high school diploma awarded to the preponderance of students in the state that is fully aligned with state standards, or a higher diploma, except that a regular high school diploma shall not be aligned to the alternate academic achievement standards.

2. Does not include a recognized equivalent of a diploma, such as a general equivalency diploma, certificate of completion, certificate of attendance, or similar lesser credential. The vast majority of students with disabilities should have access to the same high-quality academic coursework as all other students in the state that reflects grade-level content for the grade in which the student is enrolled and that enables them to participate in assessments aligned with grade-level achievement standards.

Alternate High School Diploma

Some students with the most significant cognitive disabilities may be awarded a state-defined alternate high school diploma based on alternate academic achievement standards, but that diploma must be standards-based.

Working towards an alternate diploma sometimes causes delay or keeps the student from completing the requirements for a regular high school diploma. However, students with the most significant cognitive disabilities who are working towards an alternate diploma must receive instruction that promotes their involvement and progress in the general education curriculum, consistent with the IDEA.

Further, states must continue to make a free appropriate public education (FAPE) available to any student with a disability who graduates from high school with a credential other than a regular high school diploma, such as an alternate diploma, General Educational Development (GED), or certificate of completion. While FAPE under the IDEA does not include education beyond grade 12, states and school districts are required to continue to offer to develop and implement an IEP for an eligible student with a disability who graduates from high school with a credential other than a regular high school diploma, until the student has exceeded the age of eligibility for FAPE under state law. Depending on state law, which sets the state's upper age limit of FAPE, the entitlement to FAPE of a student with a disability who has not graduated high school with a regular high school diploma could last until the student's twenty-second birthday. IEPs could include transition services in the form of coursework at a community college or other postsecondary institution, provided that the state recognizes the coursework as secondary school education under state law. Secondary school education does not include education that is beyond grade 12 and must meet state education standards.

Dual or Concurrent Enrollment Program

Increasingly, states and school districts are permitting students to participate in dual or concurrent enrollment programs while still in high school. The term "dual" or "concurrent enrollment program" refers to a partnership between at least one college or university and at least one local school district in which the student who has not yet graduated from high school with a regular high school diploma is able to enroll in one or more postsecondary courses and earn postsecondary credit. The credit(s) can be transferred to the college or university in the partnership, and it can be applied toward completion of a degree or recognized educational credential, which the student would earn after leaving high school. Programs are offered both on campuses of colleges or universities, or in high school classrooms. Examples of dual or concurrent enrollment programs include institution-specific dual enrollment programs, AP, IB, and statewide dual enrollment programs with an emphasis on implementation at one site. The Office of Special Education Programs (OSEP) has stated in prior policy guidance that, if under state law, attending classes at a postsecondary institution, whether auditing or for credit, is considered secondary school education for students in grade 12 or below and the education provided meets applicable state standards, those services can be designated as transition services on a student's IEP and paid for with the IDEA Part B funds, consistent with the student's entitlement to FAPE.

Early College High School

The term "early college high school" refers to a partnership between at least one school district and at least one college or university that allows a student to simultaneously complete requirements toward earning a regular high school diploma and earn credits that are transferable to the college or university within the partnership as part of her or his course of study toward a postsecondary degree or credential, at no cost to the student or student's family.

Summary of Performance

A summary of performance (SOP) is required for each student with an IEP whose eligibility for services under the IDEA terminates, due to graduation from secondary school with a regular high school diploma or due to exceeding the age of eligibility for FAPE under state law. The school district must provide the student with a summary of the student's academic achievement and functional performance that includes recommendations on how to assist the student in meeting the student's postsecondary goals. This summary of the student's achievement and performance can be used to assist the student in accessing postsecondary education and/or employment services.

Part Five

Living with
Learning Disabilities

Chapter 40

Coping with
a Learning Disability

Parents are always important influences in the lives of their children, but their influence is particularly important in the lives of children with learning disabilities or attention deficit hyperactivity disorder (ADHD). Parental support, encouragement, and positive reinforcement can instill children with the confidence, determination, and self-esteem they need to cope with the special challenges they face. Although parents cannot cure their children's learning difficulties, they can provide valuable social and emotional tools to help the children become strong and resilient and view their deficits as surmountable obstacles that can be overcome with hard work and optimism. Experts recommend the following parenting approaches to help give children with learning disabilities or ADHD the best chance at success.

Provide Structure and Routines

Children with learning disabilities often struggle with organization skills, so providing clear guidelines for structuring time and space and developing understandable routines can be very helpful. Visual aids—such as labels, lists, and pictures—can help children

"Coping with a Learning Disability," © 2016 Omnigraphics. Reviewed April 2019.

organize their belongings and remember how to put things away. Routines are important to help children manage time. Since many children with learning disabilities have trouble listening to and following instructions, it can be helpful to break tasks down into simple steps and communicate directions using short phrases. Parents can help children practice organization and time management skills by including them in planning activities, such as a birthday party, special meals, vacation, or planting a garden. Charting the tasks to be done, making lists, shopping for supplies, and checking off items are fun ways to develop organizational skills and promote independence.

Set Reasonable Expectations

Parents can help children with learning disabilities expand their skills by breaking complex tasks down into simple steps that the child can accomplish. After the child can perform one step without assistance, the next step can be introduced. Learning how to set the table for dinner, for instance, might begin by having the child count out the appropriate number of spoons. Next, the child can put one spoon at each place. The parent should provide initial assistance and then gradually reduce their support as the child masters the task.

Maintain Consistent Discipline

Parents should establish rules and expectations and explain them in clear, simple language. Children with learning disabilities may struggle to understand lengthy instructions and complex sentences. Reinforcement of the rules should be firm and consistent, with corrections applied in a warm and patient manner.

Practice Social Skills

Parents can help children address difficulties with personal relationships by anticipating what might happen in various social situations and practicing appropriate responses ahead of time. They can act out scenarios—such as the child wanting to join in a game on the playground—and encourage the child to come up with different approaches for solving the problem. It may be helpful for the parent to demonstrate the wrong way of handling a situation and allow the child to offer suggestions for improvement.

Focus on Strengths Rather Than Weaknesses

Children with learning disabilities are usually well aware of their areas of weakness. It is important for parents to reassure children that they are not defined by their learning disabilities. In addition to offering coping skills, parents should focus on the child's strengths, nurture their talents, and encourage them to pursue activities in which they excel, such as art, science, photography, computers, or sports.

Promote Self-Esteem

Low self-esteem is common among children with learning disabilities. As they compare themselves to peers or siblings, they notice that they struggle to perform some tasks that come easily to others, and they begin to view themselves in a negative way. Parents can help by offering frequent and specific praise for things the child does well. Concrete comments help children understand expectations, feel confident about their progress and accomplishments, and gain self-esteem. Visual evidence, such as certificates, charts, checklists, stars, and stickers, can be used to reward the child for hard work on household tasks, such as making the bed, picking up toys, setting the table, or taking out the garbage.

Offer Role Models

Parents can help children maintain a positive outlook by showing them that many successful people have had to overcome similar difficulties. Many books and videos are available that feature individuals who struggled to achieve their goals in the face of disability, illness, discrimination, or other challenges. Children may also gain inspiration from meeting highly effective members of society with learning disabilities or ADHD, such as firemen, business executives, politicians, park rangers, athletes, or celebrities.

Become an Advocate for Education

Parents of children with learning disabilities or ADHD must take an active role in ensuring that their children receive the tools and accommodations they need in order to learn. Although schools are required to develop an Individualized Education Plan (IEP) for children with disabilities, the IEP may not maximize student achievement. Parents must understand special education laws in order to be effective advocates for their children at school and ensure they get the support services to which they are entitled. Yet, parents also need to recognize that formal schooling will only be one part of the solution for their children's learning disabilities and avoid becoming excessively frustrated by dealing with the limitations of school systems.

Identify and Reinforce the Child's Primary Learning Style

Every child has a learning style that works best for them. Visual learners respond best to information they are able to see or read, for instance, while auditory learners respond best to material they can hear, and kinesthetic learners respond best to an active, hands-on approach. For parents of children with learning disabilities, it is particularly important to identify and reinforce the child's unique learning style, both at home and at school. Visual learners will benefit from using materials such as books, videos, computers, flash-cards, and visual aids such as diagrams, drawings, lists, and color coded or highlighted notes. Auditory learners will find it helpful if parents read notes or study materials aloud to them, provide a tape recorder for them to record lessons, give them access to books on tape or CD, and encourage them to use verbal repetition or word associations to memorize information. Kinesthetic learners will perform best if parents reinforce lessons with hands-on experiments, field trips, role-playing activities, model building, and memory games.

Foster Intellectual Curiosity

All children benefit from being excited and engaged in the learning process. Parents who convey a love of learning to their children can help them develop their natural curiosity and sense of wonder about the world. This spirit of inquiry can help make learning a fun, positive experience for children with ADHD or learning disabilities.

Emphasize Classifying and Categorizing Objects

Noticing similarities and differences, or picking out the relevant attributes of objects, can be difficult for children with learning disabilities. Parents can help them develop these skills by introducing simple categorization and classification of objects by color, shape, or use from an early age.

Encourage Language Usage and Math Activities

Talking with children is the most important way for parents to help them develop language skills. Children with learning disabilities sometimes experience language delays, but parents still need to keep up informal, unstructured conversation to guide their language development. Simple math skills can also be introduced from an early age in the form of counting games and number songs, as well as activities that involve estimating distances, measuring amounts, or comparing quantities.

Teach Children How to Play

To help children with learning disabilities interact with their peers in social situations, parents can help them learn to play. Children with visual-spatial difficulties may need help to develop the skills needed to stack blocks, for instance, while children who struggle with symbolic skills may need help learning to pretend. Preparing in advance for group activities and giving the child a safe environment in which to learn from their mistakes can be enjoyable for parents as well.

Build Skills for Life Success

Children with learning disabilities need to be aware that success in school is not the only means of achieving success in life. Parents should emphasize that children can still achieve their dreams and lead a happy, fulfilling life if they struggle in school. The key is to build the skills and characteristics that help people achieve life success, including self-confidence, perseverance, setting goals, being proactive, asking for help when needed, and handling stress.

Emphasize Healthy Habits

To perform at the peak of their abilities and be able to work hard and concentrate on the task at hand, it is vital that children with learning disabilities develop healthy eating, sleeping, and exercise habits. The overall health of the body has a direct impact on the brain's ability to process information. Parents should also encourage children with learning disabilities or ADHD to develop healthy emotional habits to help them express feelings of anger, frustration, or discouragement in an appropriate way and learn how to calm themselves and regulate their emotions.

References

1. Johnson, Doris J. "Helping Young Children with Learning Disabilities at Home," LD Online, 2000.

2. Kemp, Gina. "Helping Children with Learning Disabilities," HelpGuide.org, May 2016.

3. Smith, Sally L. "Parenting Children with Learning Disabilities, ADHD, and Related Disorders," Learning Disabilities Association of America, 2002.

Chapter 41

Parenting a Child with a Learning Disability

Keeping Children Safe

Everyone wants to keep their children safe and secure and help them to be happy and healthy. Preventing injuries and harm is not very different for children with disabilities compared to children without disabilities. However, finding the right information and learning about the kinds of risks children might face at different ages is often not easy for parents of children with disabilities. Each child is different, and the general recommendations that are available to keep children safe should be tailored to fit your child's skills and abilities.

There are steps that parents and caregivers can take to keep children with disabilities safe.

To keep all children safe, parents and caregivers need to:

- Know and learn about what things are unique concerns or a danger for their child.

- Plan ways to protect their child, and share the plan with others.

This chapter contains text excerpted from the following sources: Text under the heading "Keeping Children Safe" is excerpted from "Keeping Children Safe," Centers for Disease Control and Prevention (CDC), June 22, 2018; Text under the heading "Tips for Parents" is excerpted from "Intellectual Disability," Center for Parent Information & Resources, U.S. Department of Education (ED), 2017.

- Remember that their child's needs for protection will change over time.

What Parents and Caregivers Can Do

Parents or caregivers can talk to their child's doctor or healthcare professional about how to keep her or him safe. Your child's teacher or child care provider might also have some good ideas. Once you have ideas about keeping your child safe, make a safety plan and share it with your child and other adults who might be able to help if needed.

Here are some things to think about when making a safety plan for your child:

Moving Around and Handling Things

Does your child have challenges with moving around and handling things around them? Sometimes, children are faced with unsafe situations, especially in new places. Children who have limited ability to move, see, hear, or make decisions, and children who do not feel or understand pain might not realize that something is unsafe or might have trouble getting away.

Take a look around the place where your child will be to make sure every area your child can reach is safe for your child. Check your child's clothing and toys—are they suitable for her or his abilities, not just age and size? For example, clothing and toys that are meant for older children might have strings that are not safe for a child who cannot easily untangle themselves, or toys might have small parts that are not safe for children who are still mouthing toys.

Safety Equipment

Do you have the right kind of safety equipment? Safety equipment is often developed for age and size and less for ability.

For example, a major cause of child death is motor vehicle crashes. Keeping your child safe in the car is important. When choosing the right car seat, you might need to consider whether your child has difficulties sitting up or sitting still in the seat, in addition to your child's age, height, and weight. If you have a child with disabilities, talk to your healthcare professional about the best type of car seat or booster seat and the proper seat position for your child. You can also ask a certified child passenger safety technician who is trained in special needs.

Other examples of special safety equipment:

- Life jackets may need to be specially fitted for your child.

- Smoke alarms that signal with a light and vibration may be better in a home where there is a child who cannot hear.

- Handrails and safety bars can be put into homes to help a child who has difficulty moving around or a child who is at risk for falling.

- Speak to your healthcare professional about the right equipment for your child, and have this equipment ready and available before you may need it.

Talking and Understanding

Does your child have problems with talking or understanding? Children who have problems communicating might have limited ability to learn about safety and danger.

For example, children who cannot hear might miss spoken instructions. Children who have trouble understanding or remembering might not learn about safety as easily as other children. Children who have a hard time communicating might not be able to ask questions about safety. Adults might think that children with disabilities are aware of dangers when they actually are not.

Parents and caregivers may need to find different ways to teach their children about safety, such as:

- Showing them what to do

- Using pretend play to rehearse

- Practicing on a regular basis

Parents and caregivers may need to find different ways to let their children communicate that they are in danger. For example, you might teach your child to use a whistle, bell, or alarm can alert others to danger. Tell adults who take care of your child about the ways to communicate with your child if there is any danger.

It is also useful to contact your local fire department and explain any special circumstances you have, so that they do not have to rely on the child or others to explain their special needs in case of an emergency.

Making Decisions

Does your child have problems with making decisions? Children might have a limited ability to make decisions either because of developmental delays or limits in their thinking skills, or in their ability to stop themselves from doing things that they want but should not do.

For example, children with attention deficit hyperactivity disorder (ADHD) or fetal alcohol spectrum disorders (FASDs) might be very impulsive and fail to think about the results of their actions. People often put more dangerous things higher up, so that little children cannot reach them. Your older child might be able to reach something that she or he is not ready to handle safely. Check your child's environment, particularly in new places.

Some children might also have problems distinguishing when situations and people are safe or dangerous. They might not know what to do. Parents and caregivers can give children specific instructions on how to behave in certain situations that might become dangerous.

Moving and Exploring

Does your child have enough chances to move and explore? Children with disabilities often need some extra protection. But just like all children, they also need to move and explore so that they can develop healthy bodies and minds.

Some parents of children with special needs worry about their children needing extra protection. It is not possible to protect children from every bump and bruise. Exploring can help children learn what is safe and what might be difficult or dangerous. Being fit and healthy can help children stay safe, and an active lifestyle is important for long-term health.

Children with disabilities might find it hard to take part in sports and active play—for example, equipment may need to be adjusted, coaches may need extra information and support to help a child with a disability, or a communication problem may make it more difficult for some children to play as part of a team.

Talk to your child's teachers, potential coaches, care providers, or healthcare professional about ways to find the right balance between being safe and being active.

Other Concerns

Do you have other concerns? Every child is different. This is not a complete list of questions and concerns; these are just examples. Your questions and concerns may be different. Speak with your healthcare provider, teacher, or child care provider to learn more about keeping your child safe.

Tips for Parents

Learn about learning disability. The more you know, the more you can help yourself and your child.

Be patient, and be hopeful. Your child, as with every child, has a whole lifetime to learn and grow.

Encourage independence in your child. For example, help your child learn daily care skills, such as dressing, feeding him- or herself, using the bathroom, and grooming.

Give your child chores. Keep her or his age, attention span, and abilities in mind. Break down jobs into smaller steps. For example, if your child's job is to set the table, first ask her or him to get the right number of napkins. Then have her or him put one at each family member's place at the table. Do the same with the utensils, going one at a time. Tell her or him what to do, step by step, until the job is done. Demonstrate how to do the job. Help her or him when she or he needs assistance.

Give your child frequent feedback. Praise your child when she or he does well. Build your child's abilities.

Find out what skills your child is learning at school. Find ways for your child to apply those skills at home. For example, if the teacher is going over a lesson about money, take your child to the supermarket with you. Help her or him count out the money to pay for your groceries. Help her or him count the change.

Find opportunities in your community for social activities, such as scouts, recreation center activities, sports, and so on. These will help your child build social skills, as well as provide fun.

Talk to other parents whose children have a learning disability. Parents can share practical advice and emotional support. Find out more about, and connect with, parent groups.

Meet with the school and develop an IEP to address your child's needs. Keep in touch with your child's teachers. Offer support. Find out how you can support your child's school learning at home.

Take pleasure in your beautiful one. Learn from your child too. Those with learning disabilities have a special light within—let it shine.

Chapter 42

The Impact of
Disability on Parenting

People with disabilities face significant barriers to creating and maintaining families. These obstacles—created by the child welfare system, the family law system, adoption agencies, assisted reproductive technology providers, and society as a whole—are the result of perceptions concerning the child-rearing abilities of people with disabilities. But are these views informed? Does disability affect one's ability to parent?

Social science research examining the effect of disability on parenting is scarce. Historically, the absence of data has encouraged the bias against parents with disabilities. Ora Prilleltensky, professor at the University of Miami and a person with a disability, says, "Despite the growing numbers of disabled adults who are having children, parents with disabilities continue to be primarily ignored by research and social policy. The sparse literature that can be found on the topic typically focuses on the relationship between parental disability and children's well-being. In some cases, a negative impact is hypothesized, studied and 'verified;' in other cases, the correlation between indices of dysfunction in children and parental disability is explored; and in

This chapter includes text excerpted from "The Impact of Disability on Parenting," National Council on Disability (NCD), September 27, 2012. Reviewed April 2019.

others yet, the negative impact on children and the need to counsel them is taken as a given."

Drs. Megan Kirshbaum and Rhoda Olkin of Through the Looking Glass (TLG) write, "Much of the research on parents with disabilities has been driven by a search for problems in these families. The pathologizing assumptions framing such research presuppose negative effects of the parents' disabilities on their children. The perennial pairing of parents with disabilities and problems in children perpetuates the belief in deleterious effects of parental disability on children. Research reveals the widespread belief among professionals that disability severely limits parenting ability and often leads to maladjustment in children." Kirshbaum and Olkin believe that such research may perpetuate negative beliefs in the general population. Correlation and causation are often confused in the research, resulting in an impression that children's problems are caused by parents' disabilities. Contextual problems, such as poverty, the parents' history of abuse, substance use, and a lack of adequate supports, are frequently ignored, so any problems found by researchers end up being attributed to disability.

However, high-quality studies indicate that disability alone is not a predictor of problems or difficulties in children and that predictors of problem parenting are often found to be the same for disabled and nondisabled parents. According to Dave Shade, attorney, "The available evidence suggests that although parents with disabilities may have a very different approach to parenting, the presence of a disability (physical or mental) is a poor correlate of long-term maladjustment in children. Thus, although the data are far from clear, it seems safe to conclude that many parents with disabilities previously thought unable to raise a child at all may actually be able to do so, and that many more parents with disabilities may succeed in raising their children if provided appropriate support services." Echoing Shade, Paul Preston, Director of the National Center for Parents with Disabilities at TLG, says, "The implications of being raised by a disabled parent have been the source of numerous studies, public conjectures, and professional scrutiny—all of which touch upon the fundamental rights of disabled people to be parents as well as the fundamental rights of children to be raised in an environment conducive to maximal development. Despite the lack of appropriate resources for most disabled parents and their children, as well as persistent negative assumptions about these families, the vast majority of children of disabled parents have been shown to have typical development and functioning and often enhanced life perspectives and skills." In fact, clinical experience proposes that predictors of problem parenting may be the same as those for nondisabled parents; particularly, a history of physical, sexual, or substance abuse in the parent's family.

Parents with Intellectual or Developmental Disabilities

Parents with intellectual or developmental disabilities face similarly significant and detrimental discrimination, which raises the question, do intellectual and developmental disabilities affect parenting ability? According to Preston, research has historically been focused on the pathological bias against parents with intellectual and developmental disabilities, "pointing out that much of the literature on parents with intellectual disabilities has failed to distinguish between characteristics that facilitate and those that inhibit parenting abilities. Most of these studies have focused only on identifying parents with intellectual disabilities who provide inadequate child care, rather than identifying predictors of adequate child care, such as coping and skill acquisition—despite the fact that a substantial number of parents with intellectual disabilities have provided adequate care."

According to professors at the University of Minnesota School of Social Work, "Despite disproportionately greater involvement in the child welfare system, a growing body of research on the outcomes for children of parents with disabilities does not necessarily support the assumption that parents with disabilities are more likely to abuse or neglect their children. Studies have found that children of parents with intellectual and developmental disabilities can have successful outcomes."

Chris Watkins notes, "Almost all studies have found a sizeable percentage of parents with developmental disabilities to be functioning within or near normal limits. In addition, many studies have found that parents labeled 'mentally retarded' can and do benefit from training and support. Even researchers and commentators who have reached the most negative conclusions about cognitively disabled parents caution that such parents must be evaluated as individuals before reaching conclusions about their parental adequacy, or their ability to benefit from training and support."

Several researchers have used qualitative methods to investigate life experiences and outcomes of children of parents with intellectual disabilities. In Denmark, J. Faureholm interviewed 20 young adult children of mothers with intellectual disabilities. Despite the difficult circumstances of their growing up, including being bullied and ostracized by their peers, most of the children discovered an underlying personal strength that enabled them to overcome these experiences, and all but one maintained a close and warm relationship with their parents.

Similarly, in England, internationally recognized researchers Tim Booth and Wendy Booth also interviewed adult children of parents with "learning difficulties." They said, "The majority recalled happy, if not necessarily carefree, childhoods. Only three regarded their childhoods as wholly unhappy." Significantly, most of the interviewees expressed positive feelings of love and affection toward their parents, and all maintained close contact with their parents. Tellingly, those who had been removed by the child welfare system had subsequently reestablished and maintained contact with their birth parents. "In both studies, family bonds endured despite time and circumstance intervening." Recent research further demonstrates the absence of a clear correlation between low IQ and parental unfitness. In fact, studies have indicated that it is impossible to predict parenting outcomes on the basis of the results of intelligence testing. Thus, Chris Watkins says, "The available research suggests that factors unrelated to disability often have a more significant impact on parental fitness than does disability itself. The research also suggests a tremendous variance in the impact that disability has on parental fitness. Importantly, parenting services have been shown to make a difference for many parents with insufficient parenting skills. While few conclusions can be drawn about the parenting abilities of developmentally disabled parents as a group, it is clear that individual inquiry is required before decisions are made to remove children from parents."

Chapter 43

Educating Others about Your Child with a Learning Disability

One of the many vexing questions facing parents of children with learning disabilities is deciding whether and how to explain their child's diagnosis and difficulties to other people. On the one hand, parenting a child with learning disabilities may seem challenging enough without dealing with other people's reactions and opinions. On the other hand, not discussing the child's unique challenges— and explaining how they affect the child's behavior and needs—may create an uncomfortable situation or make it seem as if the parents are embarrassed or hiding something. The decision about whether to disclose the learning disability also affects the child. When other people are properly informed and educated about the child's learning disabilities, they may be better equipped to offer understanding and support. In this way, the child may feel increased comfort, trust, and confidence in seeking accommodations.

Making the Child Aware of a Learning Disability

The first step in the process of disclosure is to make the child aware of their learning difficulties. The timing of this step can be tricky, and

"Educating Others about Your Child with a Learning Disability," © 2016 Omnigraphics. Reviewed April 2019.

it must be handled in a sensitive, age-appropriate manner. In the absence of an explanation, the child will still notice that they struggle with classroom activities or need more assistance than other students. They may start to believe that they are stupid or inferior, rather than merely different in the way they process information. Yet, it is also important to avoid detailing all of the potential difficulties that could arise from the diagnosis because too much negative information could convince the child that there is no point in trying to learn. The following steps can help guide parents through the process of making a child aware of a learning disability:

- Before talking to the child, the parents should first educate themselves about the diagnosis and the full range of the child's strengths and weaknesses.

- When opening the discussion, the parents should reassure the child that they are healthy.

- Then, the parents should explain that the child's brain works differently in some ways, which will make certain tasks more difficult and other tasks easier.

- Next, the parents should reinforce the fact that they will provide all the help the child needs to be successful. The parents should be active advocates for the child at school to ensure that all available supports and accommodations are used.

- The parents must communicate clearly and make sure the child understands and feels free to ask questions.

- The parents should also discuss their expectations, as well as the child's hopes and dreams for the future. They should take a positive outlook and emphasize the power of perseverance and hard work to overcome difficulties and frustration.

- Finally, the parents should offer sincere praise and compliments to the child for hard work and positive accomplishments, and make sure the child knows that they are loved and valued.

Informing Others about a Child's Learning Disability

Although a child's diagnosis and unique learning style is personal, the details must be shared with many people who are involved with the child's life, education, and welfare. Some of the people who require a full understanding of the child's learning disability include:

- **Healthcare providers.** Doctors, nurses, social workers, psychologists, therapists, and other medical professionals who work with the child should be made aware of the child's learning disability and how it may affect the provision of healthcare services. A dentist, for instance, should be told that short appointments work better for a child with attention deficit hyperactivity disorder (ADHD) or that certain types of lights or sounds might trigger reactive behavior in a child with sensory processing disorders.

- **Education providers.** Teachers, paraprofessionals, tutors, coaches, scout leaders, camp counselors, and religious leaders who guide the child's educational and recreational experiences should also be made aware of the child's learning disability. Parents should describe the child's strengths and talents, as well as weaknesses and challenges. They should also provide examples of approaches that might aid learning and eliminate confusion or frustration for the child.

- **Strangers in the community.** Store clerks, restaurant servers, bus drivers, and other people the child might encounter in social situations do not need as much information as medical and educational providers, but parents can help smooth their interactions with the child by anticipating problems and intervening in advance. Experts suggest using a firm, positive tone to explain the child's needs, preferences, and behaviors.

- **Social acquaintances.** People who are likely to see the child regularly—including classmates, friends, and parents of friends—should be provided with some explanation about the child's learning difficulties. They at least need to know what activities might create challenges or engender disruptive behaviors.

Educating Family Members about a Child's Learning Disability

Perhaps surprisingly, immediate and extended family members can be among the most challenging people to inform about a child's learning disability. Although some family members will accept the news and immediately offer support, others may deny a problem exists or even blame the parents or the child. The closeness of family relationships—along with the fact that learning disabilities are often inherited—increases the potential for strong feelings of pain, grief, anger, and guilt. Siblings of the child with learning disabilities may feel jealous of the extra attention they receive or resentful that they may be held to different expectations. Despite the potential difficulties, however, informing and educating family members is important for both the parents and the child in order to break down barriers of communication and understanding, reduce feelings of isolation, help set realistic expectations, and expand the support system.

Experts recommend using simple, easy-to-understand language and avoiding clinical terminology. They suggest emphasizing the child's talents and positive qualities, as well as explaining their areas of difficulty. After sharing the basic information, parents should help family members come up with strategies to interact positively with the child. They should also allow the family members to ask questions and make an effort to provide thoughtful, sensitive answers. Since some people will want additional information, it may be helpful to come prepared with articles, reports, or organizations to contact for further information. Education of family members usually cannot be accomplished in one sitting, so multiple discussions may be needed. The child may be included in some of the later discussions.

When sharing information with a large family group, it may be best to begin by talking to those family members who are most likely to be supportive. These allies can help reinforce the message with others who may be more resistant. If a family member reacts with denial or blame, it may be helpful to ask a teacher, therapist, or supportive family member to intervene. It is also important to remember that some people may need time and space to process their feelings. While some family members may never fully understand the learning disability, they may still be able to find a comfortable role in the child's life and provide the child with love, attention, and support.

References

1. "Educating Others about Your Child's Learning Disability," SmartKids, January 18, 2016.

2. "Talking with Family about Your Child's Learning Disability," GreatSchools, March 18, 2016.

Chapter 44

Bullying and Learning Disabilities: What Parents Need to Know

Bullying does not just happen to the smallest kid in the class. Children who bully others target those who seem to be less powerful or not as strong. Children who bully others also often target children who seem "different." Children with disabilities are sometimes more likely to be bullied than children without disabilities.

Bullying, teasing, and harassment should not be considered normal rites of passage or "kids just being kids." The effects of bullying can be serious, including depression, low self-esteem, health problems, and even suicide. Adults can help prevent bullying by teaching children about bullying, giving them tools for what to do if they are being bullied, and taking steps to protect children's legal right not to be bullied.

What Is Bullying?

Bullying is unwanted, aggressive behavior that involves a real or perceived imbalance of power. The aggressive behavior is repeated, or has the potential to be repeated, over time.

This chapter includes text excerpted from "Disability and Safety: Information about Bullying," Centers for Disease Control and Prevention (CDC), June 22, 2018.

Types of Bullying

There are three types of bullying:

- **Physical.** Physical bullying involves hurting a person's body or possessions. Physical bullying includes hitting, kicking, pinching, spitting, tripping, pushing, taking or breaking someone's things, and making mean or rude hand gestures.

- **Verbal.** Verbal bullying is saying or writing mean things. Verbal bullying includes teasing, name-calling, inappropriate sexual comments, taunting, and threatening to cause harm.

- **Social.** Social bullying, sometimes referred to as "relational bullying," involves hurting someone's reputation or relationships. Social bullying includes leaving someone out on purpose, telling other children not to be friends with someone, spreading rumors about someone, or embarrassing someone in public.

Verbal and social bullying also can come in the form of electronic aggression (e.g., cyberbullying, using the Internet or cell phones). It can include threatening, embarrassing, or insulting emails and/or texts.

The Effects of Bullying

Children and youth who are bullied are more likely than other children to:

- Be depressed, lonely, and anxious

- Have low self-esteem

- Experience headaches, stomachaches, tiredness, and poor eating

- Be absent from school, dislike school, and have poorer school performance

- Think about suicide or plan for suicide

Some children with disabilities have low self-esteem or feel depressed, lonely, or anxious because of their disability, and bullying may make this even worse. Bullying can cause serious, lasting problems not only for children who are bullied but also for children who bully and those who witness bullying.

Ways to Prevent Bullying

Parents, school staff, and other caring adults can help prevent bullying. They can do the following:

- Explain bullying. Children do not always know when they are bullied. They might feel bad, but do not know how to talk about it. Children with disabilities that affect how they think, learn, or interact with others might need a very detailed explanation about how to recognize bullying when it happens to themselves or others.

- Teach children what to do. Children need assistance in learning what to do to protect themselves from bullying and to help others who are being bullied. They might need:

  - Very specific instructions that are tailored to them, particularly if they have disabilities that affect how they think, learn, or interact with others

  - To be encouraged to always reach out to a trusted adult

  - To learn to recognize and avoid situations where bullying occurs

Here are ways to teach children how to respond to bullying:

- Talk with them often about what they have experienced, and encourage them to think about different ways in which they could respond.

- With them, practice how to act and respond to bullying, including through the use of role play.

- Suggest ways to respond to children who bully others, including telling them to stop, use humor, walk away, and get help.

Children might not always know when they are bullying another child. Children whose disabilities impact their thinking, learning, or social skills might need extra help learning how to express themselves with respect to others.

- Protect your child's legal rights. Your child has the right not to be harassed by peers, school personnel, or other adults.

Disability harassment is discrimination that violates Section 504 of the Individuals with Disabilities Education Act (IDEA) and its regulations. Titles II and III of the Americans with Disabilities Act (ADA) also address harassment.

Chapter 45

Disability Inclusion

What Is Disability Inclusion?

Including people with disabilities in everyday activities and encouraging them to have roles similar to their peers who do not have a disability is disability inclusion. This involves more than simply encouraging people; it requires making sure that adequate policies and practices are in effect in a community or organization.

Inclusion should lead to increased participation in socially expected life roles and activities, such as being a student, worker, friend, community member, patient, spouse, partner, or parent.

Socially expected activities may also include engaging in social activities; using public resources, such as transportation and libraries; moving about within communities; receiving adequate healthcare; having relationships; and enjoying other day-to-day activities.

Disability Inclusion and the Health of People with Disabilities

Disability inclusion allows for people with disabilities to take advantage of the benefits of the same health promotion and prevention

This chapter includes text excerpted from "Disability Inclusion," Centers for Disease Control and Prevention (CDC), August 9, 2018.

activities experienced by people who do not have a disability. Examples of these activities include:

- Education and counseling programs that promote physical activity; improve nutrition; or reduce the use of tobacco, alcohol, or drugs

- Blood pressure and cholesterol assessment during annual health exams and screening for illnesses, such as cancer, diabetes, and heart disease

Including people with disabilities in these activities begins with identifying and eliminating barriers to their participation.

Why Is This Important?

Disability affects approximate 56.7 million, or nearly 1 in 5 (18.7%) people in the United States living in communities. Disability affects more than 1 billion people worldwide. According to the United Nations Convention on the Rights of Persons with Disabilities, people "with disabilities include those who have long-term physical, mental, intellectual, or sensory (such as hearing or vision) impairments, which in interaction with various barriers, may hinder their full and effective participation in society on an equal basis with others."

People with disabilities experience significant disadvantages when it comes to health, such as:

- Adults with disabilities are three times more likely to have heart disease, stroke, diabetes, or cancer than adults without disabilities.

- Adults with disabilities are more likely than adults without disabilities to be current smokers.

- Women with disabilities are less likely than women without disabilities to have received a breast cancer X-ray test (mammogram) during the past two years.

Although disability is associated with health conditions (such as arthritis, mental, or emotional conditions) or events (such as injuries), the functioning, health, independence, and engagement in society of people with disabilities can vary depending on several factors:

- Severity of the underlying impairment

- Social, political, and cultural influences and expectations

- Aspects of natural and built surroundings

- Availability of assistive technology and devices

- Family and community support and engagement

Disability inclusion means understanding the relationship between the way people function and how they participate in society and making sure everybody has the same opportunities to participate in every aspect of life to the best of their abilities and desires.

Chapter 46

Self-Esteem Issues and Children with Learning Disabilities

Self-esteem refers to positive feelings of worth, acceptance, and value that people hold with regard to themselves. Children who have high self-esteem feel proud, confident, secure, and capable. These feelings enable them to act independently, take responsibility for their actions, stand up for themselves, and face challenges. They are more likely to be resilient and keep trying if they make a mistake, and they will likely have the courage to make good decisions in the face of peer pressure. Children with low self-esteem, on the other hand, lack confidence and do not believe they have value and are worthy of respect. They are less likely to stand up for themselves or ask for help, and they are more likely to give in to peer pressure.

How Self-Esteem Develops

Self-esteem begins to develop in infancy. In childhood, when the primary influences are loving parents, most people have very positive self-esteem. Toddlers, for instance, often respond with enthusiasm when asked if they are smart or able to do something. Young children

"Self-Esteem Issues and Children with Learning Disabilities," © 2016 Omnigraphics. Reviewed April 2019.

try new things, experience repeated successes, and receive praise for their efforts. This pattern gives them confidence to face additional challenges and makes them feel good about themselves. Over time, they develop the positive characteristics associated with high self-esteem.

As children reach school age, however, they gradually begin incorporating more negative feedback from the classroom and other parts of the outside world. They experience failures, and their efforts are not always rewarded. Around the age of seven, children begin comparing themselves to their peers and realizing that others may possess stronger skills in some areas. As a result, their confidence and self-esteem may begin to wane.

Learning Disabilities and Self-Esteem

This process affects children with learning disabilities to a greater degree than most other children. Children with learning disabilities tend to experience more failure and receive more negative feedback. They also compare themselves unfavorably to their peers in terms of academic skills and performance. Schoolwork comes less easily to them and can sometimes seem impossible. Although many children with learning disabilities or attention issues are accepted by their peers, some become targets of teasing or bullying.

As a result, research suggests that children with learning disabilities tend to have lower self-esteem than their peers. After years of academic struggles and frustration, they often view themselves as being "stupid" or "slow" in comparison with other children. They tend to generalize these feelings and perceive themselves negatively in other areas of life as well. Due to low self-esteem, children with learning disabilities may lose interest in learning, develop self-defeating ways of dealing with challenges, and perform poorly, which only reinforces their low self-worth.

Ways Parents Can Impact Self-Esteem

Fortunately, parents, siblings, friends, teachers, and other influential people can help bolster children's self-esteem. Experts stress that it is possible for children to learn to improve the way they view themselves and their abilities. For parents of children with learning disabilities, being supportive yet realistic is the key to helping children build their self-esteem. While praise and positive feedback is important, it becomes meaningless if it is offered insincerely. When parents lavish praise on everything a child does, the child may begin to distrust it or overreact to negative feedback. Parents can incorporate the following suggestions to help children with learning disabilities develop higher self-esteem:

- Emphasize that the child is bright and healthy, and that they just have a deficit in a certain area of learning.

- Encourage the child's nonacademic interests, such as art, music, or sports, and highlight their areas of strength, such as kindness or a sense of humor.

- Provide an example of how to value personal strengths, while also acknowledging and working to improve upon weaknesses.

- Offer examples of successful people who have overcome learning disabilities and achieved their dreams.

- Express clear, realistic expectations instead of criticisms. For instance, instead of complaining that the child's room is always messy, ask the child to put away their toys and make their bed.

- Ensure that the child has plenty of opportunities to be successful.

- Help the child view mistakes as learning experiences for next time.

- Avoid comparing the child to other people, such as siblings or classmates, and only evaluate their performance in relation to previous efforts.

- Help the child develop positive strategies for learning and coping with challenges.

- Help the child build effective problem-solving and decision-making skills. Rather than providing solutions, help them brainstorm creative approaches and consider the possible consequences of each one.

- Teach the child to reframe negative statements.

- Help the child find friends who accept them and make them feel valued.

- Encourage the child to help others by volunteering in the community. Having something valuable to offer to other people bolsters self-esteem.

- Provide a safe haven where the child feels loved, appreciated, and supported. Studies show that children who are made to feel special by an adult develop increased hopefulness and resilience.

Self-esteem is a tremendous asset to help children manage learning disabilities successfully. Parents can play an important role in building self-confidence and empowering children with learning disabilities to overcome the challenges they face.

References

1. Cunningham, Bob. "The Importance of Self-Esteem for Kids with Learning and Attention Issues," Understood.org, 2016.

2. Lyons, Aoife. "Self-Esteem and Learning Disabilities." Learning Disabilities Association of Illinois, 2012.

3. Tracey, Danielle. "Self-Esteem and Children's Learning Problems." Learning Links, November 2012.

Chapter 47

Life Skills for Teens and Young Adults with Learning Disabilities

Although young people with learning disabilities or attention deficit hyperactivity disorder (ADHD) often face academic challenges, research indicates that problem-solving abilities and life skills may provide better indicators of future happiness and success than school grades. The key attributes, according to researchers, are social, emotional, and ethical literacy. These characteristics enable people to be creative problem solvers, flexible learners, and good decision makers in their adult lives. Parents can teach these skills and competencies through their words and actions. For instance, parents who engage in positive self-talk and model creative problem-solving strategies can help promote those capabilities in their teenagers. Young people with learning disabilities or ADHD can also benefit from training in specific life skills, such as cooking, managing finances, and driving, in order to increase their ability to function independently.

Cooking Skills

Cooking is a basic functional skill that is required for young people to become independent adults and enjoy a good quality of life. For teenagers with learning disabilities or ADHD, the process of determining what they need for a recipe, making a shopping list, obtaining ingredients, following directions, and preparing meals provides valuable real-life practice in math and reading skills.

In teaching young people with learning disabilities how to cook, it is important to choose recipes that offer the opportunity to touch on various educational goals. Cooking can allow students to work on challenges, such as prioritizing tasks and performing them in sequence, reading charts, measuring, and keeping track of time. All of these skills can be generalized to other life tasks. To maintain student motivation, it may be helpful to allow them to choose a food item that they like to eat and are likely to want to prepare at home.

The first step in the process of cooking is making a shopping list and purchasing the ingredients. Students might type the list of ingredients into a computer or use an app that generates a shopping list and includes photos of the various items. At the grocery store, students can be made familiar with the general layout of the store and assisted in identifying the aisles where different items can be found. Students should take responsibility for collecting the items, crossing them off the list, and purchasing the items.

The most important part of teaching cooking skills to young people with learning disabilities is providing directions in a way that they can understand. Depending on the student's disabilities, the recipe may need to be in large print or include photo instructions. Once the student masters the basic steps in cooking, such as using the oven and other kitchen tools, measuring ingredients, chopping, and mixing, they will be able to apply these skills to future recipes.

Managing Finances

Managing money and banking can be difficult for young adults with learning disabilities or ADHD. Teens who tend to behave impulsively, for instance, may have trouble sticking to a budget due to repeated spur-of-the-moment purchases. Similarly, young people who struggle with organization may experience problems in keeping bills and bank statements straight or balancing their checkbook. People with visual processing issues may invert or misalign numbers in check registers, leading to errors in computing the balance.

Parents can help teens with learning disabilities or ADHD avoid some of these problems by teaching and practicing money management skills. Some tips for helping young people gain competence in handling financial matters include the following:

- During the early teen years, parents should help the young person create a basic weekly budget. List sources of income, such as allowance or earnings from chores or jobs, and anticipated expenses, including clothing, entertainment, snacks, and miscellaneous expenses. Use separate envelopes for each budget category and place enough cash in each envelope at the beginning of the week to cover the anticipated expenses.

- Parents should set up a desk or table where the young person can keep all the tools needed to manage financial matters successfully, such as pencils, paper, calculator, stapler, tape, paper clips, envelopes, and stamps. Also, equip the space with an accordion file or file drawer to organize papers under different headings and a calendar to record the due dates of bills.

- By the end of high school, teens should learn the skills of using a checkbook and paying bills. Carbon checks may be helpful to provide a sample of a properly completed check and to ensure that all transactions are recorded. Some teens may prefer to manage money by using software, such as Quicken, or online banking services.

- When a young person reaches the age of 18, they should learn about the benefits and drawbacks of credit cards. Starting with a card with a low limit from a reputable bank, the teenager should be taught to pay monthly bills in full to avoid interest charges and establish a good credit history.

- Parents should also take teens with them to a variety of retail stores to help them gain consumer skills, such as locating items they commonly use, asking for assistance, and making purchases.

- Parents should also teach young people about the general workings of contracts, such as apartment leases, cell phone agreements, and gym memberships.

- Finally, parents should discuss the etiquette surrounding tipping for good service from restaurant servers, hotel bellhops, cab drivers, hair stylists, and other providers. Explain how to determine the amount of the tip and have the young person help calculate it.

Using Public Transportation and Driving

People with learning disabilities and ADHD can become socially isolated without access to transportation options. Public transportation, where available, enables people with learning disabilities to gain independence and control over their lives. It may also increase opportunities for socialization and participation in the community. Yet people with learning disabilities face some barriers to using public transportation. Travel information, such as route maps and timetables, is often presented in a way that is hard for people with learning disabilities to understand. In addition, many people with learning disabilities lack confidence or fear for their safety while using public transportation. Transportation services offered by government agencies may inspire greater confidence, but they often are not flexible enough to facilitate independent living. Proposals to resolve these problems include improving maps and timetables and assigning "travel buddies" to help increase young people's confidence as they grow accustomed to using public transportation.

Learning to drive a personal automobile can provide a great deal of independence for teenagers. For those with learning and attention issues, however, driving may create unique challenges. Young people with ADHD, for instance, may struggle to tune out distractions and focus on the road. Those with impulsivity may overestimate their driving abilities or drive too fast, which puts them at risk for accidents. Dyslexia and other reading issues can create problems for teens behind the wheel, as well. They may find it difficult to read road signs, scan the dashboard for information, or use a map or GPS device to plan a route. Other learning issues can affect a teenager's ability to see where objects are positioned in space, whether in relation to themselves or to other objects. They may experience challenges in judging distances, reading maps, or telling left from right. Recognizing these challenges enables parents to put strategies and supports in place to help teens with learning disabilities to become safe and successful drivers.

References

1. Cohen, Jonathan, and Eve Kessler. "Life Skills That Make a Difference," Smart Kids, n.d.

2. Debenham, Lucy. "Transport for People with Learning Disabilities," About Learning Disabilities, February 14, 2014.

3. "Dollars and Sense: Financial Skills for Teens with Learning Disabilities," GreatSchools, Jun 22, 2015.

4. Pulsifer, Lisa. "Teaching Cooking Skills to Students with Intellectual Disabilities," Bright Hub Education, January 7, 2012.

5. Rosen, Peg. "How Learning and Attention Issues Can Impact Driving," Understood.org, October 22, 2015.

Chapter 48

Preparing for Adulthood: Tips for Adolescents with Learning Disabilities

Life is full of transitions, and one of the more remarkable ones occurs when we get ready to leave high school and go out in the world as young adults. When a student has a disability, it is especially helpful to plan ahead for that transition. In fact, the Individuals with Disabilities Education Act (IDEA) requires it.

A Quick Summary of Transition

Transition services are intended to prepare students to move from the world of school to the world of adulthood.

Transition planning begins during high school, at the latest.

The IDEA requires that transition planning start by the time the student reaches 16 years of age.

Transition planning may start earlier (when the student is younger than 16 years of age) if the Individualized Education Program (IEP) team decides it would be appropriate to do so.

This chapter includes text excerpted from "Transition to Adulthood," Center for Parent Information & Resources (CPIR), U.S. Department of Education (ED), June 21, 2017.

Transition planning takes place as part of developing the student's IEP.

The IEP team (which includes the student and the parents) develops the transition plan.

The student must be invited to any IEP meeting where postsecondary goals and transition services needed to reach those goals will be considered.

In transition planning, the IEP team considers areas, such as postsecondary education or vocational training, employment, independent living, and community participation.

Transition services must be a coordinated set of activities oriented toward producing results.

Transition services are based on the student's needs and must take into account his or her preferences and interests.

The Individuals with Disabilities Education Act Definition of Transition Services

Any discussion of transition services must begin with its definition in law. The IDEA's definition of "transition services" appears at §300.43.

§300.43 Transition Services

a. Transition services means a coordinated set of activities for a child with a disability that:

    i. Is designed to be within a results-oriented process that is focused on improving the academic and functional achievement of the child with a disability to facilitate the child's movement from school to postschool activities, including postsecondary education, vocational education, integrated employment (including supported employment), continuing and adult education, adult services, independent living, or community participation

    ii. Is based on the individual child's needs, taking into account the child's strengths, preferences, and interests; and includes:

    • Instruction

    • Related services

    • Community experiences

444

- The development of employment and other postschool adult living objectives

- If appropriate, acquisition of daily living skills and provision of a functional vocational evaluation

b. Transition services for children with disabilities may be special education, if provided as specially designed instruction, or a related service, if required to assist a child with a disability to benefit from special education.

Considering the Definition

A number of keywords in the definition above capture important concepts about transition services:

- Activities need to be coordinated with each other.

- The process focuses on results.

- Activities must address the child's academic and functional achievement.

- Activities are intended to smooth the young person's movement into the postschool world.

You can also see that the definition mentions the domains of independent and adult living. This clearly acknowledges that adulthood involves a wide range of skills areas and activities. It also makes clear that preparing a child with a disability to perform functionally across this spectrum of areas and activities may involve considerable planning, attention, and focused, coordinated services.

Note that word—coordinated. Transition activities should not be haphazard or scattershot. Services are to be planned as in sync with one another in order to drive toward a result.

What result might that be? From a federal perspective, the result being sought can be found in the very first finding of Congress in the IDEA, which refers to "our national policy of ensuring equality of opportunity, full participation, independent living, and economic self-sufficiency for individuals with disabilities." (20 U.S.C. 1400(c)(1)) Preparing children with disabilities to "lead productive and independent adult lives, to the maximum extent possible" is one of the IDEA's stated objectives. (20 U.S.C. 1400(c)(5)(A)(ii)).

445

Students at the Heart of Planning Their Transition

For the students themselves, transition activities are personally defined. This means that the postsecondary goals that are developed for a student must take into account his or her interests, preferences, needs, and strengths. To make sure of this, the school:

- Must invite the youth with a disability to attend IEP team meetings "if a purpose of the meeting will be the consideration of the postsecondary goals for the child and the transition services needed to assist the child in reaching those goals under §300.320(b)"

- "Must take other steps to ensure that the child's preferences and interests are considered" if the child is not able to attend (§300.321(b))

When Must Transition Services Be Included in the Individualized Education Program?

What is not apparent in the IDEA's definition of transition services, but nonetheless critical to mention, is the timing of transition-related planning and services: When must transition planning begin?

The answer lies in a different provision related to the content of the IEP. From §300.320(b):

a) Transition services. Beginning not later than the first IEP to be in effect when the child turns 16, or younger if determined appropriate by the IEP Team, and updated annually, thereafter, the IEP must include:

   i. Appropriate measurable postsecondary goals based upon age-appropriate transition assessments related to training, education, employment, and, where appropriate, independent living skills

   ii. The transition services (including courses of study) needed to assist the child in reaching those goals

So, the IEP must include transition goals by the time the student is 16 years of age. That age frame, though, is not cast in concrete. Note that, in keeping with the individualized nature of the IEP, the IEP team has the authority to begin transition-related considerations earlier in a student's life if team members (which include the parent and the student with a disability) think it is appropriate, given the student's needs and preferences.

A Closer Look at What to Include in the Individualized Education Program

Breaking the provisions at §300.320(b) into their component parts is a useful way to see what needs to be included, transition-wise, in the student's IEP. This is also where the rubber meets the road, so to speak, because what is included in the IEP must:

- State the student's postsecondary goals (what she or he hopes to achieve after leaving high school)

- Be broken down into IEP goals that represent the steps along the way that the student needs to take while still in high school to get ready for achieving postsecondary goals after high school

- Detail the transition services that the student will receive to support his or her achieving the IEP goals

Writing goal statements can be a challenging business because it is not always obvious what needs to be included in a goal statement. Goal-writing is a topic worthy of an entire discussion on its own.

The Domains of Adulthood to Consider

The definition of transition services mentions specific domains of adulthood to be addressed during transition planning. To recap, these are:

- Postsecondary education

- Vocational education

- Integrated employment (including supported employment)

- Continuing and adult education

- Adult services

- Independent living

- Community participation

These are the areas to be explored by the IEP team to determine what types of transition-related support and services a student with a disability needs. It is easy to see how planning ahead in each of these areas, and developing goal statements and corresponding services for the student, can greatly assist that student in preparing for life after high school.

Types of Activities to Consider

Remember how the IDEA's definition of transition services states that these are a "coordinated set of activities" designed within a results-oriented process? Specific activities are also mentioned, which gives the IEP team insight into the range of activities to be considered in each of the domains above, including:

- Instruction

- Related services

- Community experiences

- The development of employment and other postschool adult living objectives

- If appropriate, acquisition of daily living skills and provision of a functional vocational evaluation (§300.43(a)(2))

Confused by all these lists? Putting them together, what we have is this: The IEP team must discuss and decide whether the student needs transition services and activities (e.g., instruction, related services, community experiences, etc.) to prepare for the different domains of adulthood (postsecondary education, vocational education, employment, adult services, independent living, etc.). That is a lot of ground to cover. But, it is essential ground if the student's transition to the adult world is to be facilitated. A spectrum of adult activities is evident here, from community to employment, to being able to take care of oneself, (e.g., daily living skills) to considering other adult objectives and undertakings.

Chapter 49

Employment for People with Learning Disabilities

For youth with disabilities looking ahead to life after high school, employment will be an immediate and serious consideration. And the time to consider it well and thoroughly is during the high school years, during transition planning, and through transition services that are carefully matched to the goal of employment.

Here, in this chapter, connect with resources in the employment world. Exploring what these organizations and centers have to offer can be extremely helpful when involved in planning your student's future in this area.

Getting Started

First, is employment a goal the student has for herself or himself? In what area or domain might she or he be interested? There are so many possibilities when you think about having a job, it is important for students to identify what types of jobs are suited to their interests, needs, and preferences. This alone can involve quite an inquiry, but it is a very important beginning link in the chain of planning.

This chapter includes text excerpted from "Employment Connections," Center for Parent Information & Resources (CPIR), U.S. Department of Education (ED), February 24, 2019.

Here are several resources that can help you get started.

Looking for a Job? First, Look Inside Yourself.

"Starting with Me: A Guide to Person-Centered Planning for Job Seekers" from the Institute of Community Inclusion (ICI) is a career development guide to help you make satisfying job choices. Finding satisfying work does not usually just happen by applying for a job in the newspaper. The process involves several phases—and it all begins with you.

How to Get the Most Important Person to the Table: The Young Person

This brief, also from the ICI, summarizes research on the participation of young people in person-centered planning and gives specific recommendations to help facilitators in maximize student participation.

Career Planning Begins with Assessment

On their webpage titled "Career Development," the National Collaborative on Workplace and Disability (NCWD) provides you with three lines of inquiry into career development, including the importance of assessment. The best decisions and choices made by transitioning youth are based on sound information, including appropriate assessments that focus on the talents, knowledge, skills, interests, values, and aptitudes of each individual. Here, you can find out about assessment tools to do just that.

Youthhood.Org's Job Center

The Youthood's online job center is designed for young adults with disabilities, and this section of their website targets the journey toward employment.

Understanding the Network That Is Out There to Help

There is nothing like knowing the players in the field. They are excellent sources of help, info, tools, and connections. So, visit these centers and agencies first, and explore what they offer, with an eye for what is relevant to the transition planning you are involved in.

Office of Disability Employment Policy (ODEP)
U.S. Department of Labor (DOL)
Toll-Free: 866-487-2365
Toll-Free TTY: 877-889-5627
Website: www.dol.gov/odep

The Office of Disability Employment Policy (ODEP) helps you gain an understanding of the network that exists with respect to the employment of individuals with disabilities. The ODEP provides information, training, and technical assistance to America's business leaders; organized labor, rehabilitation, and other service providers; advocacy organizations; families; and individuals with disabilities.

The National Collaborative on Workforce and Disability for Youth—Navigating the Road to Work

The National Collaborative on Workforce and Disability for Youth (NCWD/Youth) helps state and local workforce development systems better serve youth with disabilities. Its online information is phenomenal, directly pointed at the target, and rich with info for families, youth, service providers, administrators, among many others.
(www.ncwd-youth.info)

Career One-Stops—Your Pathway to Career Success

Sponsored by the DOL, this website organizes a great deal of info under one roof. Explore different careers, take self-assessments, find out about the education and training you need, and use the service locator to find workforce development services in your area.
(www.careeronestop.org)

U.S. Department of Labor—On Jobs and Self-Employment

A rich portal into the network and supports made possible by the federal government.
(www.dol.gov/odep/topics/disability.htm)

Reasonable Accommodations in the Workplace

Many individuals with disabilities need accommodations and support in the workplace. Here are two premier resources that can help you learn what is considered "reasonable," what types of accommodations can be made, and where employers can tap into specialized free guidance about accommodations.

Job Accommodation Network—The Job Accommodation Network

Job Accommodation Network (JAN) represents the most comprehensive resource for job accommodations available. Personalized technical assistance is available to employers and individuals with disabilities alike. And it is free, courtesy of the DOL's ODEP. (www.askjan.org)

Regional Americans with Disabilities Act Centers—A Gateway to Info on the Americans with Disabilities Act

There are 10 Regional Americans with Disabilities Act (ADA) National Network Centers, each serving a specific region of the country. Together, they help businesses voluntarily implement the ADA, which includes the federal mandate for reasonable accommodations in the workplace. Via the link (www.adata.org), you can find the center that serves your region and a wealth of info about employment for people with disabilities, what the ADA requires, and connections into this nationwide network of assistance.

What about a Job Coach

Job coaches play an important role in the workplace for many people with disabilities, especially those whose disabilities are severe. These professionals help the new employee learn the job and how to navigate the world of work. Support may be for a limited period of time or provided on an ongoing basis, depending on the needs of the individual. Connect-Ability gives the following suggestions to parents:

- As you work with your son or daughter's IEP team to develop work opportunities and career exploration opportunities, be sure to ask if job coaching is appropriate and how your school can provide it.

- When your daughter or son starts volunteering (or working after school or in the summer), look for natural supports (someone already working at the site, or willing to provide some of the activities listed for a job coach).

- If your son or daughter has trouble keeping a job or being successful on-the-job, consider whether a job coach might be helpful, and talk with your son or daughter about exploring this option. (Connect-Ability, 2009, "Job Coaches")

Supported Employment

You may hear the term "supported employment" (SE) used to describe a range of supports that an individual with disabilities may receive at work, but the term actually is most closely associated with its use in the Rehabilitation Act of 1973, as amended. In that context, supported employment is an approach to addressing the employment needs of individuals with the most significant disabilities, those:

- For whom competitive employment has not traditionally occurred

- For whom competitive employment has been interrupted or intermittent as a result of a significant disability

- Who, because of the nature and severity of their disability, need intensive supported employment services in order to perform designated work

For youth, especially those with significant disabilities, supported employment may be important to consider and pursue. Such services are typically available through vocational rehabilitation (VR) programs, but VR is not the only place you will find supported employment in operation. SE is considered a "place and train" model: the individual receives job-specific training after placement, rather than prevocational training before placement.

Chapter 50

Independent Living

Independent living is about life, is not it? It is about choice, seeing to your own affairs, and pursuing your talents, interests, passions, and selfhood as independently as possible. We all would like to see our young people grow to adulthood and find their place in the world, doing the best of their ability.

Disability can complicate independence, which is why independent living can be an important part of helping a young person with a disability get ready for life after high school. The more involved the disability, the more likely it is that independent living will be a subject of serious discussion and preparation.

Philosophical Underpinnings

One search of the web using the term "independent living" and it is clear to see that a great deal of passion and commitment exists in the independent living movement and community. It is rather breath-taking, in fact. You will see phrases such as: "all people achieving their maximum potential," "barrier-free society," "self-determination," "self-respect," "dignity," "equal opportunities," "consumer-driven," and "empowerment." At its heart, the passion in the independent living community is fueled by individuals with disabilities themselves. And

---

This chapter includes text excerpted from "Independent Living Connections," Center for Parent Information & Resources (CPIR), U.S. Department of Education (ED), January 24, 2019.

it is worldwide, this passion for selfhood. Consider this statement found on the website of the Independent Living Institute in Sweden. It surely captures the point:

"Independent living does not mean that we want to do everything by ourselves and do not need anybody or that we want to live in isolation. Independent living means that we demand the same choices and control in our everyday lives that our nondisabled brothers and sisters, neighbors and friends take for granted. We want to grow up in our families, go to the neighborhood school, use the same bus as our neighbors, work in jobs that are in line with our education and interests, and start families of our own. We are profoundly ordinary people sharing the same need to feel included, recognized, and loved."

You will find this sentiment, this fierce independence, echoed in a thousand websites, brochures, training materials, and resource guides because selfhood matters.

Defining Independent Living

The Center on Transition Innovations (CTI) posts the following definition of independent living.

Independent living is defined as "those skills or tasks that contribute to the successful independent functioning of an individual in adulthood." These skills are categorized into the major areas related to daily lives, such as housing, personal care, transportation, and social and recreational opportunities.

Each of these areas related to daily lives, has its own aspects and concerns that the individualized education program (IEP) team will want to consider and plan ahead for, as appropriate, the student's needs and plans.

Does the Student Need Transition Planning and Services in the Domain of Independent Living?

It is important to understand that not all students with disabilities will need an in-depth investigation of, and preparation for, independent living after high school. As the U.S. Department of Education (ED) stated in its Analysis of Comments and Changes (2006):

The only area in which postsecondary goals are not required in the IEP is in the area of independent living skills. Goals in the area of independent living are required only if appropriate. It is up to the child's IEP team to determine whether IEP goals related to the development

456

of independent living skills are appropriate and necessary for the child to receive free appropriate public education (FAPE). (71 Fed. Reg. at 46668)

Whether or not a student needs transition planning and services regarding independent living will very much depend on the nature and severity of the student's disability. As the department notes, it is up to each student's IEP team to decide if planning for independent living is needed. If the team feels that the student can benefit from transition planning and services in this domain, then independent living will be an area of discussion during IEP meetings where transition is discussed.

What Is Involved in Independent Living?

Independent living clearly involves quite a range of activities, skills, and learning needs. Consider just the three mentioned in the definition posted at the National Secondary Transition Technical Assistance Center (NSTTAC): leisure/recreation, home maintenance and personal care, and community participation. Each of these can be broken down in its own turn to include yet more skills, activities, and learning needs. Just think about what is involved in "home maintenance and personal care" alone. Everything from brushing your teeth, to shopping for food, to cooking and cleaning up afterward, to getting ready for bed, locking the front door, and setting the alarm clock for the next day can be considered as "home maintenance and personal care." It is enough to boggle the mind, all the little facets and skills of taking care of ourselves as best we can, with support or on our own.

So, how is an IEP team to take on the task of planning for a student's independent living in the future? Much will depend on the nature and severity of the student's disability. Some students will not need transition planning or services to prepare for independent living. Others will need a limited amount, targeted at specific areas of need or interest. And still others, especially those with significant support needs, will need to give independent living their focused attention.

Independent Living Centers

One of the most useful resources in the independent living area are the nationwide network of independent living centers (ILCs). ILCs are nonresidential, community-based agencies that are run by people with various disabilities. ILCs help people with disabilities achieve and maintain self-sufficient lives within the community. Operated locally, ILCs serve a particular region, which means that their services vary from place to place. ILCs may charge for classes, but advocacy services are typically available at no cost.

Chapter 51

Special Needs Trusts

A trust is a financial arrangement in which a third party holds property or assets on behalf of a beneficiary. A special needs trust (SNT)—also known as a "supplemental needs trust"—is a particular type of trust that is established on behalf of a person with special needs to provide them with financial support after their parents or other caregivers die. Some people with disabilities are unable to work to support themselves, so extra financial assistance may be necessary to ensure their future security, welfare, and quality of life (QOL). But, leaving money directly to a loved one with special needs often jeopardizes their ability to qualify for government benefits, such as Supplemental Security Income (SSI) and Medicaid.

These federal programs were established to provide a safety net of healthcare coverage and money to cover basic needs for elderly people and people with disabilities. However, the income threshold to qualify for these programs is very low. Although the value of a home, furnishings, a car, clothing, and other personal items does not count toward income for the purposes of receiving Medicaid and other government benefits, cash and investments can affect eligibility. People with disabilities who have financial resources above the threshold—even if the money comes from an inheritance or gift—are likely to lose their benefits. Special needs trusts are designed to let beneficiaries retain their eligibility for benefits while also giving them access to additional funds to cover needs and services that the government does not provide.

"Special Needs Trusts," © 2016 Omnigraphics. Reviewed April 2019.

Setting Up a Special Needs Trust

The first step in setting up a special needs trust is to create a trust document. Although a number of books and websites offer do-it-yourself instructions and forms to create a basic trust, many families seek assistance from an attorney to create a personalized trust. Knowledgeable legal advice can ensure that the trust is valid, complies with state laws, and meets the evolving needs of the beneficiary.

The trust document establishes the terms of the trust. Basically, the person who creates the trust, known as the "grantor," places funds or property in the hands of another person, known as the "trustee." The trustee has full control and discretion over the assets held in the trust, and they are legally obligated to manage the trust for the benefit of the person with disabilities, known as the "beneficiary." Once the trust document has been finalized, it must be signed by all parties and notarized in order to take effect.

Funding the Trust

The trust will then receive a tax identification number from the Internal Revenue Service (IRS), which is required to open a bank account in the name of the trust. At this point, the trust can be funded. Anyone who wants to help support the beneficiary can contribute property to a special needs trust. Most trusts are established by parents to support children with disabilities, but grandparents, siblings, friends, and others can contribute as well.

Trusts receive funds in a variety of ways. Relatives may leave property to the trust in a will, for instance, or designate the trust as a beneficiary to receive the value of stocks and bonds, a retirement plan, or a life insurance policy. Other types of property can be held in a special needs trust as well, such as jewelry, collections, cars, patents, business interests, and real estate. The key for estate-planning purposes is to leave property to the special needs trust instead of gifting it directly to the person with special needs.

Choosing a Trustee

Choosing a trustee is an important step in establishing a special needs trust. The trustee has complete control over the funds in the trust. Rather than giving money to the beneficiary directly, the trustee provides funds to purchase goods and services in accordance with the terms of the trust document. To perform this role effectively, the trustee must be familiar with the beneficiary's needs. They must also know the law in order to avoid making purchases that affect the beneficiary's eligibility for government benefits. In addition, the trustee is responsible for keeping records, paying taxes, managing trust investments, and selling tangible property in order to get cash to spend on the beneficiary.

Many families choose to hire a professional to serve as trustee. Although professionals charge an annual fee for administering the trust, this option ensures that the funds will be managed properly. In some cases, a family member who is familiar with the beneficiary's needs and has their best interests at heart will serve as co-trustee. The trust document should spell out how decisions will be made in case conflicts arise between co-trustees.

Using Trust Assets

The trustee is charged with using the trust funds to support the beneficiary. The trustee cannot give cash to the person with disabilities directly without jeopardizing their eligibility for government benefits. Instead, the trustee must use the funds to pay for goods and services that are not covered by Medicaid or SSI and that improve the beneficiary's QOL. Some of the items that can be paid for with trust assets include:

- Personal care attendants, therapies, and physical rehabilitation

- Out-of-pocket medical and dental expenses

- Educational expenses

- Recreational activities and experiences, such as vacations or concerts

- Items, such as clothing, home furnishings, or a computer

- Services, such as Internet, cell phone, housekeeping, or maintenance

- Pet food or veterinary care

A special needs trust continues to exist until the funds are depleted, the beneficiary no longer needs or is no longer eligible for government benefits, or the beneficiary dies.

Advantages and Disadvantages

The main advantage of having an SNT is that it enables the beneficiary to remain eligible for government programs and services, while also providing funds to pay for additional goods and services to enhance the beneficiary's quality of life. If the person with disabilities is unable to manage their own finances, the SNT provides a trustee to handle this function and ensure that the funds are used for their care. Finally, the funds used to create a SNT are tax-deductible.

One disadvantage of special needs trusts is the high cost involved in setting up the trust and managing the funds. In addition, some people with disabilities feel frustrated by the lack of control and independence the arrangement provides them. Finally, the passage of the Affordable Care Act (ACA) in 2010 prohibited health insurance companies from denying coverage to people with preexisting health conditions. This provision enabled many people with disabilities to obtain healthcare coverage from sources other than Medicaid. As a result, special needs trusts may no longer be necessary for the purpose of preserving eligibility for Medicaid benefits.

References

1. Elias, Stephen. "Special Needs Trusts: The Basics," Nolo, 2016.

2. Fleming, Robert. "What Are Special Needs Trusts?" Learning Disabilities Association of America, 2016.

3. Hannibal, Betsy Simmons. "How Special Needs Trusts Work," Nolo, 2016.

4. Stuart, Melissa. "The Pros and Cons of a Special Needs Trust: Ensuring Your Child's Future," Friendship Circle, September 6, 2012.

Part Six

Additional Help and Information

Chapter 52

Glossary of Terms Related to Learning Disabilities

accommodations: Techniques and materials that allow individuals with various disabilities to complete school or work tasks with greater ease and effectiveness. Examples include spellcheckers, tape recorders, and expanded time for completing assignments.

assistive technology: Equipment that enhances the ability of students and employees to be more efficient and successful. For individuals with disabilities, computer grammar checkers, an overhead projector used by a teacher, or the audio/visual information delivered through a CD-ROM (compact disk read-only memory) would be typical examples.

attention deficit disorder (ADD): A severe difficulty in focusing and maintaining attention. Often leads to learning and behavior problems at home, school, and work. Also called "attention deficit hyperactivity disorder" (ADHD).

axon: The fiber-like extension of a neuron through which the cell carries information to target cells.

basal ganglia: Deeply placed masses of gray matter within each cerebral hemisphere that assist in voluntary motor functioning.

This glossary contains terms excerpted from documents produced by several sources deemed reliable.

brain injury: The physical damage to brain tissue or structure that occurs before, during, or after birth that is verified by electroencephalography (EEG), magnetic resonance imaging (MRI), computerized axial tomography (CAT), or a similar examination, rather than by observation of performance. When caused by an accident, the damage may be called traumatic brain injury (TBI).

brainstem: The structure at the base of the brain through which the forebrain sends information to, and receives information from, the spinal cord and peripheral nerves.

cerebellum: A portion of the brain that helps regulate posture, balance, and coordination.

cerebral cortex: The intricately folded surface layer of gray matter of the brain that functions chiefly in coordination of sensory and motor information. It is divided into four lobes frontal, parietal, temporal, and occipital.

collaboration: A program model in which the learning disabilities (LD) teacher demonstrates for or team-teaches with the general classroom teacher to help a student with LD be successful in a regular classroom.

developmental aphasia: A severe language disorder that is presumed to be due to brain injury rather than because of a developmental delay in the normal acquisition of language.

dyscalculia: A severe difficulty in understanding and using symbols or functions needed for success in mathematics.

dysgraphia: A severe difficulty in producing handwriting that is legible and written at an age-appropriate speed.

dyslexia: A severe difficulty in understanding or using one or more areas of language, including listening, speaking, reading, writing, and spelling.

executive functioning: A group of skills that help people focus on multiple streams of information at the same time and revise plans as necessary.

free appropriate public education (FAPE): A term used in the elementary and secondary school context; for purposes of Section 504, refers to the provision of regular or special education and related aids and services that are designed to meet individual educational needs of students with disabilities as adequately as the needs of students without disabilities are met and is based upon adherence to procedures that satisfy the Section 504 requirements pertaining to educational setting, evaluation and placement, and procedural safeguards.

frontal lobe: One of the four divisions of each cerebral hemisphere. The frontal lobe is important for controlling movement, thinking, and judgment.

gray matter: Neural tissue, especially of the brain and spinal cord, that contains cell bodies as well as some nerve fibers, has a brownish gray color, and forms most of the cortex and nuclei of the brain, the columns of the spinal cord, and the bodies of ganglia.

hippocampus: A component of the limbic system that is involved in learning and memory.

limbic system: A set of brain structures that regulates our feelings, emotions, and motivations and that is also important in learning and memory. Includes the thalamus, hypothalamus, amygdala, and hippocampus.

midbrain: The upper part of the brainstem, which controls some reflexes and eye movements.

myelin: Fatty material that surrounds and insulates axons of some neurons.

neuron: A unique type of cell found in the brain and body that is specialized to process and transmit information.

neurotransmitter: A chemical produced by neurons to carry messages to other neurons.

perceptual handicap: Difficulty in accurately processing, organizing, and discriminating among visual, auditory, or tactile information. A person with a perceptual handicap may say that "cap/cup" sound the same or that "b" and "d" look the same. However, glasses or hearing aids do not necessarily indicate a perceptual handicap.

placement: A term used in the elementary and secondary school context; refers to regular and/or special educational program in which a student receives educational and/or related services.

plasticity: The capacity of the brain to change its structure and function within certain limits. Plasticity underlies brain functions, such as learning, and allows the brain to generate normal, healthy responses to long-lasting environmental changes.

prefrontal cortex: A highly developed area at the front of the brain that plays a role in executive functions such as judgment, decision-making, and problem-solving, as well as emotional control and memory.

premature: When a baby is born too early, before 37 weeks of pregnancy have been completed. The earlier a baby is born, the higher the risk of death or serious disability.

receptor: A protein that recognizes specific chemicals (e.g., neurotransmitters, hormones) and transmits the message carried by the chemical into the cell on which the receptor resides.

related services: A term used in the elementary and secondary school context to refer to developmental, corrective, and other supportive services, including psychological, counseling and medical diagnostic services and transportation.

self-advocacy: The development of specific skills and understandings that enable children and adults to explain their specific learning disabilities to others and cope positively with the attitudes of peers, parents, teachers, and employers.

sensitive period: Windows of time in the developmental process when certain parts of the brain may be most susceptible to particular experiences.

specific language impairment (SLI): A language disorder that delays the mastery of language skills in children who have no hearing loss or other developmental delays.

specific learning disability (SLD): The official term used in federal legislation to refer to difficulty in certain areas of learning, rather than in all areas of learning. Synonymous with learning disabilities.

synapse: The site where presynaptic and postsynaptic neurons communicate with each other.

temporal lobe: One of the four major subdivisions of each hemisphere of the cerebral cortex that assists in auditory perception, speech, and visual perceptions.

transition: Commonly used to refer to the change from secondary school to postsecondary programs, work, and independent living typical of young adults. Also used to describe other periods of major change such as from early childhood to school or from more specialized to mainstreamed settings.

white matter: Neural tissue, especially of the brain and spinal cord, that consists largely of myelinated nerve fibers bundled into tracts that help transmit signals between areas of the brain. It gets its name from the white color of the myelin.

Chapter 53

Directory of Resources Related to Learning Disabilities

General

American Speech-Language-Hearing Association (ASHA)
ASHA Action Center
2200 Research Blvd.
Rockville, MD 20850-3289
Phone: 301-296-5700
TTY: 301-296-5650
Fax: 301-296-8580
Website: www.asha.org
E-mail: actioncenter@asha.org

Association for Childhood Education International (ACEI)
1875 Connecticut Ave. N.W.
10th Fl.
Washington, DC 20009
Toll-Free: 800-423-3563
Phone: 202-372-9986
Website: www.acei.org

Resources in this chapter were compiled from several sources deemed reliable; all contact information was verified and updated in April 2019.

Centers for Disease Control and Prevention (CDC)
1600 Clifton Rd.
Atlanta, GA 30329-4027
Toll-Free: 800-CDC-INFO
(800-232-4636)
Toll-Free TTY: 888-232-6348
Website: www.cdc.gov

Center for Parent Information and Resources (CPIR)
Statewide Parent Advocacy
Network (SPAN)
35 Halsey St.
Fourth Fl.
Newark, NJ 07102
Phone: 973-642-8100
Website: parentcenterhub.org
E-mail: malizo@spannj.org

Council for Exceptional Children (CEC)
2900 Crystal Dr., Ste. 100
Arlington, VA 22202-3557
Toll-Free: 888-232-7733
Toll-Free TTY: 866-915-5000
Website: www.cec.sped.org

Disabilities, Opportunities, Internetworking, and Technology (DO-IT)
University of Washington (UW)
P.O. Box 354842
Seattle, WA 98195-4842
Toll-Free: 888-972-DOIT
(888-972-3648)
Phone: 206-685-DOIT
(206-685-3648)
Fax: 206-221-4171
Website: www.washington.edu/doit
E-mail: doit@uw.edu

Eunice Kennedy Shriver National Institute of Child Health and Human Development (NICHD)
NICHD Information Resource
Center
P.O. Box 3006
Rockville, MD 20847
Toll-Free: 800-370-2943
Toll-Free Fax: 866-760-5947
Website: www.nichd.nih.gov
E-mail: NICHDInformation
ResourceCenter@mail.nih.gov

Genetic and Rare Diseases Information Center (GARD)
P.O. Box 8126
Gaithersburg, MD 20898-8126
Toll-Free: 888-205-2311
Phone: 301-251-4925
Toll-Free TTY: 888-205-3223
Fax: 301-251-4911
Website: www.rarediseases.info.nih.gov
E-mail: GARDinfo@nih.gov

GreatSchools
2201 Bdwy.
Fourth Fl.
Oakland, CA 94612
Website: www.greatschools.org

LD OnLine
WETA Public Television
2775 S. Quincy St.
Arlington, VA 22206
Fax: 703-998-2060
Website: www.ldonline.org

Learning Disabilities Association of America (LDA)
P.O. Box 10369
Pittsburgh, PA 15234-1349
Phone: 412-341-1515
Fax: 412-344-0224
Website: www.ldaamerica.org
E-mail: info@ldaamerica.org

Learning Disabilities Worldwide (LDW)
179 Bear Hill Rd.
Ste. 104
Waltham, MA 02451
Phone: 978-897-5399
Website: www.ldworldwide.org
E-mail: help@ldworldwide.org

National Center for Education Statistics (NCES)
Institute of Education Sciences (IES)
550 12th St. S.W.
Potomac Center Plaza
Washington, DC 20202
Phone: 202-403-5551
Website: www.nces.ed.gov

National Center for Learning Disabilities (NCLD)
1 Thomas Cir N.W.
Ste. 700
Washington, DC 20005
Phone: 212-545-7510
Website: www.ncld.org

National Council on Disability (NCD)
1331 F St. N.W.
Ste. 850
Washington, DC 20004
Phone: 202-272-2004
Fax: 202-272-2022
Website: www.ncd.gov
E-mail: ncd@ncd.gov

National Institute of Mental Health (NIMH)
Office of Science Policy, Planning, and Communications (OSPPC)
6001 Executive Blvd.
Rm. 8184, MSC 9663
Bethesda, MD 20892-9663
Toll-Free: 866-615-6464
TTY: 301-443-8431
Toll-Free TTY: 866-415-8051
Fax: 301-443-4279
Website: www.nimh.nih.gov
E-mail: nimhinfo@nih.gov

National Institute of Neurological Disorders and Stroke (NINDS)
NIH Neurological Institute
P.O. Box 5801
Bethesda, MD 20824
Toll-Free: 800-352-9424
Website: www.ninds.nih.gov

National Institute on Alcohol Abuse and Alcoholism (NIAAA)
Phone: 301-443-3860
Website: www.niaaa.nih.gov
E-mail: niaaaweb-r@exchange.nih.gov

PACER Center, Inc.
8161 Normandale Blvd.
Bloomington, MN 55437
Toll-Free: 800-537-2237
Phone: 952-838-9000
Fax: 952-838-0199
Website: www.pacer.org

Smart Kids with Learning Disabilities, Inc
38 Kings N. Hwy.
Westport, CT 06880
Website: www.smartkidswithld.org
E-mail: Info@SmartKidswithLD.org

U.S. Department of Education (ED)
400 Maryland Ave. S.W.
Washington, DC 20202
Toll-Free: 800-872-5327
Website: www2.ed.gov

Aphasia

National Aphasia Association (NAA)
P.O. Box 87
Scarsdale, NY 10583
Toll-Free: 800-922-4622
Phone: 212-267-2814
Fax: 212-267-2812
Website: www.aphasia.org
E-mail: naa@aphasia.org

Assistive Technology

Family Center on Technology and Disability
Academy for Educational Development (AED)
1825 Connecticut Ave. N.W.
Seventh Fl.
Washington, DC 20009-5721
Phone: 202-884-8068
Website: www.ctdinstitute.org

Attention Deficit Hyperactivity Disorder

Attention Deficit Disorder Association (ADDA)
P.O. Box 7557
Wilmington, DE 19083-9997
Website: www.add.org

Children and Adults with Attention-Deficit / Hyperactivity Disorder (CHADD)
4601 Presidents Dr., Ste. 300
Lanham, MD 20706
Toll-Free: 800-233-4050
Phone: 301-306-7070
Fax: 301-306-7090
Website: www.chadd.org

Autism and Pervasive Developmental Disorders

Association for Science in Autism Treatment (ASAT)
P.O. Box 1447
Hoboken, NJ 07030
Website: www.asatonline.org
E-mail: info@asatonline.org

Autism National Committee (AUTCOM)
Website: www.autcom.org

Autism Network International (ANI)
P.O. Box 35448
Syracuse, NY 13235-5448
Website: www.autreat.com

Autism Research Institute (ARI)
4182 Adams Ave.
San Diego, CA 92116
Toll-Free: 833-281-7165
Website: www.autism.com

Autism Society
4340 E.W. Hwy, Ste. 350
Bethesda, MD 20814
Toll-Free: 800-3-AUTISM
(800-328-8476)
Website: www.autism-society.org

Autism Speaks, Inc.
1 East 33rd St.
Fourth Fl.
New York, NY 10016
Phone: 646-385-8500
Fax: 212-252-8676
Website: www.autismspeaks.org

Autism Spectrum Connection
P.O. Box 524
Crown Point, IN 46308
Toll-Free: 800-3-AUTISM
(800-328-8476)
Phone: 219-789-9874
Website: www.
aspergersyndrome.org
E-mail: MAAPatOasis@gmail.
com

Chromosomal Disorders

Genetics Home Reference (GHR)
8600 Rockville Pike
Bethesda, MD 20894
Website: www.ghr.nlm.nih.gov

National Human Genome Research Institute (NHGRI)
Communications and Public
Liaison Branch (CPLB)
9000 Rockville Pike
Bldg. 31, Rm. 4B09, 31 Center
Dr., MSC 2152
Bethesda, MD 20892-2152
Phone: 301-402-0911
Fax: 301-402-2218
Website: www.genome.gov
E-mail: nhgripressoffice@mail.
nih.gov

Dyslexia

International Dyslexia Association (IDA)
40 York Rd.
Fourth Fl.
Baltimore, MD 21204
Phone: 410-296-0232
Fax: 410-321-5069
Website: dyslexiaida.org
E-mail: info@dyslexiaida.org

Hearing Disorders

The Children's Hearing Institute
363 Seventh Ave.
10th Fl.
New York, NY 10001
Phone: 212-257-6138
Website: www.childrenshearing.
org
E-mail: Mwillis@
childrenshearing.org

National Institute on Deafness and Other Communication Disorders (NIDCD)
NIDCD Office of Health
Communication and Public
Liaison (OHPL)
31 Center Dr., MSC 2320
Bethesda, MD USA 20892-2320
Toll-Free: 800-241-1044
Phone: 301-827-8183
Toll-Free TTY: 800-241-1055
Fax: 301-480-0702
Website: www.nidcd.nih.gov
E-mail: nidcdinfo@nidcd.nih.gov

Vision Disorders

AAV Media, LLC
5580 La Jolla Blvd.
Ste. 78
La Jolla, CA 92037
Phone: 858-454-2145
Website: www.allaboutvision.
com

National Eye Institute (NEI)
Information Office
31 Center Dr., MSC 2510
Bethesda, MD 20892-2510
Phone: 301-496-5248
Website: www.nei.nih.gov
E-mail: 2020@nei.nih.gov

Chapter 54

Sources of College Funding for Students with Disabilities

In addition to scholarships available to the general public, minorities, and people pursuing a particular field of study, there are many scholarships specifically for students with disabilities. Below are some examples:

General

Incight provides up to 100 scholarships to help students with disabilities pay for college, vocational school, or Master's or Doctoral programs. Applicants must be residents of Oregon, Washington, or California; although, they do not have to attend a college or university in those states (spring deadline).

Incight
111 S.W. Columbia St., Ste. 1170
Portland, OR 97201
Phone: 971-244-0305
Website: www.incight.org/contact
E-mail: scholarship@incight.org

Resources in this chapter were compiled from several sources deemed reliable; all contact information was verified and updated in April 2019.

Newcombe Scholarships for Students with Disabilities are grants paid directly to colleges or universities to help students with disabilities who demonstrate financial need.

The Charlotte W. Newcombe Foundation
35 Park Place
Princeton, NJ 08542-6918
Phone: 609-924-7022
Website: www.newcombefoundation.org/about/contact
E-mail: info@newcombefoundation.org

The **American Association of Health & Disability (AAHD) Scholarship Program** is for students who are full-time undergraduates (freshman or greater status) or part-time or full-time graduate students. You must provide documentation of a disability.

Scholarship Committee
American Association on Health and Disability
110 N. Washington St., Ste. 328-J
Rockville, MD 20850
Phone: 301-545-6140
Fax: 301-545-6144
Website: www.aahd.us/initiatives/scholarship-program
E-mail: contact@aahd.us

The **Ability Center of Greater Toledo Scholarship** is for Greater Toledo, Ohio area residents with disabilities (spring deadline).

5605 Monroe St.
Sylvania, OH 43560
Voice TTY: 419-885-5733
Fax: 419-882-4813
Website: www.abilitycenter.org/contact-us/

The **Business Plan Scholarship for Students with Disabilities** is a $1,000 scholarship open to undergraduate or graduate students with disabilities who have written a business plan for a class, competition, or to start a business (spring and winter deadlines).

315 Madison Ave., 24th Fl.
New York, NY 10017
Website: www.fitsmallbusiness.com
E-mail: info@fitsmallbusiness.com

For Students Who Are Blind

The **American Foundation for the Blind** awards scholarships from $500 to $3,500 to students who are blind or visually impaired (spring deadline).

American Foundation for the Blind
1000 Fifth Ave.
Ste. 350
Huntington, WV 25701
Toll-Free: 800-232-5463
Website: www.afb.org/info/afb-2015-scholarship-application/5
E-mail: info@afb.net

The **American Council of the Blind** awards scholarships to students who are legally blind. A 3.3 cumulative point average is usually required (spring deadline).

American Council of the Blind
1703 N. Beauregard St., Ste. 420
Alexandria, VA 22201
Phone: 202-467-5081; 800-424-8666
Fax: 703-465-5085
Website: www.acb.org
E-mail: info@acb.org

The **Association of Blind Citizens** runs the Assistive Technology Fund, which covers 50 percent of the retail price of adaptive services or software for individuals who are legally blind (summer and winter deadlines).

Association of Blind Citizens
P.O. Box 246
Holbrook, MA 02343
Phone: 781-961-1023
Fax: 781-961-0004
Website: www.blindcitizens.org/assistive_tech.htm
E-mail: president@blindcitizens.org

The **Christian Record Services for the Blind** offers partial scholarships to young people who are legally blind to obtain a college education (spring deadline).

National Camps for Blind Children
A 501(c)(3) nonprofit organization
PO Box 6097
Lincoln, NE 68506-0097
Phone: 402-488-0981
Fax: 402-488-7582
Website: www.christianrecord.org
E-mail: info@christianrecord.org

The **Learning Ally's Mary P. Oenslager Scholastic Achievement Awards** are given to Learning Ally members who are blind or visually impaired and have received or will be receiving their bachelor's, master's or doctoral degree. The top three winners each receive a $6,000 scholarship and a chance to participate in a celebration in Washington, DC (spring deadline).

20 Roszel Rd.
Princeton, NJ 08540
Toll-Free: 800-221-4792
Website: www.learningally.org/NAA.aspx

The **Lighthouse Guild scholarship program** offers scholarships of up to $10,000 to help high school students who are legally blind pay for college (spring deadline).

250 W. 64th St
New York, NY 10023
Toll-Free: 800-284-4422
Phone: 212-769-7801
Website: www.lighthouseguild.org

The **National Federation of the Blind Scholarship Program** offers many scholarships from $3,000 to $12,000 to college students who are blind, in recognition of their achievements (spring deadline).

National Federation of the Blind
200 E. Wells St.
Baltimore, MD 21230
Phone: 410-659-9314
Fax: 410-685-5653
Website: www.nfb.org
Email nfb@nfb.org

The **United States Association of Blind Athletes (USABA) Copeland Scholarship** is awarded to USABA members who are legally blind and enrolled at a two-year or four-year college, university or technical school as a full-time student (fall deadline).

1 Olympic Plaza
Colorado Springs, CO 80909
Phone: 719-86-3224
Fax: 719-866-3400
Website: www.usaba.org

For Students Who Are Deaf or Hard of Hearing

The **Alexander Graham Bell Scholarship Program** offers scholarships for students who have moderately severe to profound hearing loss and are getting a bachelor's, master's or doctoral degree (spring deadline).

The **Cochlear Americas** has two scholarship programs—the **Graeme Clark Scholarship,** which is open to people who have the Nucleus® Cochlear Implant, and the **Anders Tjellstrom Scholarship,** which is open to people who have the Baha® System (fall deadline).

Cochlear Americas
The Graeme Clark Scholarship
 13059 E. Peakview Ave.
Centennial, CO 80111
Toll-Free: 800-523-5798
Telephone: 303-790-9010
Fax: 303-792-9025
Website: www.cochlear.com/us/en/connect/contact-us

The **Gallaudet University Alumni Association** provides financial assistance to graduates of Gallaudet University and other accredited colleges and universities who are deaf and are getting their graduate degree at colleges and universities not specifically for deaf or hard of hearing people (spring deadline).

800 Florida Ave., N.E.
Washington, DC 20002-3695
Phone: 202-250-2590
TTY: 202-651-5060
Fax: 202-651-5062
Website: www.gallaudet.edu

The **Sertoma Hard of Hearing or Deaf Scholarship** helps undergraduate students with clinically significant bilateral hearing loss pay for college (spring deadline).

1912 E. Meyer Blvd.
Kansas City, MO 64132
Phone: 816-333-8300
Fax: 816-333-4320
Website: www.sertoma.org

For Students with Learning Disabilities

LD Resources Foundation Awards help college students with learning disabilities pay for testing and in some cases award specific types of assistive technologies, such as Dragon Naturally Speaking (fall deadline).

LD Resources Foundation, Inc
14 Horatio Street #5H
New York, N.Y 10014
Phone: 646-701-0000
Website: www.ldrfa.org/?portfolio=award-programs
E-mail: info@ldrfa.org

The **National Center for Learning Disabilities (NCLD)** scholarships are offered to high school seniors with documented learning disabilities who are getting a higher education (winter deadline). NCLD also offers a list of scholarships for students with learning disabilities or attention deficit hyperactivity disorder (ADHD).

1 Thomas Circle N.W. #700
Washington, DC 20005
Website: www.ncld.org

Learning Ally offers the **Marion Huber Learning Through Listening Awards** for outstanding students with print or learning disabilities. The top three winners each receive a $6,000 scholarship and a chance to participate in a celebration in Washington, DC (spring deadline).

20 Roszel Rd.
Princeton, NJ 08540
Website: www.learningally.org/NAA.aspx

P. Buckley Moss Foundation Scholarships and Awards offer financial assistance to high school seniors with learning disabilities who are getting a higher education or are planning a career in the visual arts (spring deadline).

P. Buckley Moss Society
74 Poplar Grove Ln.
Mathews, VA 23109
Phone: 800-430-1320
Website: www.mosssociety.org/page.php?id=8
E-mail: society@pbuckleymoss.com

Rise Scholarships Foundation, Inc. offers scholarships for students who learn differently (winter deadline).

Website: www.risescholarshipfoundation.org
E-mail: risescholarshipfoundation@gmail.com

The **Western Illinois University Chad Stovall Memorial Scholarship** is a $500 scholarship for Western Illinois University students who have Tourette Syndrome, obsessive-compulsive disorder (OCD), or attention deficit disorder (spring deadline).

143 Memorial Hall
1 University Circle
Macomb, IL 61455 USA
E-mail: disability@wiu.edu
Phone: 309-298-2512
Fax: 309-298-2361

The **Learning Disabilities Association of Iowa** offers scholarships of $1,000 each to high school seniors planning to enroll in college or vocational programs (spring deadline).

5665 Greendale Rd., Ste. D
Johnston, IA 50131
Phone: 515-280-8558; 888-690-5324
Website: www.ldaiowa.org
E-mail: info@ldaiowa.org

Index

Index